POLICE OFFICER EXAMINATION

Preparation Guide

The Path of the Warrior

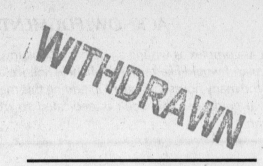

D1611281

by
Larry F. Jetmore

Captain, retired
Hartford, Connecticut
Police Department

ACKNOWLEDGMENTS

Any project as complex as writing a reference book involves many people other than the author. In particular, I would like to thank Michele Spence and Linnea Fredrickson, editors at Cliffs Notes, for the many hours they spent in editing this material and for their thoughtful and often inspirational guidance. This book is dedicated to my three grandchildren, Sean, Jr., Joshua, and Brianna.

Larry Jetmore

Also by Larry Jetmore:

Cliffs Police Management Examinations Preparation Guide

ISBN 0-8220-2075-0

FIRST EDITION

foreword

So you're interested in becoming a cop! You want to be a member of "the force," join the ranks of the thin blue line, be a hero, a "bluebelly," a new centurion—you want to serve and protect.

People enter the police profession for a variety of reasons. Perhaps you have a friend or relative on the force and admire the sense of power and security they seem to project. You might be a store detective or security guard ready to make the big jump. It could be that a recent movie or television program about police work piqued your interest. Or is it simply that you need a job and want the money, security, and retirement and benefit packages policing has to offer?

Well, becoming a police officer is not all that simple. It's become very difficult to get a job in policing. An advertisement for just one officer in a small Connecticut town with a police force of just thirty-two officers resulted in more than fifteen hundred applications! "Many are called, but few are chosen." The selection process is complicated and purposely designed to screen out candidates who don't possess what those giving the examinations feel are the intrinsic and extrinsic traits necessary to become a "good" police officer. The hiring process may consist of a job application, written and oral tests, medical and psychological screenings, a polygraph, an assessment center examination, a physical agility test, and a background investigation. Each test eliminates candidates, and the entire examination process may take several months. If you score high enough on the various tests to survive the screening process and *are* selected, you then face three to six months in a police academy, which normally eliminates ten to twenty percent of those who enter! After you're sworn in, there's a year's probation (often referred to as a "working test period") in which you won't have union protection and can be fired at any time. It may seem overwhelming, and many fine men and women drop out at various stages during the screening process because they either didn't understand what it entailed or they hadn't properly prepared themselves.

Are you discouraged yet? Well, there's a price to pay for everything of lasting value. You knew it wasn't going to be easy and you bought this book hoping to find a shortcut. There isn't one. Persistence, endurance, and motivation are the keys to success, and it's going to take a lot of hard work, dedication, and commitment. However, this book *will* give you a big edge on the competition, let you know exactly what to expect, prepare you for excellence, teach you how to achieve high scores on the examinations, and urge you toward success. The rest is up to you!

You see, I know the *real* reason you want to be a cop. You want to help people. You want to be there to make a difference in another person's life. To be a force for good! It's *OK* that you want to fight for truth, justice, and the American way. That's what cops do;

we just don't say it out loud because in today's society it sounds a little corny. In my twenty-one years as a police officer, through all the bar fights, narcotics raids, murder investigations, and senseless mayhem, I never lost sight of the primary reason we have police officers: to serve and protect the public and be there when needed. Police officers have been given awesome powers by society—to deprive people of their freedom of movement, to intervene in their lives, and even to take a life if necessary. Police work isn't a job or a career, *it's a way of life.*

We are the last of the true knights. If you have what it takes, then come, take the oath and join us in the quest. This book will provide you with the tools to begin a wonderful adventure which will last a lifetime. It's worth every sacrifice you'll have to make. But be forewarned, once you take up the shield of a warrior there is *no* going back. Your life will be changed forever. *Semper fidelis.*

Larry Jetmore

contents

1   the way

EXPLORE AND DISCOVER   3

    How to Use This Book   3
    Reading for Understanding   4
    Stimulating the Learning Process   6
    Motivation: The Key to Success   7
    Your Personal Development Action Plan   10
    Choosing a Police Department   10
        Contacting the Personnel Department   13
        How to Research a Police Department   15
    Riding With a Police Officer   17
        Tips on Riding with a Police Officer   17
    Involving Yourself with a Program   19
        Police Internships   19
        The Police Athletic League   19
        The Police Explorer Program   20
        The Police Cadet Program   20

2   beginning the quest

QUESTIONS ABOUT POLICING   25

    A Seminar   26

3   footprints from long ago

THE ORGANIZATION   43

    A Historical View of Policing   43

The Police Organization   44
  How Police Departments Are Structured   46
  Organizational Charts   46
  The Patrol Division   47
The Police Officer   50
  What Police Officers Do   50
  A Day in the Life of a Police Officer   50
  Attributes of a Good Police Officer   65
  Job Task Analysis   66

4   *moving along the path*

THE APPLICATION PROCESS   73

The Position Description   74
Residency Preference Points   79
Veterans Preference Points   83
The Rule of Three   85
Filling Out Your Application   85
Submitting Your Application   89

5   *dragons along the path*

THE WRITTEN EXAMINATION   93

Preparation for the Written Exam   93
Test-taking Strategies   94
About the Multiple-choice Practice Tests   99
  Answer Sheets   101

City of Dorchester Police Officer Examination   109
Answer Key for Dorchester Police Officer Examination   149
Answers and Analysis for Dorchester Police Officer Examination   151

City of Windsor Police Officer Examination   165
Answer Key for Windsor Police Officer Examination   203
Answers and Analysis for Windsor Police Officer Examination   205

City of Newcastle Police Officer Examination   217
Answer Key for Newcastle Police Officer Examination   247
Answers and Analysis for Newcastle Police Officer Examination   249

Writing Skills and Vocabulary Test Questions   261
Writing Skills Examination   263
Answer Key for Writing Skills Examination   277
Answers and Analysis for Writing Skills Examination   279
  Tips to Improve Your Writing Exam Skills   284

Notification of Written Examination Results   286

6   *crossroads along the path*

THE MEDICAL EXAMINATION   291

What to Expect at Your Medical Examination   291
Height and Weight Measurement   292
Body Fat Composition Measurement   295
The Vision Test   295
Color Vision Test   296
Heart and Blood Pressure Tests   296
Blood Test   297
Hearing Test   297
Respiratory Test   297
Hernia Examination   297
Urinalysis and Drug Test   298

7   *jousts along the path*

THE PHYSICAL AGILITY TEST   303

Preparation for the Physical Agility Test   304
Contact with Police Officers and Test Administrators   305
Physical Agility Test 1   306
Physical Agility Test 2   310
Physical Agility Test 3   311
Training for the Physical Agility Test   313
Physical Agility Test Preparation Guide   314
Warm-up and Flexibility Exercises   315
Event-specific and Weight Routines   317
Cool Down   324

8   *voices along the path*

THE ORAL EXAMINATION   329

The Difference Between Written and Oral Tests   329
The Oral Board   330
The Position Description   330
Conducting the Oral Examination   330
The Panelists' Viewpoint   331
Grading the Test   331
First Impression—Lasting Impression   333
Using the Advantage You Have Already Gained   334
Preparing for Your Oral Test   335
Developing Questions   335
Practicing Your Spoken Answers   335
Perfecting Your Physical Appearance   337

Appearing Before the Oral Board   340
   Questions Frequently Asked at Oral Examinations   341
   Leaving the Oral Board Examination Room   351

9   *surviving the gauntlet*

THE FINAL CHECKS   355

The Psychological Evaluation   355
The Background Investigation   357
The Polygraph Test   363
The Chief's Interview   364

10   *the gate to the way*

THE POLICE ACADEMY   369

Notification of Recruit Status   370
   The Recruit Uniform   371
   Your First Day   371
The Recruit Training Manual   373
   Additional Tips for Excelling at the Police Academy   380

11   *touchstones*

SUPPLEMENTS   385

Glossary   385
Law Enforcement Code of Ethics   393
Canons of Police Ethics   395
Duties and Responsibilities of Police Officers   399
Steps in the Justice Process and Investigation   401
Statistics   403

1
THE WAY

EXPLORE AND DISCOVER

This book is different from any you have ever read before. It's written in the old police tradition of a mentor passing on a way of life, as opposed to an instructor simply explaining how to do something. "The way" is a martial arts philosophy that seeks wisdom through a series of lifelong challenges, each of which is at a slightly higher plateau. Make no mistake about it, police officers *are* warriors and live between worlds. We see, hear, and do things others only dream about. The dangers are real, the rewards great. This book will bring you to the first plateau on the path to "the way" by preparing you for excellence in much the same way knights prepared squires. There are battles to be fought, dragons to slay, trials and pitfalls to overcome, and wild things to be done. I'm old and weary. Come, let me pass the torch to you while there is yet still time.

Although I hope you find this book interesting, it's not designed to be read for pleasure. This book is a tool to increase your knowledge and understanding. The only things required of you are a true heart, a willingness to learn, patience, and the discipline to do exactly what I tell you. You and I are going to become partners, just like it's done on the force. Since it's difficult to capture in words the gravity of what being "partners" is for anyone who isn't a cop, think of it this way. *I'm* the old veteran. I know stuff you don't. *You're* the rookie. You think you know everything, but you know nothing! I've walked the path already and know the way. My job is to be your guide, mentor, friend, bodyguard, and teacher. Your job is to be my disciple for a time. On the street, my life depends on you and your life depends on me. Other than in military combat, there isn't another profession where this interdependent relationship exists in quite the same way.

I have a personal stake in your doing well on your examinations and becoming the type of police officer both of us can be proud of. *My* badge is in a special case on the wall in the room where I'm writing this book. It's the same badge I wore for twenty-one years on the force. I wore it with honor, and I'm proud of it. So if you're going to be *my* partner you're going to have to earn your way. After you're on the force, there will come a time when a young man or woman approaches you with a wistful look and asks for advice on how to become a police officer. I hope you'll hand them a worn old copy of this book and say, "Come, let me show you the way."

> *Knowledge is of two kinds. We know a subject ourselves,*
> *or we know where we can find information upon it.*
> —Samuel Johnson

HOW TO USE THIS BOOK

The type of learning you're most accustomed to is through a teacher. Your teacher used verbal communication to pass along knowledge. You used your senses of sight and hearing; you listened and asked questions. There was give and take. Your teacher told you what to do and could even physically show you how to do it correctly. Repetition was used as a means to ensure that you were doing it right. You memorized things.

This book offers a different approach to learning. It's a guide—a "how to do it" book. Texts of this nature are usually a one-way communication process. I write; you read. Most of these types of books communicate material which has already been written before, merely putting a new coat of polish on old theory. We're going to use another method of learning, mixing the old with the new. It's called "discovery"—the process of finding out through reading, observing, and original thinking. It's part of "the way" to combine both teaching and discovery so new learning and understanding take place through a step-by-step process—pushing, pulling, and inspiring you toward excellence.

READING FOR UNDERSTANDING

The first step in discovery is to make sure you know how to read for understanding and insight, not just information. Don't read this book as you would a newspaper or a novel. Education has been described as "the only thing people will pay for but refuse to get." Most of us tend to be a little lazy and studying the material in this text and then planning a program to excel in the various examinations will be hard work! You'll

- learn how to use this book
- discover what police officers do
- find out the knowledge, skills, and abilities you'll be tested for
- understand how to excel on the various types of tests
- take practice tests and track your progress
- understand how to excel at the police academy

You need to read the book twice, using different techniques each time. The first time is easy—read through the sections without trying to learn anything in particular, only acquainting yourself with the contents of the book to get an overall picture of what's involved. Don't worry about any of the practice examinations at this stage; skip over them entirely. After reading the book through once, put it aside. You need to go shopping to gather the following things:

1. A dictionary—not a little hand copy, but a big, thick, new edition of Webster's finest.
2. A large notebook, the kind with several sections.
3. Two highlighters.
4. A police badge. Go to a flea market or police equipment store (they're in the yellow pages) and buy a police badge. Don't worry about the type of badge, just get one *you* like.

We were OK until you read that I want you to buy a badge, right? Sounds a little corny, doesn't it? Well, do you remember the scene in the movie *Rocky* where Rocky Balboa taped his boxing opponent's photograph to the bathroom mirror so it was the first thing he saw every morning? In the martial arts, we call this technique "continuous concentration." In psychology, it's termed "visualization." It's a process designed to keep your mind focused on a specific goal and motivate you toward success. You're a busy person, and people are constantly pulling you in many directions. You need to develop techniques to increase your ability to stay focused on your goal of becoming a police officer. The competition is too great to do otherwise. Get the badge and put it on your dresser, or by your alarm clock, so it's the first thing you see in the morning and the last thing you see at night. Every day from now on, when you see your badge, ask yourself what you're going to do today to prepare yourself to be a police officer.

Now that you've gathered the things you'll need, it's time to read the book a second time, and this time it's going to be harder work. Since reading comprehension is such an important component in the kinds of tests you'll be taking, we may as well start improving your ability in this area right now. Read the text very slowly, disciplining yourself to pay strict attention to every single word. While you're reading, don't allow your mind to wander. Your ability to understand what you read is an important skill in test taking.

Written communication consists of two types of words, *ordinary* words and *important* words. Tests are no different. The ordinary words are the prepositions, conjunctions, articles, adverbs, and most of the adjectives and verbs forming the skeleton on which the key concepts (the important words) hang. The very fact that you don't instantly understand a word, or a series of words, in a sentence should alert you to the need for spending time looking the word up in the dictionary and reflecting on its meaning. Most of us have developed the bad habit of skipping over words we're not familiar with, figuring we'll understand what the writer is talking about by continuing to read. This works rather well in reading newspapers, magazines, and fictional material, but it's really only scanning, not reading for understanding. Writers of instructional textbooks and test analysts write in a style which gives clues to what they think is important by using bold type, italics, quotation marks, or underlining or by discussing a term's definition. Pay attention to periods, exclamation points, and commas as well.

So get out your dictionary, notebook, pencil or pen, and highlighter. As you're slowly reading the material, sentence by sentence, develop the habit of highlighting key words and concepts. Every single time you come across a word in a sentence that you don't immediately know, I want you to look it up in the dictionary, cross the word out, and write the definition above it or in the margin. Write the heading "Key Words and Concepts" in your notebook, and list each of the words and its meaning in that section. Return and read the sentence again with the definition of the "important word" (it's important to *you* if you don't understand it) in mind.

Emphasis can change the meaning of an entire sentence. For example, here is essentially the same sentence with different emphasis on key words. Read the following out loud:

The detective asked the man if she stole the money, and he replied, "I didn't say she stole the money."

Pretty clear, right? What if I were to write it this way?

> The detective asked the man if she stole the money. The man looked surprised, pointed to himself, and shook his head, saying, "*I* didn't say she stole the money!"

Notice how a brief description of the man's body language adds to your understanding. The "I" is in italic type (suggesting emphasis), and there's an exclamation point at the end. The inference is that the *man* didn't say she stole the money, but *someone else* had said it. What if I were to write it this way?

> "I didn't say *she* stole the money."

Because the word *she* is italic, the meaning changes again. The man said someone stole the money, but he didn't say *she* was the one who did it. And what if it were written like this?

> "I didn't say she stole the *money*!"

She stole something, but it wasn't *money*.

At first glance this may seem pretty basic. It's not. Many entry-level police examinations contain sections which will require you to read a short essay and then answer four or five multiple-choice questions based on the essay's contents. So I want you to increase your ability to read with clarity and understanding in order to avoid choosing the wrong answer simply because you didn't grasp the subtle changes that little things like punctuation and key words can mean in the essay, the questions, or the answer selections.

STIMULATING THE LEARNING PROCESS

The reason I want you to write the definitions in your textbook and your personal notebook is that studies have proven that the more we stimulate our five senses in the learning process, the more apt we are to retain what we learn. We learn about seventy-five percent through the sense of sight but we *remember* only about thirty percent of what we see. So I don't want you to just sit there and read. I want you to become actively involved in the learning process and take personal responsibility for achieving your learning objectives. Get *physically* involved by writing in the margins of the book, transferring important material into your notebook, reading out loud, and taking a walk to think about the concepts presented. Thinking leads to discovery!

> *The thoughts that come often unsought, and, as it were, drop into the mind, are commonly the most valuable of any we have.*
>
> —John Locke

MOTIVATION: THE KEY TO SUCCESS

There is a single criterion which has more to do with whether you'll successfully reach your goal of becoming a police officer than any other. That criterion is **you.** How *motivated* are you? How much do *you* want it? Are *you* willing to make the sacrifices necessary, invest the time required, and make the changes in your thinking and behavior requisite to beating out the competition? Notice that I've consistently emphasized the word *you.* No one can motivate another person to *do* anything. It must come from within. I can provide the stimulus, but ultimately, success or failure is in *your* hands. Superior intelligence and/or education have little to do with entry-level police testing. That's not what the tests are designed to measure. What really matters are

- self-motivation—how much you want it
- perseverance—how much time and effort you're willing to invest to get it
- test-taking skills
- reading comprehension

Motivation is at the top of the list because if you have *motivation* you can learn the other three. I succeeded in the many police examinations I took not because I was more intelligent than the other candidates, but because I tried harder. I had the intrinsic ability to consistently sustain a high motivational level over a long period of time. Entry-level police examinations are generally regarded as difficult to prepare for because they presuppose no specific police job knowledge, experience, ability, training, or education. Consequently, many people mistakenly think they can't prepare. They believe in what I call "magical thinking." They *think* that because they're enrolled in a criminal justice program in college or did well on their SAT exam these accomplishments will somehow magically translate to high scores on civil service tests. It doesn't work that way. I prefer to explain the process of preparing people to achieve high scores on police examinations in a modified "situational leadership" framework. This framework uses "levels of readiness," which are divided into two variables, "ability" and "motivation." Here's an illustration of what I mean.

LEVELS OF READINESS

Ability	Motivation
Variables	
Knowledge: How much you know about the police examination process and what police officers really do.	*Rewards:* Money, power, status.
Education: Development gained through study or observation.	*Incentives:* Perceived recognition gained from doing it.
Training: Practicing techniques to improve test performance.	*Confidence:* Determined will to do it.
Experience: The skill or knowledge acquired from doing something.	*Self-Esteem:* Perception of how you feel about yourself.

Many of the factors contributing to the variables determining your level of readiness are under *your* direct control. You have already made an important start in acquiring knowledge by buying this book and becoming my partner. Now it's time to do a self-assessment to determine where you are today on the readiness scale. Below you'll find two thermometers. One represents "ability" and the other "motivation."

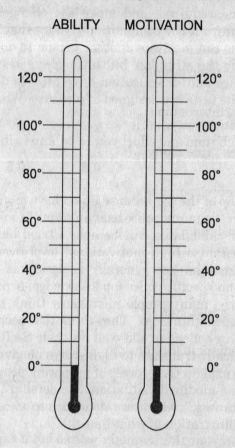

Ability is an extrinsic, *doing* variable which easily lends itself to measurement. Use the following scale to calculate your score and identify your "level of readiness" within this variable. For example, if you are currently a city or state police officer, you have a total of forty-eight points in the four categories. If you have an associate degree in criminal justice, add another thirteen, and so forth.

ABILITY LEVEL OF READINESS

Accomplishment	Knowledge	Education	Training	Experience
1. Currently a city or state police officer	15	15	8	10
2. Thorough knowledge of the contents of this book	5	5	5	0
3. Police Cadet, Explorer, internship program	2	2	0	0.5
4. Participation in a police "ride along" program	0.5	0.5	0	0
5. Attendance at two or more criminal justice seminars	0.5	0.5	0	0
6. Enrollment in a college-level criminal justice program	2	2	2	0
7. Associate degree in criminal justice or related field	5	5	3	0
8. Bachelor's degree in criminal justice or related field	7	6	4	0
9. Master's degree in criminal justice or related field	8	7	5	0
Totals				

Scorecard

110 or above = mercury in your thermometer was so hot it exploded
90-109 = very high ability
80-89 = high ability
70-79 = good ability
60-69 = fair ability
60 or below = low ability

Use a red marker to shade in your "degrees" on the "ability" thermometer.

Because motivation is an intrinsic quality varying from individual to individual, *you* have to determine your score in the motivation variable. What's meaningful to one person may not be to another. We all have different value systems, perceptions, cultures, needs, and personal expectations. Only *you* really know how motivated you are to become a police officer, and you'll have to shade in that thermometer based on your assessment of this variable. Be generous; if you took the time to purchase this book, I suspect you're pretty highly motivated. The trick is to sustain that ambition and drive over a long enough period of time, within a testing process that eliminates huge numbers of candidates simply because they didn't have the perseverance to stick with it.

Besides, you're my partner. My *job* is to constantly encourage you, and I intend to do just that throughout this book. So make your best estimate and shade in your "motivation" thermometer. Use a ruler to draw a line from your "ability" variable to your "motivation" variable so you can see exactly where you are right now. How high *is* your motivation thermometer? Can we raise it to the fever point? Where on the "ability" scale are you lacking? Education? Experience? What can you do about it? What steps can you take to raise your level of readiness in this area?

YOUR PERSONAL DEVELOPMENT ACTION PLAN

Now that we know your level of readiness, we can use this information as a tool to create a personal development and action plan to use in conjunction with this book. Our objective is to raise your level of readiness to the highest point possible, which will translate into high scores in the examination process, graduation with excellence from the police academy, and a highly successful first year as a police officer.

All goals have first steps followed by short, intermediate, and long-range plans. At the end of many of the sections of this book is a page titled "Personal Development and Action Plan." Turn now to page 21 to see your first one. On these pages, you can fill in different ways to raise your level of readiness in each specific area. It's absolutely essential that you take the steps outlined in these personal development and action plans. If you don't, your chance of securing employment in the police field is pretty slim. These action steps require only a high degree of motivation. "Rest makes rust!" Get working! Now!

> *Without faith, a man can do nothing; with it all things are possible.*
>
> —William Osler

CHOOSING A POLICE DEPARTMENT

As you now know, landing a job in the police field is becoming increasingly more difficult. However, there *are* steps you can take to get a huge lead on the other applicants even before you answer a single test question. The first step is to decide what *type* of policing you want to do. Do you want to be a police officer in a big city with a huge police force, in a medium-sized city with a force of about three hundred officers, or in a small town? As will be discussed, there are significant differences between being a police officer in a large city and a small town. Once you decide the *type* of policing you want to spend a lifetime doing, the next decision for you to make is *where* you want to do it. What factors should be taken into consideration relative to *where* you choose to apply for a position as a police officer? Knowing what type of policing is right for you and where you would prefer doing it requires researching *when* there are likely to be police positions available in the department where you want to be a police officer. When is that department likely to be *hiring*? Many candidates have been through the testing process with four or five police departments before they were successful in securing a position.

There's a lot to consider in deciding which type of policing you want to do and where you want to do it. Some of the advantages and disadvantages of different sizes of departments follow.

LARGE CITY POLICE DEPARTMENT
Population: over 250,000
Police force: over 500 officers

Advantages	Disadvantages
1. Needs to replace/hire police officers more frequently, in larger numbers due to promotions, retirement, resignations, and medical disability.	1. Bureaucratic process, large numbers of applicants, highly impersonal.
2. Likely to have its own police academy/training unit, shortening the process from selection to entry.	2. Higher crime rate, frequent calls for service, resulting in prioritized workload and less time for quality policing.
3. Likely to have a strong union, resulting in higher salary, better benefits (vacation, medical, dental, retirement, disability).	3. Frequent response to Part 1, serious criminal activity; higher degree of personal danger.
4. Wider range of assignments, greater chance for specialized assignment (arson, forensics, tactical and SWAT teams, etc.).	4. More exposure to poor working conditions due to poverty rate and high crime, resulting in higher job stress.
5. Greater opportunity for career advancement, promotion to detective, sergeant, lieutenant, captain, etc.	5. More likely to have budget reductions, resulting in poor equipment, high-mileage vehicles, dated technology.
6. Experience in all areas of policing rapidly gained due to high volume.	6. High degree of specialization, leading to lower job satisfaction at field patrol level.
7. More frequent training, education seminars, and schools.	7. Less individual supervision and management.
8. Likely to have Police Cadet, Explorer, and internship programs.	8. Uniforms often don't fit properly, require tailoring, and are of poor quality.
9. City issues uniforms, revolvers, all other police equipment and regularly replaces same at no cost to the officer.	

SMALL CITY POLICE DEPARTMENT
Population: over 100,000
Police force: fewer than 300 officers

Advantages	Disadvantages
1. Likely to consider college as a requisite to hiring and offer points added to overall score for education.	1. Low turnover rate, selects/hires singly or in small numbers.
2. May have strong union affiliation, with accompanying salary and benefit packages.	2. Large applicant pool for a small number of positions.
3. Lower crime rate, better working conditions, equipment, uniforms, and vehicles.	3. Likely to have retirement plan requiring a combination of years or service with reaching a specific age.
4. Likely to have fewer poverty zones and a higher community standard of living, resulting in better working conditions for police officers.	4. Lower crime rate results in fewer Part 1, serious criminal activity, calls for service, resulting in a longer amount of time to gain job experience.
5. Less job-related stress, lower level of danger and job-related injury.	5. Less likely to have its own police academy, resulting in a longer wait between selection and entry.
6. High degree of attention from supervision and management.	

A medium-sized city with a police department of between three hundred and five hundred officers falls somewhere between the two tables, depending on population and the size of the department.

There's still a lot to do before deciding *where* to apply. Even though police departments have the same general mission and similar organizational structures, there are definite differences from one department to another. The only way to really find out what those differences are is to visit the departments in the cities you're interested in. So, as will be discussed further, get out a map of your state and circle the cities and towns where you would consider being a police officer. You should select at least eight to ten departments to research. Make a list and prioritize it. Be realistic; the current job market may not allow you the luxury of being too picky, and there's nothing to say you can't obtain a few years of experience in one department while taking the tests for another.

Now that you have a list of police departments you're interested in, telephone the personnel department in the city or town where each is located and see what information you can find. Look up the number in the phone book, or go to the library so you'll have access to the entire state's phone books. Look under "City of _____, Personnel Department." If you don't see a heading for "Personnel Department," then just jot down the number for city hall. Prior to making your telephone calls, start a new heading in your notebook titled "Police Departments." Here's a sample of what this section in your notebook might look like.

POLICE DEPARTMENTS

Name of Department: _____

Address: _____

Name of Chief of Police: _____

Size of Department (current number of police officers): _____

Number of Officers Authorized in City Budget: _____

Number of Vacanies: _____

Police Internship Program: Yes _____ No _____ Requirements: _____

Police Cadet Program: Yes _____ No _____ Requirements: _____

Police Explorer Program: Yes _____ No _____ Requirements: _____

Ride Along Program: Yes _____ No _____ Requirements: _____

Personnel Department—Telephone Contact Date: _____ Spoke with: _____

Address: _____ Phone Number: _____

Letter to Personnel Department—Date: ____ Letter to Chief—Date: _____

Contacting the Personnel Department

In case you're not certain what to say when you call, use the following guide: "Good morning, this is Leslie Jones. Would you please connect me with someone who can answer questions relative to applying for a position in the police department?" Chances are, the person answering the telephone will be able to answer your questions and, if not, will connect you with someone who can. Do the following:

1. Ask "Are you currently accepting applications for the police department?" If the answer is *yes*, ask the person to send you an application and a copy of the police position description.

2. If the department is not currently accepting applications, ask, "Do you intend to hire police officers any time in the next six months?" Also ask for the name of the director of personnel and the name and business address of the chief of police.

3. Since the person answering your questions might not be as knowledgeable about future openings in the police department as the director of personnel, write a letter to that person. Here is a sample letter to use as a guide:

Today's date

The City of _____
Department of Personnel
Samuel T. Johnson, Director of Personnel
550 Main Street
City, State, and Zip Code

Dear Mr. Johnson:

   I am interested in applying for a position with the _____ Police Department and would greatly appreciate receiving information relative to the application process.

Sincerely,

Your name
Address
Telephone number

Also send a letter to the chief of police as follows:

Today's date

The City of _____
Police Department
Harry T. Smith, Chief of Police
135 Billingsgate Road
City, State, and Zip Code

Dear Chief Smith:

   I am very interested in becoming a police officer in your department. I would greatly appreciate your advising me when you anticipate beginning the selection process to hire new police officers.

Sincerely,

Your name
Address
Telephone number

As you're making phone calls and writing letters, jot down the information in your notebook, using the format provided in this book. You'll receive a response for every letter you write, and it's likely that at least one, if not more, of the departments you selected will be hiring in the next six months. Make your best estimate based on the information you've received and narrow your list down to about five departments.

How to Research a Police Department

The next step in your research is to visit each city on your list to find out as much as possible about the department and the type of community it serves. The best place to start is the city library. If you're polite, librarians will help you find what you want. Ask where they keep their copy of the city's annual report. You'll be referred to a thick book which describes every department in the city (police, fire, sanitation, schools, personnel, recreation, etc.) and provides statistics on the departments' budgets, number of employees, and expenditures. Look under the section for the police department. Some annual reports contain crime statistics, while others don't. If it does, this information will give you a good idea of the numbers and categories of criminal acts the department investigated. More importantly, there should be a column titled "Authorized Strength" or words to that effect, listing the number of police personnel currently in the department from chief of police to patrol officer. An example follows.

POLICE PERSONNEL

Job Position	Authorized Positions	Current Positions	Plus or Minus
Chief of Police	1	1	0
Assistant Chief	2	2	0
Captain	9	7	−2
Lieutenant	27	24	−3
Sergeant	63	62	−1
Detective	76	76	0
Officers	369	350	−19
Totals	547	522	−25

This is very important information! You know this department has nineteen fewer police officers than its budget authorizes. However, in actuality, they're going to need to hire at least twenty-four police officers just to stay at their authorized strength of 547. Here's why. They're minus two captains, three lieutenants, and one sergeant, probably because of retirements. This means that two lieutenants will be promoted to captain, creating two more vacancies in the lieutenant ranks, resulting in five vacancies for lieutenants. Five sergeants will then be promoted to lieutenant, which means they are now minus six sergeants. This means that either six detectives, six patrol officers, or a combination of both will be promoted to sergeant. Either way, it equates to six fewer patrol officers (if detectives are promoted, a patrol officer moves up to detective), and if you add that to the nineteen the department is already down, that equals twenty-four officers needed to be hired. If you factor in a prediction that any of the current personnel may soon be eligible for retirement and a ten to twenty percent failure rate in the police academy, plus any additional positions the chief may be shooting for, you may be looking at thirty-five officers or more to hire. This information will allow you to make a fairly accurate prediction whether a police department will be hiring new police officers in the near future.

I wish I could say that all police departments and city personnel units carefully study attrition rates to plan in advance when to have examinations for police officers. The truth of the matter is that hiring police officers is much more expensive than the selection process for other city departments. Hiring may boil down to whose budget the selection process for police officers impacts. Does it come out of the police department's budget or, more likely, the personnel department's budget? Does the city council or mayor have to approve the expenditure necessary for hiring and equipping thirty-five new police officers? It's an expensive process, so be aware of the politics involved.

You may be wondering why you should go through this exercise if the director of personnel has informed you that the department is not hiring and "can't anticipate" when more police officers will be needed. The reason it's important is that in city government things change rapidly. The chief and the police union may be doing some political infighting and may even prompt media references to a "lack of manpower" and "safety of the public" in order to secure the monies needed to hire enough officers to replace those who have left. If your research indicates that a police department is reduced by as many officers as in our example, then it's a good guess they will be hiring in the very near future.

You're probably thinking, "So what? When they're ready to hire, they'll send me an application because I telephoned and wrote the chief a letter." That's true, but it's *not* the reason I had you go through all of this. If you make a few phone calls and send out some letters, and a department is all set to begin the selection process, that's great. Just continue on with this book. But, chances are that's not going to be the case, and you may be better off if it's not. The reason I want you to do research and choose a specific department on which to concentrate your efforts is that you can significantly enhance your odds of becoming a police officer in a particular department if you're a Police Cadet, police intern, or Police Explorer. If possible, you need to join one of these programs. But before considering what these programs entail, let's continue the research to find the department that's right for you.

After reviewing the city's annual report, ask the librarian if there are any books on the city's police department. Some departments date to the late 1800s and the library may have a book titled something like *The History of the _____ Police Department*. If not, the origins and history of the department may be referenced in other books in the library. Ask the librarian to help you find them. Books of this nature will provide valuable insight into how the police department evolved to its present status, who the significant players were, and will also give you some sense of the "inner spirit" which all departments have. Make notes—they may help you later in your oral examination. Finally, see if the library has the city newspaper on microfilm. If not, call to see if the newspaper has it. Review the front page of the newspaper for the past two years. You'll find articles about the police department. Read them to gain an understanding of what issues involving the police were important enough to make the front page. For example, the articles may be about a civilian review board, the department changing from revolvers to semiautomatic handguns, police brutality, union/management contract negotiations, sexual harassment, police shootings, new technology purchased by the department, and so forth.

RIDING WITH A POLICE OFFICER

By now you should be starting to form an opinion about your selected police department. However, it's still too early to draw any definite conclusions. It's time to get in a cruiser and take a ride around the city with a police officer. Almost all police departments will allow you to ride with a police officer for a "tour of duty." Call the police department and ask if they have a "citizen rider" program. Explain that you're interested in a career in law enforcement and would like to ride with a police officer to learn more about the job. Your goal is to ride once on the day shift (from 8:00 A.M. through 4:00 P.M.) and at least once on the evening shift (from 4:00 P.M. through 12:00 A.M.). The reason you want to ride on both shifts is that, in most cities, policing is quite different at night when all of the business people have gone home to the suburbs. There is much more "action" on the street after dark, and riding only during the day would give you a false impression of what policing in that city is like.

> *Knowledge is power.*
> —Francis Bacon

Tips on Riding with a Police Officer

Make your ride with the police officer as profitable an experience as possible. Find out exactly where you're supposed to meet the officer (at the front desk, the front of the police station, the rear parking lot, etc.), at what time, and what the officer's name is who you're scheduled to ride with. You'll probably have to fill out a form relieving the city and the department of any responsibility if you're injured. Don't worry, the chances of your getting hurt are very remote.

Recognize that police officers seldom volunteer to have people ride with them; they're told to do it by their boss. Unless you do something to win them over, at best you'll be considered an inconvenience. Cops don't trust people quickly, so don't take it personally. You'll be given some instructions on what to do if the officer has to jump out in an emergency. (You'll probably be asked to stay in the police cruiser.) Follow these instructions to the letter. Introduce yourself, thank the officer for allowing you to ride in the cruiser (even though it may not have been his or her idea), and explain you're thinking about joining the department and that you want to get an idea of what policing is like. You'll have to play it by ear. You won't know each other, and it will be a little awkward. Police officers are just like other people in the sense that some are very approachable and will talk your ear off, while others are naturally reticent. It's up to you to get what you came for. Here are some of the things you may want to ask.

1. How long have you been with the force? What did you do before becoming a police officer?

2. Are you permanently assigned to the cruiser and a specific district (part of the city), or do police assignments change every shift?

3. Do officers change shifts every month, or does the department have a "bid shift" system where officers can select what shift they work based on seniority?

4. What's the crime rate like in the city? Are there a lot of violent crimes? How many homicides (murders) occur on average in the city each year? Is there a lot of drug activity and prostitution?

5. How is the department organized?

6. What is the police department's current method of policing? Do they use a community-oriented police strategy, crime suppression, special tactical squads? *Note: These are fairly common terms in policing. If they are unfamiliar to you, spend some time at the library before riding with the officer.*

7. Does the department have a residency requirement? If so, what is it?

8. When was the last time the department hired new officers? Do you think the department will be hiring in the near future?

9. What was the selection process like when you were hired? Can you offer any tips on how to prepare or what type of testing is used? Written tests, oral exams, assessment centers? *Note: An assessment center is not a place to go to take a test. It's a test in which candidates participate in a series of systematic, job-related, acted-out situations (often with role players) while being observed and evaluated by police experts.*

10. What was the police academy like?

11. Is the department unionized? If not, what type of affiliation or organization do officers belong to?

12. How do you feel about the department?

13. Does the department have a Police Cadet, Explorer, Athletic League, or internship program? If so, what are the requirements for joining?

14. What do you think are the chances for upward mobility or special assignment in the department?

15. What are the most significant problems facing the department?

While riding, you'll have the opportunity to observe the officer handling different situations. It's not a good idea to ask probing questions about *why* an officer handled a situation in a particular manner. Remember, your knowledge of the field is limited, and the officer doesn't have to explain his or her rationale to you. If you've been courteous, most officers will be happy to point things out and go over situations with you. Let the officer initiate this type of conversation or you're liable to find yourself limited to yes and no responses. All of this may seem a little strange to you. After all, police officers are public servants. Why wouldn't they be amenable to explaining their every action to anyone who asked? Because *you're* not one of *them.* Oh, they'll explain the law to you and how it applies to a particular situation, but if you're looking for their *personal* views on the ills of society, you've come to the wrong place.

INVOLVING YOURSELF WITH A PROGRAM

After completing research on the departments you've chosen, you're in a much better position to decide *where* to invest your time and energy. One of the questions you're eventually going to be asked at the oral examination is "What have you done to prepare yourself for a career in law enforcement?" What will *your* response be? Are *you* enrolled in a criminal justice program at your local college? Have *you* served an internship with the police department? Are *you* a Police Cadet? Have *you* joined the Police Explorers and helped young Scouts find the path to the way? Are *you* assisting the department's Police Athletic League by coaching youngsters in basketball, boxing, baseball, etc.? Choose the police department highest on your list which is most likely to be hiring in the near future and join one of these programs. A brief description of each follows.

> *The greater the difficulty, the greater the glory.*
>
> —Cicero

Police Internships

Many colleges having criminal justice programs coordinate work/study internships with local police departments. Students work part-time at the department for a period of between three to six months. They rotate through various police divisions to obtain an overall understanding of how the department operates as an organization. Three to six college credits are usually awarded for successful completion of the internship and submission of an approved research project. For example, you might spend time working in the police records unit, training academy, communications complex, forensic laboratory, property room, or one of the investigative divisions such as homicide or narcotics. Think how impressive it would be to tell an oral examination board made up of ranking members of the department about your internship in their own department! Your initial application for employment with the department has a section just for this type of information, and in the long run, it could mean your being selected over another candidate.

The Police Athletic League

The Police Athletic League (PAL) is usually found only in large police departments. Some departments have incorporated the PAL as an official, department-budgeted function and use on-duty police officers to staff and run it. Other departments recognize the PAL as a department-sponsored activity but rely on police and community volunteers to staff, operate, and fund the program. The PAL is an outreach program for young adults providing mentors within a sports framework. Whether it's basketball, football, or boxing, it gets kids off the streets and into the gym. Volunteers are always needed for the PAL, whether or not the department funds the program. You don't have to be attending college to participate and spend a few hours shooting hoops or keeping score at a game. You can do something meaningful, have some fun, and impact the police selection process all at the same time. Then, when you're asked by the oral examination panel what you've done to prepare yourself, you can say, "I spent the summer working with the department's Police Athletic League to bring rival street gangs together for a baseball tournament. The Street Boys beat the Ghetto Brothers in the final series five runs to three."

The Police Explorer Program

The Police Explorers are Scout troops sponsored by police departments and usually managed by off-duty police officers and volunteers. Participants wear distinctive uniforms resembling those worn in the police department. The group is organized along semimilitary lines. In some cities, older Scout members are allowed to ride in police cruisers, direct traffic at special events, march in parades with the police department, and work at local athletic events. Like the Police Athletic League, the Explorer program is always looking for adult volunteers to act as sponsors on outings, supervise planned programs, and attend meetings.

The Police Cadet Program

The majority of police departments still require applicants to be twenty-one years of age prior to appointment. To attract promising future candidates, some departments have created a Police Cadet program which offers paid positions within the police department. The program is specifically designed for individuals between the ages of eighteen and twenty-one. The selection process for a police cadet is similar to that for a police officer. There are written and oral examinations, a physical agility test, a medical examination, a background investigation, and a psychiatric examination. However, the testing process isn't as difficult or as in-depth as it is for police officers. Usually only a few cadet positions are available each year, and the program recruits mostly city residents. Similar to police interns, police cadets rotate through the various units and divisions of the police department. A performance evaluation is completed after each assignment, and police cadets are expected to be enrolled in college.

Obviously, many career benefits are associated with being a police cadet, but two outstanding benefits are that cadets, upon reaching the age of twenty-one, automatically enter the police academy without any further examination requirements, and their time as cadets counts toward retirement benefits.

> The only ones among you who will be really happy are those who have sought and found how to serve.
> —Albert Schweitzer

It should be obvious by now that I recommend a proactive plan for landing a job in policing. As a matter of fact, I recommend even more than that. I'm asking you to make a total commitment of your time, resources, and inner being to becoming a police officer. Read every book you can get your hands on about policing, get psyched up by watching Steven Seagal beat up the bad guys; research different departments; ride with police officers; enroll in a college criminal justice program, subscribe to police magazines such as *Law and Order* and *Police Chief* and get involved in one of the programs previously described. If there's someone especially meaningful to you (father/mother, boyfriend/girlfriend, husband/wife), get them on the team right now. Communicate with them. Tell them what your dream is and let them help you fulfill a part of it. Involve them in the process. The path is narrow in police work; don't lose the people you love along the way.

There's a scene in the latest movie adaptation of *Robin Hood* in which Kevin Costner, acting the part of Robin, kneels at his father's grave, takes out a knife, and draws the open blade against the palm of his left hand. He makes a tight fist so the blood will flow, sprinkles the blood over the grave, and makes an oath to avenge his father's death. You don't have to go quite as far as this blood oath to motivate yourself. Just *almost!* It's part of "the way."

PERSONAL DEVELOPMENT AND ACTION PLAN

What have I done today to prepare myself for a career in policing?

1. _____
2. _____
3. _____
4. _____
5. _____
6. _____
7. _____
8. _____
9. _____
10. _____

2
BEGINNING
THE QUEST

QUESTIONS ABOUT POLICING

Note: Some of the material contained in this section is covered in more detail in other sections of the book.

I'm often asked to speak at colleges and universities that offer criminal justice programs. Each of my lectures includes a question-and-answer session designed to offer students an opportunity to bridge the gap between academics (the way it's supposed to be) and the reality of the streets. I find it curious that those majoring in criminal justice programs, ostensibly to further a career goal, know so very little about how police agencies really operate. So I try to structure these sessions so that people will feel comfortable asking anything they want about policing. Having done this many times, I've noticed that some questions are asked more often than others. Many of the questions reflect a generation greatly influenced by television cop shows, movies, and, to some extent, the print media, all of which have contributed to the romanticizing and distorting of real policing. The entertainment industry, coupled with the fact that police officers work within a "closed society" (cops don't talk to anyone about their work except other cops), has created myths and half-truths about police officers and what they do, resulting in a huge gap between the reality of policing on America's streets and Hollywood's version of the supercop's world. Since you probably have many of the same questions as my students, let's list them, and then discuss them in a manner in which learning can take place.

Common Questions About Becoming a Police Officer

- Is there any difference between being a *state cop* and a *city cop*?
- What *qualifications* do I have to have?
- What *type* of *test* is given?
- What *type* of *department* does _____ (city) have?
- How many *"men"* are on the force?
- How many *women* are on the force?
- How do you feel about *women* police officers?
- How much does police work *pay*?
- Would I have to *live in the city* in which I was a police officer, or could I live somewhere else and commute to work?
- Is there a *height/weight* requirement?
- How *long* does it *take* to become a *police officer*?
- What's the *police academy* like? *How long* does it last?

- Will they take me if I *wear glasses*?

- *How long* does it take to make *detective*?

- Have you ever *shot* anyone?

- What type of *gun* do cops carry?

- If someone *smoked marijuana* in high school, would it prevent them from becoming a police officer?

- If someone got a *ticket for speeding,* would that stop them from becoming a police officer?

- If someone was arrested for *breach of the peace* or *disorderly conduct,* would it prevent them from becoming a police officer?

- Do they give a *drug test*?

- How does someone go about *applying* to become a cop?

A SEMINAR

Creating a list of questions and answers provides you with only a limited learning experience. Because this is a book, and we can't see or speak directly to one another, communication is one-sided. We need to find a way to change that to enhance your understanding of the knowledge I'm trying to transfer from me to you. So, let's pretend you're enrolled in a criminal justice program at your local community college. It's a small class with only twenty-three students. We've just come back from a fifteen-minute break, and the next forty-five minutes is devoted to a question-and-answer session on any aspect of policing.

Rather than stand behind a lectern, I've asked you and the other students to move your seats into a semicircle so everyone can see each other. At the top of the semicircle, where the opening is, I've plopped down in a chair. It's obvious that I'm trying to create an atmosphere where people will feel comfortable asking questions. Once you've all moved your chairs and are seated again, it's time for me to begin.

"OK, lets get started. I'll be happy to give you my opinion and advice on any aspect of policing. This session is intended to be very informal, so please don't be afraid to ask anything you want."

Nobody says anything. There's an awkward silence. The whole group stares at me intently, and then they look at one another. Some people begin squirming around in their seats with polite little smiles on their faces, while others have pens poised to take notes as if there were going to be a test on this stuff. They're not used to this type of teaching. If I want to loosen them up, I'll have to change the mood in the classroom.

"Listen folks, this is a gift. It's extra. You don't have to take notes. Your professor won't test you on this, and chances are, none of you will ever see me again. I don't even know your names. I don't work here. I'm just a guest speaker. If you don't ask any questions, it's going to be a long forty-five minutes." This little speech usually works, and sure enough, a hand from a student sitting next to you tentatively goes up.

"Mr. Jetmore, there seem to be all kinds of different police agencies. State, local police, the FBI, and sheriffs' departments, among others. *Is there any real difference between, say, working for the state police and working for a local police department?*"

Smiling, I thank heaven for small favors. What a perfect question to start things rolling.

"That's an important question which has significance for everyone in this room. Not only *are* there differences between state, city, and town police agencies, but also important variables from city to city and town to town. Primarily, state police officers (sometimes called troopers) are responsible for criminal and traffic-control-related activities occurring on state highways. They have jurisdiction (statutory police arrest powers) throughout the state and can make arrests in any city or town within the state's borders. However, the general rule of thumb is that state police officers cover the state highways, including entrance and exit ramps. All police matters occurring *off* the highways and ramps are usually the responsibility of the local city or town police department, although there is some overlap.

"Obviously, city and town police officers also have arrest powers on state highways and ramps within their city's or town's geographical limits. So do agents of the Federal Bureau of Investigation (FBI) and the Drug Enforcement Administration (DEA), motor vehicle inspectors, and a host of other federal, state, and local officials. An agreement is reached (sometimes in writing—a 'reciprocal compact'—but more often not) that the state cops take the highways and the town and city cops have the rest. This arrangement prevents disputes over who is responsible for what and when.

"Those towns not having an organized police department, due to the infrequency of crime, traffic accidents, etc., are covered by the state police from a centralized location. In addition to regular state police officers, some states have 'resident state troopers.' The town pays all or a portion of the resident state police trooper's salary and often provides an office for the trooper in exchange for having the officer stationed in the town. This provides the town with faster and more personalized police services. In some ways, this arrangement is similar to that of the sheriff of the Old West.

"So, for the most part, state police officers are responsible for traffic control and the maximum movement of traffic along state highways. In contrast, city police officers are responsible primarily for crime prevention, crime detection, and the arrest of people who commit criminal acts. The larger the city, the greater the contrast between individual departments. In bigger cities, like Dallas, Los Angeles, Detroit, or New York, for example, police officers patrolling a district (a specified area of the city for which the officer is responsible) may respond to thirty or forty calls for service in a single eight-hour tour of duty! These calls for service (calls into the police station from the public reporting a crime or requesting assistance or criminal activity the officer comes across while on patrol) may range from something as simple as the need to tow a car blocking a driveway to an active street robbery, mugging, or drive-by shooting. Compare this to the situation in a small town where an officer might respond to only five calls for service in an eight-hour shift, the highlight of which could be escorting the manager of the local McDonald's to the bank to make a night deposit.

"The reason this is so important to *you* is that the city's or town's type of police agency, size of department, and political structure will directly affect the quality of life of its police officers. All of you in this classroom should be taking a broadbased approach to choosing a police department. For instance, does the department you're interested in have a residency requirement? Will you have to live there or within a specified distance of the city? If you *are* required to live within the boundaries of the city, would you *want* to live and raise a family there? Is it a place your wife or husband (think years into the future) will want to live? What is the school system like? Would you want your children to attend school there? How much will housing and transportation to and from work cost? If you're already a resident, does the testing process offer 'residency points' on the exam? Some cities add from five to ten points to a person's overall score if he or she is a city resident.

"The larger the city, the greater the size of the police department, and the greater the size of the department, the more opportunities there are for promotion and/or selection for specialized assignment. A big-city police department has a wide range of job assignments, considered by some to be more prestigious than just 'wearing the bag' (being a uniformed street cop). Big city means a crimes against persons division (homicide squad, robbery detail, and warrant unit), crimes against property division (burglary and auto theft squads), vice and narcotic division (drugs, prostitutes, pornography, and gambling), intelligence division (organized crime and gangs), evidentiary services division (forensics, photography, blood stains, and murder scenes), traffic division (motorcycle and accident-investigation specialists), special weapons assault teams (SWAT) or emergency response teams or tactical units, bomb squads, crime prevention officers, canine officers, community relations specialists, and more. Large police departments have a higher turnover rate. People retire. That means increased opportunity for promotion to detective, sergeant, lieutenant, captain, assistant chief, and even chief of police! And, if you're interested in street action, the big city is the place to go.

"A smaller city or town, with just ten police officers, for example, is probably going to have only a chief of police, one or two sergeants, and maybe eight police officers. The eight officers are expected to provide police services for the town twenty-four hours a day, three hundred sixty-five days a year. Police departments, unlike other state and local agencies, are open twenty-four hours a day, and officers make house calls! That means if you're the newest member on the force, you can expect to spend your first few years working the 'dog shift' (midnight to eight). Forget about being with your family on Christmas or any other holiday, for that matter. Small-town cops are generalists. They do everything. If an arrest is made, there is no 'paddy wagon' to call to transport prisoners to headquarters or a 'booking room' as there is in a big city. *You* bring the prisoners in, search them, take their property, fingerprint and photograph them, and put them in a cell. In a larger city, these tasks are usually performed by specialists.

"That doesn't mean big-city cops are any *better* than those in smaller cities and towns. All have courageous men and women. I just want to be sure you understand that there are many differences between individual police departments."

Several more hands pop up, and I point to the student sitting closest to me.

"Mr. Jetmore, my name's Paula. *What qualifications do police departments require for applicants?*"

"Well, there are some pretty standard qualifications and others unique to individual departments. Most require applicants to be twenty-one years of age. Others allow candidates to apply as early as eighteen. A *few* allow persons under these ages to apply as long as they'll turn the mandatory age by the time their police academy class graduates.

All require you to be a United States or naturalized citizen, have at least a high school diploma or a general equivalency diploma (some require college), and have a state driver's license or the ability to obtain one. You'll have to have vision correctable to twenty/twenty for most places, twenty/forty for others, and pass a medical examination and a physical agility test. Some departments have a strict height/weight and/or weight-in-proportion-to-height requirement, while others allow for ten to twenty percent waivers in weight and up to a one-inch waiver in height. Residency requirements vary from requiring you to live in the city or town to specifying a maximum number of miles and/or driving time away from the city. Some departments don't have a residency requirement at all.

"The position description, which is usually given to you along with the application for employment (or is published in the newspaper), specifies the type of testing procedure, which may consist of written and oral examinations, an assessment center test, a medical examination, a background investigation, a psychological evaluation, a polygraph test, and a physical agility test. Sometimes you're not told about *all* of what's entailed because the process occurs in stages over several months, and the initial application is used primarily to screen out unqualified candidates. Many more applicants apply than there are openings for on the force. There's no doubt that it's a tough selection process. Don't forget, we give cops guns!"

All the hands are up now. People are really starting to get into this.

You ask, *"What are the tests that you mentioned like?"*

"I could teach an entire college course just on civil service testing. Everything about the process is a test. If we define a test as anything which eliminates candidates from the process, then your initial application for employment is a 'test.' What they're trying to do by testing candidates is to predict who's going to be most successful on the job. If all applicants possessed the same knowledge, skills, abilities, and personal characteristics, there wouldn't be a need for testing.

"Let's say a department is forecasting that twenty-five of its members will retire and another five will resign or leave for other reasons in the next two years. They want to hire thirty police officers. Knowing that ten to twenty percent of those entering the police academy won't graduate, they establish a number of thirty-six police officers to hire to finally get the thirty they want. The chief also knows from past experience that if he or she starts advertising today, it could be nine or ten months before any of these newly hired police officers hit the streets. So the city personnel department advertises in the paper and in magazines such as *Police Chief* and *Law and Order*. More progressive departments might also send representatives to college campuses, advertise on the radio, and send "recruiters" to local community centers, churches, and military separation centers. But all of this provides only a large pool of hopeful candidates. Because of the number of applicants, the economy, and the declining job market, a department can afford to be very selective. After the cutoff date for receiving applications, a letter is sent advising *qualified* candidates that their applications have been received (or that further information is needed, such as a copy of a high school diploma) and that they will be contacted with the date, time, and location of the *written examination*.

"The written examination is given first because it readily lends itself to testing large numbers of people. It's economical, court defensible, easy to administer, simple to score, and it allows for the ranking of candidates. It also eliminates large numbers of people from the process because the passing score can be adjusted to whatever grade the tester wants. Multiple-choice questions are almost always used to insure objectivity and that there is only one correct answer. The written examination is similar to a basic achievement or aptitude test. It tests your ability to use analytical thinking and demonstrate reading comprehension and common sense. It may have a writing component, usually contains a memory and observation test (such as showing you a series of photographs or mug shots and asking you to recall specific details about them later in the test), and sometimes has a math component. Often, police phrasing and language are used in the questions and in the types of situations the test puts you in, but you're not expected to know specific police rules, regulations, or procedures.

So, two thousand people apply and a couple of hundred are eliminated in the initial application process because they don't have the basic qualifications or they don't produce requested documentation. That leaves eighteen hundred people to take the written test, of which two hundred don't show up. Obviously, they can't handle sixteen hundred people in the next phase—either the oral examination or medical evaluation—so they notify only the cream of the crop, say the highest one hundred twenty-five scores on the written test, depending upon affirmative-action needs. There is, of course, a problem if only one hundred twenty-five white males go forward in the process. The courts have prohibited the use of tests which tend to disproportionately reject members of various classes of people for reasons which can't be shown to be job related. So, if you were scoring the test and had the results in front of you, you might look to see how many females and how many different races are in the top one hundred twenty-five scores and adjust the passing mark upward or downward, depending on the results, to get the right mix in the pool of candidates to go forward in the process. (Most experts agree that a police department should reflect the racial balance of the community it serves.)

"There's nothing that says that everyone who obtains a mark of seventy percent is automatically entitled to go forward in the selection process. The cutoff grade may be eighty-eight percent, and many candidates may have achieved that score. So letters go out to everyone who took the written examination. You're informed that your score is 87.99 percent, but that you didn't do well enough to make the cut and are eliminated from the process. Wow! After getting such a high mark, that's pretty hard to swallow. The examinations for police officer have become very competitive. Expect to have to score in the nineties to secure a position. The written examination *can* be prepared for, and I would urge you to do so. Practice makes perfect. If you don't succeed on the first try, use the knowledge you gained in taking the test on the next department's test you take.

"In some police departments, the next test is the *oral examination*. In others, it's the *medical*, or, as it's sometimes referred to, the *physical exam*. The medical examination is given before the physical agility test to ensure that the applicant is physically able to perform the exercises involved. The city certainly doesn't want a lawsuit if a candidate has a heart attack on the obstacle course.

"The oral exam is designed to measure the intrinsic, personal qualities of a candidate. This is often done by asking questions about how you would respond to a situation outlined by a panel scoring you on a variety of different elements. These may include decision-making ability, judgment, oral communication, organizational integrity (putting departmental goals ahead of personal goals), appearance, poise, etc. For example, one of the oral panelists might ask, 'You're a police officer and observe a man commit a serious crime. He's coming at you with a large, lead pipe yelling that he's going to kill you. How would you handle this situation?' Oral boards can be intimidating if you don't understand what's involved. You *can* study for them, like any other test, and, if you're prepared and use common sense, you won't have a problem achieving a high mark.''

> *Rotten wood cannot be carved.*
> —Chinese proverb

"The medical examination is really no different from those that all of you have gone through before. You're provided with a detailed questionnaire to record your medical history and current condition. Don't lie (it will come back to haunt you later), but don't volunteer information either. Then it's height, weight, blood pressure, blood test, chest X-ray, hearing test, urinalysis, and vision test, which also includes color vision. Either the job announcement or correspondence from the personnel department will inform you of the requirements for the medical examination. It's a good idea to find out what they are way ahead of time because failure to pass the medical examination will eliminate you from the process. Often, there are lifestyle changes you can make in order to pass the physical if you're aware of the department's standards in advance.

"There may be some differences in the types of evaluation used by a particular department on the *physical agility test,* but usually it involves a series of exercises such as push-ups; sit-ups; a vertical jump; pull-ups; stretches (such as sit and reach); distance running (two miles or so); stair climbing or a step test; and an obstacle course or agility run, which re-creates police situations by having you climb over a wall while carrying a weight or pull a weighted dummy along the floor for a distance. You're competing against time, minimum performance levels, other candidates, or all three. Some departments give the physical agility test a score which they 'weight' against the other examinations, while others simply use a pass/fail system.

"Let's see, I've covered the written, oral, medical, and physical agility tests a little bit. What's left? Oh, the *psychological evaluation*. Don't worry, you probably won't be sitting down with a psychiatrist or psychologist. The evaluation is normally a paper-and-pencil test asking a series of questions to evaluate whether you're a mature, stable, well-adjusted person capable of working with others. They need to make sure you don't have an emotional or personality maladjustment. There isn't a grade, and to be rejected solely as a result of the test, a psychologist or psychiatrist would have to be able to show that you're not emotionally and/or mentally fit to perform the duties of a police officer.

"That leaves the *background investigation* and *polygraph test*. The background is simple. Don't lie on your application. Don't stretch the truth either. In most police departments, detectives are assigned to complete background investigations on candidates. You'll have completed a detailed personal history statement and answered in-depth questions relative to your past and current employment, medical history, academic credentials, credit, previous residences, and so on. The background investigation team will obtain all your academic records, visit or call previous employers, check to see if you've been arrested or convicted of a crime, perform a credit check, and inspect your motor vehicle driving record. The object is to determine if you're a responsible and reliable person. If you've lied on your medical history questionnaire or about your academic credentials, prior employment, etc., it will *eliminate* you from further consideration in the selection process.

"The polygraph examination, commonly referred to as the lie-detector test, isn't done in all police departments because it's very expensive and many question its reliability and accuracy. Polygraph examinations aren't currently admissible in criminal proceedings. Your part is very simple. Just tell the truth. A professional polygraph examiner will hook you up to a machine which records changes in blood pressure, pulse, and breathing on a moving chart as the examiner asks you a series of questions. Polygraph specialists interpret emotional responses and changes in blood pressure and breathing to assist them in determining if a person is telling the truth."

All of the hands in class are up again. The young woman sitting on your left asks, *"What's the normal proportion of males to females on police forces across the United States?"*

"It varies too much from city to city to give you a concrete, statistical answer, but women are making their mark in policing just as they are in every other profession. However, I don't want to sugar-coat the fact that policing is still very much male dominated, and female police officers are the exception rather than the rule. Right now I would be surprised to see many police departments in which females comprise more than seven or eight percent of the force. Generally, the larger and more progressive the department, the more female police officers you'll find. I expect the number of women applying for police positions to continue to grow rapidly and the percentages to gradually come up as time goes on."

The young woman persists, saying, "I assumed most of that, but what do *you* personally feel about women on the force?"

The class waits expectantly. Many are women, and an ever so slight note of hostility was in the young woman's voice as she asked the question. This challenge causes me to get up and walk around the outside of the circle and grab an empty chair, which I squeeze between her and the next student.

"Would you mind if I ask your name?"

She looks me dead in the eye. "It's Mary."

"Mary, we've only known each other for a couple of hours. Tell me, what do you honestly think my answer will be?"

Mary hesitates, but only for a second, and says, "Well, I really don't know, but you seem to be a pretty straight shooter. If you're not *afraid* to tell us what you *really* think, I'm betting you would rather have a man beside you in a fight than a woman. Right?"

I shrug. "So, in other words, you think my answer will be that if a woman wants to be a lumberjack, she should be able to handle her end of the log. It's not a fair question, Mary, because 'fighting,' or a police combat situation, is such a minute part of what we do. Statistically, the average police officer never fires his or her weapon over a twenty-year career! But, to be honest, if you had asked me that question during the first few years I was a cop, I would have said, 'You're damn right I want another guy with me. Women can't handle combat, and I don't want to get killed.'

"My viewpoint *now* is that people have different strengths and weaknesses, different skills and abilities. Over the years, I've been in combat with men and women police officers by my side many times. I was commander of a SWAT team for four years. Some women were excellent in combat, some not. Some men were excellent in combat, some not. In emergency situations I often had to choose who would do what job and when. It's really quite simple. You choose the *person* who is best at the skill needed. If I needed a sniper, it was the person who had the most training and experience and was the best shot under pressure. If I needed a hostage negotiator, it was the person who was best for *that* type of situation. If I needed someone to break down a door with a sledge hammer, the same criteria applied. In other words, when lives are at stake, you don't have the luxury of being sexist. It's whoever can get the job done best.

"So, to answer your question directly, in most cases, you're not going to be able to choose who is or isn't with you in a fight. It happens without planning. If the combat is hand to hand, I'd rather have the added size and strength of most men. If it's not hand to hand, then it really doesn't matter, male or female. The police officers I served with always were there when the bell rang. None of them ever backed up in a fight, male or female."

Looking at the faces in class, I think I won that one, but it's hard to tell. Unfortunately, I'm a lot older than these kids. "More questions?"

"Mr. Jetmore, my name is Mark. How much do most police jobs start you out with?"

"You mean how much does the job pay?"

"Yeah," Mark grins.

"Well, Mark, again it depends a lot on where in the country you are." Getting up, I grab a thick manila folder off the desk in front of the class and move over toward the blackboard.

"Let me put some statistics on the board from a recent survey completed by the Labor Relations Information System out of Portland, Oregon. You'll be interested to know that they surveyed 332 cities with populations of more than fifty thousand, and the average entry-level salary for a police officer was $25,824." Writing quickly on the board, I produce a table, which is replicated on the next page.

ENTRY-LEVEL AND TOP-LEVEL POLICE OFFICER SALARIES
Selected U.S. Cities

City	State	Entry-Level Wage	Top-Level Wage
Anchorage	Alaska	$52,032	$59,296
Los Angeles	California	37,824	49,644
Miami	Florida	27,984	43,452
Detroit	Michigan	27,852	36,792
Boston	Massachusetts	27,708	35,604
Phoenix	Arizona	27,036	40,056
New York	New York	25,900	42,912
St. Louis	Missouri	24,060	34,728
Dallas	Texas	23,892	32,016
Scranton	Pennsylvania	14,688	26,928

"As you can see, there's a wide range of entry- and top-level salaries for police officers. It's not surprising that the survey also showed that the average number of police officers per capita tends to rise in relationship to the population size of the city. Take a look at these statistics."

Population Category	Officers/1,000
50,000–75,000	1.78
75,000–100,000	1.79
100,000–250,000	1.85
250,000–500,000	2.17
over 500,000	2.55

"The number of officers in Phoenix, Arizona, is 2,041, with a population of nearly one million; Los Angeles has 8,212 officers, with a population of 3.4 million; and New York City has 27,156 police officers to serve a population of nine million. Also, keep in mind that most police agencies have excellent benefit packages. These may include paid medical and dental plans, a uniform allowance or yearly stipend to purchase uniforms, twelve or so paid holidays, and two weeks vacation to start and three weeks, usually, after five years of employment. Plus, many police departments (especially those which are unionized) have a twenty-year retirement plan with no age limit, which means if you went on the job at age twenty-one, you could theoretically retire at age forty-one, with fifty percent of whatever your pay was at that time for the rest of your life! Also, policing is one of the few jobs left where you can affect another person's life in a positive way every single day."

"Mr. Jetmore, my name is Paul." (They're not even bothering to raise their hands now.) *"What type of physical requirements do most police departments have?"*

"Well, Paul, by physical requirements, I take it you mean height, weight, vision, and stuff like that?" Paul nods.

"I hate to keep telling all of you that it varies, but it does. Not just department to department, but again, it depends on what part of the country you live in. Generally speaking, the courts have ruled that *job requirements* must be shown by the employer to be specifically related to *job performance*. In order to ensure that their standards are nondiscriminatory and court defensible, many, but far from all, police agencies have rescinded specific height and weight requirements and now talk in terms of height *in proportion* to weight. So some departments have thrown out the old height/weight charts and have gone to body fat composition as determined by a skinfold measurement test as a superior method of judging overall body composition. Height requirements might pose a problem for some, because you can be too short or too tall, but at least weight is something you can control and do something about.

"Not so with vision, however. This is an area which can readily be tied to police officer job performance, and the only real question is what standard a department uses. If you're concerned, have an eye exam. Wearing glasses is not a problem, but generally, correctable vision (with glasses or contact lenses) of twenty/twenty or twenty/forty is a good rule of thumb as a requirement for most departments."

After answering Paul's question, it's time for a drink of water. I head over to the podium, where there's a pitcher and some glasses. There's a charged air in the classroom, and people are talking excitedly among themselves. "Further questions?" A hand shoots up.

"Hi, I'm Bob. *How long does it take to become a police officer?"*

"The best way I can answer your question, Bob, is to have you think of policing as a *way of life* rather than a job. The mechanical process of applying for the *job,* taking the various tests, and going through the police academy usually takes around ten months—*if* everything goes smoothly. That's figuring four months for the various tests (figure less if it's a small department) and twenty-two weeks for the police academy, give or take a couple of weeks. However, some police departments swear you in (have you take the oath of office) before you enter the academy. In that case, you might technically be a police officer trainee, but it's really in name only. The 'way of life' part comes in because, even after you graduate from the academy and pin on your shield, it will take you years to *become* a police officer. It's *not* just a matter of graduating from a police academy, pinning on a badge, and wearing a gun. You have to earn your shield on the street, and only *you* will really know when you've arrived."

Bob's hand is up again, and I point in his direction. He asks, *"What's the police academy like?"*

"The police academy is part college classroom and part Marine boot camp. It's where we separate the 'wannabes' from the 'almosts.' You see, in most police organizations, all of the testing is done by civilians, not cops. The city personnel unit handles most of the testing, especially the initial application process, written test, psychological exam, and medical exam. Police personnel may get involved with the oral testing, background investigation, and physical agility test, but in many cases, it's not until candidates arrive at the police academy that they're under *our* control for the first time. Remember *this:* policing is a *doing* profession. You have to be able to apply what you learn.

"For example, I can give everyone in the academy a class on handcuffs and handcuffing techniques, and they can all regurgitate the information back to me with a median class average of ninety-eight percent. Pretty good class average, right?" Everyone agrees.

"Wrong. It's good only if the candidates can *apply* handcuffing techniques, which means they have to demonstrate that ability by handcuffing someone who doesn't want to be handcuffed and may be bigger than they are. Yes, there are classes such as Constitutional Law, History of Police, Forensics, Laws of Arrest, and Search and Seizure which are purely academic. But we already know you can retain data. That's what the initial testing was all about.

"What we don't know is what's *inside* you, your intrinsic qualities. We don't know about stuff like courage, inner strength, honor, integrity, and whether you're racist. We don't know your concept of justice, truth, ethics, morality, and self-discipline. The kinds of things which really matter! So, if I yell in your ear, make you do a few push-ups, call you a name, and embarrass you a little, can you take it? If not, policing isn't for you. See, if you make a mistake in the factory or office, someone loses money. But if you fly off the handle and make a mistake with a *gun,* someone *dies!* What do you say when the bullet comes out and you've shot a little five-year-old boy or girl? 'Oops, I made a mistake!'? So the police academy is the place to separate those who have what it takes from those who don't. People with average intelligence won't have a problem, academically, in the police academy if they're motivated and study hard. But those who are lacking in inner strength had better find it quick!"

> *Character is made by what you stand for; reputation by what you fall for.*
>
> —Roger Quillen

As soon as I stop speaking almost every hand in class pops up. "Let's see, who hasn't had a chance to ask a question. How about you, sir?"

"Mr. Jetmore, *how long does it take to make detective*? Those of us who graduate with a degree in criminal justice will have a better chance, won't we?"

"No, not in the way *you* mean. You'll have a better chance than someone without college only because you've had a lot of recent practice taking tests and your reading comprehension is probably better. But you can't get overconfident. The written test won't know you graduated from college, and the *type* of written test given is different from those you're used to. It's not until the oral test that you'll have an opportunity to tell the examination board what you've done to prepare yourself for a career in policing. But all of that just gives you an edge in getting on the job, not in making detective. Police officers make detective because they've developed unique skills that can't be found in a book. They catch crooks. You need to get several years of practical police experience, like walking a beat and going on hundreds of police calls, before you're ready to turn in your silver badge for a gold one. Learning about being a cop in the classroom is one thing; being a cop on the street is another."

I think I hurt their feelings a little. Maybe it was a hard blow, but someone has to tell these kids the truth once in awhile. "Does anyone have any further questions?"

I point toward several raised hands, and a student who looks a little older than the rest asks, *"What type of guns do most police officers carry?"*

"Until very recently the Smith and Wesson thirty-eight caliber, six-shot revolver was carried by most police officers across the United States. Many departments are now choosing to arm their officers with semiautomatic handguns, such as the Colt forty-five and the Glock nine millimeter. This change has come about in response to the superior firepower available to and frequently used by today's criminals and also because of officer-involved shootings with multiple suspects. Semiautomatics provide officers eighteen to twenty cartridges as opposed to the six available with the revolver. Read any big-city newspaper, and you'll find an article about some drug dealer who shot a bunch of other drug dealers with an Uzi submachine gun in a battle over turf."

Everyone laughs again, and a voice from somewhere says, "What's wrong with that? Let them kill one another!" The rest of the class joins in general agreement that this would be an excellent outcome.

Smiling, I shake my head in disbelief. "You know, for a bunch of college kids so involved in social issues, you amaze me. You're so caught up in the paradigm of fighting the 'war on drugs' that you don't yet understand that this whole thing isn't about the residue of some plant. Nor do you understand that while the drug dealers are shooting at one another, they often miss and kill some little kid who just happened to be in the wrong place at the wrong time. No, this is about poverty, oppression, lack of job skills, money, power, the breakdown of the nuclear family, and a criminal justice system that burst at the seams years ago. Don't get me started, or we'll be here all night.

"The question was about the type of guns police officers carry. It's more important for you to know that in a police department *you* won't have a vote in the decision. Policing is not a democracy. The *department* will decide exactly what gun you'll carry while on duty and, in most cases, the type of firearm you can carry off duty while in the city or town in which you're a police officer. Most police departments issue you the weapon. Others have *you* purchase it. *All* prescribe the type, caliber, and even the kind of cartridge that goes in the gun. Policing is very much a semimilitary profession, with all kinds of rules and regulations. You'll be issued a large, thick manual containing a department order telling you what make, model, and caliber handgun; the length of its barrel; its color; the type of grips allowed; the type of holster it must be worn in, including its color; the type of belt the holster can be affixed to and where it's to be worn on the belt; and the exact type of cartridge, down to the number of grains of powder, which can be put into the gun. Then, the department will train you with the weapon, requiring you to obtain a minimum score on the firing range to be issued the firearm in the first place, and have you requalify at least once yearly in order to keep it. Any further questions about guns?"

A young woman asks, *"Have you ever shot anybody?"*

"No, thank God, I haven't had to do that. I've come very close, as do all police officers, but I never had to pull the trigger. I've been with officers on several occasions when they had to use deadly physical force to protect themselves or others from being killed. In each case, it had a drastic effect on their lives. One minute you're giving a citizen directions, and the next you're five blocks away, shooting someone trying to kill another person with a machete. But, as I mentioned before, the average police officer serves twenty years and never fires his or her service revolver off the police firing range."

Somewhere along the line, I'd gotten a little excited, left my chair, and begun pacing around the circle. The hands are back up.

"Mr. Jetmore, if someone smoked marijuana in high school, would it prevent them from becoming a police officer?"

"It's interesting that all of you use the term 'someone,' as if you're asking about a friend who missed tonight's class." They all begin laughing again. I think I may have won them over.

"Up until a relatively short time ago, the discoverable use of illegal drugs would have automatically disqualified a person from becoming a police officer. The law enforcement profession has uniquely compelling reasons to have a drug-free police department. The integrity and public confidence in law enforcement is eroded when its members use drugs, and the potential for corruption is promoted by illegal drug use. The public has every right to expect that those who are sworn to protect and serve them will be physically and mentally prepared to do their job.

"However, most departments have recognized that there *is* a significant difference between drug experimentation, drug abuse, and the sale of drugs. For example, do we automatically disqualify an otherwise exceptional candidate who freely admits during the polygraph that he or she tried a marijuana cigarette in the ninth grade? Or how about those who admit to stealing some records or tapes from a department store when they were in the seventh grade? Contrast this with a candidate who lies on the application for police employment about a drug arrest and lies on the polygraph test, and *then* the truth is found out. It's a judgment call, and several factors must be taken into consideration. What kind of drug was it? When was the drug last used? What was the frequency of its use and the circumstances under which it was used? These factors will all be weighed against the totality of information gathered in the hiring process about the candidate. So there's a good chance that if a person tried a marijuana cigarette in high school, but has not used drugs since, and everything else in the person's background is in good order, it won't prevent that individual from becoming a police officer."

Looking around the classroom at the students' faces, I'm not convinced they're ready to move on to another area. "OK, what about this is bothering everybody?"

A young man says, *"You mentioned something earlier about a drug test in the hiring process. How does that work?"*

"It's really nothing to worry about. As part of your medical exam to become a police officer you'll be required to submit to a urinalysis drug screening which uses a reliable scientific method involving chemical synthesis or extraction. In plainer English, you'll be asked to give a urine specimen in an unobserved, private setting. Usually, the types of drugs tested for are marijuana, cocaine, opiates (such as heroin and morphine), amphetamines, barbiturates, methadone, and phencyclidines. The test used by most police departments usually is not sensitive enough to detect these substances if they were used more than a year earlier. There are tests which can detect your use of these drugs at any period in your life, but they are too expensive for most departments. The drug test you'll probably be given is designed to test for recent drug use, not three or four years ago."

Several more students raise their hands. "Mr. Jet," (I'm Mr. Jet now) "how about *speeding tickets or someone who has been arrested for a minor crime like disorderly conduct*? I have a friend who was arrested during a protest against nuclear weapons."

I laugh. "There's that 'friend' popping up again. Those types of minor offenses probably wouldn't prevent a person from being hired as a police officer. A speeding ticket and perhaps another traffic violation over a period of several years isn't a problem. However, a repeated pattern of traffic violations, such as reckless driving, drunken driving, evading responsibility, and the like, along with other negative factors about the candidate, could certainly result in another person's being chosen for the job. It's the same for a person with a minor misdemeanor arrest record. When did it happen? What were the circumstances involved? What are the chances of it happening again? Obviously, conviction for a felony precludes appointment as a police officer. Your best bet is to be totally honest during your interviews. Things like motor vehicle and criminal arrest records are very easily checked.

"Well, we've gone beyond our allotted time for this class. How about one more question?"

You ask, *"Where do we go to get the application to apply for a police job?"*

"If it's a city or town police department, you can obtain one at the personnel department in the city or town hall. During a recruiting drive, police departments also have applications at their front desks. If it's a state police job you're looking for, obtain an application at the state personnel department. Use your phone book and call them. They'll usually mail you an application or at least send an interest card for you to fill out. The main thing to remember is *don't give up on the process*. If you really want a job in policing, there's one out there for you."

> *Everything comes to him who hustles while he waits.*
> —Benjamin Franklin

3

FOOTPRINTS
FROM LONG AGO

THE ORGANIZATION

If you're going to become a police officer, you should have at least a general idea of the historical background of policing, how police departments are organized, and what police officers do. Learning about these concepts will establish a framework to help you understand the examination and screening process used to select people to become police officers. The more you understand about the process, the better you can prepare. The better prepared and motivated you are, the higher final score on the examinations you will receive. The higher your final mark, the better chance you'll have of reaching your goal of becoming a police officer.

A HISTORICAL VIEW OF POLICING

Laws of Hammurabi

The concept of having a person or group specifically responsible for enforcing customs, beliefs, values, social order, and codes of conduct has been around for a long time. The origins of policing can be traced as far back as 2100 B.C. to the king of Babylon and a collection of customs known as the laws of Hammurabi. The laws, or code, of Hammurabi contained references to "messengers" who acted as enforcers of these codes of conduct and they are viewed by historians today as the forerunners of police officers.

The Metropolitan Police Act of 1829

France and other Continental countries had professional police forces as early as the seventeenth century. However, it's generally agreed that the first truly organized, modern police department was established by the English parliament on September 29, 1829, with the passing of the "Metropolitan Police Act." It named Sir Robert Peel as administrator of an organized police force located in Westminster (a short distance from London). It was the first police force to wear uniforms, which consisted of a blue swallow-tailed coat, a leather stock, and a reinforced top hat. A rattle was carried to sound the alarm and summon help. Similar to the police badge of today, a letter was fastened to the collar of the coat, designating what division the constable belonged to, followed by a personal number. The only weapon carried was a wooden truncheon.

Within a year, the new force consisted of a thousand men under the overall direction of two police commissioners: Charles Rowan, a retired lieutenant-colonel from the 52nd Light Infantry, and barrister Richard Mayner. Headquarters was eventually established at 4 Whitehall Place, the rear of which opened into a large courtyard called Scotland Yard, and a police station was established there. From the beginning, the department was associated with the now famous Scotland Yard. The department moved in 1885 to a building on the Thames River, called New Scotland Yard, and again in 1967 to another building off Victoria Street, retaining the famous name. It was under Charles Rowan's guidance that the police began using military principles of organization. A general order issued to the new police department in 1829 by Commissioner Rowan is as timely today as it was then:

> It should be understood at the outset, that the principal object to be obtained is the prevention of crime. To this great end, every effort of the police is to be directed. The security of persons and property, the preservation of the public tranquility and all other objects of a police establishment would thus be better effected than by the detection and punishment of the offender after he succeeded in committing the crime.

Within the decade, Sir Robert Peel was recognized as a national hero, and his men were commonly referred to as "Peelers" or "Bobbies." It's quite a tribute to Robert Peel that, even today, police officers in England are still called bobbies. By 1839, the English parliament had passed an act empowering justices to establish police forces in the counties and, in 1856, required every borough and county to have a police force.

First United States Police Departments

In the United States, it wasn't until 1833 that the first organized, paid police department was formed in Philadelphia—followed by Boston in 1838, New York in 1844, Chicago in 1851, New Orleans and Cincinnati in 1852, Baltimore and Newark in 1857, and Providence in 1864. The first state police department was formed in 1835 and became known as the Texas Rangers. They were responsible for dealing with "cattle rustlers, outlaws, Indians, and marauding Mexicans from across the border."

During the late 1800s, police officers were called constables, and many people believe the word "cop" came from the initials for "*constable on patrol*." Others think cop is a shortened form of the word "copper," a reference to the copper badges worn by many police officers.

At the federal level, the United States Postal Inspectors were formed in 1829, the Secret Service in 1865, and the United States Border Patrol in 1886. Canada's Northwest Mounted Police Force was founded in 1873 and in 1920 became known as the Royal Canadian Mounted Police.

THE POLICE ORGANIZATION

For all its contemporary technology, automation, and forensic science, policing today retains the basic premise for which police departments were originally formed:

1. To protect life and property against criminal acts.

2. To preserve the peace and ensure the safe movement of traffic.

Textbooks on police management now speak in terms such as "controlling crime, maintaining order, and providing services," but they're really saying the same thing in a different way. Today, there are approximately 298,000 police officers in the United States, most of them in the larger cities. Although differences exist in structure, organization, diversity of tasks, and management styles, all police departments face common problems and perform the same general duties. Only the scale, volume, and complexity of the departments' responsibilities differ. In other words, the chords may change, but the melody stays the same.

Down through the years, the responsibilities of the police have been described, revised, and added to many times. A 1970 project of the American Bar Association to identify what the role of the police should be in society is included here to provide a description of the purpose of police organizations (the ABA findings are adapted by the author to reflect the more recent social service roles of the police):

THE PURPOSE OF POLICE ORGANIZATIONS

1. To protect life and property against crime.
2. To create a belief in the minds of criminal offenders that the commission of a criminal act will quickly lead to arrest and prosecution.
3. To provide assistance to people who are the victims of criminal acts, disasters, and accidents.
4. To ensure equal and impartial protection of constitutional and legal rights, such as that of peaceful assembly and access to public facilities.
5. To render aid to those who can't care for themselves, such as the homeless, the physically or mentally incapacitated, children, and the aged.
6. To facilitate the safe movement of traffic and pedestrians.
7. To secure the willing cooperation and support of the public in observing the law through educational and crime-prevention programs.

As can be seen from the outline, the majority of police responsibilities are not specifically related to the enforcement of the law. Many are social-service, peace-keeping, and order-maintenance functions. It's estimated that between eighty and ninety percent of a police officer's time is now spent on these types of activities. It's long been an axiom in policing that officers have to be part lawyer, social worker, doctor, psychiatrist, judge, and Good Samaritan. That's why the most important skill of a good police officer is the *ability to communicate with people* from all walks of life. This skill is so important that communication is the most tested-for skill in the selection process for police officers.

In 1968, the International Association of Chiefs of Police issued a planning report to the Commonwealth of Massachusetts which stated:

> The ultimate goal of law enforcement in society should be to reach a high level of citizen compliance with the law through voluntary means with minimal enforcement.

As a student of law enforcement, it's important for you to understand that the police are supplements to, not substitutes for, community involvement, participation, and planning on how to reduce crime. Every citizen has a right to expect that the police will equally protect the rights of *all* citizens in the community. Police departments are part of local or state government, *not* independent bodies of government, and they are only one segment of a larger system in the criminal justice process consisting of police, courts, and prisons. Don't forget, an arrest by a police officer *is not proof* that a person committed a crime. If that were the case, we wouldn't need courts. America is a free society, and a carefully designed system of checks and balances ensures at least the perception of fairness and equitable treatment.

> *No one can make you feel inferior without your consent.*
> —Eleanor Roosevelt

How Police Departments Are Structured

The majority of police departments operate under local city government and control. In most states, the head of the police department (chief of police) is protected by state statute from being fired without a public hearing showing "just cause." He or she reports directly to a local official, usually a mayor or city manager and in some cases a police commission. On the following pages are examples of organizational charts for a large police department and for a smaller one. However, an organizational chart, with boxes for positions, job duties, and lines of authority, provides only a pattern of interrelationships among the jobs within an organization. The chart is not the organization; people are!

Although the general responsibilities of all police departments are similar, departments' operational systems and internal structures vary across the country. Still, universal concepts used to establish police objectives are the same whether you become an officer in a small town in Wyoming or in a big city like Los Angeles.

Organizations are created to accomplish things which can't be done by individuals. They have specific goals—a job to do. The first step in carrying out police departments' goals of prevention of crime and disorder, protection of property, and preservation of the peace is to identify specific objectives and job tasks:

- What kind of work needs to be done?
- How is it to be done?
- Who is going to do it?
- Where is it to be done and when?

Organizational Charts

The objectives given above and the individual job tasks needed to accomplish them must be grouped according to similarity and purpose and then arranged and subdivided into specific functions so the work can be distributed according to a logical plan.

In police organizations, members are divided into groups according to what kinds of police services they perform. These groups are often referred to as "bureaus"—for example, the "detective bureau" or in large departments, the "investigative services bureau." Bureaus are subdivided into smaller work units called "divisions." Thus, the investigative services bureau might be made up of the crimes against persons division (homicide and robbery), the crimes against property division (burglary and auto theft), and so on. The largest bureau in a big police department is the field services bureau, under which the patrol division operates. The patrol division is often referred to as the "backbone of the police department" because the officers assigned to it make up the vast majority of the force and provide direct services to the citizens of the community.

The Patrol Division

The primary method of accomplishing the police mission is through the patrol division, and since almost all entry-level officers are assigned there after graduation from the police academy, this book will concentrate on its organization. The patrol division provides police coverage for the entire city twenty-four hours a day, seven days a week, by assigning police officers where they are needed most often at a specific time of day. The need for police officers varies according to time. They are distributed according to a statistical formula based on the frequency of crime and other related factors. Because crime is usually most frequent between the hours of 1600 and 2400 (4:00 P.M. and 12:00 A.M.), more officers work that shift than, say, the 2400 to 0800 shift (12:00 A.M. to 8:00 A.M.), which has the least amount of crime.

The officers in the patrol division are distributed throughout the city according to a geographic plan, within specific time frames, allowing for variations in patrol work by day of week and time of day. Thus, the functions performed by officers (nature of the job tasks) may be divided into time (police shifts), place of performance, (where functions are performed—districts, beats, etc.), how officers are distributed (in vehicles, called cruisers, or on foot, called foot beats), and the level of authority needed to assure that the job is being done right (communication and supervision). This coordination of effort assists the organization in being efficient, effective, and productive. To further accomplish these goals, the officers are organized into a structure made up of individual units with specific responsibilities so there will be no duplication of effort. Lines of authority and responsibility are definite and direct. In law enforcement, these responsibilities are divided into levels of authority and grouped into functions, or services performed, called "line" and "staff." Police organizations are directed and controlled through a vertical chain of command called "ranks." The titles of ranks vary from department to department. (An example is: chief of police, assistant chief, captain, lieutenant, sergeant, detective, and officer, with each having different levels of authority and responsibility.) This chain of command is necessary to give the organization control and ensure that effective communication takes place so people will understand their roles in relationship to the organization and each other. The various line and staff functions are listed following.

Staff Functions

Staff functions are services which assist the administrators and supervisors of a police department in making the work of line personnel more effective. Some examples are personnel and training activities, planning and research, public relations, community relations, detention, records, communications, identification services, property and maintenance activities, and the forensic laboratory.

ORGANIZATIONAL CHART: LARGE POLICE DEPARTMENT

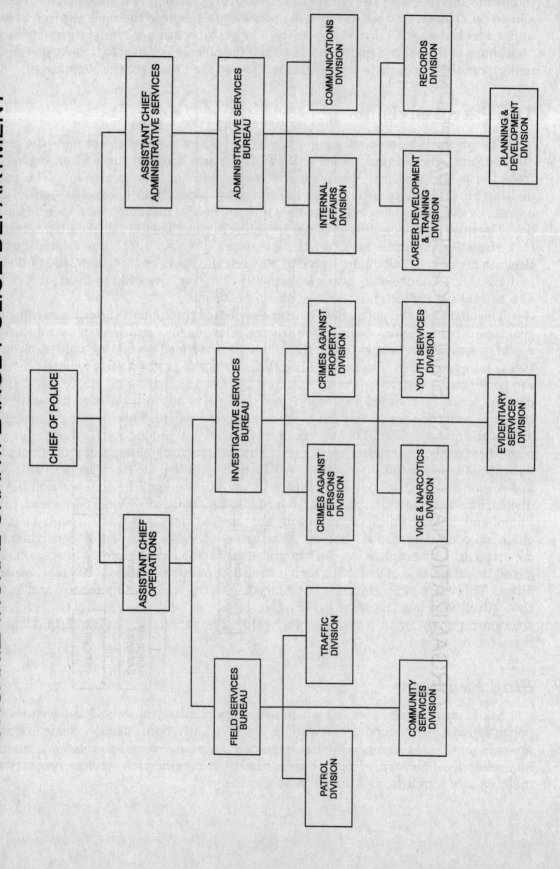

ORGANIZATIONAL CHART: SMALL POLICE DEPARTMENT

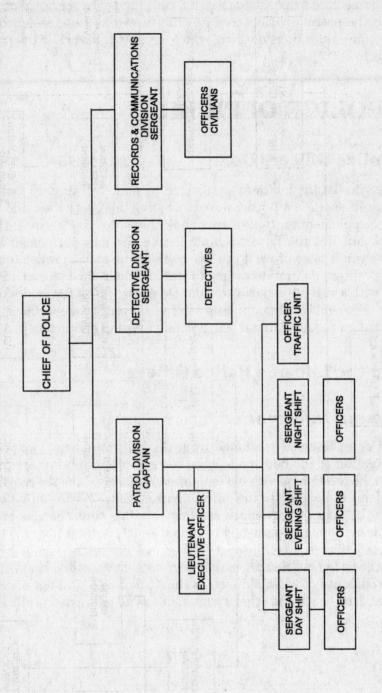

Line Functions

Line functions are those services performed by officers engaged in activities directly related to immediate response to citizens' calls for police service. For example, officers assigned to the patrol division are line officers, while those assigned to the training, records, or communications division, which support the work of the patrol division, are staff officers.

THE POLICE OFFICER

What Police Officers Do

It's easy to list the job tasks performed by police officers. In fact, the question of what police officers *do* is often answered by listing their activities, and you'll find such a list in the Supplement section of this book. Lists are like recipes: they give you the ingredients, but not the flavor. Simply listing the jobs performed by police officers doesn't give you a taste of what it's like to really be one. In order to fully understand what police officers *do*, it's necessary to walk in their shoes for awhile. So let's spend some time with a real-life cop named John Douglas—just a few hours to give you a taste of the job. Remember, though, this isn't a pretend police officer like you see on television. He's a regular human being among a cast of characters just like you and me.

A Day in the Life of a Police Officer

Background Information

Officer John Douglas graduated from the police academy two years ago in a city with a population of 363,000 and a police force of 582. John is married, and he and his wife, Karen, have a four-month-old daughter, Kimberly. Like the majority of officers on the force, John is assigned to the patrol division. Since he has only two years with the department, he doesn't have much seniority and his shift changes every month. This month, Officer Douglas is assigned to Squad A, 0740–1600 hours. The city is divided into districts. Officers patrol districts either in a car (a cruiser) or by walking a beat. Officers in the patrol division are assigned to work cruisers and beats at specific times of the day through use of what's known as the "police roll" (a huge sheet of heavy paper with the districts, beats, and other assignments of all police patrol officers written on it).

POLICE ROLL CALL
City of Newcastle Police Department

Patrol Division   **Day: Wednesday**
Date: July 12, 19—

Unit	Day Watch Squad A	On Duty	Off Duty	Regular Days Off	Approved Day Off	Sick/Injured/ Vacation
1	Franklin	0700		M & T		
3	~~Jenkins~~ (Sherman)	0700		T & W		
5	~~Pawlina~~ (Sicoras)	0700		W & Th		
7	Davis	0700		Th & F		
9	Jones	0700		F & S		
11	Fenimore	0700		S & Su		
13	~~Faggaini~~ (Boyce)	0700		Su & M		sick
15	Stamilio	0700		M & T		
17	~~Archer~~ (Brady)	0700		T & W		
19	Rodriguez	0700		Th & F		
2	Terbush	0800		F & S		
4	Delgado	0800		S & Su		
6	~~Reid~~ (Douglas)	0800		Su & M		vacation
8	Fallon	0800		S & Su		
10	Luthringer	0800		S & Su		
12	Nelson	0800		Su & M		
14	Coleman	0800		M & T		
16	~~Deep~~ (Shapiro)	0800		T & W		
18	Reeves	0800		Su & M		

Beats

Unit		On Duty		Regular Days Off		
114	Spellman	0700		S & Su		
115	Dakin	0800		Su & M		
116	Sullivan	0800		Su & M		
117	Prevost	0800		S & Su		

Relief List

Unit		On Duty		Regular Days Off		
3	Sherman	0700		F & S		
5	Sicaras	0700		Th & F		
	Riccio			W & Th		
13	Boyce	0700		S & Su		
17	Brady	0700		Su & M		
6	Douglas	0800		M & T		
16	Shapiro	0800		Su & M		

Since districts, and sometimes beats, need to be covered seven days a week, twenty-four hours a day, the regular (senior) officers have staggered days off, some Monday and Tuesday, some Tuesday and Wednesday, some Wednesday and Thursday, and so on. Just like regular people, police officers get sick, take vacations, and have deaths in their families. Officers on what's known as the "relief list," like our man John, fill in for officers regularly assigned to cruisers and beats who are not working on that particular day. So where Officer Douglas works in the city frequently changes. One day he might be downtown walking a beat and the next in a cruiser patrolling a different section of the city. He could also be assigned to administrative tasks, such as to the booking room (where arrested persons are processed), to guard an arrested person being treated at a hospital, or to the front desk. There are many different job assignments in the patrol division. These frequent changes of assignment familiarize John with every part of the city, providing him the opportunity to perform a variety of job functions.

Today, John is assigned to District 6, to a cruiser that covers part of downtown. It's July, and the city's in the middle of a heat wave. It's been over ninety degrees for the past six days.

A NEW DAY

At 5:00 A.M., a gentle poke in the ribs makes John Douglas sleepily open his eyes.

"The baby's crying. It's your turn," Karen said.

John went back to sleep. The next jab in his ribs was harder and more insistent. He groaned, rolling out of bed. He could hear the howling from the crib from both the next room and the little intercom on the bedstand next to Karen that her mother had bought them, "just in case."

"OK, OK, OK, I'm coming," John muttered. As he approached the crib, the crying stopped. He tiptoed over, hoping that by some miracle little Kimberly had gone back to sleep. He peeked into the crib and was greeted by two big, blue eyes and a toothless smile as bright as sunshine. When Kimberly saw her dad, she waved her arms and legs in excitement. John smiled in spite of himself, picked up the baby, and gave her a hug. "Hi, sweetheart, are you ready for some breakfast?"

In the kitchen, he took a bottle out of the refrigerator and popped it into the microwave. When he thought it was done, he squirted a little of the formula from the heated bottle onto his arm to test it. "Ow, Ow. Much too hot!" The baby looked at him, bewildered, and started crying again. He grabbed a coffee mug, plopped the bottle in, and ran cold water over it. Retest. "It's OK now." He inserted the nipple into Kimberly's mouth, but she cried even louder and shook her head. "Apparently *still* not the right temperature," John thought.

Karen shuffled into the kitchen. "Give her to me. You men are so useless. Go on, get ready for work." In about two seconds, Kim was happily drinking her bottle, and Karen smiled up at John, waving her hand for him to go.

"Thanks, hon, I'll get up with the baby tomorrow."

Karen laughed. "Sure you will. Now go make some money."

An hour later, John was crawling along in commuter traffic with everyone else. The car's transmission was going, and it kept slipping in and out of gear. Even this early, it was already seventy-eight degrees. Something was wrong with the car's thermostat.

Heat was pouring in from the engine compartment, and he couldn't get it to stop. He shook his head in disgust. "I've got to get a new car."

Finally pulling into the police parking lot at the rear of the station, he hopped out and looked under the front end to see if transmission fluid was leaking. As he was looking under the car, he was joined by Officer Pedro Rodriguez, who had graduated from the police academy with him.

"Hey, Johneee, Qué pasa, hombre?"

John straightened up and laughed, slapping Rodriguez's palm in a short five. "I don't know what's wrong with the damn thing. I think the transmission's shot."

Rodriguez shrugged. "Well, life's a bite."

At the station's rear door, John slid his identification card into the slot.

"How's the baby, man?" Pedro asked.

"It's a whole new life. Karen made me get up early this morning to give Kim her bottle."

Pedro rolled his eyes. "Yeah, I've been there. It's something else, isn't it?"

The patrolmen's locker room was a madhouse. John had tried to describe it to Karen once, but all he could think to compare it to was a football team's locker room before a game. Since Karen had never been in one, it was difficult for her to picture what he was talking about. Forty-five men and four women were on Squad A—the women, of course, had their own locker room. Some officers wore their full uniforms from home to work, while others changed in the locker room. Sometime last night a pipe had broken, or a sink had overflowed, and a thin film of water covered the floor. Guys were cussing and griping as usual. "If it wasn't the water, it would be something else," John thought.

He took off his civilian clothes (Bermuda shorts, T-shirt, and sneakers) and began changing into his uniform. Grabbing his new, lightweight, bulletproof vest, he hesitated, thinking how hot it was going to get outside. Some guys didn't wear the vest because of the heat or rationalized that it restricted their movement in a fight. John thought about Karen and Kim and slipped it over his head, tightening the Velcro straps on each side. It was getting late, so he quickly put on his uniform and gun belt. Taking his badge out of his wallet, he pinned it over the left breast of his uniform. Even after two years, he still got a thrill every time he put on his badge. He removed a five from his wallet and stowed the wallet in his locker along with his watch and ring.

He slipped another watch (just a face without a strap) into his pocket. He'd seen an old-timer do this, and when he'd asked him about it the guy had said, "No sense losing your wallet in a foot chase through back yards and over fences or breaking your watch or hand in a fight."

John ran a cloth diaper over his shoes, restoring the spit shine, and then began making his way through the puddles and down the corridor into the squad room, a spacious area in which all the furniture had been removed except for a large podium. The walls were lined with cork bulletin boards from which hung mug shots, wanted posters, union information, and three-by-five cards with for-sale ads on everything from houses and campers to motorcycles, guns, and knives. John's department didn't permit officers to sit at desks for roll call; they "fell in" military style. People jammed into the room—reading newspapers, drinking coffee, gossiping, and generally milling about. The old-timers had staked out one corner and snarled at anyone who even looked like they were going to come near them.

ROLL CALL

At exactly 0740 hours, Sergeant Donnelly, six feet, four inches and a solid 230 pounds, entered, bellowing, "Fall in for roll call!" Lieutenant Jenkins and Captain Anderson followed him in. Since John was still considered a rookie by everyone but his fellow academy graduates, by tradition, he and the other newer officers fell into the front two ranks. Donnelly yelled, "Dress right dress. Ready front. Attention to roll call." All the officers, in military formation, stood at attention seven ranks deep. Donnelly positioned himself alongside the first rank, a couple of steps to one side and slightly in front, and came to attention with a click of his heels.

Captain Anderson, standing at the podium, began calling the roll. "Officer Terbush, unit two."

"Here, sir."

"Officer Delgado, unit four."

"Here, sir."

"Officer Douglas, unit six."

"Here, sir."

After the roll was called and everyone was accounted for, Donnelly quickly inspected the officers' uniforms, spending the most time with the newer officers in the first two ranks. By the time he reached the veterans in the last rank, he just glared and grunted. After the inspection, the captain read the "orders of the day," consisting of several memos from the chief about phone courtesy, the necessity to completely fill out reports, and the like. Lieutenant Perkins took over, running through a short, boring lecture on estimating the time of death by rigor mortis and post-mortem lividity stains.

WORKING THE STREET

At exactly 0755 hours, Donnelly barked, "OK, troops, fall out!" The room erupted into a din of backslapping, laughter, and "I'll meet you there for coffee." Everyone piled out of the room to pick up portable radios at the front desk. John handed the duty officer his chit for the radio and headed out to the parking lot, where cruisers had been left by officers who had worked the midnight shift. He finally found the vehicle marked six, his cruiser for the day.

John was assigned to what's known as a "late car." Officers working the day shift work either from 0640 to 1500 (an early car) or from 0740 to 1600, as John was today. Cops in the day early cars were relieved by people working the early cars on the evening shift (1440 to 2300), and cops in day late cars and "beat officers" were relieved by people working late cars on the evening shift (1540 to 2400). They, in turn, were relieved by early and late nightshift officers. This happened every day, seven days a week, 365 days a year.

John's first task after locating his cruiser was to fill out the vehicle and equipment inspection form and turn it in to Sergeant Donnelly. Cops all over the parking lot were beginning to inspect their vehicles, and beat officers were climbing into the back seats of cruisers to be transported to their walking areas throughout the city. John tried to spot Hank Sullivan and Paul Dakin, who had beats in his district. Not seeing either of them, he opened the cruiser door, tossed his briefcase onto the front passenger seat, and jammed his nightstick into the space between the seats so the handle protruded, close at hand. He fired up the cruiser, turned the air conditioner to high, and quickly tested the vehicle's strobe lights and siren system. Although he flicked the switch on the police radio, which began busily chattering, he hadn't "gone on the line" yet, so he ignored what was being being said and pushed the button to open the trunk. He inspected the first-aid kit, oxygen tank, flares, slim jim, and blankets. Unzipping the shotgun case, he removed the weapon, checked the chamber, and then loaded it with three cartridges of buckshot, followed by a deer slug and two more cartridges of buckshot. As he was doing this, Sullivan and Dakin ambled over.

"Careful you don't shoot your foot off, son," Sullivan said.

"Yeah, we don't want to be stuck in the station all day just because you shot your big toe off," Dakin added.

Both men seemed to find their routine enormously funny. John just laughed because he knew it didn't pay to try to match wits with twenty-year guys. They'd beat you every time. Sullivan and Dakin opened the cruiser's rear doors and began checking the back seat for weapons, drugs, or anything a prisoner could use to hurt a cop. The rear of the cruiser was known as the "cage" because it had heavy wire mesh separating the front and rear seats so that prisoners placed in the back couldn't get at the officers in front. Once the rear doors were closed, they couldn't be opened from inside. The beat cops lifted the bench-type rear seat to see if the officer using the car on the previous shift had overlooked anything after transporting a prisoner. As John slid into the front seat, Sullivan said, "It's clean."

John nodded his thanks while making a mental note to check out the rear seat after dropping off the two men. He had once found a knife and another time a bag of dope tucked under the rear seat, and he knew he wouldn't feel comfortable until he checked it out himself.

As John's cruiser reached the front of the line to give the inspection form to Sergeant Donnelly, the sergeant leaned a heavy forearm into the window and pushed his cap back with his thumb. "Make sure you drop these two lowlifes off on their posts right away. I don't want them spending half the morning riding around with you. If they don't go on the line in twenty minutes, they're gonna take the blue goose (bus) out to their beats from now on."

"OK, Sarge," John agreed and pulled out onto an access road to the highway and downtown. He checked out Sullivan and Dakin in the rearview mirror but neither spoke. While he knew the two men had worked for Donnelly for a long time, John wasn't sure of their relationship. Sullivan lit a cigar, and at the same moment, the air conditioner rattled, sputtered, and died. John cranked down his window. It was going to be a long day.

John lifted the radio mike off its holder and "went on the line" by depressing the red mike button, saying, "Unit six, car six, Officer Douglas, on the line."

The police dispatcher immediately acknowledged. "Unit six, you're on the line at 0810 hours."

As the other cruisers went on the line, the police dispatcher's map of the city began lighting up. Green lights indicated cruisers available for dispatch to calls; red lights marked cruisers already on calls. The process had been automated for years, and, for the most part, computers decided which officers handled which calls (computer-aided dispatching), but the map helped the dispatcher see graphically who was available.

John pulled onto the highway, merging with the still-heavy commuter traffic. The big Ford LTD cruiser, light blue with white trim, had a bar of police lights mounted on top, a spotlight just forward and to the right of the driver's side rearview mirror, and the word "Police," with "Unit 6" in smaller letters just below, across the left and right doors and trunk. When John moved into the middle lane, all the traffic in front of him shied to the right or left to let the police cruiser pass. "No one likes a police car directly behind them," he thought.

He took the State Street exit, figuring Sullivan and Dakin probably wanted to be dropped off at the intersection of Main and State, which bordered both of their beats. After dropping them off, he watched the two cops make their way down the sidewalk to their favorite coffee shop. Almost exactly twenty minutes from the time the sergeant had issued his warning, John heard both officers go on the line with the police dispatcher, using their portable radios. He wasn't surprised. Donnelly was no one to fool with, and for him to issue them this little warning, especially in front of John, he figured they must have really messed up.

The police radio had been squawking almost nonstop, and John wasn't particularly happy with the way everyone had been using it lately. He'd discussed his reasoning with Karen, explaining that every radio transmission is *supposed* to use ten-series police radio codes, and it bothered him that a lot of officers weren't using them properly. For example, if the dispatcher said, "Unit twenty, ten-two," it meant *return to headquarters*. John had been taught in the police academy that there were two main reasons radio codes are used: to save radio air time and to prevent criminals from knowing where police officers are located. When an officer depressed the radio button to talk, everyone on that frequency could hear what was being said, but no one else could speak while he or she was transmitting. Even though this only took a few moments, it could literally mean life or death to an officer who had only a second to yell into the radio, "Unit three. Ten-zero, Main and State!" Translation: "Officer Jenkins in unit three is in bad, bad trouble at the corner of Main and State and needs a lot of help, *right now*." If Officer Jenkins had only that brief second to use his portable radio to transmit the message, but another officer was going on and on over the radio, no one would hear Officer Jenkins's cries for help or even know he was in trouble. So short, concise messages in code are supposed to be given over the police radio. There may be different frequencies or channels on the radio for other functions or for dividing large numbers of personnel over the entire city into radio zones with different radio channels, but however you cut it, two people couldn't talk at once.

John had also explained to Karen that a lot of folks have police scanners and can hear the radio transmissions being broadcast. Criminals could buy scanners, too. It wouldn't take a person with a scanner very long to figure out how many police officers were working, where their districts and beats were, when shift changes occurred, and so forth, and to use this information to pull off a bank robbery, burglary, auto theft, etc. So police codes are supposed to be used, but, being human, police officers and dispatchers sometimes developed the bad habit of using a code and then following it up with unnecessary verbiage, such as "Unit two, ten-two to the station." Or "Unit two, see the woman at 167 Sigourney Street, apartment A-2, on a ten-sixty-seven, burglary into her apartment." All that should have been said was, "Unit two, ten-sixty-seven, Mrs. Fleming, 167 Sigourney Street, apartment A-2, code one." "Code one" meant "It's past tense—the burglary isn't going on now; the bad guy is gone." For the first few months, John had carried a printed copy of the radio codes with him, but they eventually became second nature. So, although the radio was going almost nonstop, John had developed the ability to tune it out while at the same time being aware of where all the police officers around him were and what was being said. He worried that the careless use of the radio might cause someone to get hurt.

THE ACCIDENT

He still wanted to check the back seat, so he pulled behind a restaurant into a parking lot and hopped out to check. Satisfied, he was just getting back in when he received a radio call. "Unit six, see Mrs. Tyler on a ten-thirty, Main and Park, at 0855 hours."

John grabbed the mike. "Ten-four. Unit six."

One of the problems working days and having a downtown cruiser was that officers responded to a lot of fender-bender traffic accidents. For the most part, people still thought police officers "investigated" *all* traffic accidents and became irritated when they found out that wasn't the case. In John's department, they investigated only accidents in which there was personal injury and/or more than $1,000 dollars of damage to either car (not combined), and/or an *obvious* traffic violation. There were exceptions, of course, such as accidents involving drunk drivers or the evasion of responsibility (hit and run).

John's department had conducted a study which showed that thousands of hours per year were being spent investigating minor accidents. In fact, the consultant who did the study produced a report indicating there were so many minor accidents, involving major chunks of officer's time, that if the department could reduce the time spent to under thirty minutes for each accident, it would be the equivalent of adding two additional officers to the force! So, for the most part, officers responded to the scene, had the cars moved out of the way of traffic, and handed the drivers forms so they could exchange the information needed by their insurance companies. John didn't like responding to these types of calls because he sensed the people's disappointment when they found out he wasn't really going to "do" anything.

Traffic near the site of the accident was backed up coming and going on both sides of Main Street. John looked for a way to get through and, not seeing any, hit his strobe lights and siren. Motorists inched over to the right so he could get by, and he caught brief glimpses of their faces. "Traffic jams really stress people out," he thought. Some people were scowling; others looked a little apprehensive; one guy was pounding his fist on the steering wheel in frustration; and a little girl in the back of one of the cars smiled and waved at him as he went by. He returned her wave, thought about Kimberly and what she was going to be like at that age, and felt a little better. As he pulled into the intersection, he quickly grasped the situation. A station wagon going south on Main Street had collided with a newer-model Cadillac coming east on Park Street. The right front fender and door of the wagon were pushed in, and the left front fender of the Caddy was slightly damaged. On the sidewalk, across from the scene of the accident, John saw a man wearing a crumpled business suit, who appeared to be in his late fifties, standing next to a young woman holding a small baby. None of them appeared to be hurt, but the man was impatiently motioning to him and looked irritated. John couldn't quite make out what the man was saying, but his body language indicated that he wanted John to hurry.

He turned the car's siren off but left the flashing lights on, parking the cruiser in the middle of the street behind the wagon. He notified the dispatcher that he had arrived. "Unit six. I'm ten-eight. Let me have another cruiser here to do traffic."

The dispatcher replied with, "Unit six, your arrival time is 0905. Unit nineteen, assist unit six with traffic, Main and Park."

Grabbing his police hat, John got out and quickly walked around the wreck, surveying the roadway. He noticed a long, black line of heavy skid marks leading back from the Caddy across Main Street into Park Street. He stood there for a moment, looking east and then up at the traffic light. It appeared to him that the driver of the Caddy had jammed on his brakes, leaving the skid marks, while the driver of the wagon had probably been almost at a standstill, preparing to turn left onto Park Street, going east. Considerable headlight glass and debris from the accident littered the road. Traffic was gridlocked, and people were blowing their horns.

John walked to the sidewalk and started to introduce himself. "Hi, I'm . . ."

"It's about damn time you got here," the man interrupted in a deep Texas drawl. "I called from my car phone over twenty minutes ago. Where the hell have you been, having a cup of coffee?"

John smiled. The guy was only about five feet, seven inches but must have weighed three hundred pounds. His suit was much too tight and his stomach hung over a big, square belt buckle depicting a cowboy lassoing a steer. Instead of a standard tie, he had on a bolo with a steer's head design. Cops quickly size up people, and John thought to himself, "Salesman, rented car, late, stressed out." John ignored what the man had said, assuming the guy was just upset over the accident, and spoke to the woman holding the baby. "I'm Officer Douglas. Is anyone hurt?"

The man suddenly stepped forward, close to him, between John and the woman. "Look, I'm in a hurry. No one's hurt. This pretty little lady wasn't looking where she was going and ran the light. Just give her a ticket so I can get the hell outta here. I'm late for a meeting."

John looked the man in the eye and pointed to a lamppost a few feet away. Softly, but firmly, he said, "Please go stand over there." The man looked at the lamppost, back at John, and then at unit nineteen, which had pulled up and parked on the other side of the intersection with the flashing lights on.

The man opened his mouth, then closed it. John still pointed. The man ducked his head, muttered something under his breath, and walked to the exact spot John had indicated.

John turned his attention back to the woman. "Now, are you all right, ma'am?"

"Yes, Officer. We're both OK. I just banged my knee."

John saw that her knee was slightly swollen and that a small laceration had caused some blood to flow. "You stay here. I'll be right back." John trotted to his cruiser, where Officer Rodriguez was directing traffic around the accident scene. "Hey, Pedro. The lady hurt her knee. I'm bringing my cruiser over so she can sit down."

"OK John, I've got all day." Rodriguez stopped traffic while John moved his cruiser. He turned off the flashing lights and hit the button to pop open the car's trunk to get to the first-aid kit. The salesman, he noticed, was still muttering and glaring in John's direction.

"This guy's gonna be trouble," John thought. "Ma'am, why don't you have a seat in my cruiser while I patch up your leg?"

As she eased onto the front passenger seat, she said, "My name's Mary Tyler, Officer. I don't think you have to do anything. My knee's OK."

John used a couple of alcohol wipes and a gauze bandage to clean the area around the small wound but felt mildly awkward doing it.

Sensing this, the woman suggested, "Let me have those, and I'll stick the bandage on. Would you please hold the baby for a minute?" John took the baby, wrapped in an oversized, light blue blanket, and watched as she quickly cleaned her knee and applied the bandage. "There, good as new," she said.

As John handed the baby back, he glanced at the salesman, who was now smirking and emphatically pointing to his watch.

"Why don't you tell me what happened?" John asked the woman.

"Well, I was going down Main Street on the way to the doctor for Samantha's checkup. His office is a little ways from here down on Park Street, so I needed to make a left turn. I was stopped at the red light behind two or three other cars, and when my turn came, I moved forward with my signal on and stopped, waiting for oncoming traffic to go by. Then, all of a sudden, *pow!* I mean, I didn't even see him *coming*. I was looking up Main Street toward traffic and over to the left. I heard this screeching sound, but I didn't see the car coming at me until it hit the side of my car!"

"What color was the light when he hit you?"

Mary shrugged. "He must've had a red light. I don't know for sure. The light was green when I pulled into the intersection, and a few seconds later, he hit me."

"OK. Do you know if there are any witnesses?"

"Sure. Other cars must have seen what happened, but they all left." She had become apprehensive and her eyes showed incipient tears.

"Don't worry, Mary, everything will be all right," he reassured her. "Do you have your license and registration?"

She passed him her license from her purse. "The registration is in the car. Do you want me to get it?"

"No, you stay here with the baby. I'll get it for you." He found the slip in the glove compartment and went to speak with the salesman once again. The man sweated in the heat and was obviously growing more hostile.

"How much longer is this gonna take?"

"Not too long," John answered. "Why don't you tell me what happened?"

The salesman was disbelieving. "I already told you. She blew the light and hit my car!"

"Start from the beginning. You were driving down Park Street, and then what happened?"

"Jeez," the man said disgustedly. I was driving down Park Street. The light for me was green. As I was going through the intersection, she slammed into my car."

"Did you see her coming before the accident?"

"Naw, she must have been doing a hundred miles an hour. All I know is *blam!* She hit me!"

"Oh really? Then why all the skid marks?"

"What skid marks?"

"The ones on the street."

"How do you know those are mine? Anybody could have made them."

"Because they lead right up to the back of your car and they're fresh."

"Well, I don't know about any skid marks. All I know is she blew the light and smashed into me."

"You never hit your brakes?"

The man looked away. "Yeah, at the last minute, I might have jammed them on."

"Let's see your license and registration."

"It's a rented car. I guess the registration is in the glove compartment." The salesman took out his wallet and made a big production out of sifting through it looking for his driver's license. "Musta left it back at the hotel room or forgot it at home. Hell, I've been driving for over thirty years."

"Do you have any identification?"

The guy produced a credit card issued to Kenneth R. Forster. John took a small notebook from the pocket of his uniform shirt and jotted down the name. "What's your date of birth and home address, Mr. Forster?"

"January 20, 1934. I live at 116 South Street in Houston, Texas."

"OK. We have a reciprocal agreement with the state of Texas, and I can check your license over the radio." John noted Forster's sudden stillness and suspected that the man didn't have a license, had a suspended license, or was wanted for something. "I wonder why he didn't just take off," he thought.

John walked back to the cruiser. "How are you doing, Mary?"

"I'm fine. The baby's getting kinda fidgety because of the heat, but we'll be OK."

"It won't be much longer." He turned the radio to frequency four, designated specifically for checking motor vehicle and wanted person information. "Unit six," John said.

The dispatcher replied, "Unit six, come in."

"Unit six. Give me a ten-thirteen and ten-eighteen (driver's license and wanted person information) on Kenneth R. Forster. That's *F* as in Frank, *O*–ocean, *R*–Robert, *S*–Sam, *T*–Tom, *E*–Eddie, *R*–Robert. D.O.B. 1/20/34, of 116 South Street, Houston, Texas."

"OK, Unit six, but it'll take awhile because it's out of state."

John took a spinwheel from the trunk to measure the skid marks. He liked it better than a tape measure because he could use it by himself. The spinwheel, a long pole ending in a wheel, provided accurate measurements by allowing officers to simply push a button on the handle, place the wheel on the pavement, and walk whatever distance was necessary. He placed the wheel at the end of the skid marks near the rear wheels of the Cadillac and walked across Main Street following the skid marks to where they began a little past the intersection into Park Street. The odometer on the wheel read forty-three feet, nine inches. "So," John thought, "he jammed on his brakes while still on Park Street, before entering the intersection, and then continued through and hit the station wagon. He's coming down Park, probably isn't familiar with the area, and either doesn't see the light or is looking for a street sign. He looks up, sees the light is red, and jams on his brakes. It's too late, but he almost gets the car stopped and swerves slightly to the right before hitting the wagon. That would account for the relatively minor damage to both cars."

John heard the dispatcher calling him and pulled his portable out to listen.

"Unit six, your ten-eighteen is negative. Ready to copy on your ten-thirteen?"

"Ten-four. Unit six," John responded.

"Kenneth R. Forster, D.O.B. 1/20/34, of 116 South Street, Houston, Texas. Operator's license suspended as of 4/28. He's a white male, with brown eyes."

John OK'd the dispatch and jotted the information in his notebook. This changed things. John knew that in this state, driving while your license was suspended was a booking offense. He would have to arrest the salesman and take him to the police station to post a "promise to appear" bond. If he didn't show up on his court date, he'd forfeit the money, and a rearrest warrant would be issued.

John advised Rodriguez of the situation. "I've got to go to the restaurant on the corner and see if there are any witnesses. Keep an eye on him for me."

John saw that Forster was watching him warily. As he neared the restaurant, he thought again, "I wonder why the guy stuck around and didn't just take off." The Main Street Coffee Shop, just a few feet down from Park had small tables covered by checkered table cloths, a couple of chairs to each table. A deli ran the length of the far wall, ending in a small counter and cash register. There were only six customers—two waiting at the counter and the others at the tables. John made a general announcement. "Excuse me, folks. Did anyone see how the accident outside happened?"

He watched the reactions closely. There wasn't much chance of finding a witness, because too much time had gone by, but it was worth a shot. The two guys at the counter listened and then went back to getting their coffee.

One of two other men dressed in business suits and sitting at a table, offered a comment. "We just got here, Officer."

John nodded at them. His attention had been drawn to an older couple sitting at a table next to a window which looked out onto Main and the scene of the accident. The woman was anxiously whispering something to the man and pointing at John. The man shook his head, and both of them glanced at John as he walked over.

John thought, "They saw it. The woman wants to tell and the man doesn't."

"Hi folks. I'm Officer John Douglas." He grabbed a chair from an adjoining table. "You saw the accident happen?" The couple looked at one another, and the woman took the man's hand and nodded. He sighed.

"Yes, Officer. I saw the accident happen. It's funny. Our car is parked right outside. After we came in, I realized I'd left my cigarettes in the car, so I went back to get them. I was standing by the driver's door taking out my keys when I heard tires screeching and looked up and saw the Cadillac go through the light and hit the station wagon."

"How do you know the light was red?"

"Well, I heard the tires and it startled me. I saw it coming down Park and looked up at the light and saw it was red. The whole thing only took a second. The guy went through the light, tried to swerve at the last minute, and hit the station wagon, which must have stopped to take a left onto Park. The guy in the Cadillac got out and started screaming at the lady in the wagon who had a baby with her, so I stuck around outside for a couple of minutes to make sure she would be OK. The guy got back in his car, but he couldn't get it started. I think he flooded it, or something happened to the engine in the accident. The lady came in the restaurant and asked them to call the police. The only reason we're still here is that we're waiting for our daughter to meet us, and she's a little late."

John flipped open his notebook. "Can I have your name and address please?"

"Will I have to testify in court? I don't even know these people."

"Well, look at it this way. That could have been *your* daughter out there, and you'd want someone to speak up for her, wouldn't you?"

"Yeah, I guess you're right. My name is Henry Walker, and I live at 118 Stonington Street."

"What's your phone number, Mr. Walker?"

"It's 232-7258."

"Your age?"

"I'm sixty-seven years old."

John closed his notebook and patted Walker on the shoulder. "Thank you very much, sir. Now, one last thing. Please show me exactly where you were standing when you saw the accident."

The two men went outside, and Walker took John to his car and pantomimed putting the key in the lock and looking up. John took a quick measurement, pacing the distance from where Walker said he was standing to the corner of Main and Park. He returned, saying, "That's all I need, sir. You probably won't have to testify in court, so don't worry about it. You did the right thing." He shook hands with Walker, now all smiles and seeming very pleased with himself. "Please thank Mrs. Walker for me, too." John watched the man walk back into the restaurant, where he was rewarded with a hug from his wife.

Back at his cruiser, John told Mary about the witness to the accident and about the driver of the Caddy. "The guy's license is suspended, so I'll have to take him down to the station."

"Do you have to?"

"Yes, I do. Your car is drivable, so do you want to just drive it off, or would you like me to call someone for you?"

"No, I'll drive it home. I want to call my husband and our insurance agent. How did you ever find the witness?"

John laughed. "It was easy, I just asked. Sometimes it works that way."

"Thanks, Officer, I really appreciate all you've done."

John tore a piece of paper from his notebook and handed it to her. "Here's all the information you'll need for your insurance. I've also written my name and the police case number. Because of your injury, you'll have to report the accident to the Motor Vehicle Department within five days. You can get the form from your agent or at any Motor Vehicle office."

As John walked her to her car, she said, "You're very good at this, aren't you?"

"We believe in customer service, ma'am." He helped secure the baby in the car seat, and then he and Rodriguez stopped traffic so she could pull out. She gave them a wave and was gone.

As the wrecker for the Cadillac pulled up, Forster marched into the street. "What the hell's going on? I don't want my car towed."

John said, "Your license is suspended, Mr. Forster. You'll have to come down to the station with me."

Forster's face was flushed and he clenched his right fist. "Like hell I will." John moved close to the man and spoke softly, but firmly. "Ken, right now you're in just a *little* trouble, but if you don't lighten up, you're in for a real hornet's nest." Rodriguez had started toward the two men. He could tell by John's stance and the way he was talking to the guy that there might be trouble.

Forster caught the movement and looked from John to Rodriguez and then back. "I don't want any trouble, Officer. I understand you're just doing your job."

The tension of the moment had eased, and John knew from past experience that it was going to be OK now. He took Forster to the cruiser, quickly patted him down, and put him in handcuffs. He didn't particularly like putting someone charged with a motor vehicle offense in handcuffs, but it was department policy, so he did it. "Better to be safe than sorry," he thought.

John notified the dispatcher that he was on his way to the station with the prisoner. "I'm curious, Mr. Forster, why did you stick around? You knew your license was suspended and the police were on the way."

Forster laughed. "Well, I thought about it, but my damn car wouldn't start. Besides, how was I supposed to know you could check my license two states over? I figured you'd give her a ticket, and the most I could get was failure to carry my license. Look, Officer, I'm a salesman. I have to be able to drive to make a living. I got in a little trouble back home with a few too many brewskis."

"How did you rent the car without a license?"

Forster snorted. "Where have *you* been? Throw a couple of hundred-dollar bills on the counter, and they don't care. They handed me a form, and I filled it out. I put my driver's license number down on the form. That's all they want."

After dropping Forster off at the booking room, John returned to his district and pulled onto a side street which had been having problems with cars being broken into. He might as well work on the traffic accident report and related paperwork where he might do some good. After finishing his paperwork, he notified the dispatcher that he was "clear" and available for another call. It was now 1015 hours. The call had taken him an hour and twenty minutes.

OFFICER IN TROUBLE

John answered a couple of other minor calls—a car blocking a driveway (moved by the time he got there) and a homeless alcoholic who had passed out on the sidewalk in front of city hall. John called an ambulance for the man and stood by until he was on the way to the hospital. He was beginning to get a little hungry and was trying to decide where to have lunch when a frantic message blared from the radio.

"Unit one-sixteen. Get me some help on Allyn Street." It was Officer Hank Sullivan. John immediately engaged the cruiser's flashing lights and siren and took off. This was unusual. Veterans like Sullivan rarely called for help. It was a matter of pride with them that they could handle anything by themselves. So John knew Sullivan was probably in *real* trouble. He was only a block away and could get there quickly. Before the dispatcher even had a chance to send help, John picked up the mike.

"Unit six on the way!"

"Okay, six! Unit eight, assist one-sixteen and six on Allyn St! Unit one-sixteen, what is your exact location?"

No answer. "This isn't good," John thought. He reported in. "Unit six. I'm on Allyn St. I'm going to try the bus station. Unit eight, you check out the train station."

Officer Frank Fallon in unit eight answered, "Okay, unit six, but I'm a ways off."

The bus depot was on the corner of Allyn and Church. Half of its large parking lot was used for buses and the other half for cars picking up people and dropping them off. The terminal was open twenty-four hours a day and often frequented by drug dealers, drunks, prostitutes, and petty thieves. John knew Sullivan tried to keep a tight rein in and around the station and had a kind of semiofficial office in the back. He thought it was a fair bet Sullivan was there.

As John pulled swiftly into the lot, he saw a crowd gathered around the terminal's front doors. Several people waved him on. "Unit six. There's a crowd gathered at the entrance to the bus terminal. One-sixteen must be inside. I'm stepping out!"

"OK, six. Let us know. Unit eight, do you copy?"

"Unit eight. Ten-four. I'm still a ways off!"

Sergeant Donnelly radioed in, "Unit forty-two. I'm only two blocks away. I'll respond!"

"OK, Unit forty-two, at 1138 hours."

John was out of the cruiser almost before it came to a stop and running to the front of the building. Shouts from the crowd—"In there!" He flung open the glass doors to a large, open waiting room filled with plastic chairs. The room was completely empty! A ticket clerk pointed frantically. John hit the door to the men's room at a dead run. He could hear shouts inside, he thought from Sullivan, but he couldn't distinguish words. He pushed open the door, keeping his hand on his service revolver. Sullivan was bent backward over a sink by a burly, bearded guy in motorcycle leather. The guy had Sullivan's nightstick, and before John could react, he smashed the cop in the face with it, crushing his nose and splitting his cheekbone from ear to chin. Blood gushed.

John had drawn his gun. "Drop it, or I'll shoot!" Sullivan slumped to the floor, hands over his face, moaning. The leather man turned toward John. The guy was a giant—had to go six feet, six inches and maybe 240 pounds. Sullivan's blood coated his face and upper body. His eyes had a crazed sheen. Leather man took a step forward.

John yelled again, "Drop it, or you're a dead man!" His finger tightened on the trigger. The guy was only eight feet away. He knew he couldn't miss. The .45 automatic was leveled at the guy's chest. The giant growled and threw the nightstick in the corner, where it landed with a clang. He swayed from side to side, bearlike, and charged. In one smooth move John holstered his weapon, stepped slightly to the left and braced his left leg. Twisting his hip to gain power, he drove the heel of his right palm up into the bridge of the giant's nose. The force of the blow and the man's forward momentum combined to triple the energy of the karate strike, stopping the giant dead in his tracks. With a sick, crunching sound, the man's head snapped back, and he dropped to his knees and then to the floor.

John quickly straddled him and was cuffing him when he looked up to see Sergeant Donnelly standing in the doorway, gun drawn. Donnelly had arrived just as the giant charged. The entire incident had happened in the blink of an eye, and Donnelly had seen the whole thing. John yanked the giant to his feet, safely in cuffs.

Donnelly holstered his weapon. "You done real good, kid. I've never seen anyone throw a shot like that."

The sergeant was beaming. It was as though John had passed a special test or made it through some rite of passage. He had never seen Donnelly so jubilant. Within the next few minutes, it seemed as though half the department arrived on the scene, crowding into the bus terminal's waiting room. Sullivan was whisked away to the hospital in one ambulance, while the giant was hustled into another and taken to a different hospital under police guard.

AFTER-ACTION REPORT

John later found out that Sullivan had interrupted the giant selling methamphetamines in the bus station's bathroom. He'd tried to grab both the giant and the kid he was selling to and had ended up in a hand-to-hand struggle with the big guy. It had gone on for quite awhile. The giant had finally managed to wrestle Sullivan's nightstick away and hit him with it just as John arrived. It took forty-eight stitches to close the gash on

Sullivan's face, and his nose and cheekbone were broken. He would later become John's mentor and teach him the tricks of the trade. Everything except how to fight. He knew John Douglas could do that.

John had broken a bone in his hand when he hit the giant, but in the excitement of the fight, it was some time before he realized it. His right hand was put in a cast, and he was told to take a few weeks off. On the way home, his car broke down on the highway, and no one would stop to pick him up. He finally had to hoof it to the nearest exit and find a phone. Karen's mother came and got him. She scolded him about his car before she noticed the cast on his hand. The giant sued everyone—John, Sullivan, Donnelly, the chief of police, the bus station, and the hospital. John, however, did get out of feeding the baby for awhile, and he did receive considerable attention from Karen when he got home that night.

> *One can never consent to creep when one feels an impulse to soar.*
>
> —Helen Keller

Attributes of a Good Police Officer

The purpose of this short story isn't *just* to give you an idea of what it's like to be a police officer. It's also intended to help you prepare your study program for the various examinations you'll be taking. So I want you to read the entire essay again, but this time, see if you can pick out the knowledge, skills, abilities, and personal traits exhibited by Officer John Douglas throughout his day at work. Take out a piece of paper and, as you read the story again, jot down the things he did that *you* think make him a good police officer. What are his positive traits? Before you start, read the following definitions of the terms *knowledge, skill, ability*, and *personal trait*:

Knowledge: A systematic body of information which a person possesses as a result of formal education, life experience, or training.

Skill: The minimum mental or physical performance necessary to execute a task successfully.

Ability: Possession of knowledge and aptitude necessary to perform a function which is either mental or physical.

Personal Trait: A predisposition on the part of a person to behave in a certain way.

Do you have your list ready? OK, I'll grant you that Officer Douglas is already partially trained. He graduated from the police academy, completed his year's probationary training period, and has two years overall experience on the job. However, the testing process is largely a prediction of the degree to which you can develop these same attributes *after* receiving training. Knowing what knowledge, skills, abilities, and positive personal traits police officers should have can guide you in your studying. Compare your list with the model list below.

Knowledge, Skills, Abilities, and Personal Traits Exhibited by Officer John Douglas

1. The primary task of police officers is to serve the public. They must be able to interrelate and communicate effectively with people from a wide variety of cultural and economic backgrounds and deal with them in a calm, dignified, professional manner.

2. Police officers must possess a high ethical standard, have the emotional maturity to be calm and objective in all situations, be courageous and poised, and be free of bias or prejudice.

3. Police officers must have a high degree of intelligence and initiative and have the ability to assume a great deal of responsibility. They must adapt quickly to changing situations and be able to solve problems and make decisions quickly.

4. Police officers should be students of human behavior, displaying an understanding of their fellow human beings and a willingness to help when needed.

5. Police officers must be able to adapt their thinking and methods of operation to sociological and technological change.

6. They must possess the physical and psychological characteristics necessary to perform the duties of a police officer.

7. Police officers must have a keen sense of organizational integrity and loyalty to their community, department, and fellow officers.

Job Task Analysis

In creating entrance-level police examinations, test experts spend a great deal of time performing a "job task analysis." A job task analysis is a systematic process defining the tasks and/or behaviors needed to perform a job successfully over a period of time. What is it that police officers *do*? How do they do it? What steps are required? What unique characteristics are important? What job tasks do police officers spend most of their time performing? What personal traits are necessary to perform the job over time? Once the test expert has the answers to these questions, a series of tests can be designed to find out who among the candidates has the knowledge, skills, abilities, and personal traits needed. Following is a sample of what a test expert might find are some of the knowledge, skills, abilities, and personal traits needed for an entry-level police officer.

Job Task Analysis: KSAT (Knowlege, skills, abilities, and traits)

Knowledge

The candidate knows

- how to operate a motor vehicle.
- the basic elements of human behavior, differentiating between criminal and noncriminal.
- English grammar, usage, spelling, and sentence and paragraph construction.

Skills

The candidate is skilled in

- writing clearly, concisely, and completely.
- verbal communication.
- physical activity, manual dexterity, and motor coordination.
- adapting behavior and communication style to fit the needs of a particular situation.
- identifying suspicious behavior in a variety of settings.
- methods of proper note-taking.
- drawing accurate diagrams.
- determining the need for and using reasonable physical force.

Abilities

The candidate is able to

- acquire the skills and knowledge necessary for satisfactory performance of police duties and responsibilities.
- react quickly to changing situations.
- maintain a level of physical and mental fitness allowing satisfactory performance of demanding tasks and duties.
- understand verbal and written instructions.
- listen actively and understand the communication of others.
- memorize.
- write a clear, concise, thorough report from the information gathered.
- follow orders and the chain of command.
- take constructive criticism.
- make independent decisions when guidelines are not present.
- prioritize from most to least important activity.
- use, understand, and transmit radio codes and communications.
- receive abuse in language and behavior and remain professional in manner.
- separate facts from opinions.
- remain objective when conducting investigations.
- know when to seek supervisory assistance.
- analyze facts and come to reasonable conclusions.
- work alone under adverse conditions.

Traits

The candidate will be

- a self-motivated achiever.
- courteous, tactful, and pleasant.
- positive in attitude.
- self-disciplined.
- honest and have integrity.
- able to handle stress.
- compassionate.
- decisive.
- realistic and practical.
- willing to work alone.
- patient.
- able to maintain a sense of humor.
- self-confident.
- able to use good judgment and common sense.
- willing to learn new skills and techniques.
- willing to follow instructions.
- willing to work alternating schedules.
- able to maintain objectivity.

It's quite a list, isn't it? Looks to me like they're looking for a saint! But don't let all of this scare you. You don't have to have every one of these traits; nor do you have to have them at a one hundred percent, pure as snow, level. It's the combination that counts, and the more you can put on the plus side of the column, the better your chances of becoming a police officer will be. Besides, partner, I know a lot of the tricks of the trade and, between us, you'll do just fine.

> *Enthusiasm finds the opportunities, and energy makes the most of them.*
>
> —Henry Hoskins

PERSONAL DEVELOPMENT AND ACTION PLAN

What have I done today to prepare myself for a career in policing?

1. _____

2. _____

3. _____

4. _____

5. _____

6. _____

7. _____

8. _____

9. _____

10. _____

4

MOVING
ALONG THE PATH

THE APPLICATION PROCESS

Your first *test* in the selection process is filling out an application for employment as a police officer. The reason I consider this a test is that your application will be reviewed by the city personnel department and compared with the qualifications outlined in the position description. If your application doesn't show that you have the minimum qualifications, you will be disqualified as a candidate.

The previous section discussed your writing the director of personnel and the chief of police to express your interest in becoming a police officer. If you did so, chances are good you'll be notified when the city is accepting applications. The method of notification ranges from sending a postcard advising you where to obtain an application to sending an application along with a position description. However, Murphy's Law being what it is, your initial inquiry letter may have been lost in the system, eaten by a computer, or garbled during data entry into another name and address entirely. So, since almost all cities advertise for police applicants, get in the habit of checking your newspaper's help-wanted section. Advertisements for police positions vary in the amount of information offered. Here are several examples of what you can expect newspaper recruitment notices to look like.

POLICE OFFICER

$33,072–$39,624

Qualifications: 21 years of age
High school graduate or equivalency
Valid state driver's license

Selection: Examination process includes written, physical agility, oral, and medical examinations and background investigation. The list established from these exams will be used to fill vacancies as they occur throughout the next year.

Women and minorities are encouraged to apply.
Application deadline: April 13, 19—.

City of Dorchester
Department of Personnel
125 Main Street
Dorchester, —
(406) 728-9323

THE CITY OF WINDSOR

Police Officer

Applications being accepted for the position of police officer through December 19, 19—. Salary $532 per week. Must be 21 yrs., U.S. or nat. citizen, H.S. or GED, state driver's license, reside within 10 miles by end of probation period. Application and position description available at City Hall, Dept. of Personnel, Room 328, 155 State St. Phone: 443-3421.

THE CITY OF NEWCASTLE
Department of Personnel
425 Main Street
Newcastle, —

Police Officer
Salary: $36,420

Applications now being accepted for open, competitive examinations for the position of police officer. Qualifications: 18 years of age at time of appointment, United States or naturalized citizen, high school or GED diploma, valid state driver's license. Must successfully pass a written examination, physical examination, drug test, physical agility test, oral examination, polygraph examination, background investigation, and psychological examination. Closing date for applications: Sept. 18.

THE POSITION DESCRIPTION

Running advertisements in newspapers and magazines is very expensive, so only a minimum amount of information is given. The position description, which usually accompanies the application, contains more detailed information. Here are the position descriptions for our three cities that ran ads in the newspaper.

The City of Dorchester
an equal opportunity employer
announces an employment opportunity for

POLICE OFFICER—Salary range: $33,072–$39,624
(Note: above salary range is effective for period 7/1/— through 6/30/—. Salary and benefits are subject to collective bargaining.)

Position

Vacancies are in the Police Department of the city of Dorchester. Under supervision, performs law enforcement duties involving the protection of life and property, the prevention of crime, and the apprehension of criminal suspects. Performs public service duties involving noncriminal calls for service and the preservation of peace. Works 40 hours on shift rotation schedule involving weekends and holidays. Performs related work as required.

Minimum Requirements

Age: Must be 21 by June 16, 19—.
Education: High school graduation or equivalency diploma. A copy of high school diploma or GED certificate must be submitted with application.
Physical condition: Must pass a thorough medical examination.
Vision: Without correction, must be 20/20 or better in one eye and 20/40 or better in the other eye.
Driver's license: Must possess or be eligible to obtain a valid state driver's license.
Verification: All experience and qualifications will be verified.

Examination

The examination process consists of a written test, a physical agility test, an oral examination, a medical examination, a background investigation (which includes a polygraph examination), an interview with the Chief of Police, and a working test period, or probationary period, of one year (beginning on the date sworn in). All parts of the examination are designed to determine the ability of applicants to learn and perform the duties of police officers, as stated above, in an inner-city environment. Qualified applicants will be scheduled to begin the examination process on or about April 20, 19—.

Note: Dorchester residents shall have ten percent added to their passing grade. A Dorchester resident preference point request form must be signed and submitted with the application for residents who claim ten percent.

Applications will be accepted until April 13, 19—. Applications are obtained from and submitted to

Department of Personnel
Municipal Building
125 Main Street
Dorchester, —
Telephone: (406) 728-9323

Exam No. 1093

The City of Windsor
an equal-opportunity employer
announces

an examination for the position of
POLICE OFFICER: Salary—$532–$742

Last Date for Filing Applications

Applications must be postmarked or on file at the office of the Department of Personnel, Room 328, City Hall, 155 State Street, Windsor, —, on or before December 19, —.

Rating Procedure

Applicants who meet the minimum requirements and other criteria established by the city of Windsor will be rated according to their merit and relative fitness to perform the duties of the position.

Examination Process

The Department of Personnel will review all applications received at the discretion of the Director of Personnel. The number of applicants admitted to the examination process may be limited to those applicants whose background and experience as stated on the application would indicate skills and qualifications of most benefit to the department and the city of Windsor.

The examination for this position will consist of the following parts:

Written exam: 50%
Oral exam: 50%

As a condition of employment, all prospective appointees shall be required to undergo a physical examination by a physician chosen by the city, a background investigation, and a physical agility test.

Requirements

21 years of age at time of appointment
United States citizen or naturalized citizen
High school diploma or GED
Valid state driver's license
Vision correctable to 20/20
Live within a 10-mile radius of city by end of the probationary period

Supervision Received

Works under the supervision of an officer of higher rank who reviews work for conformance to department standards, regulations, and applicable laws.

Examples of Duties

- Patrols on foot, in a police vehicle, or by other means
- Enforces state statutes and local ordinances
- Arrests criminal offenders
- Provides such services to the public as department policy and regulations direct
- Maintains order at parades, rallies, demonstrations, and other public assemblies
- Performs other related duties as required

THE CITY OF NEWCASTLE invites applications for the position of

POLICE OFFICER

General Qualifications and Requirements

- You *must* be at least 18 years of age at the time of appointment.
- You *must* be a United States or a naturalized citizen.
- You *must* possess a high school diploma or GED.
- You *must* possess a valid state driver's license.
- Your application for the position of police officer *must* be postmarked by *September 18.*
- You *must* pass a written examination that will be held on *October 8.*
- You *must* pass a physical examination and a drug test that will be held on *October 15 and 16.*
- You *must* pass a physical agility test that will be held on *October 28.*
- You *must* pass an oral examination that will be held on *November 19.*
- You *must* pass a polygraph examination and extensive background check.
- You *may* be required to take a psychological examination.
- You *must* have vision correctable to 20/20, reside within 12 air miles of Newcastle, and be a nonsmoker.

Examples of Duties

- Patrols an assigned area to establish a police presence.
- Enforces state laws and city ordinances.
- Interacts with citizens to receive/investigate complaints.
- When necessary, arrests criminal suspects, initiates booking process, or issues summonses.
- Investigates motor vehicle accidents to determine causes and issues summonses as necessary.
- Renders first aid to sick and injured persons and victims of crimes.
- Makes written reports on accidents, investigations, and other activities by completing department forms.
- Completes follow-up on assigned investigations.
- Performs related duties as required.

Required Knowledge, Skills, and Abilities

- Ability to learn police procedures and techniques, the law, departmental guidelines, and all aspects of recruit training.
- Ability to reason logically, handling situations with good judgment and common sense.
- Good powers of observation, vision, and hearing.
- Ability to communicate well, to speak and listen effectively.
- Ability to read and write effectively.
- Ability to deal effectively with people, knowing when and how to use such skills as tact, understanding, leadership, and firmness.
- Ability to calmly handle emergencies and tense situations.
- Good physical condition, strength, and agility.

Brief Description of the Written Examination

The written examination is a "multiple-choice" test. The questions have been designed to assess important qualities needed to be a successful police officer—such as:

Judgment: You will be asked to apply judgment and common sense to situations which a police officer might encounter.

Ability to learn police materials: You will review a study booklet containing police-related materials, followed by questions based on these materials.

Powers of observation: You will be shown a series of "wanted posters" and will be required to remember details of the posters.

Motivation and interest: This section of the test will assess your work interests and preferences.

The written examination will take approximately 2½ hours to complete.

Brief Description of the Physical Agility Test

Test 1: Skinfold assessment, blood pressure, vision test, height and weight
Test 2: Push-ups—muscular endurance
Test 3: Sit-ups—muscular endurance
Test 4: Sit- and-reach—flexibility
Test 5: Agility run—ability to change speed and direction quickly
Test 6: Vertical jump—muscular explosiveness and strength of legs
Test 7: 1.5-mile run—cardiorespiratory endurance

Important Parts of the Position Description

Contained in the position description are two areas you should pay close attention to: "Minimum Requirements" and "Methods of Selection" (also called "Examination"). Highlight the important words contained in these sections.

The minimum requirements section outlines the basic qualifications required to apply for the job. For example, what is the age requirement? Do you have to be twenty-one years old, or does the city you're interested in accept candidates who are eighteen? Since the selection process lasts so long, could you apply at age twenty if you would turn twenty-one prior to final selection and entry into the police academy? Do you meet the physical requirements of the job—vision, height/weight, etc.? Is your driver's license current?

The methods of selection (examination) section is the most important part of the position description. It explains the type and various parts of the examination, the skill level and depth of understanding required, the relative weights of each type or part of the test, and the minimum passing score, if there is one. For example, how much of the final grade does the written examination represent? How about the oral examination? Does each count fifty percent of the total, or does the physical agility test receive a numerical grade as opposed to pass/fail? Like the residency and veterans preference points, are additional points added for a college education?

There are sections of this book devoted specifically to preparing you for the various types of examinations, but the above factors may influence where you choose to apply.

Prior to completing the actual application for employment, you should give your attention to two additional areas: "Residency Preference Points" and "Veterans Preference Points."

RESIDENCY PREFERENCE POINTS

Regardless of the type of test mechanism used (written examination, oral board, assessment center, physical agility test, medical exam, etc.), each applicant who successfully completes the process receives a final numerical score. Because of the large number of applicants and the types of tests used, the numerical rankings often result in only *tenths* of a point separating the top few candidates. Just six or seven *full* points may be between the person who comes out first and the top ten percent of the rest of the list. It's almost certain there will be just tenths of a point between those who "make it" and the first few who don't! When residency and/or veterans preference points (often ten percent of a resident applicant's final passing grade) are factored into this numerical equation, the final hiring list changes dramatically. For example, if a police department intends to hire twelve persons, consider the following list of applicants who have taken all of the tests. (The written examination and oral examination each count fifty percent of the final grade.)

POLICE EXAMINATION TEST RESULTS

Name	Written Test	Oral Test	Final Grade	Resident
1. Paul Drake	94%	90.20%	92.10%	
2. John Plummer	89	94.50	91.75	
3. Thomas Brown	92	88.50	90.25	
4. Pauline Simms	88	92.50	90.25	
5. Douglas Johnson	91	86.50	88.75	
6. Carol Jenkins	86	90.00	88.00	
7. Pablo Morales	93	82.80	87.90	
8. Jose Mendoza	91	84.30	87.65	X
9. Frank Rudewicz	87	88.30	87.65	X
10. Ronald Faggaini	88	85.20	86.60	X
11. James Peters	90	83.00	86.50	X
12. Mark Edwards	90	80.50	85.25	
cutoff --				
13. James Donnelly	91%	74.50%	82.75%	X
14. Joseph Kubiak	92	72.80	82.40	
15. Ted Mendito	89	75.50	82.25	
16. Barbara Moriarty	88	76.00	82.00	X
17. Ralph Murray	88	75.00	81.50	X
18. Sean Sullivan	87	76.00	81.50	
19. Anthony Mendoza	87	74.00	80.50	
20. Judith Johnson	90	70.50	80.25	
21. James Lynch	88	72.00	80.00	X
22. Ann Macrino	89	70.00	79.50	X
23. Lawrence Fleming	88	70.50	79.25	X
24. Jose Lopez	87	71.50	79.25	X
25. Sandra Young	86	72.00	79.00	

Note that only 6.85 percentage points separate Paul Drake, who came out number one with a final grade of 92.10 percent, and Mark Edwards, who is number twelve with a grade of 85.25 percent. However, if a ten percent premium is added to the final passing grade for those who are "residents" of the city, it changes the numerical makeup and standing of the entire list. Following are the revisions to the list after ten percent was added to the final passing grade of applicants who are residents.

POLICE EXAMINATION TEST RESULTS
(after adding ten percent for residency)

Name	Written Test	Oral Test	Residency Points	Final Grade
1. Jose Mendoza	91%	84.30%	8.76	96.41%
2. Frank Rudewicz	87	88.30	8.76	96.41
3. Ronald Faggaini	88	85.20	8.66	95.26
4. James Peters	90	83.00	8.65	95.15
5. Paul Drake	94	90.20	0.00	92.10
6. John Plummer	89	94.50	0.00	91.75
7. James Donnelly	91	74.50	8.27	91.02
8. Thomas Brown	92	88.50	0.00	90.25
9. Pauline Simms	88	92.50	0.00	90.25
10. Barbara Moriarty	88	76.00	8.20	90.20
11. Ralph Murray	88	75.00	8.15	89.65
12. Douglas Johnson	91	86.50	0.00	88.75

- Carol Jenkins, 88%, went from 6th to 14th.
- Pablo Morales, 87.90%, went from 7th to 15th.
- Mark Edwards, 85.25%, went from 12th to 19th.
- James Donnelly went from 13th to 7th.
- Barbara Moriarty went from 16th to 10th.
- Ralph Murray went from 17th to 11th.

- Jenkins, Morales, and Edwards fell on the list due to residency points and were not selected.
- Donnelly, Moriarty, and Murray rose on the list due to 10% of their final passing grade being added to their score, and they were selected.

The only reason Donnelly, Moriarty, and Murray rose high enough on the list (within the top twelve) to beat out the other applicants is that residency points were added to their scores. So, how can you use this information to your advantage? If the department you're most interested in offers residency points and your research indicates a high probability the city is going to hire police officers in the near future, you *may* wish to consider moving to that city. I know it's a big risk, but let's consider what's involved. First, find out the exact definition of "residency." Would you have had to live in the city a year, six months? Would you only need to show proof of current residency prior to the test? Is having ten percent of your final passing grade added to your score worth moving into the city, finding an apartment, changing your driver's license and vehicle registration, and having your mail sent there? What if something goes wrong and they decide to postpone hiring police officers until the following year because of budget constraints? It's a big decision—one that only you can make depending on your individual circumstances. However, it could make the difference in your scoring high enough on the tests to get the job! An example of a residency preference form follows.

DORCHESTER RESIDENT PREFERENCE POINTS
REQUEST FORM

Your name: _____

Address: _____

         (street address)   (apartment #)   (city)   (state)   (zip code)

Title of job you are applying for: _____

Exam number: _____

Eligibility Requirements (Personnel Rules and Regulations, Rule VI.8)

"In any open, competitive examination for entry-level classification, a Dorchester resident shall have ten percent (10%) added to his or her passing grade. An entry-level classification is one for which there exists no lower-level classification in which an employee could normally gain the necessary experience and training to qualify for promotion to that classification. Proof of eligibility for Dorchester resident preference shall be provided by the applicant in a manner prescribed by the Director of Personnel."

Proof of Eligibility

If you wish to exercise your right as a Dorchester resident, you must sign the statement below and submit it with your application. If this form is not submitted to the Department of Personnel with your application, you cannot submit it at a later date. A separate form must be filled out for each and every application you submit to the Department of Personnel for open, competitive, entry-level examinations.

Special Note

The Department of Personnel reserves the right to request further proof of residence. The Department of Personnel will routinely verify the addresses of applicants requesting ten percent under the Dorchester resident preference system.

Please Read Carefully Before Signing Below

I certify that the address listed above is my actual residence and that I presently reside at this address on a continuous basis. I understand that false or inaccurate information regarding my address may result in my disqualification for employment or my dismissal, if employed. I hereby request ten percent added to my passing score and understand that these preference points will be added to my score only if I pass all parts of the examination process for the job.

_____   _____

        (signature—please sign in ink)   (date)

Requiring police officers to live in the city or town they serve and offering extra points on the final score for residency are controversial issues in policing. Many people think officers who live in the city they serve will be more sensitive to multicultural issues and will thus better serve the public. Others think that after an officer spends a full work day being exposed to the psychological and physiological stresses of policing, it's helpful to live in another environment. Those cities offering extra points in the testing process for residency obviously have come to the conclusion that it's important for an officer to live within the community he or she serves.

VETERANS PREFERENCE POINTS

Many cities also offer preference points for honorably discharged veterans who served in time of war. The definition of "time of war" varies from World War II, Korea, and Vietnam to the "conflicts" the United States has been involved in during the past decade. Normally, *five points* are added to the applicant's final passing grade. Notice that these are *full* points, not percentage points of the final grade. So resident applicants could receive ten percent for residency and an additional five points added to their score if they were veterans who met the above criteria. An example of a veterans preference points form follows.

VETERANS PREFERENCE

Your name (please print)_____

Title of job you are applying for_____

Eligibility

In any examination for initial employment, an honorably discharged veteran of the Army, Marine Corps, Navy, Coast Guard, or Air Force of the United States who has served in time of war shall have five points added to his or her passing grade.

Service in Time of War

Section 27-403 of the General Statutes defines "service in time of war" as service of 90 or more days unless separated from service because of a service-related disability rated by the Veteran's Administration during the following:

World War II: December 7, 1941, to December 31, 1946
Korean hostilities: June 27, 1950, to October 27, 1953
Vietnam era: January 1, 1964, to July 1, 1975

Proof of Eligibility

Proof of eligibility for veterans preference points shall be provided by veterans in the form of DD-214, a certified copy, photostatic copy, or other satisfactory evidence of honorable service. Proof of eligibility must be submitted at the time of the examination. If you wish to exercise veterans preference and meet the above eligibility requirements, answer all parts listed below and submit the form with your application. If a part does not apply to you, check "no."

	Yes	No
1. Have you ever served on active duty in time of war in the United States military service?	☐	☐
2. Have you ever been discharged from the armed services under less than honorable conditions?	☐	☐
3. Do you claim 5 points preference based on active duty in the armed forces during time of war?	☐	☐

4. List dates, branch, and serial number of all active service in time of war.

From _____ to _____

Branch of service _____

Serial number _____

A false answer to any question above may be grounds for not employing you or for dismissing you after you begin work.

I certify that all of the statements made by me are true, complete, and correct to the best of my knowledge and belief and are made in good faith.

_____   _____
(signature—please sign in ink)   (date)

THE RULE OF THREE

In many cities, the selection process is further complicated by city personnel rules which allow the department head (chief of police, fire chief, head of public works, etc.) to select *any* of the *top three* candidates for a vacant position regardless of their numerical ranking on the list! This is often referred to as the "rule of three." Refer to the list back on page 81. If only one vacant position existed, the chief could choose either Jose Mendoza, Frank Rudewicz, or Ronald Faggaini to enter the police academy. Realistically, the rule of three comes into play at the bottom portion of the list. From the list, the chief could "pass over" number twelve, Douglas Johnson, and select number thirteen, James Lynch.

Residency and veterans preference points, along with the rule of three, all have an impact on the final list of who is selected to become a police officer and who isn't. If you're a Police Cadet, have completed an internship, have served in the Police Athletic League or Explorers, or are a member of a protected class, the chief of police might "reach down" a bit on the list and select *you,* jumping over others, if you score high enough on the exams to be in contention.

> *Not everything that is faced can be changed, but nothing can be changed until it is faced.*
>
> —James Baldwin

FILLING OUT YOUR APPLICATION

Your application for employment is your first "test" in the selection process. It will be reviewed by the city personnel department, and if you pass the written examination and physical agility test, the background investigation team will use your application to begin the process of checking your credentials. A surprisingly high number of applicants are screened out of the examination process simply because they didn't follow the directions in filling out their applications. They also neglect to attach requested documents, such as a copy of their high school diploma. Following is an example of what an application for a police department looks like.

THE CITY OF DORCHESTER
An Equal Opportunity Employer

APPLICATION FOR EMPLOYMENT
Department of Personnel
125 Main Street
Dorchester, —

Print in ink or type.

1. Job you are applying for: _____
   (use title on job announcement)

   Exam number: _____

2. Your name: _____
   (last)   (first)   (middle)

3. Your address: _____
   (number and street—RD, PO box)   (apt. #)

   _____
   (city)   (state)   (zip code)

4. How long have you lived at this address? _____

5. Your telephone number: Home _____
                           Work _____

6. Your date of birth: _____

7. Have you ever been convicted of any offense other than a minor traffic violation?
   Yes _____ No _____
   Note: Conviction is not necessarily disqualifying. Give the facts and dates of your convictions in space 8.

8. Use this space to explain any items in spaces 1–7.

9. Education:
   (A) Did you graduate from high school? Yes _____ Month _____ Year _____
                                           No _____
                                           Highest grade completed _____
   (B) If you have a high school equivalency certificate, give the year and place the
       certificate was granted. Year _____ Place _____
   (C) List the last high school or trade school you attended.

   _____
   (name of school)   (location)   (dates attended)   (course)

(D) List any colleges, business schools, or trade schools you attended.

(name of school)	(location)	(courses/major)	(dates attended)	(degree)

(name of school)	(location)	(courses/major)	(dates attended)	(degree)

(E) Other training: Special courses, work training programs, armed forces training. Give name and location where training was given, certificate (if any), dates attended, subject of training, number of hours weekly, and other details related to the job for which you are applying.

_____

_____

_____

10. Experience: Start with your present or last job and work back, listing all paid or unpaid, full or part time work, military service, and summer jobs performed during the last 10 years. Use additional sheets of paper if you need more space. Work performed more than 10 years ago may be given if it applies to the job you want.

Is it OK if we contact your present employer?   Yes _____ No _____

_____

(start date)	(end date)	(name/address of present/last employer)

(salary)	(hours per week)	(name/title/phone number of your supervisor)

_____

(your reason for leaving)

_____

(your present or last job title)	(your duties)

(start date)	(end date)	(name/address of next previous employer)

(salary)	(hours per week)	(name/title/phone number of your supervisor)

_____

(your reason for leaving)

_____

(your previous job title)	(your duties)

11. Special skills or abilities: Show licenses, including driver's machines you operate, languages other than English you speak, read, and write well, typing and shorthand speed, and any other special abilities or knowledge relating to the job you want. Some veterans may be eligible for special preference. Check with the Department of Personnel.

_____

_____

_____

Certification

I certify that all statements made on or in conjunction with this application are true, complete, and correct to the best of my knowledge and belief and are made in good faith. I understand that incomplete, false, or inaccurate information may result in the rejection of this application and that false information may result in my dismissal if employed.

_____   _____
(signature of applicant)   (date)

Compliance Information

The following information is needed for compliance with government selection requirements and for EEO reports. It will be detached when your application is filed, and the information on it will not be considered in the employment process.

1. Your name: _____

2. Job applied for: _____

3. Your sex (please check): Male _____   Female _____

4. Describe yourself in terms of one of the following groups. Check one.

  (A) American Indian _____

  (B) Black/Afro-American _____

  (C) White/Caucasian: _____

  (D) Hispanic/Spanish _____

  (E) Oriental/Asian-American _____

  (F) Other _____
         (please specify)

Don't complete your application in handwriting unless the directions specifically require you to do so. Type it. As mentioned previously, it will be reviewed by the city personnel office and the background investigation team. It might even end up in the hands of your oral board panel. Be certain _all_ the blocks are filled in completely. Obviously, you're not going to lie about any of the information you place on the application for employment, but I would caution you not to stretch the truth either.

Important Sections of the Application

There are several sections of the application form which are especially important. For example, review *item 7* on our sample application: "Have you ever been convicted of any offense other than a minor traffic violation?" Notice the words *convicted* and *offense*. An offense is normally defined as a felony, misdemeanor, or violation, all of which are "crimes." *Convicted* means you were arrested for an *offense* (crime) and were found or plead guilty in a court of law. If you were arrested but found *innocent*, or the case (charges) was *dismissed,* then you haven't been convicted of an offense and should check "no." If you *were convicted* for an offense, by all means check "yes." When the application asks for the "facts" concerning a conviction, this is your opportunity to *mitigate* what otherwise might disqualify you as a candidate. For example, if you're now twenty-two but at sixteen you were arrested and convicted of "criminal trespass," point out the fact that this happened six years ago and that the "trespass" consisted of you and some friends crawling through an open window of the high school gym to play basketball.

The next section deserving special attention is *item 9-E,* "Other Training." Even if you received a wage for your work and have already included it elsewhere on the application, if you served as a Police Cadet, completed a police internship, or were a member of the Police Athletic League or Police Explorers, place this information in that section. If you received *any* work-related training, this is the area to highlight it.

At a minimum, your present or most recent employer will be contacted by the background investigation team. What your boss says about your work performance and behavior is important. It's sometimes difficult to tell an employer you've applied for a job someplace else and are asking for a good recommendation. The best way to handle it is to be completely honest and inform your employer, and/or whomever you list on your application that you report to, that you've applied for a position with the police department and have given his or her name as an employment reference. Explain why you want to become a police officer and what the examination process entails. You'll be in a much better position than you would if your boss received a phone call or visit "cold." You may have to take some time off work to take the various examinations, and if you've been honest and up front with your boss, it's likely to go a lot smoother.

SUBMITTING YOUR APPLICATION

Once you've completed typing out your application, make a copy of it for your records and, if possible, hand deliver it. Obtain the name of the person you give it to and request that it be dated and time-stamped in your presence. Sometimes there are ties on entry-level police examinations. For example, if there were twelve vacancies, and two applicants had the same final score, then usually whoever received the higher score on the *written examination* would be placed higher on the list. If both applicants received the same written test score, then the tie is usually broken by who handed in their application *first.* These facts are usually not mentioned in the position description and probably won't be known by the person to whom you hand your application. They're part of many cities' personnel rules for civil-service examinations, and it often takes a team of lawyers to make sense out of those rules. So don't be surprised if the clerk in the personnel office says, "Oh, you don't need to go through all of that. Just leave it in the basket." Be polite but insistent. It could turn out to mean the difference between your getting the job or not!

> *Experience is not what happens to you. It is what you do with what happens to you.*
>
> —Aldous Huxley

PERSONAL DEVELOPMENT AND ACTION PLAN

What have I done today to prepare myself for a career in policing?

1. _____
2. _____
3. _____
4. _____
5. _____
6. _____
7. _____
8. _____
9. _____
10. _____

5

DRAGONS ALONG THE PATH

THE WRITTEN EXAMINATION

The city will set a date after which no further applications for the position of police officer will be accepted. Expect to wait several weeks past the cutoff date before you receive a letter advising you of the date, time, and location of the written examination. The letter will instruct you to bring either two forms of identification (for example, your birth certificate and social security card) or a picture identification, such as a driver's license, to the examination. Some cities include an identification number which you must detach from the bottom of the letter and bring with you to the exam. Due to the large number of applicants, police entry-level examinations are often held at high schools or colleges, frequently on a Saturday.

PREPARATION FOR THE WRITTEN EXAM

The Test Site

Don't be late for your test because you *think* you know how to get there. Once the examination begins, the test proctor may not let you in the room. Drive to the test site several days before the exam. It's not just a matter of knowing how to get there and estimating the driving time. You'll also want to check the availability of parking and the *exact* location of the test. For instance, if the test is given at a city college or municipal building, you may have to park on the street or in a parking garage. How far away is this from the test site? How will this affect your travel-time estimate? What about inclement weather and traffic conditions? What if the test is to be given in a college gymnasium? Do you know the *exact* location of the gym? You'd better find out; it may not be as easy to find as you think. It makes sense to take these basic precautions. It *doesn't* make sense to get stressed out right before you sit down to take a test in which you're competing against hundreds of other people! Plan to arrive at the test location at least forty-five minutes before the test is scheduled to begin.

What to Wear

The written examination doesn't grade you for appearance, so wear comfortable clothing. The test may last up to three hours. Your personal comfort is important. You'll probably be sitting in one of those uncomfortable chairs with a small, attached desktop, so dress accordingly.

What to Bring

Bring the following items with you on test day:

- several number two pencils
- large pad of paper
- durable eraser
- highlighter
- driver's license
- two other forms of identification
- watch
- calculator

Your Physical Condition

Get a good night's rest before taking the test. Don't make the mistake of staying up late the night before. You want to be as sharp as possible on test day. If you wear glasses, don't forget to bring them.

What to Expect

When you arrive at the exam location, expect to have to stand in line to check in prior to being allowed into the examination room. There may be tables set up outside the room to check your identification and/or the number sent you by the personnel department.

Police entry examinations are given under strict conditions. There will be at least one representative from the city's personnel department and one or more test proctors, depending on the number of applicants. Choose a seat in the front row where you can hear the test directions well and where you'll have fewer distractions—distractions which can lead to careless mistakes. Listen carefully to the test proctor. You'll be told exactly how much time you have to take the examination, and you'll be given specific instructions concerning the different sections of the test. Ask if it's permissible to use a calculator on any math questions.

TEST-TAKING STRATEGIES

Using Time Effectively

Time is important in test taking. Once you're told to begin, quickly review all parts of the examination to estimate how long it will take to complete the test. A minute and a half per question on a one-hundred-question, multiple-choice exam would take 150 minutes (two and a half hours). In a three-hour test, that would leave only thirty minutes for review. Check the time frequently to be sure you're on schedule. You'll get a good idea of how long it takes to complete the various sections of these types of tests by taking the practice examinations in this book.

The Test Booklet and Answer Sheet

Read the instructions in the test booklet carefully. If there's something you don't understand, ask! Be sure you have *all* the test materials that the oral and written instructions indicate you should have. Usually, computer-type answer sheets, similar to those included in this book, are used for entry-level police examinations. Follow the oral and written directions and use the type of pencil indicated by the exam proctor. Fill in your answers completely, and don't make any notations or marks on the answer sheet that might confuse the computer into taking points away from you. Make sure you put your name on the test and/or the computer answer sheet. This is especially important when the answer sheet is separate from the test booklet.

Understanding Questions and Answers

Police entry-level examinations are multiple-choice tests, but they are not as straightforward as those you may have taken in high school or college. Although the examination doesn't require applicants to have knowledge of police technical language, rules, regulations, or procedures, it does pose questions designed to measure analytical thinking, reasoning, judgment, observation, memory, common sense, grammar, writing, and problem solving, all written in police vernacular. Your research and reading about different departments, along with your participation in a police internship, Athletic League, Explorers, and/or Cadet program and the time you spent riding with police officers, will give you a big edge over other people taking the test in understanding police terminology.

To measure your knowledge, skills, ability, and personal traits, test analysts often create reading passages which relate a series of facts, definitions, rules, procedures, descriptions, situations, and events from which you must

- analyze the facts presented in the reading passage and use deductive reasoning and/or practical judgment to choose the most correct answer to the question
- choose the most appropriate course of action from among several options
- choose the next logical step in an ongoing progression

Before you begin the written examination, ask the proctor if you're allowed to mark on the test booklet. As you're taking the exam, you'll move rapidly in some sections, confident that you've chosen the most correct answer. You'll find other sections more complicated, and you may make the mistake of looking for hidden meanings or reading into the questions. When you reach a roadblock on the test, use the following procedure to increase your comprehension of the question and answer choices.

1. If the section you're working on includes an essay or paragraph to read, followed by multiple-choice questions, carefully read the material, circling each word you don't know the meaning of. You can usually get a good idea of what the word means by reading the entire selection.

2. Go back to the word you circled and substitute another word you feel more comfortable with. Use the same process for the question and answer choices. An example:

Test Question: You are a police officer walking your beat, and at 12:10 P.M. you are approached by a citizen who informs you he just came from a restaurant located a short distance away. While in the restaurant's washroom, he observed a man who took a small pistol out of his pocket and placed it on the sink while washing his hands. The first thing you should do is

The key words in this question are *12:10 P.M., citizen, restaurant, short distance away, washroom, small pistol,* and *first thing you should do.* Circle these words and write directly above them, if they are not absolutely clear to you as they are, *noon, person, public place, close by, bathroom, gun,* and *protect life and property.* Mentally change the question to read: "You are a police officer walking your beat, and around *noon* you're approached by a *person* who says he just came from a *restaurant/public place* located *close by* and he saw a man in the *bathroom* put a *gun* on the sink while he washed his hands." Since a police officer's primary duty is to protect life and property, what should you do first? Let's look at the answer choices offered for this test question:

(A) continue questioning the citizen to obtain his full name, address, and telephone number.
(B) immediately respond to the scene and take appropriate police action.
(C) obtain a description of the suspect, notify the police dispatcher via radio of the information received, and respond to the scene with the citizen.
(D) go to a phone booth with the citizen and call in the information to the police communication center via telephone.

Use the same process of circling key words for the answer choices. Answer (A) is straightforward and needs no further explanation. Answer (B) might be changed to "run to the scene" (a person with a gun is an emergency situation) "and, depending on what is found, react to it." Answer (D) might read, "walk to the nearest phone booth with the citizen and call the police dispatcher to explain the situation." As you might have guessed, (C) is the correct answer. The question doesn't provide information about how much time has passed since the citizen saw the man in the bathroom, but since the restaurant is a "short distance away" and the citizen informed the officer he "just came from a restaurant," you can infer that only a short time has passed. The fact that a man has a gun in the bathroom of a restaurant, especially at a time it's likely to be crowded, calls for immediate police response by more than one police officer. The police radio is the fastest means of communicating the information received to all other police officers and to the police dispatcher. Further details, such as the citizen's name, address, and phone number and his familiarity with handguns enabling him to describe the weapon as a pistol as opposed to a gun, can be discussed enroute to the scene. This answer does not imply that the officer will bring the citizen inside the restaurant. It merely indicates that time is important and that the officer is reacting proactively, as opposed to passively, because this is what the situation calls for.

If the test proctor does not allow writing on the exam booklet, which is sometimes the case, write the confusing terms on a separate piece of paper.

Marking Questions and Answers

If you're allowed to write in the test booklet, highlight or underline key words in both the question and answer choices. If you come to a question you're not sure of, skip it, but put a check mark next to the number of the question on both the test booklet and the answer sheet. *If you use this method, be sure you completely erase all the check marks from the answer sheet before time is called so the computer doesn't identify them as wrong answers.* In almost every entry-level police examination, someone skips a question and then gets the answer sheet out of sequence, resulting in a very low score. Using check marks will help you avoid this disaster.

As you read the questions, circle the letter of the correct answer in the booklet and then transfer your selection to the answer sheet. Most multiple-choice tests have either four or five answer choices. You can usually eliminate two of the answers as being obviously wrong. If it's allowed, cross out the letter of these answers in the examination booklet. In a four-answer spread, you've increased your odds, if you're guessing, from one in four to one in two. You now only have to select the *best* answer of the remaining two, which are often similar. Read the question again and then read the answers. Make sure you know what the question is asking.

Many answer choices contain words called *specific determiners*. Specific determiners that are too broad often indicate the *wrong* selection. Examples of such specific determiners are

only, all, never, nothing, everyone, none, must

Words that often indicate the *right* answer are

could, might, usually, sometimes, any, often, generally, rarely, occasionally, frequently, possibly, normally

Above all, make sure you don't get stuck on any question. Remember, all the questions count the same, so if you hit a question that seems very complex or difficult, mark it, fill in a guess answer, and move on. There's no point in agonizing over it, wasting valuable test time, or letting it throw you so completely that you lose concentration on following questions.

Returning to Unanswered Questions

Never leave a question unanswered unless the oral or written instructions indicate that you don't lose credit for questions left blank. Often, as you're taking the test, another question will refresh your memory about one of the questions you've taken a guess on. Then you need merely to go back to the questions you've checked and select the right answer. If this isn't the case, carefully read the question again, circling key words and phrases and substituting your own words in questions and answers. The most difficult questions often leave you with two answer alternatives which directly contradict one another (an either/or situation), yet both seem somehow to be correct. If you're still stuck, stay with your best guess.

Changing Answers

It seems that every time I've taken a test and changed an answer, I changed a right answer to a wrong one. Test-taking statistics indicate that this is most often the case. Unless you're positive, don't change your answers. Trust your initial instincts. If you do change an answer, make sure to completely erase the original answer mark. Be sure, too, to review all of your answers if you have time remaining at the end of the test, making sure you haven't carelessly filled in wrong answer choices even though you knew the right answer. It can happen, so double-check.

> *Enthusiasm finds the opportunity, and energy makes the most of it.*
>
> —Henry Hoskins

ABOUT THE MULTIPLE-CHOICE PRACTICE TESTS

The content of police entry-level examinations varies across the country. However, the general theory involved in testing for the required knowledge, skills, abilities, and personal traits remains constant. It doesn't matter whether you're taking the written examination in Dallas, Texas, or Salt Lake City, Utah. The testing principles are the same.

The three multiple-choice tests contained in this guide are representative and deal with broad-based testing principles and theory common to all entry-level police examinations. The object of taking practice examinations is to increase your skill in taking the type of written tests most often used. People who practice taking tests do better than those who don't, all other factors excluded. The practice tests that follow are presented as if they were tests for the cities of Dorchester, Windsor, and Newcastle. Because writing skills are important to police work, and because more departments are adding spelling and grammar questions to written tests, the three practice tests are followed by a fourth test on writing skills.

Before you take the practice multiple-choice examinations, read again the section on improving your techniques for taking multiple-choice tests (pp. 94–98). Make the conditions in which you take the practice tests as realistic as possible. Find a quiet place, free from interruptions. Follow the directions carefully. Use the standard computer-type answer sheets provided; the vast majority of police entry-level examinations use them. Take the entire examination in one sitting, in the time allotted, without using references. Don't look ahead to the answer key to see how you're doing. Manage your time and highlight key words in the questions and answer selections. Don't read information that isn't there into the question or change your answers unless you're positive of another answer. Experiment with the test booklet by marking out answer choices as you eliminate them, etc.

After finishing your test, compare your selections with the answer key immediately following the test. Answers and analysis follow each practice test. Be sure to read *all* of these.

Good luck!

CITY OF DORCHESTER POLICE OFFICER EXAMINATION
ANSWER SHEET

cut here

1. Ⓐ Ⓑ Ⓒ Ⓓ Ⓔ	26. Ⓐ Ⓑ Ⓒ Ⓓ Ⓔ	51. Ⓐ Ⓑ Ⓒ Ⓓ Ⓔ	76. Ⓐ Ⓑ Ⓒ Ⓓ Ⓔ
2. Ⓐ Ⓑ Ⓒ Ⓓ Ⓔ	27. Ⓐ Ⓑ Ⓒ Ⓓ Ⓔ	52. Ⓐ Ⓑ Ⓒ Ⓓ Ⓔ	77. Ⓐ Ⓑ Ⓒ Ⓓ Ⓔ
3. Ⓐ Ⓑ Ⓒ Ⓓ Ⓔ	28. Ⓐ Ⓑ Ⓒ Ⓓ Ⓔ	53. Ⓐ Ⓑ Ⓒ Ⓓ Ⓔ	78. Ⓐ Ⓑ Ⓒ Ⓓ Ⓔ
4. Ⓐ Ⓑ Ⓒ Ⓓ Ⓔ	29. Ⓐ Ⓑ Ⓒ Ⓓ Ⓔ	54. Ⓐ Ⓑ Ⓒ Ⓓ Ⓔ	79. Ⓐ Ⓑ Ⓒ Ⓓ Ⓔ
5. Ⓐ Ⓑ Ⓒ Ⓓ Ⓔ	30. Ⓐ Ⓑ Ⓒ Ⓓ Ⓔ	55. Ⓐ Ⓑ Ⓒ Ⓓ Ⓔ	80. Ⓐ Ⓑ Ⓒ Ⓓ Ⓔ
6. Ⓐ Ⓑ Ⓒ Ⓓ Ⓔ	31. Ⓐ Ⓑ Ⓒ Ⓓ Ⓔ	56. Ⓐ Ⓑ Ⓒ Ⓓ Ⓔ	81. Ⓐ Ⓑ Ⓒ Ⓓ Ⓔ
7. Ⓐ Ⓑ Ⓒ Ⓓ Ⓔ	32. Ⓐ Ⓑ Ⓒ Ⓓ Ⓔ	57. Ⓐ Ⓑ Ⓒ Ⓓ Ⓔ	82. Ⓐ Ⓑ Ⓒ Ⓓ Ⓔ
8. Ⓐ Ⓑ Ⓒ Ⓓ Ⓔ	33. Ⓐ Ⓑ Ⓒ Ⓓ Ⓔ	58. Ⓐ Ⓑ Ⓒ Ⓓ Ⓔ	83. Ⓐ Ⓑ Ⓒ Ⓓ Ⓔ
9. Ⓐ Ⓑ Ⓒ Ⓓ Ⓔ	34. Ⓐ Ⓑ Ⓒ Ⓓ Ⓔ	59. Ⓐ Ⓑ Ⓒ Ⓓ Ⓔ	84. Ⓐ Ⓑ Ⓒ Ⓓ Ⓔ
10. Ⓐ Ⓑ Ⓒ Ⓓ Ⓔ	35. Ⓐ Ⓑ Ⓒ Ⓓ Ⓔ	60. Ⓐ Ⓑ Ⓒ Ⓓ Ⓔ	85. Ⓐ Ⓑ Ⓒ Ⓓ Ⓔ
11. Ⓐ Ⓑ Ⓒ Ⓓ Ⓔ	36. Ⓐ Ⓑ Ⓒ Ⓓ Ⓔ	61. Ⓐ Ⓑ Ⓒ Ⓓ Ⓔ	86. Ⓐ Ⓑ Ⓒ Ⓓ Ⓔ
12. Ⓐ Ⓑ Ⓒ Ⓓ Ⓔ	37. Ⓐ Ⓑ Ⓒ Ⓓ Ⓔ	62. Ⓐ Ⓑ Ⓒ Ⓓ Ⓔ	87. Ⓐ Ⓑ Ⓒ Ⓓ Ⓔ
13. Ⓐ Ⓑ Ⓒ Ⓓ Ⓔ	38. Ⓐ Ⓑ Ⓒ Ⓓ Ⓔ	63. Ⓐ Ⓑ Ⓒ Ⓓ Ⓔ	88. Ⓐ Ⓑ Ⓒ Ⓓ Ⓔ
14. Ⓐ Ⓑ Ⓒ Ⓓ Ⓔ	39. Ⓐ Ⓑ Ⓒ Ⓓ Ⓔ	64. Ⓐ Ⓑ Ⓒ Ⓓ Ⓔ	89. Ⓐ Ⓑ Ⓒ Ⓓ Ⓔ
15. Ⓐ Ⓑ Ⓒ Ⓓ Ⓔ	40. Ⓐ Ⓑ Ⓒ Ⓓ Ⓔ	65. Ⓐ Ⓑ Ⓒ Ⓓ Ⓔ	90. Ⓐ Ⓑ Ⓒ Ⓓ Ⓔ
16. Ⓐ Ⓑ Ⓒ Ⓓ Ⓔ	41. Ⓐ Ⓑ Ⓒ Ⓓ Ⓔ	66. Ⓐ Ⓑ Ⓒ Ⓓ Ⓔ	91. Ⓐ Ⓑ Ⓒ Ⓓ Ⓔ
17. Ⓐ Ⓑ Ⓒ Ⓓ Ⓔ	42. Ⓐ Ⓑ Ⓒ Ⓓ Ⓔ	67. Ⓐ Ⓑ Ⓒ Ⓓ Ⓔ	92. Ⓐ Ⓑ Ⓒ Ⓓ Ⓔ
18. Ⓐ Ⓑ Ⓒ Ⓓ Ⓔ	43. Ⓐ Ⓑ Ⓒ Ⓓ Ⓔ	68. Ⓐ Ⓑ Ⓒ Ⓓ Ⓔ	93. Ⓐ Ⓑ Ⓒ Ⓓ Ⓔ
19. Ⓐ Ⓑ Ⓒ Ⓓ Ⓔ	44. Ⓐ Ⓑ Ⓒ Ⓓ Ⓔ	69. Ⓐ Ⓑ Ⓒ Ⓓ Ⓔ	94. Ⓐ Ⓑ Ⓒ Ⓓ Ⓔ
20. Ⓐ Ⓑ Ⓒ Ⓓ Ⓔ	45. Ⓐ Ⓑ Ⓒ Ⓓ Ⓔ	70. Ⓐ Ⓑ Ⓒ Ⓓ Ⓔ	95. Ⓐ Ⓑ Ⓒ Ⓓ Ⓔ
21. Ⓐ Ⓑ Ⓒ Ⓓ Ⓔ	46. Ⓐ Ⓑ Ⓒ Ⓓ Ⓔ	71. Ⓐ Ⓑ Ⓒ Ⓓ Ⓔ	96. Ⓐ Ⓑ Ⓒ Ⓓ Ⓔ
22. Ⓐ Ⓑ Ⓒ Ⓓ Ⓔ	47. Ⓐ Ⓑ Ⓒ Ⓓ Ⓔ	72. Ⓐ Ⓑ Ⓒ Ⓓ Ⓔ	97. Ⓐ Ⓑ Ⓒ Ⓓ Ⓔ
23. Ⓐ Ⓑ Ⓒ Ⓓ Ⓔ	48. Ⓐ Ⓑ Ⓒ Ⓓ Ⓔ	73. Ⓐ Ⓑ Ⓒ Ⓓ Ⓔ	98. Ⓐ Ⓑ Ⓒ Ⓓ Ⓔ
24. Ⓐ Ⓑ Ⓒ Ⓓ Ⓔ	49. Ⓐ Ⓑ Ⓒ Ⓓ Ⓔ	74. Ⓐ Ⓑ Ⓒ Ⓓ Ⓔ	99. Ⓐ Ⓑ Ⓒ Ⓓ Ⓔ
25. Ⓐ Ⓑ Ⓒ Ⓓ Ⓔ	50. Ⓐ Ⓑ Ⓒ Ⓓ Ⓔ	75. Ⓐ Ⓑ Ⓒ Ⓓ Ⓔ	100. Ⓐ Ⓑ Ⓒ Ⓓ Ⓔ

CITY OF WINDSOR POLICE OFFICER EXAMINATION
ANSWER SHEET

1. Ⓐ Ⓑ Ⓒ Ⓓ Ⓔ	26. Ⓐ Ⓑ Ⓒ Ⓓ Ⓔ	51. Ⓐ Ⓑ Ⓒ Ⓓ Ⓔ	76. Ⓐ Ⓑ Ⓒ Ⓓ Ⓔ
2. Ⓐ Ⓑ Ⓒ Ⓓ Ⓔ	27. Ⓐ Ⓑ Ⓒ Ⓓ Ⓔ	52. Ⓐ Ⓑ Ⓒ Ⓓ Ⓔ	77. Ⓐ Ⓑ Ⓒ Ⓓ Ⓔ
3. Ⓐ Ⓑ Ⓒ Ⓓ Ⓔ	28. Ⓐ Ⓑ Ⓒ Ⓓ Ⓔ	53. Ⓐ Ⓑ Ⓒ Ⓓ Ⓔ	78. Ⓐ Ⓑ Ⓒ Ⓓ Ⓔ
4. Ⓐ Ⓑ Ⓒ Ⓓ Ⓔ	29. Ⓐ Ⓑ Ⓒ Ⓓ Ⓔ	54. Ⓐ Ⓑ Ⓒ Ⓓ Ⓔ	79. Ⓐ Ⓑ Ⓒ Ⓓ Ⓔ
5. Ⓐ Ⓑ Ⓒ Ⓓ Ⓔ	30. Ⓐ Ⓑ Ⓒ Ⓓ Ⓔ	55. Ⓐ Ⓑ Ⓒ Ⓓ Ⓔ	80. Ⓐ Ⓑ Ⓒ Ⓓ Ⓔ
6. Ⓐ Ⓑ Ⓒ Ⓓ Ⓔ	31. Ⓐ Ⓑ Ⓒ Ⓓ Ⓔ	56. Ⓐ Ⓑ Ⓒ Ⓓ Ⓔ	81. Ⓐ Ⓑ Ⓒ Ⓓ Ⓔ
7. Ⓐ Ⓑ Ⓒ Ⓓ Ⓔ	32. Ⓐ Ⓑ Ⓒ Ⓓ Ⓔ	57. Ⓐ Ⓑ Ⓒ Ⓓ Ⓔ	82. Ⓐ Ⓑ Ⓒ Ⓓ Ⓔ
8. Ⓐ Ⓑ Ⓒ Ⓓ Ⓔ	33. Ⓐ Ⓑ Ⓒ Ⓓ Ⓔ	58. Ⓐ Ⓑ Ⓒ Ⓓ Ⓔ	83. Ⓐ Ⓑ Ⓒ Ⓓ Ⓔ
9. Ⓐ Ⓑ Ⓒ Ⓓ Ⓔ	34. Ⓐ Ⓑ Ⓒ Ⓓ Ⓔ	59. Ⓐ Ⓑ Ⓒ Ⓓ Ⓔ	84. Ⓐ Ⓑ Ⓒ Ⓓ Ⓔ
10. Ⓐ Ⓑ Ⓒ Ⓓ Ⓔ	35. Ⓐ Ⓑ Ⓒ Ⓓ Ⓔ	60. Ⓐ Ⓑ Ⓒ Ⓓ Ⓔ	85. Ⓐ Ⓑ Ⓒ Ⓓ Ⓔ
11. Ⓐ Ⓑ Ⓒ Ⓓ Ⓔ	36. Ⓐ Ⓑ Ⓒ Ⓓ Ⓔ	61. Ⓐ Ⓑ Ⓒ Ⓓ Ⓔ	86. Ⓐ Ⓑ Ⓒ Ⓓ Ⓔ
12. Ⓐ Ⓑ Ⓒ Ⓓ Ⓔ	37. Ⓐ Ⓑ Ⓒ Ⓓ Ⓔ	62. Ⓐ Ⓑ Ⓒ Ⓓ Ⓔ	87. Ⓐ Ⓑ Ⓒ Ⓓ Ⓔ
13. Ⓐ Ⓑ Ⓒ Ⓓ Ⓔ	38. Ⓐ Ⓑ Ⓒ Ⓓ Ⓔ	63. Ⓐ Ⓑ Ⓒ Ⓓ Ⓔ	88. Ⓐ Ⓑ Ⓒ Ⓓ Ⓔ
14. Ⓐ Ⓑ Ⓒ Ⓓ Ⓔ	39. Ⓐ Ⓑ Ⓒ Ⓓ Ⓔ	64. Ⓐ Ⓑ Ⓒ Ⓓ Ⓔ	89. Ⓐ Ⓑ Ⓒ Ⓓ Ⓔ
15. Ⓐ Ⓑ Ⓒ Ⓓ Ⓔ	40. Ⓐ Ⓑ Ⓒ Ⓓ Ⓔ	65. Ⓐ Ⓑ Ⓒ Ⓓ Ⓔ	90. Ⓐ Ⓑ Ⓒ Ⓓ Ⓔ
16. Ⓐ Ⓑ Ⓒ Ⓓ Ⓔ	41. Ⓐ Ⓑ Ⓒ Ⓓ Ⓔ	66. Ⓐ Ⓑ Ⓒ Ⓓ Ⓔ	91. Ⓐ Ⓑ Ⓒ Ⓓ Ⓔ
17. Ⓐ Ⓑ Ⓒ Ⓓ Ⓔ	42. Ⓐ Ⓑ Ⓒ Ⓓ Ⓔ	67. Ⓐ Ⓑ Ⓒ Ⓓ Ⓔ	92. Ⓐ Ⓑ Ⓒ Ⓓ Ⓔ
18. Ⓐ Ⓑ Ⓒ Ⓓ Ⓔ	43. Ⓐ Ⓑ Ⓒ Ⓓ Ⓔ	68. Ⓐ Ⓑ Ⓒ Ⓓ Ⓔ	93. Ⓐ Ⓑ Ⓒ Ⓓ Ⓔ
19. Ⓐ Ⓑ Ⓒ Ⓓ Ⓔ	44. Ⓐ Ⓑ Ⓒ Ⓓ Ⓔ	69. Ⓐ Ⓑ Ⓒ Ⓓ Ⓔ	94. Ⓐ Ⓑ Ⓒ Ⓓ Ⓔ
20. Ⓐ Ⓑ Ⓒ Ⓓ Ⓔ	45. Ⓐ Ⓑ Ⓒ Ⓓ Ⓔ	70. Ⓐ Ⓑ Ⓒ Ⓓ Ⓔ	95. Ⓐ Ⓑ Ⓒ Ⓓ Ⓔ
21. Ⓐ Ⓑ Ⓒ Ⓓ Ⓔ	46. Ⓐ Ⓑ Ⓒ Ⓓ Ⓔ	71. Ⓐ Ⓑ Ⓒ Ⓓ Ⓔ	96. Ⓐ Ⓑ Ⓒ Ⓓ Ⓔ
22. Ⓐ Ⓑ Ⓒ Ⓓ Ⓔ	47. Ⓐ Ⓑ Ⓒ Ⓓ Ⓔ	72. Ⓐ Ⓑ Ⓒ Ⓓ Ⓔ	97. Ⓐ Ⓑ Ⓒ Ⓓ Ⓔ
23. Ⓐ Ⓑ Ⓒ Ⓓ Ⓔ	48. Ⓐ Ⓑ Ⓒ Ⓓ Ⓔ	73. Ⓐ Ⓑ Ⓒ Ⓓ Ⓔ	98. Ⓐ Ⓑ Ⓒ Ⓓ Ⓔ
24. Ⓐ Ⓑ Ⓒ Ⓓ Ⓔ	49. Ⓐ Ⓑ Ⓒ Ⓓ Ⓔ	74. Ⓐ Ⓑ Ⓒ Ⓓ Ⓔ	99. Ⓐ Ⓑ Ⓒ Ⓓ Ⓔ
25. Ⓐ Ⓑ Ⓒ Ⓓ Ⓔ	50. Ⓐ Ⓑ Ⓒ Ⓓ Ⓔ	75. Ⓐ Ⓑ Ⓒ Ⓓ Ⓔ	100. Ⓐ Ⓑ Ⓒ Ⓓ Ⓔ

Name: _____

SSN: _____ / _____ / _____

CITY OF NEWCASTLE POLICE OFFICER EXAMINATION
ANSWER SHEET

1. Ⓐ Ⓑ Ⓒ Ⓓ Ⓔ	26. Ⓐ Ⓑ Ⓒ Ⓓ Ⓔ	51. Ⓐ Ⓑ Ⓒ Ⓓ Ⓔ	76. Ⓐ Ⓑ Ⓒ Ⓓ Ⓔ
2. Ⓐ Ⓑ Ⓒ Ⓓ Ⓔ	27. Ⓐ Ⓑ Ⓒ Ⓓ Ⓔ	52. Ⓐ Ⓑ Ⓒ Ⓓ Ⓔ	77. Ⓐ Ⓑ Ⓒ Ⓓ Ⓔ
3. Ⓐ Ⓑ Ⓒ Ⓓ Ⓔ	28. Ⓐ Ⓑ Ⓒ Ⓓ Ⓔ	53. Ⓐ Ⓑ Ⓒ Ⓓ Ⓔ	78. Ⓐ Ⓑ Ⓒ Ⓓ Ⓔ
4. Ⓐ Ⓑ Ⓒ Ⓓ Ⓔ	29. Ⓐ Ⓑ Ⓒ Ⓓ Ⓔ	54. Ⓐ Ⓑ Ⓒ Ⓓ Ⓔ	79. Ⓐ Ⓑ Ⓒ Ⓓ Ⓔ
5. Ⓐ Ⓑ Ⓒ Ⓓ Ⓔ	30. Ⓐ Ⓑ Ⓒ Ⓓ Ⓔ	55. Ⓐ Ⓑ Ⓒ Ⓓ Ⓔ	80. Ⓐ Ⓑ Ⓒ Ⓓ Ⓔ
6. Ⓐ Ⓑ Ⓒ Ⓓ Ⓔ	31. Ⓐ Ⓑ Ⓒ Ⓓ Ⓔ	56. Ⓐ Ⓑ Ⓒ Ⓓ Ⓔ	81. Ⓐ Ⓑ Ⓒ Ⓓ Ⓔ
7. Ⓐ Ⓑ Ⓒ Ⓓ Ⓔ	32. Ⓐ Ⓑ Ⓒ Ⓓ Ⓔ	57. Ⓐ Ⓑ Ⓒ Ⓓ Ⓔ	82. Ⓐ Ⓑ Ⓒ Ⓓ Ⓔ
8. Ⓐ Ⓑ Ⓒ Ⓓ Ⓔ	33. Ⓐ Ⓑ Ⓒ Ⓓ Ⓔ	58. Ⓐ Ⓑ Ⓒ Ⓓ Ⓔ	83. Ⓐ Ⓑ Ⓒ Ⓓ Ⓔ
9. Ⓐ Ⓑ Ⓒ Ⓓ Ⓔ	34. Ⓐ Ⓑ Ⓒ Ⓓ Ⓔ	59. Ⓐ Ⓑ Ⓒ Ⓓ Ⓔ	84. Ⓐ Ⓑ Ⓒ Ⓓ Ⓔ
10. Ⓐ Ⓑ Ⓒ Ⓓ Ⓔ	35. Ⓐ Ⓑ Ⓒ Ⓓ Ⓔ	60. Ⓐ Ⓑ Ⓒ Ⓓ Ⓔ	85. Ⓐ Ⓑ Ⓒ Ⓓ Ⓔ
11. Ⓐ Ⓑ Ⓒ Ⓓ Ⓔ	36. Ⓐ Ⓑ Ⓒ Ⓓ Ⓔ	61. Ⓐ Ⓑ Ⓒ Ⓓ Ⓔ	86. Ⓐ Ⓑ Ⓒ Ⓓ Ⓔ
12. Ⓐ Ⓑ Ⓒ Ⓓ Ⓔ	37. Ⓐ Ⓑ Ⓒ Ⓓ Ⓔ	62. Ⓐ Ⓑ Ⓒ Ⓓ Ⓔ	87. Ⓐ Ⓑ Ⓒ Ⓓ Ⓔ
13. Ⓐ Ⓑ Ⓒ Ⓓ Ⓔ	38. Ⓐ Ⓑ Ⓒ Ⓓ Ⓔ	63. Ⓐ Ⓑ Ⓒ Ⓓ Ⓔ	88. Ⓐ Ⓑ Ⓒ Ⓓ Ⓔ
14. Ⓐ Ⓑ Ⓒ Ⓓ Ⓔ	39. Ⓐ Ⓑ Ⓒ Ⓓ Ⓔ	64. Ⓐ Ⓑ Ⓒ Ⓓ Ⓔ	89. Ⓐ Ⓑ Ⓒ Ⓓ Ⓔ
15. Ⓐ Ⓑ Ⓒ Ⓓ Ⓔ	40. Ⓐ Ⓑ Ⓒ Ⓓ Ⓔ	65. Ⓐ Ⓑ Ⓒ Ⓓ Ⓔ	90. Ⓐ Ⓑ Ⓒ Ⓓ Ⓔ
16. Ⓐ Ⓑ Ⓒ Ⓓ Ⓔ	41. Ⓐ Ⓑ Ⓒ Ⓓ Ⓔ	66. Ⓐ Ⓑ Ⓒ Ⓓ Ⓔ	91. Ⓐ Ⓑ Ⓒ Ⓓ Ⓔ
17. Ⓐ Ⓑ Ⓒ Ⓓ Ⓔ	42. Ⓐ Ⓑ Ⓒ Ⓓ Ⓔ	67. Ⓐ Ⓑ Ⓒ Ⓓ Ⓔ	92. Ⓐ Ⓑ Ⓒ Ⓓ Ⓔ
18. Ⓐ Ⓑ Ⓒ Ⓓ Ⓔ	43. Ⓐ Ⓑ Ⓒ Ⓓ Ⓔ	68. Ⓐ Ⓑ Ⓒ Ⓓ Ⓔ	93. Ⓐ Ⓑ Ⓒ Ⓓ Ⓔ
19. Ⓐ Ⓑ Ⓒ Ⓓ Ⓔ	44. Ⓐ Ⓑ Ⓒ Ⓓ Ⓔ	69. Ⓐ Ⓑ Ⓒ Ⓓ Ⓔ	94. Ⓐ Ⓑ Ⓒ Ⓓ Ⓔ
20. Ⓐ Ⓑ Ⓒ Ⓓ Ⓔ	45. Ⓐ Ⓑ Ⓒ Ⓓ Ⓔ	70. Ⓐ Ⓑ Ⓒ Ⓓ Ⓔ	95. Ⓐ Ⓑ Ⓒ Ⓓ Ⓔ
21. Ⓐ Ⓑ Ⓒ Ⓓ Ⓔ	46. Ⓐ Ⓑ Ⓒ Ⓓ Ⓔ	71. Ⓐ Ⓑ Ⓒ Ⓓ Ⓔ	96. Ⓐ Ⓑ Ⓒ Ⓓ Ⓔ
22. Ⓐ Ⓑ Ⓒ Ⓓ Ⓔ	47. Ⓐ Ⓑ Ⓒ Ⓓ Ⓔ	72. Ⓐ Ⓑ Ⓒ Ⓓ Ⓔ	97. Ⓐ Ⓑ Ⓒ Ⓓ Ⓔ
23. Ⓐ Ⓑ Ⓒ Ⓓ Ⓔ	48. Ⓐ Ⓑ Ⓒ Ⓓ Ⓔ	73. Ⓐ Ⓑ Ⓒ Ⓓ Ⓔ	98. Ⓐ Ⓑ Ⓒ Ⓓ Ⓔ
24. Ⓐ Ⓑ Ⓒ Ⓓ Ⓔ	49. Ⓐ Ⓑ Ⓒ Ⓓ Ⓔ	74. Ⓐ Ⓑ Ⓒ Ⓓ Ⓔ	99. Ⓐ Ⓑ Ⓒ Ⓓ Ⓔ
25. Ⓐ Ⓑ Ⓒ Ⓓ Ⓔ	50. Ⓐ Ⓑ Ⓒ Ⓓ Ⓔ	75. Ⓐ Ⓑ Ⓒ Ⓓ Ⓔ	100. Ⓐ Ⓑ Ⓒ Ⓓ Ⓔ

WRITING SKILLS EXAMINATION
ANSWER SHEET

1. Ⓐ Ⓑ Ⓒ Ⓓ Ⓔ	26. Ⓐ Ⓑ Ⓒ Ⓓ Ⓔ	51. Ⓐ Ⓑ Ⓒ Ⓓ Ⓔ	76. Ⓐ Ⓑ Ⓒ Ⓓ Ⓔ
2. Ⓐ Ⓑ Ⓒ Ⓓ Ⓔ	27. Ⓐ Ⓑ Ⓒ Ⓓ Ⓔ	52. Ⓐ Ⓑ Ⓒ Ⓓ Ⓔ	77. Ⓐ Ⓑ Ⓒ Ⓓ Ⓔ
3. Ⓐ Ⓑ Ⓒ Ⓓ Ⓔ	28. Ⓐ Ⓑ Ⓒ Ⓓ Ⓔ	53. Ⓐ Ⓑ Ⓒ Ⓓ Ⓔ	78. Ⓐ Ⓑ Ⓒ Ⓓ Ⓔ
4. Ⓐ Ⓑ Ⓒ Ⓓ Ⓔ	29. Ⓐ Ⓑ Ⓒ Ⓓ Ⓔ	54. Ⓐ Ⓑ Ⓒ Ⓓ Ⓔ	79. Ⓐ Ⓑ Ⓒ Ⓓ Ⓔ
5. Ⓐ Ⓑ Ⓒ Ⓓ Ⓔ	30. Ⓐ Ⓑ Ⓒ Ⓓ Ⓔ	55. Ⓐ Ⓑ Ⓒ Ⓓ Ⓔ	80. Ⓐ Ⓑ Ⓒ Ⓓ Ⓔ
6. Ⓐ Ⓑ Ⓒ Ⓓ Ⓔ	31. Ⓐ Ⓑ Ⓒ Ⓓ Ⓔ	56. Ⓐ Ⓑ Ⓒ Ⓓ Ⓔ	81. Ⓐ Ⓑ Ⓒ Ⓓ Ⓔ
7. Ⓐ Ⓑ Ⓒ Ⓓ Ⓔ	32. Ⓐ Ⓑ Ⓒ Ⓓ Ⓔ	57. Ⓐ Ⓑ Ⓒ Ⓓ Ⓔ	82. Ⓐ Ⓑ Ⓒ Ⓓ Ⓔ
8. Ⓐ Ⓑ Ⓒ Ⓓ Ⓔ	33. Ⓐ Ⓑ Ⓒ Ⓓ Ⓔ	58. Ⓐ Ⓑ Ⓒ Ⓓ Ⓔ	83. Ⓐ Ⓑ Ⓒ Ⓓ Ⓔ
9. Ⓐ Ⓑ Ⓒ Ⓓ Ⓔ	34. Ⓐ Ⓑ Ⓒ Ⓓ Ⓔ	59. Ⓐ Ⓑ Ⓒ Ⓓ Ⓔ	84. Ⓐ Ⓑ Ⓒ Ⓓ Ⓔ
10. Ⓐ Ⓑ Ⓒ Ⓓ Ⓔ	35. Ⓐ Ⓑ Ⓒ Ⓓ Ⓔ	60. Ⓐ Ⓑ Ⓒ Ⓓ Ⓔ	85. Ⓐ Ⓑ Ⓒ Ⓓ Ⓔ
11. Ⓐ Ⓑ Ⓒ Ⓓ Ⓔ	36. Ⓐ Ⓑ Ⓒ Ⓓ Ⓔ	61. Ⓐ Ⓑ Ⓒ Ⓓ Ⓔ	86. Ⓐ Ⓑ Ⓒ Ⓓ Ⓔ
12. Ⓐ Ⓑ Ⓒ Ⓓ Ⓔ	37. Ⓐ Ⓑ Ⓒ Ⓓ Ⓔ	62. Ⓐ Ⓑ Ⓒ Ⓓ Ⓔ	87. Ⓐ Ⓑ Ⓒ Ⓓ Ⓔ
13. Ⓐ Ⓑ Ⓒ Ⓓ Ⓔ	38. Ⓐ Ⓑ Ⓒ Ⓓ Ⓔ	63. Ⓐ Ⓑ Ⓒ Ⓓ Ⓔ	88. Ⓐ Ⓑ Ⓒ Ⓓ Ⓔ
14. Ⓐ Ⓑ Ⓒ Ⓓ Ⓔ	39. Ⓐ Ⓑ Ⓒ Ⓓ Ⓔ	64. Ⓐ Ⓑ Ⓒ Ⓓ Ⓔ	89. Ⓐ Ⓑ Ⓒ Ⓓ Ⓔ
15. Ⓐ Ⓑ Ⓒ Ⓓ Ⓔ	40. Ⓐ Ⓑ Ⓒ Ⓓ Ⓔ	65. Ⓐ Ⓑ Ⓒ Ⓓ Ⓔ	90. Ⓐ Ⓑ Ⓒ Ⓓ Ⓔ
16. Ⓐ Ⓑ Ⓒ Ⓓ Ⓔ	41. Ⓐ Ⓑ Ⓒ Ⓓ Ⓔ	66. Ⓐ Ⓑ Ⓒ Ⓓ Ⓔ	91. Ⓐ Ⓑ Ⓒ Ⓓ Ⓔ
17. Ⓐ Ⓑ Ⓒ Ⓓ Ⓔ	42. Ⓐ Ⓑ Ⓒ Ⓓ Ⓔ	67. Ⓐ Ⓑ Ⓒ Ⓓ Ⓔ	92. Ⓐ Ⓑ Ⓒ Ⓓ Ⓔ
18. Ⓐ Ⓑ Ⓒ Ⓓ Ⓔ	43. Ⓐ Ⓑ Ⓒ Ⓓ Ⓔ	68. Ⓐ Ⓑ Ⓒ Ⓓ Ⓔ	93. Ⓐ Ⓑ Ⓒ Ⓓ Ⓔ
19. Ⓐ Ⓑ Ⓒ Ⓓ Ⓔ	44. Ⓐ Ⓑ Ⓒ Ⓓ Ⓔ	69. Ⓐ Ⓑ Ⓒ Ⓓ Ⓔ	94. Ⓐ Ⓑ Ⓒ Ⓓ Ⓔ
20. Ⓐ Ⓑ Ⓒ Ⓓ Ⓔ	45. Ⓐ Ⓑ Ⓒ Ⓓ Ⓔ	70. Ⓐ Ⓑ Ⓒ Ⓓ Ⓔ	95. Ⓐ Ⓑ Ⓒ Ⓓ Ⓔ
21. Ⓐ Ⓑ Ⓒ Ⓓ Ⓔ	46. Ⓐ Ⓑ Ⓒ Ⓓ Ⓔ	71. Ⓐ Ⓑ Ⓒ Ⓓ Ⓔ	96. Ⓐ Ⓑ Ⓒ Ⓓ Ⓔ
22. Ⓐ Ⓑ Ⓒ Ⓓ Ⓔ	47. Ⓐ Ⓑ Ⓒ Ⓓ Ⓔ	72. Ⓐ Ⓑ Ⓒ Ⓓ Ⓔ	97. Ⓐ Ⓑ Ⓒ Ⓓ Ⓔ
23. Ⓐ Ⓑ Ⓒ Ⓓ Ⓔ	48. Ⓐ Ⓑ Ⓒ Ⓓ Ⓔ	73. Ⓐ Ⓑ Ⓒ Ⓓ Ⓔ	98. Ⓐ Ⓑ Ⓒ Ⓓ Ⓔ
24. Ⓐ Ⓑ Ⓒ Ⓓ Ⓔ	49. Ⓐ Ⓑ Ⓒ Ⓓ Ⓔ	74. Ⓐ Ⓑ Ⓒ Ⓓ Ⓔ	99. Ⓐ Ⓑ Ⓒ Ⓓ Ⓔ
25. Ⓐ Ⓑ Ⓒ Ⓓ Ⓔ	50. Ⓐ Ⓑ Ⓒ Ⓓ Ⓔ	75. Ⓐ Ⓑ Ⓒ Ⓓ Ⓔ	100. Ⓐ Ⓑ Ⓒ Ⓓ Ⓔ

cut here

Department of Personnel

*The City
of
Dorchester*

Name: _____

SS No.: _____

Date: _____

POLICE OFFICER EXAMINATION
NUMBER 1093

General Examination Directions

This examination consists of four sections, each of which will be given to you at specific times during the examination. Each individual section has directions for taking that part of the examination. You will be provided with a computerized answer sheet on which you must record your answer selections using the pencil provided. Print your *name* and the *examination number* on *both* the answer sheet and the examination booklets.

Time: 3 hours
100 Questions

SECTION 1 OF 4

Booklet 1 of 7: Information

Directions

The following section tests your ability to read and understand practical police and legal concepts. You will be given *twenty minutes* to read the information contained in this booklet. At the end of twenty minutes, *this booklet will be collected,* and you will be given questions that apply to the information you have read. Choose the *most* correct answer.

PROBABLE CAUSE

The Fourth Amendment to the United States Constitution states:

> The right of the people to be secure in their persons, houses, papers, and effects, against unreasonable searches and seizures, shall not be violated, and no warrants shall issue, but upon probable cause, supported by oath or affirmation, and particularly describing the place to be searched, and the persons or things to be seized.

In order for an arrest to be legal, it must comply with Fourth Amendment requirements. An arrest based on *less* than probable cause is illegal and negates all the evidence obtained as a direct result of that arrest. One of the most important decisions a police officer is faced with is *when* to place a person under arrest. Arrest is defined as the "taking of a person into custody to answer for a crime he or she is alleged to have committed." The decision to arrest depends upon the existence of probable cause. A police officer must determine in his or her own mind whether enough probable cause exists to make a legal arrest.

The United States Supreme Court has defined probable cause in the following manner:

> Probable cause exists where the facts and circumstances within the officers' knowledge and of which they have reasonable, trustworthy information, are sufficient in themselves to warrant a man of reasonable caution in the belief that an offense has been committed. (*Brinegar* v. *United States*, 338 U.S. 160)

Another definition of probable cause is "less than proof, but more than mere suspicion that a crime is being, has been, or will be committed."

The only limitation in the above definitions is that the facts be taken in good faith by the officer and that the officer can show that the circumstances acted upon were reasonable. The arresting officer must have more than mere suspicion to act upon. The police officer must show the facts or circumstances which led to the belief that the arrested person committed a crime. When reviewing probable cause, the court will view the facts through the eyes of the experienced police officer and not those of a layperson. Police officers are expected to use their training and experience in determining probable

111

cause. Any facts may be used to build probable cause as long as they are taken in good faith by the police officer. In providing probable cause, there are no rules of evidence. Hearsay evidence may be used to build probable cause. Following is a partial list of guilt-laden facts which, by themselves or in combination, may be used to build probable cause.

- flight
- furtive movements
- hiding
- attempts to destroy evidence
- admissions or confessions
- evasive answers
- unreasonable explanations
- unusual or suspicious conduct
- identification of a suspect by a witness
- contraband or weapons in plain view
- knowledge that a crime was committed
- hearsay information from a fellow officer or informant

If the information available at the moment of arrest is not sufficient to make probable cause, the arrest is illegal, even though other incriminating evidence may come to light later. The question of probable cause is ultimately decided by a court at a pretrial hearing. It is up to the defense to raise the question, which is then decided by a judge. The arresting officer, under oath, lays out all the facts until it has been proven to the judge that probable cause existed for the arrest.

The exact time the arrest took place may become the critical aspect in proving probable cause. As soon as an arrest is made, no further facts which have not already been discovered may be used to establish probable cause. For this reason, the defense will try to prove that the arrest took place as early as possible in order to eliminate as many incriminating facts as possible. The prosecution, on the other hand, will try to prove that the arrest took place as late as possible in order to include as many incriminating facts as possible.

The burden of proof at the probable-cause hearing is to establish a reasonable ground for belief in guilt, not beyond a reasonable doubt, as in a trial. Probable cause is determined by whether or not a police officer's actions were reasonable and prudent in view of the totality of circumstances as they appeared at the moment of arrest.

Name: _____

Exam No.: _____

SECTION 1 OF 4

Booklet 2 of 7: Questions

Directions

You have *twenty-five minutes* to answer questions 1 through 10 based on the "Probable Cause" reading section.

1. Which amendment to the United States Constitution deals with arresting a person using probable cause?

   (A) First Amendment
   (B) Second Amendment
   (C) Third Amendment
   (D) Fourth Amendment

2. Officer Jones placed Robert Franklin under arrest for larceny (shoplifting). Officer Jones did not have probable cause to arrest Robert Franklin. The arrest is

   (A) legal. If Officer Jones arrested Robert Franklin for shoplifting, Jones must have had evidence that Franklin did it.
   (B) illegal. If Officer Jones did not have probable cause to arrest Robert Franklin, the arrest was illegal.
   (C) legal. Even though Officer Jones did not have probable cause to arrest Robert Franklin, Jones had suspicion that Franklin committed larceny.
   (D) illegal. Larceny is a misdemeanor; a police officer cannot arrest a person for committing a misdemeanor.

3. In order for a police officer to have probable cause to arrest a person,

   (A) the officer needs proof beyond a reasonable doubt that a crime was committed.
   (B) the officer needs proof that a crime was committed.
   (C) the officer needs less than proof but more than mere suspicion that a crime was committed.
   (D) the officer needs a preponderance of evidence that a crime was committed.

4. While walking her beat, Officer Jennings heard what sounded like a gunshot coming from a nearby park. Entering the park, she was approached by a "witness" who said he saw a man take a handgun from his pocket and shoot at a pigeon. The witness pointed to a man standing by a fountain in the park. Officer Jennings approached the man, who, upon seeing the officer, began running. The officer chased the man, captured him, and placed him under arrest. Searching him, the officer found a pistol in the man's pocket. The pistol

   (A) can be used to establish probable cause. The witness told the officer he saw the man shoot at a pigeon with it.
   (B) cannot be used to establish probable cause. The officer found it after the man was arrested.
   (C) can be used to establish probable cause. The officer had more than mere suspicion a crime had been committed.
   (D) cannot be used to establish probable cause. The man may have a permit for the pistol.

5. Using the information in question 4, which of the following facts may be used by Officer Jennings to build probable cause?

   (A) She heard what sounded like a gunshot come from the park and was told by a witness that he saw a man take out a handgun and shoot at a pigeon.
   (B) The witness pointed out the man who shot at the pigeon, and the officer found a pistol on him after he was arrested.
   (C) The suspect ran when approached by Officer Jennings.
   (D) all of the above
   (E) (A) and (C) but not (B)

6. Using the information in question 4, the arrest of the man was

   (A) legal. The officer had facts and circumstances which would lead a police officer to believe that the man committed a crime.
   (B) illegal. The officer did not have enough "guilt-laden" facts to believe that the man committed a crime.
   (C) legal. The officer found the pistol in the man's pocket.
   (D) illegal. The officer violated the man's Fourth Amendment right not to be searched without a search warrant.

7. Which of the following "guilt-laden" facts can be used in establishing probable cause?

   (A) the name of a person being arrested
   (B) a person's suspicious conduct
   (C) the race of a person being arrested
   (D) the fact that a person lives in a high-crime area

8. In a pretrial hearing to decide probable cause,

   (A) the defense will try to prove that the arrest took place as late as possible to show the officer did not act in good faith.
   (B) the prosecution will try to prove that the arrest took place as early as possible so a search after arrest can be used as evidence.
   (C) the burden of proof is to establish a preponderance of evidence that a crime was committed.
   (D) none of the above

9. One of the most important decisions a police officer must make is

   (A) when to place a person under arrest.
   (B) how to place a person under arrest.
   (C) where to place a person under arrest.
   (D) what state statute number to arrest the person for.

10. When reviewing probable cause, the court will view the facts through the eyes of

   (A) the average person.
   (B) the layperson.
   (C) the prosecutor.
   (D) an experienced police officer.

SECTION 2 OF 4

Booklet 3 of 7: Questions

Directions

This part of the examination tests your ability to use practical judgment, establish priorities, and demonstrate reasoned thinking. You have *eighty minutes* to answer questions 11 through 60. Choose the *most* correct answer.

11. You are a police officer and respond to the scene of a motor vehicle accident involving serious injuries. The accident is located just over the crest of a steep hill. It is dark, the hill is covered with ice, and cars coming over the hill are sliding. What is the first thing you should do upon arrival?

    (A) Place flares at the top of the hill to warn motorists.
    (B) Request, via radio, that additional police officers be sent to the scene.
    (C) Care for the injured.
    (D) Ask the drivers to move their vehicles.

12. You are a police officer chasing a man on foot who just shot a clerk at the Town Line Package Store. The suspect runs across a street into the next city, where you do not have police jurisdiction. You are only a few seconds behind the suspect. You should

    (A) continue chasing the suspect and apprehend him.
    (B) stop chasing the suspect and radio your location.
    (C) continue chasing the suspect until a police officer from that city joins you.
    (D) stop chasing the suspect but fire a warning shot to stop him.

13. The owner of an apartment building is informed by the city building inspector that the elevator in the building is seriously defective, dangerous, and should not be used. The building inspector has temporarily turned off the elevator and put up a warning sign advising people not to use it. The owner of the building removes the sign and turns the elevator back on. The elevator cable snaps and several people are seriously injured. The apartment building owner

(A) committed a crime, acting intentionally, recklessly, and with negligence.
(B) was negligent but did not commit a criminal act.
(C) was reckless but not negligent.
(D) was reckless and negligent, but this is a civil not a criminal matter.

14. You are a police officer and observe a man who grabs some fruit from an outdoor stand and begins running down the sidewalk. The owner of the stand yells for you to "arrest that man!" You chase him down an alley, at the end of which is a tall, chainlink fence, which he begins climbing. It's obvious that he will get away. You should

(A) draw your service weapon, order the man to stop, and if he ignores your command, fire one shot to prevent his escape.
(B) identify yourself as a police officer, order the man to stop, and if he ignores your command, shoot to wound the man.
(C) identify yourself as a police officer, order the man to stop, and if he ignores your command, resume regular patrol duties.
(D) identify yourself as a police officer, order the man to stop, and if he ignores your command, notify the police dispatcher of the location, the man's description, and that he is wanted for a minor larceny.

15. You are a police officer and have arrested a person for murder. He has been handcuffed but is belligerent and is resisting your efforts to put him in the cruiser. You and your partner are unable to place him in the cruiser. As a police officer, you would be justified in

(A) striking the prisoner on the head with your nightstick.
(B) kicking the prisoner in the groin.
(C) forcibly pushing the prisoner into the cruiser.
(D) punching the prisoner in the stomach to loosen him up.

16. A husband and wife are having a loud argument in the lobby of a hotel. The manager calls the police, and you arrive at the scene. The hotel manager wants the couple arrested for creating a disturbance. Both the husband and wife have apologized and are ready to check out of the hotel. You should

(A) arrest both persons on the complaint of the manager.
(B) arrest whichever person admitted to starting the argument if the manager agrees to be a witness in court.
(C) warn both parties and allow them to leave.
(D) arrest both parties if the manager signs a complaint.

17. A person enters a home through an open door. He is apprehended inside by the police, arrested, and advised of his constitutional rights, and admits that he entered thinking valuable jewelry was inside. The police contact the homeowners who advise that there was no jewelry inside. The arrest was

   (A) improper, due to the absence of the jewelry.
   (B) proper, but since the police were advised by the owners that no jewelry was inside, the arrested person will have to be set free.
   (C) improper, since the door was open and no jewelry was inside.
   (D) proper, regardless of whether the door was open or jewelry was inside.

18. Which of the following is the most valid purpose for the existence of a law enforcement code of ethics?

   (A) to elevate the standards of the profession
   (B) to encourage police officers to appreciate the full responsibility of their office
   (C) to create a system to assure that public internal investigations are fair
   (D) to earn the support and cooperation of the public

19. You are a police officer directing traffic at a busy intersection. A motorist stops and informs you that there is a bad accident three blocks up the street. You should

   (A) ask the motorist for a ride, leave your post, and respond to the scene of the accident.
   (B) radio the information to the police dispatcher and remain at your post.
   (C) radio the police dispatcher as you are walking to the scene, directing traffic as you go.
   (D) ask the motorist to return to the scene to assist those involved in the accident until the police arrive.

20. Late at night, you are dispatched to the scene of a burglary into a large warehouse. Upon arrival, you observe that the front door is wide open, and you see a man on the floor unconscious, bleeding from a wound to the head. Your most appropriate course of action is to

   (A) radio the information in, but wait for backup prior to going inside.
   (B) park the police cruiser close enough to shine the vehicle's spotlight in the doorway while waiting for backup.
   (C) radio the information in and then cautiously approach and enter the building to give aid to the unconscious man.
   (D) radio the information in, then cautiously approach the building and take up a position outside.

21. Which of the following most accurately describes the primary function of the police?

   (A) to arrest those who break the law
   (B) to serve the public
   (C) to prevent crime and disorder
   (D) to reduce the opportunity to commit crimes

22. Of the following crimes, on which do police patrol efforts have the most effect?

    (A) homicide
    (B) domestic disputes
    (C) sexual assault
    (D) auto theft

23. The police department receives an anonymous call that a woman is yelling for help inside apartment 402 located at 152 Main Street. You respond, knock on the door, and hear faint cries for help inside. Your most appropriate course of action is to

    (A) call the fire department and enter through a window.
    (B) guard the door and have another officer obtain a search warrant to enter the apartment.
    (C) enter the apartment with a passkey from the building superintendent.
    (D) immediately break the door down.

24. A woman is arrested for robbing a convenience store located next to the train station. The robbery occurred at 3:00 P.M. The woman's alibi is that she was on a train leaving a station seventy-five miles away and traveling at thirty miles per hour toward the city. The train left at 1:00 P.M. If the train's speed was constant, what time did it arrive?

    (A) 1:45 P.M.
    (B) 2:15 P.M.
    (C) 2:30 P.M.
    (D) 3:30 P.M.

25. In order to park in a handicapped parking space, vehicle operators must display a state-approved permit in the window. You observe a car parked in a handicapped space without a permit. As you are writing out a parking ticket for the vehicle, you are approached by an elderly woman on crutches. She informs you that it is her car and that she lost her permit several days ago. You should

    (A) issue the woman a ticket for parking in a handicapped space without a permit.
    (B) not issue the ticket and explain to the woman where to get a new handicapped parking permit.
    (C) severely warn the woman, not issue the ticket, but advise her that you will tow her vehicle if it happens again.
    (D) issue the woman a ticket for parking in a handicapped space and advise her where to get another permit.

CITY OF DORCHESTER WRITTEN EXAMINATION / 123

26. While on routine patrol working the midnight shift, you find the rear door to a jewelry store unlocked. You notify police communications, enter, and find that nothing appears to have been disturbed. The store owner responds to the scene, confirms that nothing is stolen, and is so appreciative that he takes out a fifty-dollar bill and wants to give it to you. You should

   (A) accept the money so as not to embarrass the jewelry store owner, but turn it in to the department.
   (B) accept the money with the understanding that you will donate it to the Police Athletic League.
   (C) refuse the money and arrest the store owner for attempted bribery.
   (D) refuse the money, explaining to the jewelry store owner that you were merely doing your job.

27. You respond to the scene of a fight in progress on a city street. Upon arrival, you observe one man strike another man in the face with his fist. The man who was struck falls to the ground, takes out a handgun, and shoots and kills the man who struck him. He immediately hands the gun over to you claiming he shot the man in self-defense. You should

   (A) arrest the man who did the shooting.
   (B) arrest the man who struck the shooter in the face.
   (C) take the gun, but make no arrest, since it was a case of self-defense.
   (D) take the gun, obtain the shooter's name and address, and turn the case over to the detective division.

28. You and another officer respond to the scene of a burglary into a liquor store. You both enter and find the premises ransacked but no one inside. You observe the other officer take several small liquor bottles off the shelf and place them in his jacket pocket saying, "Help yourself, no one will ever know." You should

   (A) instruct the officer to put the liquor back but remain silent about the matter.
   (B) request a supervisor to the scene and report what you saw the officer do and say.
   (C) say nothing but refrain from taking anything yourself.
   (D) leave money to cover the liquor which was taken.

29. Your police cruiser is parked between two other vehicles. As you are pulling out, the front end of your cruiser slightly nudges one of the cars, cracking its taillight. There is no damage to the police vehicle, and apparently no one saw the accident. The car you struck is several inches into a "no parking tow zone." You should

   (A) place a ticket on the car for parking in a tow zone.
   (B) take no action. The parked vehicle suffered only a cracked taillight, and there is no damage to the police vehicle.
   (C) try to locate the owner of the vehicle. If you cannot, you should leave a note with your name, department address, and phone number and report the matter to your supervisor.
   (D) make a notation in your notebook of the car's license plate number in case the owner reports the damage.

30. Of the following crimes, which one does police patrol have the least effect in reducing?

   (A) homicide
   (B) domestic disputes
   (C) sexual assault
   (D) auto theft

31. The most effective method of reducing crime is to

   (A) increase the number of police officers.
   (B) reduce the societal causes of crime.
   (C) increase public awareness.
   (D) incarcerate all persons who break the law.

32. You hear over the police radio the following description of a suspect wanted for a purse snatch: "White male, five feet, eight inches, 165 pounds, brown hair, wearing a red jacket, jeans, and sneakers." Which of the following makes the suspect easiest to spot?

   (A) white male, five feet, eight inches, 165 pounds
   (B) white male, five feet, eight inches, 165 pounds, wearing jeans
   (C) white male, wearing a red jacket, five feet, eight inches, 165 pounds
   (D) white male, five feet, eight inches, 165 pounds, brown hair

33. While driving home after work, you observe a dumpster engulfed in flames. The dumpster is located in an alley next to a wood-framed building. Your most appropriate course of action is to

   (A) call the fire department.
   (B) attempt to extinguish the fire.
   (C) evacuate the building.
   (D) notify police headquarters.

34. An audible alarm outside a convenience store has gone off twice during your tour of duty. The police dispatcher radios you that the alarm is going off again. You should

   (A) respond to the scene to ensure that the property is secure.
   (B) inform the dispatcher that it must be a false alarm.
   (C) drive by the location, but don't waste valuable time checking the building.
   (D) ask for a city electrician to disconnect the alarm.

35. A police sergeant, your immediate supervisor, gives you an order you don't understand. You should

   (A) ask a more experienced officer what the sergeant meant.
   (B) wait until later and ask another sergeant what the order meant.
   (C) write a report to your sergeant asking for clarification.
   (D) tell your sergeant you don't understand the order.

36. There is an emergency hostage situation. A man is holding three people at gunpoint and has already shot one other person. You have been instructed to position yourself in front of an elevator and not allow anyone to use it or go upstairs. The hostage situation is on the fourth floor. A woman approaches you, says that she lives on the second floor and needs to get into her apartment. You should

(A) explain the situation, escort her to the apartment, but use the stairs.
(B) explain the situation, escort her to the apartment, but use the elevator.
(C) explain the situation and advise her she will have to wait until the matter is resolved.
(D) explain the situation and allow her to go upstairs if she signs a form relieving the department of responsibility.

37. While walking your beat, you observe a vehicle with its driver's window smashed out. There is a large rock on the passenger seat and a screwdriver sticking out of the ignition. It would be most logical to think that

(A) the owner lost the keys to the vehicle.
(B) someone had attempted to steal the vehicle.
(C) the owner is repairing the vehicle.
(D) the vehicle has been abandoned.

38. In which of the following circumstances would it be least advisable to use a police cruiser's flashing lights and siren?

(A) responding to the scene of a serious motor vehicle accident
(B) responding to the scene of a silent burglar alarm
(C) responding to the scene at which shots have been fired
(D) responding to the scene of a person who suffered a heart attack

39. There has been a heavy snowstorm. For the past three days, you have observed a vehicle parked on a city street that has not been moved. It is a BMW. The location is a high-crime, poverty-stricken area. It would be most appropriate to

(A) make a notation in your log of the make, model, and license plate number of the vehicle.
(B) write out a parking ticket for the vehicle.
(C) determine if the vehicle is stolen.
(D) leave a note on the windshield for the owner to contact the department.

40. Which of the following is an indicator of criminal behavior?

(A) the manner in which a person is dressed
(B) a person's race
(C) speech patterns repeatedly used
(D) none of the above
(E) all of the above

41. You are in the middle of an intersection directing traffic. A woman approaches you, highly distraught, and says that her seven-year-old daughter is missing. The first thing you should do is

    (A) tell the woman to go to the nearest phone and call the police.
    (B) tell the woman to go to the police station and report her daughter missing in person.
    (C) ask the woman where she lost the child.
    (D) escort the woman to the sidewalk, obtain a description, and broadcast it to all officers via radio.

42. You are directed by your sergeant to go to 142 Adams Street, apartment A-2, and serve an arrest warrant for Samuel Johnson, D.O.B. 1/11/48, charged with assault in the second degree. You knock on the door, and a man answers. You should

    (A) place him under arrest.
    (B) determine his identity.
    (C) advise the man you have an arrest warrant for Samuel Johnson.
    (D) place the man under arrest and advise him of his constitutional rights.

43. Which of the following terms is concerned with the presence or absence of drugs and/or poisons in body fluids or organs?

    (A) serology
    (B) toxicology
    (C) neurology
    (D) biology

44. Review the diagram below. Vehicle 1 and vehicle 2 were stopped at the red traffic signal. Vehicle 2 was struck in the rear by vehicle 3, causing vehicle 2 to strike vehicle 1 in the rear. Which vehicle or vehicles were most at fault in the accident?

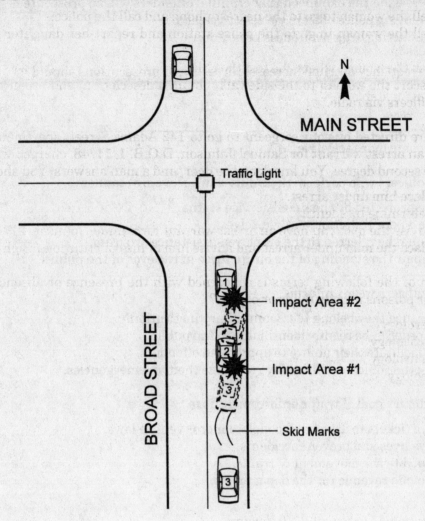

(A) vehicle 1
(B) vehicles 2 and 3
(C) vehicle 3
(D) vehicles 1 and 3

45. You respond to the scene of a landlord/tenant dispute. The landlord informs you that the tenant is five days past due in her rent, and he wants her evicted. The tenant says she has withheld the rent because the landlord will not fix her broken sink. You should

(A) tell the tenant to pay the rent or you will arrest her.
(B) tell the landlord to fix the tenant's sink or you will arrest him.
(C) tell both parties that this is a civil, not a police, matter.
(D) tell the tenant to pay a portion of the rent.

46. Crime prevention most clearly means

    (A) reducing the opportunity for criminals to commit crimes.
    (B) increasing the likelihood that criminal offenders will be prosecuted.
    (C) deploying police officers via selective patrol.
    (D) conducting drug-awareness programs.

47. As the frequency of crime increases, arrests and prosecutions should

    (A) remain stable.
    (B) increase.
    (C) decrease.
    (D) become more selective.

48. Police officers who perform their duties in a slovenly manner

    (A) are protected by their civil-service status.
    (B) are a poor reflection on themselves.
    (C) should be referred to the employee-assistance program.
    (D) impair the standing of the entire force in the eyes of the public.

49. Police officers wear uniforms

    (A) because they belong to a semimilitary institution.
    (B) in order to be readily identifiable to the public.
    (C) to facilitate their ability to apprehend offenders.
    (D) so other officers will readily recognize them in emergencies.

50. The primary goal of traffic enforcement is to

    (A) give tickets to drivers who violate motor vehicle laws.
    (B) save lives and prevent accidents.
    (C) expedite the movement of traffic.
    (D) provide revenue for the department.

Answer question 51 based on the following.

There are three basic ways in which murder can be committed. A person is guilty of murder when

    (1) he or she intentionally kills another person.
    (2) he or she intentionally causes a suicide by force, duress, or deception.
    (3) he or she causes the death of a nonparticipant while committing a felony or fleeing from a felony.

51. Mary Williams is backing her car into a parking space on a busy city street. As she's backing up, a small child steps off the curb, and Mary runs over the child, killing him. Mary

    (A) can be charged with murder. She intentionally backed the car up, killing the child.
    (B) cannot be charged with murder. There was no intent. It was an accident.
    (C) can be charged with murder. She did not post a proper lookout while backing.
    (D) cannot be charged with murder. The child is the parent's responsibility.

52. While on patrol in a high-crime area late at night, you observe a fourteen-year-old girl hitchhiking on a city street. Hitchhiking is prohibited by city ordinance and is punishable by a twenty-five dollar fine. You should

    (A) set up a surveillance to determine if the girl is engaging in prostitution.
    (B) stop the girl and issue her a ticket for hitchhiking.
    (C) stop the girl and determine why she is hitchhiking.
    (D) wait until the girl is picked up and then give her a ticket.

53. Crime is more likely to occur in locations with a

    (A) high-density population.
    (B) high level of commercial property.
    (C) high level of residential property.
    (D) high level of vehicular traffic.

54. The primary objective of police vehicular patrol is

    (A) to prevent crime from occurring.
    (B) to provide rapid response to criminal behavior.
    (C) to provide emergency medical response capability.
    (D) to arrest criminal offenders.

55. People are motivated toward goals through which of the following?

    (A) desires
    (B) self-motivation
    (C) wants
    (D) stimulus response

56. You're working the front desk in the lobby of police headquarters. A man enters and asks directions to a location. You do not know how to get there. You should

    (A) direct the man as close to the location as possible.
    (B) give the man a map of the city so he can figure out how to get to the location.
    (C) tell the man you don't know how to get there and make every effort to find out.
    (D) suggest that the man buy a street guide at a local store.

Answer questions 57 and 58 based on the following.

> Law enforcement officers bear the heavy responsibility of maintaining in their own conduct the honor and integrity of all government institutions. Officers shall guard themselves against being placed in a position in which any person can expect that special consideration is being given. Thus, officers should be firm in refusing favors, or gratuities, large or small, which can, in the public's mind, be interpreted as capable of influencing their judgment in the discharge of their duties.

57. According to the passage, the acceptance of gifts is

    (A) acceptable as long as the officer is off duty.
    (B) acceptable if done in private out of the public domain.
    (C) not acceptable if the gift is larger than normal.
    (D) not acceptable under any circumstances.

58. According to the passage, if you, as a police officer, were about to give a ticket to a motorist for speeding, but then the motorist said he was the brother of a fellow police officer, you should

    (A) extend professional courtesy and not issue the ticket.
    (B) tell the motorist to give the ticket to his brother to fix.
    (C) issue the motorist the ticket.
    (D) issue the motorist the ticket but tell him you're not going to hand your copy in.

59. While you are walking your beat, a man approaches you and says there is a gun in a dumpster located in a parking lot around the corner. The first thing you should do is

    (A) go to see if the gun is there.
    (B) determine the man's identity.
    (C) call detectives to the scene.
    (D) call a supervisor to the scene.

Answer question 60 based on the following.

> The law enforcement officer shall be concerned equally in the prosecution of the wrongdoer and the defense of the innocent.

60. According to the passage,

    (A) police officers have as much obligation to prove a person innocent as to prove a person guilty.
    (B) if a police officer doesn't have absolute proof, he or she shouldn't arrest a person.
    (C) police officers should spend more time in proving people innocent than in proving people guilty.
    (D) police officers should not arrest anyone unless they have a warrant.

SECTION 3 OF 4

Booklet 4 of 7: Information

Directions

You have *ten minutes* to read the following state statutes. At the end of ten minutes, you will be issued a booklet containing test questions 61 thorugh 95 and given *thirty additional minutes* to answer the questions. Questions 61 through 75 are based on the following reading passages. Questions 76 through 95 are based on reading passages preceding these questions. *You may retain the booklet containing the state statutes for reference while taking this portion of the examination.*

STATE STATUTES

53a-30: Definitions

1. "Physical injury" means impairment of physical condition or pain.

2. "Serious physical injury" means physical injury which creates a substantial risk of death, or which causes serious disfigurement, serious impairment of health, or serious loss or impairment of the function of any bodily organ.

3. "Deadly physical force" means physical force which can reasonably be expected to cause death or serious physical injury.

4. "Deadly weapon" means any weapon, whether loaded or unloaded, from which a shot may be discharged, or a switchblade knife, gravity knife, billy, blackjack, bludgeon, or metal knuckles.

5. "Dangerous instrument" means any instrument, article, or substance which, under the circumstances in which it is used or attempted or threatened to be used, is capable of causing death or serious physical injury, and includes a motor vehicle.

53a-18: *Use of reasonable physical force or deadly physical force generally*

The use of physical force upon another person which would otherwise constitute an offense is justifiable and not criminal under any of the following circumstances:

1. A parent, guardian, teacher, or other person entrusted with the care and supervision of a minor or an incompetent person may use reasonable physical force upon such minor or incompetent person when and to the extent that he or she reasonably believes it is necessary to maintain discipline or to promote the welfare of such minor or incompetent person.

2. A person acting under a reasonable belief that another person is about to commit suicide or to inflict serious physical injury upon himself or herself may use reasonable physical force upon such person to the extent that he or she reasonably believes it is necessary to thwart such result.

3. A duly licensed physician, or a person acting under the physcian's direction, may use reasonable physical force for the purpose of administering a recognized form of treatment which the physician reasonably believes to be adapted to promoting the physical or mental health of the patient.

53a-19: *Use of physical force in defense of person*

(a) Except as provided in subsections (b) and (c), a person is justified in using reasonable physical force upon another person to defend himself or herself or a third person from what is reasonably believed to be the use or imminent use of physical force, and he or she may use such degree of force which is reasonably believed to be necessary for such purpose; except that deadly physical force may not be used unless the individual reasonably believes that such person is (1) using or about to use deadly physical force, or (2) inflicting or about to inflict great bodily harm. (b) Notwithstanding the provisions of subsection (a), a person is not justified in using deadly physical force upon another person if he or she knows that the necessity of using such force can be avoided with complete safety (1) by retreating, except that the individual shall not be required to retreat if in his or her dwelling or place of work and not the initial aggressor, or the individual is a peace officer or a private person assisting such peace officer at his or her direction, or, (2) by surrendering possession of property to a person asserting a claim or right thereto, or (3) by complying with a demand that he or she abstain from performing an act which he or she is not obliged to perform. (c) Notwithstanding the provisions of subsection (a), a person is not justified in using physical force when (1) with intent to cause physical injury or death to another person, he or she provokes the use of physical force by such other person, or (2) he or she is the initial aggressor, except that the use of physical force upon another person under such circumstances is justified if the actor withdraws from the encounter and effectively communicates to such other person intent to do so, but such other person notwithstanding continues or threatens the use of physical force, or (3) the physical force involved was the product of combat by agreement not specifically authorized by law.

53a-25: Felony, definition of

Any offense for which a person may be sentenced to a term of imprisonment in excess of one year is a felony.

53a-26: Misdemeanor, definition of

Any offense for which a person may be sentenced to a term of imprisonment of not more than one year is a misdemeanor.

SECTION 3 OF 4

Booklet 5 of 7: Questions

Directions

You have *thirty minutes* to answer the questions 61 through 95. Answer questions 61 through 75 based on the "State Statutes" reading section.

61. Paul Jennings is arrested for the sale of narcotics, convicted, and sentenced to prison for three years, suspended after two years served. He committed a

    (A) felony.
    (B) misdemeanor.
    (C) violation.
    (D) tort.

62. You respond to the scene of an active bar fight. Investigation reveals that Jimmy Joiner struck Mark Mayson over the head with a liquor bottle, causing a laceration requiring four stitches to close. Mayson suffered

    (A) physical injury.
    (B) serious physical injury.
    (C) deadly physical injury.
    (D) physical impairment.

63. Under which of the following circumstances can a police officer use deadly physical force?

    (A) to defend himself or herself or to defend a third person from the imminent use of physical force
    (B) to defend himself or herself or to defend a third person from the use of deadly physical force
    (C) to defend himself or herself against the imminent use of deadly physical force
    (D) to defend a third person against the use of deadly physical force

64. Gladys stabbed Paul in the chest with a pair of scissors. The scissors are a

    (A) dangerous instrument.
    (B) deadly weapon.
    (C) dangerous article.
    (D) illegal weapon.

65. Johnny Johnson was convicted of credit card theft, sentenced to a prison term as a repeat offender for eleven months, and ordered to pay a fine of five thousand dollars. Johnson committed a

    (A) felony.
    (B) misdemeanor.
    (C) violation.
    (D) tort.

66. You are called to a local high school on a complaint from the parents of a fourteen-year-old student that a teacher assaulted the student. You investigate and determine that the student was engaged in a violent fight in the school cafeteria with another student. In separating the students, the teacher "grabbed" the student by the arm. The student was not injured. The teacher's use of force was

    (A) not justified. A teacher has no legal right under state statutes to use force on a minor.
    (B) justified. A teacher may use reasonable physical force to maintain discipline.
    (C) not justified. Technically the teacher committed an assault and should be arrested.
    (D) justified, but a warrant should be sought for the teacher's arrest so a judge can decide.

67. A man is on the window ledge of a high-rise apartment building threatening to jump. A police officer grabs his arm, pulling him backward to safety. The man suffers a broken wrist. The officer's use of force is

    (A) improper. The resulting injury was an excessive use of force.
    (B) proper. The officer's use of force was reasonable given the circumstances.
    (C) improper. The officer should have been able to talk the man off the ledge.
    (D) proper; however, the officer should have made sure there was a net below.

68. A police officer responds to the scene of a bank robbery. Upon the officer's arrival, a man exits the bank wearing a mask and brandishing a shotgun. The suspect fires at the officer, misses, and hits a bystander. The officer returns fire, mortally wounding the suspect. The officer's use of force was

    (A) not justified. The officer could have retreated in safety.
    (B) justified. The officer's life was in imminent danger.
    (C) not justified. The officer should have waited to see if the suspect would give up.
    (D) justified. The suspect was the initial aggressor.

69. A man enters a package store, takes out a small pocket knife, and demands money. The store owner refuses. The man yells an obscenity, puts the knife back in his pocket, and leaves the store. The store owner takes a handgun from under the counter, follows the man outside the store, and shoots the man in the back. The store owner's use of force was

    (A) justified. The man had threatened him with a knife and tried to rob him.
    (B) not justified. The store owner did not warn the man to stop prior to shooting him.
    (C) justified. Other people's lives might later be threatened by the man.
    (D) not justified. The store owner was not in his place of business or in danger of suffering great bodily harm when he shot the man.

70. Peter, the owner of Pete's Pizza Express, was shot in the chest during a robbery attempt on his store. Peter suffered

    (A) physical injury.
    (B) serious physical injury.
    (C) mortal injury.
    (D) substantial risk of death.

71. Which of the following best reflects a situation in which a police officer may use deadly physical force?

    (A) as a last resort
    (B) whenever necessary
    (C) when legally justified
    (D) in specific circumstances

72. Several children are playing at a construction site on a Saturday. One of the children falls into a gravel pit and fractures his ankle. The police are called, but an ambulance team overhears the radio transmission and arrives first. An emergency medical technician (EMT), after speaking over the radio to a doctor at the hospital, forcibly restrains the child, administering a sedative because the child is hysterical and further aggravating his injury. The use of force by the EMT was

    (A) technically not justified. The EMT could use force only at the direction of a police officer.
    (B) justified. The EMT used reasonable force under the direction of a licensed physician.
    (C) not justified. This is a violation of state statutes.
    (D) justified, but the EMT should have waited for parental consent.

73. Which of the following is a "deadly weapon"?

    (A) a steak knife
    (B) an unloaded target pistol
    (C) a motor vehicle
    (D) both (B) and (C)

74. A woman walking home alone was robbed. She gave a description of her assailant as a white male, five feet, eight inches tall, with an earring in his left ear and wearing a baseball hat, blue jacket, and brown pants. A police officer observes a man fitting that exact description one block away from where the robbery took place. The officer steps out of the cruiser and observes the suspect turn and begin to run. The officer chases the suspect several blocks, yelling for him to stop. He finally stops and then takes a swing at the officer, who blocks the punch and wrestles him to the ground. The officer's use of force was

(A) not justified. The officer did not have proof the man committed a crime when he began chasing him.
(B) justified. The officer used reasonable force to defend himself.
(C) not justified. The officer could have retreated without using force.
(D) justified. The man committed a robbery.

75. Using the information in question 74, a police officer would have been least justified in using

(A) physical force.
(B) reasonable physical force.
(C) deadly physical force.
(D) the minimum amount of force necessary.

Answer questions 76 through 84 based on the following.

On May 12, at 2:15 P.M., Officer Ronald Fleming observed a 1988 Chevrolet with Texas license plate number JK 1049 travel north on Main Street and go through the red traffic signal at the intersection of Main Street and Asylum Avenue. Officer Fleming engaged his cruiser's flashing lights and siren and notified the police dispatcher that he had stopped the vehicle at 1400 Main Street.

As Officer Fleming approached the vehicle, he observed two people in the car: the driver and a passenger in the right front seat. Officer Fleming observed that the passenger threw an object out the vehicle's window and that the object went under the rear of a parked, 1990 Ford van, New Jersey license plate number VXK 15. At 2:27 P.M., Officer Sean Phelps arrived at the scene, and Officer Fleming advised Officer Phelps that he had observed the passenger throw an object out the window and that it had landed under the Ford van.

The object was retrieved by Officer Phelps and found to be a plastic bag containing ten small bags of white powder. Each of the small bags was marked with five stars and later found to be cocaine. The driver of the vehicle, Pedro Gonzalez, of 113 Stonington Street, apartment B, was arrested for failure to obey a traffic control signal and possession of cocaine with intent to sell. The passenger of the vehicle, Julio Gonzales, of 131 Stonington Street, was arrested for possession of cocaine with intent to sell.

76. The suspect vehicle was traveling

    (A) north on Stonington Street.
    (B) south on Main Street.
    (C) north on Main Street.
    (D) south on Stonington Street.

77. At what time did Officer Phelps arrive at the scene?

    (A) 2:15 P.M.
    (B) 2:27 P.M.
    (C) 2:51 P.M.
    (D) 3:27 P.M.

78. The suspect vehicle was a

    (A) 1990 Ford, Texas license plate number VXK 14.
    (B) 1988 Chevrolet, Texas license plate number VXK 15.
    (C) 1990 Chevrolet, New Jersey license plate number JK 1049.
    (D) 1988 Chevrolet, Texas license plate number JK 1049.

79. The object thrown from the suspect vehicle landed under a

    (A) 1988 Ford van.
    (B) 1990 Chevrolet.
    (C) 1990 Ford van.
    (D) 1988 Chevrolet.

80. The object thrown out the suspect vehicle's window was thrown by the

    (A) driver and landed under the Chevrolet.
    (B) passenger and landed under the Ford.
    (C) driver and landed under the Ford.
    (D) passenger and landed under the Chevrolet.

81. Officer Ronald Fleming

    (A) notified the police dispatcher he was stopping the suspect vehicle at 1400 Main Street.
    (B) did not notify the police dispatcher.
    (C) notified the police dispatcher that he had stopped the suspect vehicle at the intersection of Main Street and Asylum Avenue.
    (D) notified Officer Phelps that he observed the suspect vehicle at 1400 Main Street.

82. The object thrown from the suspect vehicle was

(A) retrieved by Officer Fleming and found to be ten bags of cocaine.
(B) retrieved by Officer Phelps and found to be a plastic bag containing ten smaller bags of cocaine.
(C) retrieved by Officer Phelps and found to be a bag of cocaine marked with five stars.
(D) retrieved by Officer Fleming and found to be five bags of cocaine with ten stars marked on them.

83. Officer Fleming

(A) advised Officer Phelps that he saw the driver of the suspect vehicle throw an object out the window.
(B) did not advise Officer Phelps that he saw the passenger in the suspect vehicle throw an object out the window.
(C) advised Officer Phelps that he saw the passenger in the suspect vehicle throw an object out the window.
(D) advised the police dispatcher that he saw the passenger in the suspect vehicle throw an object out the window.

84. Which of the following is not true?

(A) Officer Phelps saw one of two people in the suspect vehicle throw an object out the window.
(B) Twelve minutes elapsed between the time Officer Fleming first saw the suspect vehicle and the time Officer Phelps arrived at 1400 Main Street.
(C) Officer Fleming told Officer Phelps that he saw two people in the suspect vehicle throw an object out the window.
(D) A plastic bag containing ten other bags was found under the Ford van.

Answer questions 85 through 95 based on the following.

On July 5 at 11:17 P.M., Officer Edward Pawlina received a call via police radio dispatching him to 1432 Albany Avenue on a complaint from Mrs. Jennings in apartment B-9 that a car was being broken into in the rear parking lot of the building. A second police cruiser, operated by Officer Janice Peters, was dispatched to back up Officer Pawlina at 11:19 P.M. Officer Pawlina radioed Officer Peters to meet him in the parking lot of a school a short distance from 1432 Albany Avenue so they could proceed to the scene on foot and surprise the suspects. Proceeding on foot, the officers entered the parking lot and observed a 1987 Chevrolet Caprice with both doors open, two youths inside the vehicle, and another youth outside who appeared to be acting as a lookout. As the officers got closer, the lookout yelled "Cops!" and began running. The two youths inside the car got out and also began running. Officer Pawlina notified the police dispatcher via portable radio at 11:35 P.M. and began pursuing one of the youths that had been in the vehicle. Officer Peters chased after the lookout, caught him, placed him in handcuffs, and brought him back to the car. His name was Jamie Loranger, age fourteen, of 1454 Albany Avenue, apartment

A-3. Officer Pawlina also caught his suspect, John Lorenzo, age fourteen, of 1445 Albany Avenue, apartment B-3. Officer Pawlina notified the police dispatcher that two suspects were in custody at 11:57 P.M. Inspection of the vehicle revealed the stereo to have been removed and damaged and to be lying on the front seat. The vehicle had been stolen. Jamie Loranger said that the third youth involved was Michael Meehan, age fifteen, of 1454 Albany Avenue, apartment C-3.

85. How much time elapsed between Officer Pawlina's receiving the original call and notification to the police dispatcher that two suspects were in custody?

(A) thirty-seven minutes
(B) forty minutes
(C) forty-two minutes
(D) thirty-five minutes

86. Suspect Jamie Loranger was

(A) observed inside the vehicle and captured by Officer Pawlina.
(B) observed outside the vehicle and captured by Officer Peters.
(C) chased by Officer Peters but captured by Officer Jennings.
(D) chased by Officer Peters but not captured.

87. Which of the following youths were in the car?

(A) Jamie Loranger and Michael Meehan
(B) Michael Meehan and John Loranger
(C) John Lorenzo and Michael Meehan
(D) Jamie Loranger and John Lorenzo

88. Which of the following suspects was placed in handcuffs?

(A) Jamie Loranger
(B) Michael Meehan
(C) James Loranger
(D) Michael Lorenzo

89. Which of the following statements is false?

(A) One of the youths lives at 1544 Albany Avenue, apartment C-3.
(B) Twenty-two minutes elapsed between the time the chase began and the time Officer Pawlina notified the dispatcher that two suspects were in custody.
(C) One of the suspects lives at 1454 Albany Avenue, apartment A-3.
(D) There were two suspects inside and one outside the vehicle.

90. Which of the following statements is true?

(A) John Lorenzo is fourteen and lives at 1454 Albany Avenue, apartment A-3.
(B) Michael Meehan is fifteen and lives at 1445 Albany Avenue, apartment C-3.
(C) Jamie Loranger was inside the suspect vehicle.
(D) Jamie Loranger lives at 1454 Albany Avenue, apartment A-3.

91. The vehicle reported stolen was a

    (A) 1987 Chevrolet Caprice.
    (B) 1987 Chevrolet Spectrum.
    (C) 1987 Chevrolet Celebrity.
    (D) 1987 Chevrolet Malibu.

92. Which of the following statements is true?

    (A) The vehicle had one door open and three youths inside.
    (B) The vehicle had both doors open and two youths inside.
    (C) The vehicle had been stolen, and its stereo was damaged.
    (D) John Lorenzo acted as a lookout.
    (E) both (B) and (C) but not (A) and (D)

93. The vehicle was

    (A) stolen, and its stereo was found to be on the car's floor.
    (B) not stolen, and its stereo was found to be on the seat.
    (C) stolen, and its stereo was found to be on the seat.
    (D) not stolen, but the ignition was "popped."

94. Which of the following individuals yelled "Cops!"?

    (A) Jamie Loranger
    (B) Jamie Jennings
    (C) John Lorenzo
    (D) Michael Meehan

95. Officer Peters and Pawlina were

    (A) justified in chasing the suspects.
    (B) not justified in chasing the suspects. They did not commit a crime.
    (C) justified in chasing the suspects but could not arrest them because of their age.
    (D) not justified in placing one of the suspects in handcuffs.

SECTION 4 OF 4

Booklet 6 of 7: Information

MEMORY AND OBSERVATION

Directions

This section of the examination tests your ability to observe and retain information. The following consists of a drawing which you will be allowed to observe for *five minutes*. The drawing will then be taken from you, and you will be required to answer questions 96 through 100 in *ten minutes* based on what you have observed, without looking at the drawing again. For each question, select the most correct answer. Do not begin until you are told to do so by the exam proctor.

SECTION 4 OF 4

Booklet 7 of 7: Questions

Directions

You have *ten minutes* to answer questions 96 through 100 based on the drawing.

96. What are the last three digits of the license plate number of the vehicle closest to the two men?

    (A) 455
    (B) 554
    (C) 545
    (D) 555

97. In which hand is the suspect holding a gun?

    (A) in his left hand
    (B) in his right hand
    (C) in both hands
    (D) There is no gun in the drawing.

98. Which of the two men is wearing a black leather jacket?

    (A) the victim
    (B) the suspect
    (C) neither the victim nor the suspect
    (D) both the victim and the suspect

99. Which of the two men is wearing sneakers?

    (A) the suspect
    (B) the victim
    (C) both the suspect and the victim
    (D) neither the suspect nor the victim

100. Which of the two men is wearing dark-colored trousers?

    (A) the suspect
    (B) the victim
    (C) the suspect and the victim
    (D) neither the suspect nor the victim

ANSWER KEY FOR CITY OF DORCHESTER POLICE OFFICER EXAMINATION

1.	D	26.	D
2.	B	27.	A
3.	C	28.	B
4.	B	29.	C
5.	E	30.	B
6.	A	31.	B
7.	B	32.	C
8.	D	33.	A
9.	A	34.	A
10.	D	35.	D
11.	B	36.	C
12.	A	37.	B
13.	A	38.	B
14.	D	39.	C
15.	C	40.	D
16.	C	41.	D
17.	D	42.	B
18.	D	43.	B
19.	B	44.	C
20.	C	45.	C
21.	B	46.	A
22.	D	47.	B
23.	C	48.	D
24.	D	49.	B
25.	B	50.	B

51. B	76. C
52. C	77. B
53. A	78. D
54. A	79. C
55. B	80. B
56. C	81. A
57. D	82. B
58. C	83. C
59. B	84. C
60. A	85. B
61. A	86. B
62. A	87. C
63. C	88. A
64. A	89. A
65. B	90. D
66. B	91. A
67. B	92. E
68. B	93. C
69. D	94. A
70. B	95. A
71. A	96. A
72. B	97. B
73. B	98. B
74. B	99. A
75. C	100. B

ANSWERS AND ANALYSIS FOR CITY OF DORCHESTER POLICE OFFICER EXAMINATION

Section 1

1. **(D)** The first paragraph of the reading passage quotes the Fourth Amendment, which specifically uses the words *probable cause* in the context of seizing or arresting a person.

2. **(B)** Circle the words *did not* in the question. The reading passage clearly states: *An arrest based on less than probable cause is illegal.* This eliminates answers (A) and (C). Circle the word *cannot* in answer (D). Larceny is theft or stealing. It doesn't make sense that a police officer *cannot* arrest a person for theft. The correct answer is (B); without probable cause, the arrest is illegal.

3. **(C)** If a police officer needed *proof* that a crime was committed (A or B), we wouldn't need courts. Preponderance of evidence (D) is a term used in civil, not criminal, cases. Proof beyond a reasonable doubt (A) is the standard for conviction, not for arrest. The reading passage clearly defines probable cause as *less than proof but more than mere suspicion* that a crime was committed.

4. **(B)** The key to the answer to this question is *when* Officer Jennings placed the man under arrest. The reading passage states that the factors which make up probable cause end at the moment of arrest. The officer found the pistol in the man's pocket *after* she placed him under arrest. This eliminates answers (A) and (C). Answer (D) can easily be eliminated by reasoning that, even if he *did* have a permit for the pistol, it would be unreasonable to think a permit would justify his firing the pistol in a park where others could get hurt.

5. **(E)** The passage lists twelve *guilt-laden* facts which can be used to establish probable cause. Look at answer (D), all of the above. For (D) to be the correct answer, (A), (B), and (C) would *all* have to be valid statements in determining probable cause. Answer (B) is incorrect, although a true statement. The fact that the pistol was found on the man *after* he was arrested *cannot* be used to build probable cause. Choices (A) and (C) are valid statements and contain *guilt-laden* facts permissible in establishing probable cause. Since the question asks *which of the following,* the correct answer is (E)—both (A) and (C) but not (B).

6. **(A)** If the officer had probable cause, the arrest is legal. Since the officer had facts and circumstances which led her to believe the man committed a crime, she did have probable cause to arrest. This eliminates answers (B) and (D). Since we know the pistol can't be used in the determination of probable cause (C), the correct answer is (A), which is almost word for word from the reading passage.

7. (B) Don't read into the question; take each answer selection at face value. A person's name (A), race (C), or address (D) can't be used to establish probable cause. Answer (B), suspicious conduct, is on the list in the reading section. That doesn't mean that this one fact alone would be enough to arrest a person, but suspicious conduct along with other *guilt-laden* facts could result in the establishment of probable cause.

8. (D) How good is your reading comprehension under the pressure of taking a test? Circle the word *late* in answer (A) and the word *early* in answer (B). In each case it should be just the opposite, so (A) and (B) are incorrect answers. The reading passage states, *The burden of proof . . . is to establish a reasonable ground for belief in guilt,* . . . Thus, (C) is also incorrect. The correct answer is (D), none of the above.

9. (A) Circle the words *most important* in the question. Answer choices (B), (C), and (D) are all decisions in the sense that they are elements in the arrest process. However, the reading passage states, *One of the most important decisions a police officer is faced with is when to place a person under arrest.* The *when* in this sense does not mean simply the time of day but whether or not to arrest and at what point in an investigation to arrest.

10. (D) Answer (C) is obviously wrong because a *prosecutor* is the government's attorney, and if probable cause were viewed through the eyes of the state, it would automatically unbalance the fairness aspect of adjudication. The reading passage says that . . . *the court will view the facts through the eyes of the experienced police officer and not those of a layperson.*

Section 2

11. (B) Circle the words *first thing you should do upon arrival*. Many test questions will require you to prioritize a list of plausible choices of action. Even without previous law-enforcement experience, you can still put yourself in the position of an officer arriving at this accident scene and visualize the *first* thing you would do among the answer choices. Note the words *serious injuries,* meaning more than one person is hurt. Note that it's dark, that the accident is located just over the crest of an icy hill, and that cars are coming toward the accident scene and sliding. *You* are alone and pull up at the scene. You *evaluate* the situation, and it's obvious that further help will be needed (B). In order of priority, the *next* thing a police officer should do is keep the accident scene from getting worse (A) by placing flares at the top of the hill, because it won't help the injured (C) if they are struck by another car while you are caring for them.

12. (A) What makes the most sense among the answer selections? Does it make sense that a person who has just shot someone and is being chased by a police officer can cross a boundary line with the officer right behind him and then just wave at the officer from the other side? Of course not, so (B) can be eliminated. If we eliminate (B), then (C) also doesn't make sense; nor does (D)—especially the thought that a police officer would be required to stop at an imaginary line but then be allowed to

shoot across it! The key to the answer is in the question, *You are only a few seconds behind the suspect.*

13. (A) This is a difficult question requiring you to reason out the answer. What information does the question provide which directly ties into the answer choices? The building inspector has inspected the elevator and found it to be seriously defective and dangerous. He felt so strongly about the danger that he disabled the elevator, put up a warning sign not to use it, and contacted the building owner. The owner *intentionally* removed the sign and turned the elevator back on. So we know the owner purposefully disregarded a dangerous situation that put other people, who *did not know* the risk, into danger. This is what makes his actions criminal as opposed to civil—(B) and (D) can be eliminated. What's the difference between negligent and reckless? You're reckless when your negligence leads to your or someone else's injury or potential injury. The building owner acted intentionally (on purpose), was negligent (should have repaired the elevator and not allowed anyone to use it until it was repaired), and was reckless (knowingly put others in harm's way) (A).

14. (D) Can a police officer kill a person for stealing a piece of fruit? If you answered (A) or (B), that's what you're saying. Answer (C) implies that if the thief doesn't stop when you tell him to, you'll just go back to what you were doing prior to the incident. Answer (D) is the most plausible choice because it makes the most sense. You're going to use your portable radio to inform all the other officers in the area that a person fitting a specific description is wanted for a crime.

15. (C) The general rule of thumb for the use of force in police work is that only the minimum amount of force necessary to overcome a person's resistance may be used. The prisoner is in handcuffs. With use-of-force questions, always choose the least amount of force that will get the job done. So out of choices to strike (A), kick (B), punch (D), and push (C), the least severe of these options is forcibly pushing the prisoner into the cruiser. Note also that (C) is the only choice which fulfills the objective—to get the prisoner into the cruiser.

16. (C) Note that the disturbance did not occur in the presence of the officer, that it is no longer occurring, and that both people are ready to leave. Answers (A) and (D) suggest that if a person makes a complaint (the manager), a police officer is *required* to make an arrest. Common sense should tell you that this is not the case. Answer (B) would require the husband and/or wife to make a statement which could then be used by the police to file criminal charges on one or the other. Generally speaking, a husband or wife cannot be compelled to give evidence against each other. The most correct answer is the one that solves the problem—warn them and allow them to leave (C).

17. (D) If you answered (A), (B), or (C), then anyone can come into your home, go into every room, and as long as they don't actually take anything, it's OK! Does the fact that the door to a home is left open mean that anyone can enter? Common sense should point you to answer (D) as the correct choice.

18. (D) Circle the word *most*. In order to choose the most correct answer you must determine if all the answer selections are true and/or valid statements and then prioritize them from *most* important to least. Our system of laws relies for the most part on voluntary compliance. The support and cooperation of the public (D) is the cornerstone of effective law enforcement.

19. (B) The bad accident is located three blocks away. The police radio is the fastest method of getting police response to the scene. In policing, the general rule of thumb is to remain at your post unless an emergency situation requiring your immediate response is occurring close to you. It doesn't make sense to leave the intersection and direct traffic for three blocks as offered in answer (C) or to ask the person who just informed you of the accident to go back and handle the matter (D). Police officers ride in citizens' vehicles (A) only in the movies.

20. (C) Again, think of yourself as a police officer. You see a person unconscious and bleeding. Would you shine a light on him from a car and wait, as offered in answer (B)? Your obligation and first priority is to the victim, even at the expense of allowing a suspect to escape. Answers (A), (B), and (D) all indicate waiting. If you were a private citizen, that might be the correct response, but as a police officer, you're expected to lay down your life, if necessary, to protect people.

21. (B) Because of the use of the word *primary* in the question, you're again being asked to prioritize the answer selections. Arrest (A) is only a very small part of a police officer's job. Although it's important to prevent crime and disorder (C) and to reduce the opportunity to commit crimes (D), the primary function of the police department is to serve the public (B).

22. (D) For the most part, police patrol occurs outdoors. Most homicides (A), domestic disputes (B), and sexual assaults (C), occur indoors. Police patrol has little effect on preventing these crimes. Of all the answer choices, patrol would have the most effect in preventing auto theft (D).

23. (C) The key to the answer to this question is what gets the job done as quickly as possible with a minimum use of force. Answers (A) and (B) take too long. Additionally, (B) implies that police officers need to wait for search warrants prior to entering premises even in noncriminal cases when their intent is to save lives, which is not true. Eliminating (A) and (B) leaves two choices. Which among them is the easier method of getting the job done with a minimum use of force? The correct answer is (C). Reading into the question and asking what if the superintendent wasn't home or trying to estimate how much time it would take to find the super as opposed to breaking down the door (D) is a trap intentionally set by the person designing the test question.

24. (D) This is simple math computation. The train left at 1:00 P.M. and traveled thirty miles each hour. It would then arrive at 3:30 P.M., thirty minutes after the robbery occurred.

25. (B) The question explains what the law is and the punishment for violation, a ticket. It's a judgment situation, one as old as policing. Enforce the letter of the law or serve and protect? Answer (C) is the easiest one to eliminate. Police officers don't threaten people, as the answer implies by using the words *severely warn* and *tow her vehicle*. Both answers (A) and (D) result in issuing a ticket to an *elderly woman on crutches,* who obviously is handicapped and says she did have the required permit but lost it. State permits are easily checked. A police officer not only shouldn't issue the elderly woman a ticket (B) but should help her to her car.

26. (D) The only person who gives you something for nothing is your mother. Absolute rule: **never, ever accept anything under any circumstances—no matter how the gratuity might be rationalized.** Answers (A) and (B) are obviously wrong, regardless of the intent to transfer the money from the officer's hands to a charity (B). The only way the situation can be attempted bribery (C) is if the store owner offered the money to the officer to obtain a benefit resulting from the capacity as a police officer—for example, a person who offers a police officer money to overlook a speeding offense. The correct answer is (D), refuse the money and explain to the store owner you were only doing your job.

27. (A) Note that the officer is present and observes the entire incident. Answer (B) is wrong; you can't arrest someone who is dead. Is a person justified in killing another for hitting him in the face and knocking him down? Of course not, not unless a person's life is in imminent danger. That is not the case in this situation, so it's not self-defense, answer (C). A crime, murder, occurred in front of a police officer. If you answered (D), it means you would merely take the murderer's name and address and allow him to walk away. The correct answer is (A), place the man under arrest.

28. (B) The officer committed a crime. Answers (A), (C), and (D) are not only ethically wrong, but are also criminal offenses. When answering this type of question, the correct answer always involves either immediately reporting the matter to a supervisor or taking direct action to stop it, such as a case in which a police officer was criminally assaulting a prisoner. The only acceptable answer is (B).

29. (C) Regardless of how minor the damage, the officer is involved in a traffic accident and subject to at *least* the same rules as a private citizen. Answer (A) is an abuse of power, and even if a technical parking violation is involved, issuing a ticket doesn't explain what will be done about the accident. Like answer (A), answers (B) and (D) imply that the police are above the law and are not required to inform anyone of the accident or the damage the officer caused the other vehicle's taillight. Answer (C) makes the most sense and, except for the added requirement of notifying a supervisor, is what *any* person in this situation would be expected to do.

30. (B) This is similar to but the exact opposite of question 22. Circle the word *least*. Since we know police patrol occurs mostly outside, answer (D) can be eliminated because, of the choices offered, auto theft is *most* reduced by patrol efforts. Police patrol has little effect on homicide, sexual assault, or domestic disputes. However, of the three, arguments and assaults between family members are least likely to be affected by a police car driving down the street or a police officer walking by.

31. (B) Circle the words *effective, reducing,* and *crime* in the question. Answer (D), putting people in prison who commit crimes obviously isn't working. Our courts and prisons are full, and the crime rate is not decreasing. Although I'll bet you answered (A), there is no evidence that increasing the number of police officers has a *direct* relation to reducing crime. Increasing public awareness (C) is important. But modern telecommunication technology makes us more "aware" now than at any other time in history, yet crime has not been reduced. The most effective method of reducing crime is to impact poverty, drug abuse, unemployment, etc. (B) the root causes of crime within our society.

32. (C) Circle the words *easiest to spot* in the question. Now, look at the answer choices. All four tell you that the suspect is a white male, is five feet, eight inches tall, and weighs 165 pounds. Answer (B) offers jeans, (C) a red jacket, and (D) brown hair. A red jacket is easier to spot than either jeans or brown hair.

33. (A) Remember this. If you're a police officer and lives are at stake (and most times even if they aren't), you're never off duty. As is the solution to many test questions, the solution to this one is to determine what's the quickest way to get the job done, to put the fire out. Don't read into the question. Calling the fire department (A) is the correct answer.

34. (A) Imagine *not* responding only to later find that this time it was a real burglary and that several men backed a truck up to the store and stole all the merchandise! If you answered (B), (C), or (D), you would have a lot of explaining to do. Police officers always respond.

35. (D) This is another commonsense question. If your boss tells you to do something, and you don't understand what he or she wants done, ask for clarification. This is especially true in policing, where lives are at stake. If you have any doubt, consider the situation in question 36.

36. (C) Circle the words *emergency hostage situation*. If you got this question wrong, circle and underline ten times the words *You have been instructed to position yourself in front of an elevator and not allow anyone to use it or go upstairs.* In answers (A), (B), and (D), the officer allows the woman to go upstairs. The correct answer is (C), explain, but no matter what else happens, *no one is getting past you to go upstairs.*

37. (B) Let's see, window smashed, large rock on the seat, screwdriver sticking out of the ignition. The only commonsense answer is (B), someone tried to steal the car.

38. (B) Circle the word *least*. Flashing lights and siren mean it's very important to get to the scene quickly, and it doesn't matter who knows the officer is coming. Answers (A) accident and (D) heart attack meet that criteria. This leaves a choice between (B) silent burglar alarm and (C) shots fired. The use of the term *silent* as opposed to *audible* in (B) should give you a hint that it's the right answer. The reason the alarm is *silent* as opposed to *audible* is to catch the burglar inside. When responding to silent alarms, police officers use their vehicle's flashing lights and siren to get close to the scene but then cut them off far enough away so the burglar won't know they're coming. So between choices (B) and (C), the most correct answer is (B), responding to the scene of a silent alarm.

39. (C) What information does the problem provide? Circle the words *heavy snowstorm, three days, vehicle parked on a city street, has not been moved, BMW* (very expensive car), and *high-crime, poverty-stricken area*. If you were just going to write a ticket (B), make a note in a log (A), or leave a note on the windshield (D), you missed the point of the question. After a heavy snowstorm, police officers make it a *point* to check vehicles within their areas meeting the above criteria to determine if they're stolen.

40. (D) A person's manner of dress, race, or manner of speaking have *nothing* to do with criminal behavior. The correct answer is (D), none of the above.

41. (D) Notice that the child is only seven years old. Time is important. Note also that the question asks what the *first* thing you should do is. When you become a police officer, please don't ask people to go to the phone and call the police (A). You *are* the police. The same holds true of advising people to go to the police station to report an incident to the police (B). Asking the woman where she *lost* the child (C) is insulting. A child is not a license or credit card. The officer is in the middle of an intersection with cars going by. The *first* thing the officer should do is escort the woman out of the intersection to the sidewalk, obtain a description of the child, and advise all officers that she is missing and what she looks like via radio. The answer is (D) because it's the quickest way to locate the missing child.

42. (B) Answers (A) and (D) imply that you will arrest anyone who comes to the door as long as it's a man. What if the man who answers the door isn't Samuel Johnson? On the other hand, if you automatically advise the man who comes to the door that you have an arrest warrant for Samuel Johnson (C), many criminals would simply deny that they were in fact he. The best answer is the simple one, find out who he is (B).

43. (B) This is a vocabulary question. However, you know the answer isn't (D) biology. Look at the stem of the word *toxic*ology. Now, look at the question. Circle the words *drugs and/or poisons*. *Toxic* means deadly. The correct answer is toxicology (B).

44. (C) The diagram and the way the question is worded are designed to make you think that the answer couldn't be as simple as it is. Two cars, vehicle 1 and vehicle 2, were stopped for a red light. Vehicle 3 comes down the road and plows into vehicle 2, and the force of the collision causes vehicle 2 to move forward and strike vehicle 1. Vehicle 3 is at fault.

45. (C) Even though you're not a police officer yet, there is enough information here for you to reason out the correct answer. The key to eliminating answers (A) and (B) is the threat of arrest. Police officers don't arrest people for not paying their bills or not fixing sinks. Eliminating (A) and (B) leaves a choice between (C) and (D). Is it the role of the police to tell people to pay or not pay their rent as offered in choice (D)? No. The correct answer is (C), this is a civil matter, not a police matter.

46. (A) To prevent is to keep from happening. Answer (B) does not directly prevent crime; prosecution occurs after a crime has been committed and the criminal has been caught. Drug-related crimes (D) are only a part of the overall crime picture. Deploying (sending) police officers via selective patrol (selective patrol is in areas with a high rate of crime) (C) once again is specific to only a narrow band of criminal activity. The most correct answer is (A), reduce the opportunity for criminals to commit crimes.

47. (B) The more crimes committed, the more criminals get caught by the police, resulting in more prosecutions.

48. (D) Answers (A) and (C) can be crossed out immediately if you know the meaning of the word *slovenly*. *Slovenly* means careless or untidy. Even though answer (B) is true, the most correct answer is (D), impair the standing of the entire force in the eyes of the public, because the impact on an entire organization is more important than that on a single individual.

49. (B) Wearing a uniform has little to do with catching crooks (C). Don't forget, the emphasis is on serving the public. Belonging to a semimilitary profession (A) is partially correct, and so is (D), emergency situations. Are either of them the most correct answer? The *most* correct answer is (B), to be readily identifiable to the public.

50. (B) Giving tickets (A) and making money (D) are not the *goals* of traffic enforcement. Moving traffic quickly (C) pales when compared to saving lives and preventing accidents (D).

51. (B) The reading selection states that for Mary to be charged with murder, her actions must be intentional (on purpose). This eliminates answers (A) and (C). We now have a choice between (B) and (D). Even if the child *was* the responsibility of the parents, that has nothing to do with whether Mary could be charged with murder. The most correct answer is (B), cannot be charged with murder, because there was no intent. It was an accident.

52. (C) Circle the words *high-crime area, late at night,* and *fourteen-year-old girl.* The question informs you that hitchhiking is illegal. However, the officer's main concern should be to find out why the girl is hitchhiking, especially late at night in a high-crime area. Is she a runaway or missing person? Does she need help? In answers (B) and (D), the emphasis is incorrectly on giving a ticket. Answer (A) needlessly puts the young girl in danger. The correct answer is (C), start by finding out *why* she is hitchhiking.

53. (A) The more people living proximate to one another, the more crime is likely to occur.

54. (A) The primary objective of having police officers is not to arrest criminals (B) and (D), but to prevent crime from occurring in the first place (A). Response to medical emergencies (C) is important, but it's not the primary objective of having police officers.

55. (B) Since desires (A) and wants (C) are the same thing, you can eliminate both because there can't be more than one correct answer. (Unless a test gives you an anwer choice such as "both (A) and (B)"). Motivation comes from within (B). Other people and stimuli (D) only supply the incentive.

56. (C) People often stop at police headquarters to ask for directions and rightfully expect police officers to be familiar with the city. Answer (D), telling a person to go to a store and purchase a street guide, or (B), giving the person a map to figure out the way himself, reflects poorly on the department and the officer. The most correct answer is the honest one, (C). Tell the person you don't know and find out for him.

57. (D) A police officer *cannot accept gratuities at any time.*

58. (C) A police officer cannot give any person special consideration and must treat all people equally.

59. (B) Note that the question asks what the *first* thing you should do is. There's no sense calling a supervisor (D) or detectives (C). There is no *scene* until the gun is actually located. Before seeing if the gun is there (A), first determine the man's identity (B). If the gun *is* located and later found to be a murder weapon, there will be many questions to ask the man who told the officer the gun was in the dumpster. Find out who he is.

60. (A) Contrary to popular belief, a police officer has as much obligation to defend the innocent as to arrest the guilty.

Section 3

61. (A) A felony is defined as any offense for which a person may be sentenced to a term of imprisonment in excess of one year.

62. (A) *Serious physical injury* means there is a likelihood of death. A laceration requiring four stitches is not life threatening. The term *deadly physical injury* (C) does not appear in the reading passage. Physical impairment (D) is an element of physical injury. If you answered (B), serious physical injury, instead of the correct answer (A), physical injury, it's because you reasoned that a person hit over the head with a liquor bottle receiving a gash requiring four stitches must be *serious*. You must answer these types of questions strictly by the legal definitions contained in the reading section, not according to the normal definitions used in day-to-day conversation.

63. (C) Circle the words *deadly physical force* and substitute the word *kill*. If you answered (A), then you're suggesting that a police officer can kill a person for kicking the officer in the shin (physical force). Answers (B) and (D) would both be correct if the word *imminent* were inserted. To use deadly physical force, the police officer or a third person must be in *imminent* danger of being killed. For example, a police officer couldn't shoot a suspect having a gun in a holster until the suspect took the gun out and the officer believed the suspect was about to shoot the officer. At that point, the officer could use deadly physical force in defense.

64. (A) The reading section lists *deadly weapons* and also gives the definition of a *dangerous instrument*. Even though the scissors was used to stab a person in the chest, it is *not* a deadly weapon. Deadly weapons are constructed for and have one purpose, to *kill*. Scissors are not constructed to kill; they are used to cut paper or other material.

65. (B) Don't let the term *repeat offender* confuse you into choosing felony (A). If the person was sentenced to a prison term of less than one year, it's a misdemeanor (B).

66. (B) The reading section states that a teacher may use *reasonable* physical force upon a minor to the extent the teacher believes necessary to maintain discipline.

67. (B) The reading section states that reasonable physical force may be used to prevent a person from committing suicide, so answers (A) and (C) can be eliminated. If you selected (D), you're reading into the question. Given the totality of circumstances, the officer's use of force was proper (B).

68. (B) According to the reading section, answers (C) and (D) would be considerations only if the question asked about the use of force by a private citizen. Answer (A) can also be eliminated. Police officers are not required by law to retreat to safety; they're obligated to protect lives. The correct answer is (B), justified. The officer's life was in imminent danger.

69. (D) The key to this answer is whether the store owner was *in* his premises *and* in fear of *great bodily harm* when he fired the shot. Both elements must be present for the store owner to be justified in using deadly physical force. This same reasoning makes (C) incorrect, along with the use of the word *might* in the answer selection. Although answer (A) is a true statement, it is removed in time and location from the firing of the shot. The store owner was no longer in his place of business, and the fact that he shot the man in the back would indicate that he was not in fear of great bodily harm. Whether or not the store owner warned the man to stop (B) does not mitigate his improper use of deadly force. Even if he had warned the man to stop, the store owner would not be justified in shooting him.

70. (B) There are only two types of injury defined in the reading section, *physical injury* and *serious physical injury*. Mortal injury (C) is not mentioned. Substantial risk of death (D) is an element within the definition of serious physical injury. The correct answer is (B), Peter suffered serious physical injury.

71. (A) In this question, you're asked to select from answer choices which are all essentially correct. Circle the words *best reflects* in the question. In policing, the use of *any* type of force, not just deadly physical force, is as a last resort. For example, even though a police officer might legally be justified in shooting and killing a twelve-year-old child pointing a loaded pistol at the officer, our society expects that the officer would do so only after every other method to handle the situation had failed (A).

72. (B) The reading section states that a *duly licensed physician* (doctor) or a person acting under the doctor's direction may use reasonable physical force to treat a patient. Was the force used by the EMT under the direction of a doctor? Was the force used by the EMT reasonable under the circumstances? The answer to both questions is *yes,* so answers (A) and (C) can be eliminated. Since this is an emergency situation, it would be unreasonable for the EMT to have to wait for parental consent (D). The correct answer is (B).

73. (B) The reading section defines what deadly weapons are by listing them. The only answer choice on that list is (B), an unloaded target pistol. It doesn't matter whether the pistol is loaded or unloaded according to the reading passage.

74. (B) The first five sentences of the question are filler. The suspect took a swing at the officer (attempted to assault him), a criminal offense in itself even if the suspect didn't commit the robbery. Answer (A) is wrong because of the word *proof.* Answer (C) is not correct; police officers are not required to retreat. Answer (D) would be incorrect even if the suspect *did* commit a robbery. It's not the *type* of crime that justifies an officer's using force; it's the actions of the suspect. The correct answer is (B), justified. The officer used reasonable physical force to defend himself.

75. (C) Circle the word *least* in the question. Deadly physical force (C) means to kill. The officer would be *least* justified in killing the suspect.

76. (C) The suspect vehicle was traveling north on Main Street.

77. (B) Officer Phelps arrived at the scene at 2:27 P.M.

78. (D) The suspect vehicle was a 1988 Chevrolet, Texas license plate number JK 1049.

79. (C) The object thrown from the suspect vehicle landed under a 1990 Ford van.

80. (B) The object thrown out the suspect vehicle's window was thrown by the passenger and landed under the Ford.

81. (A) Officer Ronald Fleming notified the police dispatcher that he was stopping the suspect vehicle at 1400 Main Street.

82. (B) The object thrown from the suspect vehicle was retrieved by Officer Phelps and found to be a plastic bag containing ten smaller plastic bags of cocaine.

83. (C) Officer Fleming advised Officer Phelps that he saw the passenger in the suspect vehicle throw an object out the window.

84. (C) Officer Fleming did not tell Officer Phelps that he saw two people in the suspect vehicle throw an object out the window.

85. (B) Officer Pawlina received the call at 11:17 P.M. and notified the police dispatcher that two suspects were in custody at 11:57 P.M. The elapsed time was forty minutes.

86. (B) Suspect Jamie Loranger was observed outside the vehicle and captured by Officer Peters.

87. (C) The two youths in the car were John Lorenzo and Michael Meehan.

88. (A) Suspect Jamie Loranger was placed in handcuffs.

89. (A) Circle the word *false* in the question. Answer (C) is true. Jamie Loranger lives at 1454 Albany Avenue, apartment A-3. Answer (D) is true. There were two suspects in the vehicle, John Lorenzo and Michael Meehan, and one suspect outside the vehicle, Jamie Loranger. Answer (B) is true. Officer Pawlina notified the dispatcher at 11:35 P.M. that he was pursuing a suspect and at 11:57 P.M. that two suspects were in custody, which is an elapsed time of twenty-two minutes. Answer (A) is false. None of the suspects lives at 1544 Albany Avenue, apartment C-3.

90. (D) Circle the word *true* in the question. Answer (A) is false. John Lorenzo is fourteen, but he lives at 1445 Albany Avenue, apartment B-3, *not* 1454 Albany Avenue, apartment A-3. Answer (B) is false. Michael Meehan is fifteen, but he lives at 1454 Albany Avenue, apartment C-3, *not* 1445 Albany Avenue, apartment C-3. Answer (C) is false. Jamie Loranger was *not* inside the vehicle. The correct answer is (D). Jamie Loranger lives at 1454 Albany Avenue, apartment A-3.

91. (A) The vehicle reported stolen was a 1987 Chevrolet Caprice.

92. (E) Circle the word *true* in the question. Answer (A) is false. The vehicle had *both* doors open and *two* youths inside. Answer (D) is false. Jamie Loranger, *not* John Lorenzo, acted as a lookout. Answer (B) is *true*. The vehicle had both doors open and two youths inside. Answer (C) is *true*. The vehicle had been stolen, and its stereo was damaged. The correct answer is (E)—both (B) and (C) but not (A) and (D).

93. (C) This question calls for a process of elimination. You're looking for a *true* statement. Answer (A) is incorrect. The car was stolen, but the stereo was found on the seat, *not* the floor. Answers (B) and (D) are incorrect. The vehicle *was* stolen. The correct answer is (C). The vehicle was stolen, and its stereo was found on the seat.

94. (A) Jamie Loranger was the lookout and yelled "Cops!" as the officers approached.

95. (A) The totality of circumstances offered in the reading section would lead a reasonable person to believe a crime was being committed, which eliminates answer (B). Age (C) is not a limiting factor in whether an officer can place a person under arrest. A police officer can place an arrested person in handcuffs (D). The correct answer is (A). The officers were justified in chasing the suspects.

Section 4

96. (A) The last three digits of the license plate number closest to the two men are 455.

97. (B) The suspect is holding a gun in his right hand.

98. (B) The suspect is wearing a black leather jacket.

99. (A) The suspect is wearing sneakers.

100. (B) The victim is wearing dark-colored trousers.

CITY OF WINDSOR
POLICE OFFICER EXAMINATION
TEST 10628

Name: _____

Social Security No.: _____

Today's Date: _____

General Examination Directions

This examination consists of three sections. Each section has specific directions for taking that part of the examination and will be given to you at different times during the examination process. Use the examination booklets, answer sheet, and pencils provided. Print your *full name* on *both* the answer sheet and the examination booklets.

Time: 3 hours
100 Questions

DO NOT OPEN THIS TEST BOOKLET UNTIL TOLD TO DO SO

SECTION 1 OF 3

Booklet 1 of 5: Questions

Directions

The following section tests your ability to apply analytical thinking, practical judgment, and to establish priorities and utilize reasoning in police situations and in applying legal concepts. You have *ninety-five minutes* to answer questions 1 through 70. Choose the *most* correct answer.

1. While on foot patrol on a busy city street, you observe a man relieving himself in an alley between two buildings. As you approach, he begins to run. You should

    (A) yell for the man to stop, but allow him to escape since a warning is sufficient.
    (B) fire one warning shot in the air to stop the man.
    (C) pursue and apprehend the man.
    (D) determine if there are any witnesses to the man's indecent exposure.

2. You stop a motorist for driving through a red light. He doesn't have his driver's license with him. The least acceptable form of identification to write him a summons would be

    (A) an official, state photo majority card.
    (B) a social security card.
    (C) an out-of-state library card.
    (D) a photo identification card from a local employer.

3. While on patrol you observe a boy, who appears to be about four years old, standing alone and crying in front of a department store. Pedestrian traffic is heavy. You should

    (A) use the radio to ask the police dispatcher if any children have been reported missing.
    (B) approach the child and ask where his parents are.
    (C) take no immediate action, but make a note in your log to return later to see if the child is still there.
    (D) notify the juvenile squad to investigate the matter and continue your vehicular patrol.

4. You are informed by your sergeant of a recent rash of burglaries in a warehouse district near the waterfront. While on foot patrol late at night, you check the rear of a warehouse and find fresh pry marks next to a window. The window is slightly open, and you observe a pry bar inside on the floor. It would be most logical to think that

(A) the owner of the building is inside.
(B) the warehouse has been burglarized.
(C) repairs are being done by workers.
(D) the sergeant is testing to see if you're checking the warehouses.

5. You are off duty and observe a man knock a woman down, take her purse, and begin running. The woman is lying on the sidewalk and appears to be having an epileptic seizure. The first thing you should do is

(A) render first aid to the woman.
(B) pursue and capture the assailant.
(C) notify police headquarters via phone.
(D) ask someone to care for the victim and then pursue the assailant.

6. You hear the following description over the radio: "Wanted for murder: John Anderson, age forty-two, white male, five feet, nine inches, 165 pounds, black hair, brown eyes, last seen wearing a sweatshirt, jeans, and sneakers." Of the following, which contains the least important descriptive factor in picking the suspect out of a crowd?

(A) white male, wanted for murder, age forty-two, five feet, nine inches, 165 pounds, black hair, brown eyes, wearing a sweatshirt, jeans, and sneakers
(B) white male, John Anderson, age forty-two, five feet, nine inches, 165 pounds, black hair, wearing a sweatshirt, jeans, and sneakers, wanted for murder
(C) white male, age forty-two, five feet, nine inches, 165 pounds, black hair, wearing jeans, sneakers, and a sweatshirt
(D) white male, five feet, nine inches, 165 pounds, black hair, brown eyes, sweatshirt, jeans, and sneakers

7. Which of the following would make a stolen vehicle easiest to spot in heavy traffic?

(A) a crack in the left front headlight
(B) a large emblem in the rear window reading "St. Elmo's College"
(C) all tires clearly marked "Goodyear"
(D) two large, plastic dice hanging from the rearview mirror

8. In which of the following circumstances would it be most appropriate for a police officer to fire her weapon?

   (A) after a foot chase, in which the officer lost her radio, in order to alert other officers to her location
   (B) to stop a suspect from striking a woman in the face with his fist
   (C) to stop a suspect from stabbing a dog to death with a knife
   (D) to prevent a suspect from striking a man in the head with a baseball bat

Answer question 9 based on the following.

   A basic purpose of patrol is to create an impression in the minds of potential offenders there is no opportunity for successful misconduct.

9. Based on the above, it most logically follows that

   (A) police officers should patrol high-crime areas using conspicuous and unpredictable patrol patterns in unmarked cars.
   (B) police patrol has no relationship to crime prevention.
   (C) police patrol should be conducted primarily in densely populated residential areas.
   (D) police officers should patrol high-crime areas in marked cruisers using both conspicuous and unpredictable patrol patterns.

10. A police vehicle's gasoline tank holds 18.4 gallons of fuel when full. The gas tank fuel dial reads three-fourths full. How many gallons of gasoline remain in the gas tank?

   (A) 9.2 gallons
   (B) 13.8 gallons
   (C) 14.4 gallons
   (D) 14.6 gallons

Answer question 11 based on the following.

An officer is never justified in using physical force to punish a suspect placed in custody or to retaliate for verbal abuse.

11. According to the reading passage, in which of the following cases would a police officer be justified in using physical force?

 (A) A prisoner in handcuffs being transported for assault tells an officer he is HIV-positive and begins spitting at him. The officer slams on the vehicle's brakes so the prisoner will be propelled forward, hitting his face on the cage behind the front seat.
 (B) As an officer is leading a handcuffed prisoner to the cruiser, the prisoner begins swearing at the officer. The officer intentionally pushes the prisoner, making him fall off a curb into the roadway.
 (C) A prisoner with handcuffs behind his back begins kicking a police officer. The officer grabs the prisoner's leg forcing him to the ground.
 (D) A male prisoner makes a sexual remark to a female police officer and she slaps him in the face.

12. While on patrol in the downtown area, you observe a vehicle stopped in the middle of the street blocking traffic. The driver is slumped over the wheel. You should

 (A) notify the police dispatcher to send you a "back up" and arrest the driver.
 (B) notify the police dispatcher to send a wrecker for the vehicle.
 (C) determine why the driver is slumped over the wheel.
 (D) notify the police dispatcher and direct traffic until assistance arrives.

13. You have been sent by the police dispatcher to respond to a call involving a car blocking a driveway. While enroute, you're flagged down by a pedestrian who advises you there is a "drunk" lying unconscious on the sidewalk. Your most appropriate course of action is to

 (A) ask the citizen to stay with the victim until another officer arrives.
 (B) notify headquarters via radio and continue to the original call.
 (C) determine the condition of the unconscious man.
 (D) ask for another patrol unit to check the man and continue to the original call.

Answer question 14 based on the following.

Officers are considered to be available for duty at all times and are required to take action even when off duty.

14. The above statement most clearly means

 (A) police officers work twenty-four hours a day.
 (B) a police officer must take action upon observing a person breaking the rules.
 (C) officers have a responsibility to intervene if a crime occurs in their presence, even when off duty.
 (D) officers are salaried employees and must take appropriate action, even when off duty.

15. Preserving a crime scene most clearly means

   (A) maintaining it in the same physical condition as it was left by the criminal.
   (B) taking pictures of the scene of the crime.
   (C) sketching the crime scene.
   (D) dusting the crime scene with preservation powder for fingerprints.

16. You are a police officer administering first aid to a person who is suffering an apparent heart attack. While doing so, you observe an approaching vehicle swerving from lane to lane. The vehicle strikes your police cruiser, and the driver backs up and flees the scene at a high rate of speed. Your most appropriate course of action would be to

   (A) immediately pursue the vehicle and apprehend the driver.
   (B) notify the police dispatcher and engage the vehicle in pursuit.
   (C) continue giving first aid to the victim and notify the police dispatcher via portable radio of a description of the vehicle.
   (D) flag down a motorist and ask the person to follow the vehicle and obtain its license plate number.

17. You're a police officer investigating a one-car motor vehicle accident. You pace off the distance from a light pole to the final resting position of the vehicle. You walk fourteen and one-half paces. If one pace equals three feet, how far was the car from the light pole?

   (A) forty-two feet
   (B) forty-three feet, six inches
   (C) forty-four feet
   (D) forty-four feet, six inches

Answer question 18 based on the following.

Manslaughter in the Second Degree with a Motor Vehicle—53a–56b.
A person is guilty of manslaughter in the second degree with a motor vehicle when: (a) while operating a motor vehicle under the influence of intoxicating liquor or any drug or both, (b) he or she causes the death of another as a consequence of the effect of such liquor or drug.

18. According to the above statement, in which of the following circumstances could a person be charged with Manslaughter in the Second Degree with a Motor Vehicle—53a–56b?

   (A) a drunk driver who hits a child with his vehicle and leaves the scene
   (B) a drunk driver who hits an elderly man with his vehicle, causing injuries requiring his hospitalization
   (C) a person driving under the influence of cocaine who backs up into a pedestrian, causing his death
   (D) a driver who recklessly passes a school bus striking an oncoming vehicle, killing three people

19. While on patrol, you're approached by a girl, about ten years old, who hands you a wallet she says she found in a dumpster. Your most appropriate course of action is to

   (A) open the wallet and determine if anything is in it
   (B) berate the child for looking in the dumpster
   (C) determine where the child lives
   (D) notify the child's parents

Answer questions 20 through 22 based on the following.

   At 10:45 P.M., while on routine patrol, Officers Harvey Young and Maria Rodriguez were dispatched to 1438 Nelton Court, apartment D, on a complaint from Janice Rodriguez about a domestic dispute occurring at 1438 Nelton Court, apartment C. Upon arrival at the location, the officers spoke with Mrs. Rodriguez, who stated that at 10:40 P.M., she heard a woman she believed to be Maria Ortiz arguing loudly with a man. She also heard the sound of furniture breaking and of Maria Ortiz crying hysterically. The officers went to 1438 Nelton Court, apartment C, knocked on the door, and were admitted by Silvia Ortiz, age fourteen, who was crying. When asked by the officers where her mother was, Silvia Ortiz pointed to the bedroom and ran into the bathroom, locking the door. The officers noted most of the living room furniture was badly damaged. The bedroom door opened, and a man, later identified as Pedro Ortiz, came out yelling at the officers to get out of his apartment. Silvia Ortiz could be heard yelling from the bathroom, "He killed my mother." Pedro Ortiz attacked the officers, was arrested, and was placed in handcuffs. The officers found Maria Ortiz on the floor in the bedroom, unconscious and badly beaten. She was taken to a local hospital via ambulance. Janice Rodriguez agreed to care for Silvia Ortiz until relatives could be located.

20. Which address did the officers initially respond to?

   (A) 1438 Nelton Court, apartment C
   (B) 1438 Nelson Court, apartment D
   (C) 1483 Nelton Court, apartment C
   (D) 1438 Nelton Court, apartment D

21. The name of the complainant was?

   (A) Maria Rodriguez
   (B) Maria Ortiz
   (C) Janice Rodriguez
   (D) Silvia Ortiz

22. The officers were admitted to 1438 Nelton Court, apartment C, by

   (A) Silvia Ortiz.
   (B) Janice Rodriguez.
   (C) Maria Rodriguez.
   (D) Maria Ortiz.

23. While on foot patrol during the midnight shift, you hear an audible alarm sounding. Investigating, you find the front window of a jewelry store broken and a small rock on the ground surrounded by glass fragments splattered with blood. It would be most logical to think that

   (A) the rock was thrown from a distance of more than six feet.
   (B) the rock was placed in a cloth and used to break the window.
   (C) the person who broke the window was cut.
   (D) because of the alarm sounding, the glass broke and cut the burglar.

24. During the initial stages of a police investigation, you place a person under arrest, handcuff him, and put him in your police cruiser. Further investigation leads to the discovery of facts proving him innocent. You should

   (A) release him and inform him of the new evidence.
   (B) bring him to headquarters and place him in a cell until court convenes.
   (C) telephone a state prosecutor to obtain permission to let him go.
   (D) take him to headquarters for fingerprints and a photograph.

25. A police officer responds to a complaint from Mrs. Collins of a burglary into her home. Upon arrival, the officer learns from Mrs. Collins, an elderly woman, that she just returned from a trip, found her home burglarized, and immediately notified the police. The first thing the officer should do is

   (A) ensure that the burglar isn't still in the house.
   (B) preserve the scene of the crime.
   (C) locate the point of entry used by the burglar.
   (D) determine if anything is missing.

26. Officer Jenkins responds to a complaint from Joseph Murphy that the trunk of his car was broken into and a briefcase valued at $150 was stolen containing the following property:

1 35-mm camera valued at	$325.00
1 35-mm camera lens valued at	75.00
4 rolls of 35-mm film each valued at	3.99
1 calculator valued at	10.99

   In completing his case incident report, which of the following should Officer Jenkins list as the total value of the property stolen from Joseph Murphy's vehicle?

   (A) $426.95
   (B) $462.95
   (C) $576.95
   (D) $597.76

Answer questions 27 through 29 based on the following.

Special Order 14-11: Precautionary Measures RE: Arrest. When making an arrest, officers must have regard for both their safety and that of the prisoner. Officers are responsible for delivering the prisoner safely to the court or place of lawful detention.

1. Keep prisoners in front of you, never allowing them behind you or at your side where they are able to seize your gun or other weapons.

2. Never allow prisoners to place their hands in their pockets. Upon arrest, all prisoners shall be handcuffed with their hands behind the back.

3. Always consider an accused to be armed. Take no chances, even after a prisoner has been carefully searched. The prisoner should be searched for dangerous weapons at the time of arrest and placed in handcuffs.

4. When circumstances permit, always obtain assistance when arresting an armed or dangerous criminal.

27. While on foot patrol in a high-crime housing project, Officer John Barnes interrupts a narcotics transaction in the hallway of an apartment building. He arrests one of the participants for possession of cocaine. The other gets away. While escorting the prisoner outside, the man takes a gun out of his jacket pocket. A struggle ensues. The officer disarms the man and places him in handcuffs. According to Special Order 14-11, Officer Barnes

    (A) should have placed the prisoner in handcuffs when the arrest was made.
    (B) should have obtained assistance prior to making the arrest.
    (C) should have shot the prisoner as soon as the arrested person displayed a gun.
    (D) should have remained in the hallway with the prisoner until assistance arrived.

28. According to Special Order 14-11, which of the following statements is false?

    (A) All prisoners should be placed in handcuffs at the time of their arrest.
    (B) After a prisoner is carefully searched and handcuffed, he or she may be allowed to stand at either side of the officer.
    (C) A person arrested for a minor crime must be handcuffed behind the back.
    (D) Prisoners should be considered armed even if they are in handcuffs and have been carefully searched.

29. Officer Robert Nelson observes a vehicle make an improper turn, almost causing an accident. Upon stopping the motorist, Officer Nelson learns that there is a valid arrest warrant for the driver for murder, and he is to be considered armed and dangerous. According to Special Order 14-ll, Officer Nelson should

   (A) approach the vehicle cautiously, with his weapon drawn, and arrest and handcuff the suspect.
   (B) notify police headquarters and use the cruiser's loudspeaker to order the man out of the car with his hands raised in the air.
   (C) if possible, wait for assistance prior to placing the suspect under arrest.
   (D) if possible, have the suspect pull to the curb and place both hands out of the driver's window until the officer can safely approach.

30. Police officers spend most of their time handling calls relating to noncriminal, social-service functions. Of the activities listed below, which does not fall into this category?

   (A) issuing a parking ticket on a crowded downtown street
   (B) processing a prisoner after an arrest
   (C) responding to a medical emergency
   (D) responding to a report of a homeless person sleeping in a doorway

31. If conspicuous patrol in marked cruisers is the most effective method of minimizing the opportunity for criminal behavior, it logically follows that this type of patrol should be performed in proportion to

   (A) the number of total officers on the force.
   (B) the amount of crime occurring within a specific area.
   (C) vice-related activities occurring on the street.
   (D) the number of noncriminal calls for service received by a police department statistically averaged over time.

32. Statistics indicate that one area of a city is more prone to vehicular speeding than others. One tactic used to prevent motorists from speeding is placing a conspicuously marked, unoccupied, patrol unit on the street where the speeding is occurring. The purpose of this tactic is to

   (A) enforce state statutes relative to motor vehicle offenses.
   (B) reduce the cost of personnel associated with traffic enforcement.
   (C) act as a deterrent.
   (D) to reduce the number of traffic accidents.

33. The mission of the police department is often described as "serving and protecting the public." Of the following, which does not fall into that category?

   (A) counseling a small child about the dangers of playing at a construction site
   (B) bringing a stranded motorist to a phone during a snowstorm
   (C) bringing a stray animal to the humane society
   (D) all of the above
   (E) none of the above

34. A series of incidents have been reported in which motorists, while driving along the street, have had their windshields smashed by someone throwing an object from an overpass. You are assigned to stake out the area in which this has been occurring, and you observe a fourteen-year-old boy, who plays baseball with your son, throw a soda bottle off the overpass, nearly striking a vehicle. You apprehend the youth. Your best course of action would be to

(A) take the youth home to his parents and explain the situation.
(B) arrest the youth.
(C) issue a stern warning explaining the consequences which could have resulted from his action.
(D) take the youth home but write a report on the incident.

35. Officer Peter Prete arrests a man for assault in the first degree and transports him to the lockup. Which of the following items of personal property should be taken from the prisoner prior to his being placed in a cell?

(A) his belt
(B) his shoelaces
(C) a pen knife with a blade less than one inch long
(D) all of the above

Answer questions 36 through 46 based on the following.

At 11:50 A.M., Officer Paul Reid is dispatched to the intersection of Union Place and Allyn Street on the report of a two-car, personal injury, motor vehicle accident. The weather is clear and the roadway is dry. Upon arriving at the scene, Officer Reid observes that two vehicles have collided in the intersection. A 1993 Chevrolet Vega, registration number AU 134, is facing south on Union Place with moderate damage to the left front. A 1991 Chevrolet Caprice, registration number BL 694, is up against the left front of the Vega and facing in a westerly direction with minor damage to the right front.

The operator of the Vega is John Simmons, D.O.B. 7/14/49, of 1411 Hanover Street. He has a minor laceration to his forehead but declines medical attention. Simmons states that he was driving his car south on Union Place at approximately twenty-five miles per hour when he heard the screech of brakes and suddenly saw a car coming at him into the intersection. He jammed on his brakes, but before he could further react, the Caprice struck the left front of his car. Simmons states that the Caprice was going "very fast."

The operator of the Caprice is Ralph Johnson, D.O.B. 6/21/52, of 110 Main Street. He states that he was driving west on Allyn Street at approximately twenty miles per hour and stopped for the stop sign at the intersection of Allyn Street and Union Place. He saw the Vega coming south on Union Place but thought he had enough time to make a left turn. As he entered the intersection, the Vega "suddenly sped up" and struck his car.

Officer Reid locates a witness to the accident, Robert Anderson, D.O.B. 8/14/54, of 145 Union Place. Anderson states that he was standing at the corner of Union Place and Allyn Street, heard tires squealing, and saw the Caprice coming west on Allyn Street "at a fast speed." Anderson further states that he saw the Caprice go through the stop sign at Allyn and Union Place "without even slowing down" and strike the Vega, which was coming south on Union Place. Anderson states, "There's skid marks in the road," referring to the Caprice.

Following is Officer Reid's diagram of the accident scene.

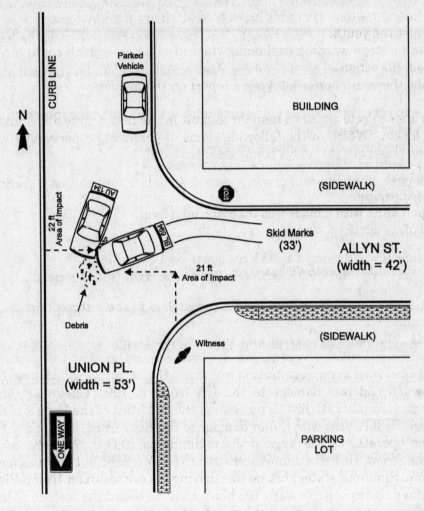

36. How many feet of skid marks did the Caprice leave in the roadway on Allyn Street?

   (A) twenty-one feet
   (B) twenty-two feet
   (C) thirty-three feet
   (D) forty-four feet

37. Which of the following statements is true?

    (A) John Simmons, D.O.B. 6/21/52, lives at 1141 Hanover Street and was operating the Vega.
    (B) John Simmons was driving south on Union Place in a vehicle which left thirty-three feet of skid marks.
    (C) The registration number of the vehicle going west on Allyn Street is BL 694.
    (D) Ralph Johnson, D.O.B. 6/21/52, lives at 110 Main Street, was driving a Caprice, and said he was traveling at approximately twenty-five miles per hour.

38. Based on the reading section and diagram, which of the following probably had the most effect in causing the accident?

    (A) the driver of the Caprice going through the stop sign at the intersection of Allyn Street and Union Place
    (B) the speed of the two vehicles involved
    (C) the constricted narrowness of Allyn Street
    (D) the parked vehicle, which was a view obstruction for vehicles traveling west on Allyn Street

39. Which of the following statements is true?

    (A) Johnson was driving a 1992 Vega south on Union Place.
    (B) The driver of the vehicle with damage to the right front received a laceration to the forehead.
    (C) Anderson was standing at the southeast corner of Union Place and Allyn Street.
    (D) The weather was a contributory factor in the accident.

40. According to the reading section and diagram of the accident, which of the following is a true statement?

    (A) John Simmons lives at 141 Hanover Street and was driving a 1991 Caprice.
    (B) Anderson lives at 145 Union Place and was driving a 1993 Vega.
    (C) John Simmons was driving south on a one-way street.
    (D) The vehicle with registration number AU 134 had minor damage to the left front.

41. Of the following, which constitutes the primary evidence indicating fault in this accident?

    (A) statements made by Simmons
    (B) statements made by Anderson
    (C) statements made by Johnson
    (D) the weather conditions at the time of the accident

42. The primary physical evidence at the accident scene is the

    (A) stop sign
    (B) the witness
    (C) the one-way street sign
    (D) the skid marks

43. The parked vehicle is facing

    (A) west on Allyn Street
    (B) north on Union Place
    (C) east on Allyn Street
    (D) south on Union Place

44. The width of Union Place is

    (A) twenty-one feet
    (B) twenty-two feet
    (C) thirty-three feet
    (D) fifty-three feet

45. The person most at fault in this traffic accident was the driver of the

    (A) 1993 Vega.
    (B) 1992 Caprice.
    (C) 1992 Vega.
    (D) 1991 Caprice.

46. The most logical elements in determining fault in this accident are

    (A) physical evidence and eyewitness statements.
    (B) statements by Simmons and physical evidence.
    (C) statements by Johnson and Anderson.
    (D) statements by Simmons and Johnson

Answer questions 47 through 50 based on the following reading section.

PHOTOGRAPHIC IDENTIFICATION

Photographs commonly referred to as "mug shots" are often shown by the police to witnesses and victims of criminal acts in order to determine the identity of the person who committed the crime. In determining whether photographic identification procedures have violated a suspect's constitutional rights, the courts will determine if the methods used by the police in showing photographs were unnecessarily suggestive. Photographic-identification procedures may be suggestive if the police in any way indicate that a particular picture they are showing to the victim or witness is the suspect.

To avoid situations which might prove to be unnecessarily suggestive, police should adhere to the following recommended procedures.

1. The photographic array should contain at least eight photographs. A single photo should never be used.

2. Photographs should be of similar types. Police photographs should not be mixed with Polaroids or colored photos with black-and-whites.

3. The officer should not indicate through words or actions that a particular photograph is of the person believed to be the suspect.

4. Witnesses and/or victims of criminal acts should never view photographs together or communicate during the identification procedure.

5. Photographs should be of persons with similar physical appearances.

47. A package store was robbed at gunpoint several days ago. Based on a description supplied by the victim of the robber, a police officer obtains a mug shot of a person he believes is a suspect in the robbery. The officer brings the mug shot to the victim who identifies it as the person who committed the crime. According to the reading section

(A) the officer's actions were proper. The package store owner identified the suspect from a mug shot.
(B) the officer's actions were improper. He should have put the suspect's photograph in with at least three other mug shots.
(C) the officer's actions were proper. The victim did not ask to see the mug shots, so it wasn't unnecessarily suggestive.
(D) the officer's actions were improper. Showing a single mug shot is unnecessarily suggestive.

48. A woman has been the victim of a purse snatch. She is brought to headquarters to look at photographs to see if she can identify her assailant. According to the reading section, which of the following is incorrect procedure?

(A) The victim was shown forty Polaroid mug shots, all of which were in black and white and of similar types.
(B) The victim was not allowed to view the mug shots in the company of her husband, who witnessed the crime.
(C) The victim was shown fifty mug shots of suspects with dissimilar physical appearances.
(D) The officer left the victim alone and did not suggest that he believed any person in the photographs was the person who committed the crime.

49. According to the reading section, which of the following statements is correct?

(A) A single photograph should never be used.
(B) Color photographs should not be mixed with black-and-white photographs.
(C) Police officers should not tell the victim of a crime that a photograph the victim is looking at is thought to be the suspect.
(D) all of the above

50. The primary purpose of showing photographs to witnesses and victims of crimes is to

(A) ensure the constitutional rights of a person accused of committing a crime.
(B) provide a procedure to ensure that the use of photographs by police is not unnecessarily suggestive.
(C) determine who committed the crime.
(D) justify the arrest of a suspect in a criminal indictment.

51. While on patrol, you observe a vehicle with its emergency flashers on travelling at a speed over the posted limit. You stop the vehicle and the driver points to a female passenger who is in obvious distress. The driver says that his wife is in labor and that he is driving her to the hospital. Your most appropriate course of action is to

(A) issue the driver a summons for speeding.
(B) caution the driver for operating the vehicle over the posted speed limit and allow him to proceed.
(C) give the driver of the vehicle a police escort to the hospital.
(D) call for an ambulance to take the woman in labor to the hospital and issue the driver a summons for speeding.

52. At 10:50 P.M., you are sent to investigate a complaint from an anonymous caller of "shots fired" in a parking lot behind a school building. Upon arrival, you observe no one in the area, but on the ground next to a dumpster, you find a shotgun shell casing. A short distance away, you also find a loaded .38 caliber, six-shot revolver with one empty cylinder. It would be most logical to think

(A) the shotgun shell casing came from the revolver.
(B) the revolver was fired, and the one empty cylinder resulted in the shotgun shell casing being ejected onto the ground.
(C) the shotgun shell casing did not come from the revolver.
(D) both the revolver and a shotgun were fired in the parking lot.

53. A body is found floating in a river at 1:45 P.M. Examination by the medical examiner at the scene reveals a fresh wound to the skull which occurred "less than two hours ago." An autopsy later reveals that the victim died of strangulation at least three hours prior to the head wound. It would be most logical to think that

(A) the victim was struck in the head, strangled, and then thrown into the water.
(B) the victim died of strangulation caused by drowning.
(C) the victim was strangled, struck in the head, and then thrown into the water.
(D) the victim was thrown into the water, hitting his head, and drowned.

54. A police officer arrests a man in possession of 392 grams of cocaine. If there are twenty-eight grams in an ounce and sixteen ounces in a pound, which of the following statements is true?

(A) The officer seized 3.5 pounds of cocaine.
(B) The officer seized 3.5 ounces of cocaine.
(C) The officer seized 11,480 grams of cocaine.
(D) The officer seized fourteen ounces of cocaine.

55. Officer James Peters responds to a local hospital on a complaint of a sexual assault. The victim informs Officer Peters that she does not feel comfortable relating the details of the incident to him and would rather speak to a female officer. Officer Peters should

(A) have a female police officer interview the victim.
(B) advise the victim that she will have to give details in court of what occurred, so she may as well tell him.
(C) caution the victim that time is of the essence if she wants the police to catch the person who assaulted her.
(D) advise the victim that the crime is actually against the state and not her and that she is required to give him the details.

56. You observe a vehicle with all four windows rolled down parked in a lot. There is no front license plate and the rear of the vehicle is up against a building, making the back plate unreadable. The glove compartment is open, and papers are scattered throughout the vehicle's interior. It would be most logical to think that

(A) the vehicle is stolen.
(B) the vehicle is abandoned.
(C) the vehicle was involved in an accident.
(D) the owner left the vehicle in that condition.

57. An axiom often used to describe the mission of the police is "to serve and protect." This most clearly means to serve and protect

(A) the people living within the city.
(B) the taxpayers within the city.
(C) any person the officer encounters.
(D) people from criminal behavior.

58. A police officer pursues a suspect vehicle thirteen city blocks. The suspect vehicle then makes a sudden turn into an alley. The police vehicle passes the alley, traveling another six blocks before the officer realizes the suspect has eluded him. The officer turns around, driving back to the alley. Each city block is one-tenth of a mile. How far did the police officer travel in total?

(A) 1.3 miles
(B) 2.0 miles
(C) 2.3 miles
(D) 2.5 miles

59. Police community relations are influenced most by the

(A) interactions between police officers and citizens.
(B) dedicated efforts of a department community-relations unit.
(C) department's relationship with the press.
(D) efforts of the department's chief of police.

60. Which of the following terms has the same meaning as regulation?

   (A) rule
   (B) policy
   (C) procedure
   (D) goal

Answer questions 61 and 62 based on the following.

At 11:50 P.M., Officers Robert Nelson and Peter Hopkins are parked adjacent to The Gaslight Bar and Grill and hear the sound of gunshots coming from inside. Entering the bar, which is crowded with customers, the officers observe a man bleeding from a gunshot wound to his left hand. The victim tells the officers that a woman standing next to the entrance to the women's restroom did the shooting. As the officers approach the suspect, she suddenly takes an object out of her coat pocket, placing it into her purse, and runs into the restroom, closing the door.

61. The officers should

   (A) wait for the woman to come out of the restroom and arrest her.
   (B) ask a female patron of the bar to go into the restroom and ask the woman to step out so the officers can speak with her.
   (C) pursue the woman and take her into custody.
   (D) call for a female police officer to respond to the scene.

62. Which of the following is the first thing the officers should do upon making contact with the suspect?

   (A) establish her identity
   (B) ensure their safety by taking the purse from the suspect
   (C) ask her if she shot the victim
   (D) ensure that no other women are in the restroom

63. In a criminal trial, the primary role of the defense attorney is to

   (A) cause the jury to doubt the guilt of his or her client.
   (B) discredit the testimony of police officers.
   (C) cause the jury to determine justice.
   (D) see that the guilty are punished and the innocent go free.

64. You are a police officer working the front desk of police headquarters. During your shift, a juvenile has been killed by a hit-and-run driver. The parents have not been notified, and you have been instructed by your supervisor not to give the child's name out to the press. A reporter comes to headquarters asking for the name of the child. You should tell the reporter

    (A) that the police do not know the name of the child.
    (B) that it's against police regulations to provide the name of an accident victim.
    (C) that you will not give out the name of the child until proper notification of next of kin has been made.
    (D) to ask your supervisor for the name.

65. While on patrol in the early morning hours, you observe an apartment building engulfed in flames. You notify headquarters via radio and begin knocking on doors, alerting tenants to evacuate because of the fire. An elderly man refuses to leave his apartment. The fire is rapidly spreading. You should

    (A) notify headquarters and request further instructions.
    (B) remove the elderly man to a position of safety.
    (C) ask other tenants to take the man out of the apartment.
    (D) allow him to make an informed choice and take responsibility for his own actions.

66. You respond to the rear of a local high school on a report from a "concerned citizen" of students using drugs in the parking lot. Approaching on foot, you observe a female student, about seventeen years old, smoking marijuana. After placing her under arrest she gives you two "dime bags" of marijuana from her coat pocket. The student says that if you let her go she will tell you whom she bought the marijuana from. Your most appropriate course of action would be to

    (A) release the student if she supplies the name of the person she bought the marijuana from.
    (B) offer to destroy the two "dime bags" of marijuana and arrest her only for the marijuana cigarette if she cooperates.
    (C) turn the case over to the narcotics squad.
    (D) proceed with the arrest process, making no deals or promises.

67. Sociologists contend that crime can never be totally eliminated. Of the following, which criminal act is most likely to be eliminated by the police?

    (A) prostitution
    (B) murder
    (C) robbery
    (D) none of the above

68. You respond to the scene of an assault. Upon arrival, you find a woman has been badly beaten and must be taken to the hospital. Of the following, which is the most important question a police officer should ask the victim?

    (A) the name of her assailant
    (B) what time the assault took place
    (C) if the victim wants to prefer charges against her assailant
    (D) where the incident took place

69. You are a police officer on foot patrol during the day in a busy downtown area. You notice that a small crowd has formed on the sidewalk next to an intersection. Responding, you find a woman lying on the sidewalk with a laceration to the back of her head. After administering first aid, your next most immediate responsibility is to

    (A) clear the sidewalk area of the crowd so pedestrian traffic can move freely.
    (B) complete a report on the incident.
    (C) determine if a crime has been committed.
    (D) call for a police photographer to photograph the scene.

70. While on patrol, you receive a radio dispatch that there has been a shooting at a grocery store. Upon arrival, you learn that the store was robbed. Four customers are in the store, and you are assigned by your sergeant to interview them. Of the following, the first thing you should determine is

    (A) the exact time the robbery took place.
    (B) if the customer was present when the robbery took place.
    (C) a description of the suspect.
    (D) if the suspect got into a vehicle.

SECTION 2 OF 3

Booklet 2 of 5: Information

Directions

This portion of the examination is designed to measure your ability to observe, retain information, and draw reasonable conclusions and references from what you have observed. The following page contains pictures which you will be allowed to study for several minutes. The pictures will then be taken away from you, and you will be required to answer questions about the pictures. You will not be able to look at the pictures again after the test proctor advises you that the time period has elapsed. Choose the *most* correct answer.

Questions 71 through 80 are based on a series of six pictures and information relative to the person in the picture. You will be given *five minutes* to observe the pictures and information, after which they will be taken from you. You will then be given *twenty minutes* to answer questions 71 through 80. **Do not begin until you are told to do so by the examination proctor.**

Frank Scarleti   Alias: John D'Amico
Born: 6/3/53   Height: 5'9''   Weight: 180 lbs.
Hair: black   Eyes: brown
Convicted of: assault in the first degree with a firearm
Scars or Marks: large mole on left forearm

Rita Moreno   Alias: Delores Rodriguez
Born: 4/10/65   Height: 5'3''   Weight: 135 lbs.
Hair: brown   Eyes: brown
Convicted of: murder
Scars or Marks: none

Raymond Armeti   Alias: Gilbert Shasha
Born: 12/10/47   Height: 5'10''   Weight: 175 lbs.
Hair: gray   Eyes: brown
Convicted of: insurance fraud
Scars or Marks: tattoo of eagle on left shoulder

Jose Melendes   Alias: Pedro Gonzalez
Born: 3/9/40   Height: 5'6''   Weight: 175 lbs.
Hair: gray   Eyes: black
Convicted of: possession of narcotics
Scars or Marks: missing index finger, left hand

Barbara Johnson   Alias: Richard Brown
Born: 9/18/55   Height: 5'6''   Weight: 135 lbs.
Hair: blonde   Eyes: blue
Convicted of: injury risk to a minor
Scars or Marks: none

John Cunningham   Alias: Pete the Hammer
Born: 8/16/57   Height: 5'11''   Weight: 175 lbs.
Hair: gray   Eyes: brown
Convicted of: bank robbery
Scars or Marks: large burn on back of right hand

SECTION 2 OF 3

Booklet 3 of 5: Questions

71. Which of the persons was convicted of murder?

    (A) Barbara Johnson
    (B) John Cunningham
    (C) Rita Moreno
    (D) Frank Scarleti

72. Which of the persons is missing a finger on the left hand?

    (A) Raymond Armeti
    (B) Jose Melendes
    (C) John Cunningham
    (D) Barbara Johnson

73. Which of the persons has a tattoo?

    (A) Raymond Armeti
    (B) Rita Moreno
    (C) Jose Melendes
    (D) John Cunningham

74. Which of the persons has a large mole on the left forearm?

    (A) Jose Melendes
    (B) Raymond Armeti
    (C) Barbara Johnson
    (D) Frank Scarleti

75. Barbara Johnson's alias is

    (A) Rita Moreno.
    (B) Frank Scarleti.
    (C) Richard Brown.
    (D) Delores Rodriguez.

76. Which of the following facts is true of the person convicted of bank robbery?

    (A) His alias is Pete the Hammer.
    (B) His eyes are brown.
    (C) He has a large burn mark on the back of his right hand.
    (D) all of the above
    (E) both (A) and (C), but not (B)

77. Jose Melendes was convicted of

    (A) insurance fraud.
    (B) bank robbery.
    (C) possession of narcotics.
    (D) assault in the first degree with a firearm.

78. All of the following are true of Barbara Johnson except

    (A) height five feet, six inches.
    (B) born 6/18/45.
    (C) convicted of injury/risk to a minor.
    (D) alias is Richard Brown.

79. The person convicted of insurance fraud is

    (A) Raymond Armeti.
    (B) Rita Moreno.
    (C) Frank Scarleti.
    (D) Jose Melendes.

80. The person convicted of assault in the first degree with a firearm is

    (A) Frank Scarleti.
    (B) Raymond Armeti.
    (C) John Cunningham.
    (D) Jose Melendes.

SECTION 3 OF 3

Booklet 4 of 5: Information

Directions

This section tests your ability to read and understand practical police and legal concepts. You will be given *thirty minutes* to read the information contained in Booklet 4. It contains two reading sections with information on different police subjects. **Do not open the examination booklets until told to do so by the examination proctor.** At the end of thirty minutes, the booklet will be taken from you and you will be given questions that apply to the information you have read. You will have *thirty minutes* to answer these questions. Choose the *most* correct answer.

READING SECTION 1: PATROL METHODOLOGY

Patrol

A department's patrol division is often referred to as the "backbone of the police department" because it's through the patrol division that the department provides direct services to the community which it serves. Although there are many types of police patrol, this booklet will concentrate on *foot* and *vehicular* patrol.

Foot Patrol

A combination of factors contribute to whether a specific area of the city can be served more effectively through the use of foot patrol than through the use of vehicular patrol. Factors indicating that foot patrol may be advantageous include:

1. A high demand for police services within a small geographic area.

2. High-density population within a small geographic area, such as housing projects, shopping malls, amusement centers, bars, and parks.

3. Locations having high volumes of pedestrian and/or vehicular traffic, such as downtown or in business areas.

The size and boundaries of foot patrols are influenced by the numbers and types of calls for police services within walking distance in a specific area and natural boundaries such as rivers, parks, bridges, and highways. There are several advantages and disadvantages of foot patrol. Advantages include:

1. Officers on foot patrol can make more person-to-person contact with citizens, increasing the department's ability to perform community-relations services.

2. Officers on foot can respond to lower-priority calls, relieving line patrol vehicles from having to respond to minor calls for service.

3. Officers on foot can devote more attention to traffic congestion, illegal parking, information gathering, and deterring illicit activity such as prostitution and gambling.

Disadvantages of foot patrol include:

1. Police officers in vehicles can cover larger areas in less time than can officers on foot. Foot patrol restricts mobility and the size of the area which can be covered.

2. The capacity of officers on foot to pursue a criminal is limited.

3. Officers on foot patrol are limited to the equipment they can carry with them, while patrol vehicles can be equipped with emergency equipment, such as first-aid supplies, flares, oxygen, and special weapons.

4. Officers in vehicles can respond faster to emergency situations than can officers on foot.

5. Supervision of foot patrols is more time consuming and costly than is supervision of officers in vehicles.

Vehicular Patrol

To determine the effectiveness of vehicular patrol, many of the same factors used in determining the need for foot patrol are used. These include the type of, frequency of, and need for police services; the size, geography, and topography of the area; density of population and vehicle and pedestrian traffic within an area; and the safety of the police officer. The advantages of vehicular patrol include:

1. Officers in vehicles can cover larger areas more frequently and with greater speed than can officers on foot.

2. Patrol vehicles can be equipped with first-aid, fire, and inclement weather equipment, along with special weapons.

3. Officers in vehicles can respond to emergency situations faster than can officers on foot.

Whether on foot or in a vehicle, officers should ensure that their patrol efforts don't establish a pattern which a criminal can observe and use to aid in the planning and commission of a crime. Patrol should be done randomly, with no obvious pattern, visiting different parts of the beat or district at different times and with no systematic pattern.

READING SECTION 2: FIREARM GUIDELINES

Police officers are issued firearms and trained in their use. Generally, the reason officers carry guns is to protect themselves and the public they serve. As law enforcement officers sworn to protect life and property, officers must be constantly aware of the sanctity of human life and the moral implications of the use of deadly force. Situations encountered by police officers necessitating the use of a firearm are the most critical judgment decisions a police officer is called upon to make.

The use of a firearm by a police officer is *deadly force*. Police officers may use deadly force only as a last resort and when it is reasonable and necessary to protect themselves or another person from the imminent danger of death or serious bodily injury. Firearms may also be used to put to death an animal which presents an immediate, serious physical threat to the officer or a third party, or one so badly injured that humaneness demands its immediate removal from further suffering. The use of firearms is *prohibited*

1. where the lives of innocent persons could be endangered by the use of a firearm.

2. for firing at or from a moving vehicle unless the occupants of the vehicle are using deadly physical force which can reasonably be expected to kill the officer or a third person.

3. for firing warning shots or sounding a call for assistance.

SECTION 3 OF 3

Booklet 5 of 5: Questions

Answer questions 81 through 90 based on the "Patrol Methodology" reading section.

81. Which of the following is not an advantage of vehicular patrol over foot patrol?

    (A) increased opportunity to perform community-relations work
    (B) greater mobility
    (C) faster response in emergency situations
    (D) may be equipped with emergency supplies

82. Of the following, which is the primary benefit of foot patrol?

    (A) It allows the officer to learn a specific area of the city.
    (B) It increases the ability to check doors on the midnight shift.
    (C) It provides physical fitness for officers.
    (D) It relieves vehicle patrol units from responding to minor calls.

83. Which of the following is not a contributing factor in favor of deciding to establish a foot beat?

    (A) low-density population within a large geographic area
    (B) high volume of pedestrian traffic
    (C) high volume of vehicular traffic
    (D) high crime in a densely-populated area

84. Officer James Johnson takes his lunch break at the same restaurant at the same time every day. This practice should be

    (A) encouraged. Supervisors will know where the officer is at a specific time.
    (B) discouraged. Merchants may complain the officer is only frequenting one establishment.
    (C) encouraged. It assists in community relations.
    (D) discouraged. The officer is establishing a pattern which could be observed by a criminal.

85. All of the following are factors in determining the boundaries of foot patrol except

    (A) the number and types of calls for police services.
    (B) the political make-up of the area to be patrolled.
    (C) natural boundaries.
    (D) safety of police officers.

86. Which of the following is the most costly to a police department?

    (A) one officer patrolling on foot
    (B) two officers patrolling together on foot
    (C) one officer patrolling in a vehicle
    (D) two officers in the same vehicle patrolling one area

87. Which of the following calls for police service would be most appropriately responded to by an officer on foot patrol?

    (A) report of a vehicle speeding up and down a city block
    (B) report of a man suffering a heart attack
    (C) report of a vehicle blocking a downtown driveway
    (D) report of a three-car, personal-injury, traffic accident on a busy downtown street

88. Which of the following is a disadvantage of vehicular patrol?

    (A) It allows the carrying of special equipment.
    (B) It does not allow frequent citizen contact.
    (C) It allows frequent coverage of an area.
    (D) It is highly mobile.

89. Which of the following should be inspected most often by an officer on foot?

    (A) a bar
    (B) an office building
    (C) a large shopping mall
    (D) residential property

90. Whether patrol is by vehicle or on foot, the most effective description of how patrol should be conducted is

    (A) at random.
    (B) in the most economical manner.
    (C) selectively.
    (D) by routine aggressive patrol.

Answer questions 91 through 100 based on the 'Firearm Guidelines' reading section.

91. According to the reading section, the use of firearms by a police officer is prohibited in each of the following except

    (A) to fire at a shoplifting suspect.
    (B) to kill a dog which is biting and dragging an infant by the neck.
    (C) to kill a dog on a metal leash foaming at the mouth.
    (D) to kill a man coming at the officer with a plastic bat.

92. Which of the following most accurately describes a situation in which firearms may be used by a police officer?

    (A) The officer's life is in danger.
    (B) The life of a third person is in danger.
    (C) The officer's life is in imminent danger.
    (D) A third person is in danger of serious physical injury.

93. Officer Doherty interrupts a drug transaction and chases one of the drug dealers on foot. The suspect gets in a vehicle and is pulling away. The officer fires one round from her service revolver to stop the vehicle. According to the reading section, the officer's actions are

    (A) reasonable. The suspect committed a serious crime and would have gotten away.
    (B) prohibited. The suspect did not commit a felonious act.
    (C) prohibited. The occupants of the vehicle are not using deadly force against the officer or another person.
    (D) reasonable. The vehicle could turn toward the officer, placing her in danger.

94. According to the reading section, an officer may fire at a motor vehicle if

    (A) the vehicle is coming at the officer or a third party.
    (B) the vehicle is being operated by a felony suspect.
    (C) there is imminent danger of deadly force being used against the officer by the vehicle's occupant.
    (D) the vehicle is heading toward a truck carrying gasoline.

95. According to the reading section, officers may use their firearms

    (A) to defend themselves against the imminent use of deadly physical force.
    (B) to defend a third person against the imminent use of physical force.
    (C) to defend themselves or a third person against the imminent use of force.
    (D) to put to death an animal presenting a threat to people.

96. Officer Jones is confronted by a young child pointing a loaded BB gun at him. The officer

    (A) would be justified in killing the child.
    (B) would be justified in shooting the child in the shoulder.
    (C) would not be justified in using his firearm.
    (D) would be justified in shooting the child in the foot.

97. According to the reading section, a police officer who has a legal right to use his firearm

    (A) should do so only as a last resort.
    (B) should consider the moral implications of the use of deadly force.
    (C) should do so only when all other means of controlling the situation are insufficient.
    (D) all of the above

98. Officer Jenkins observes a man stab and kill another man in a crowded bar. The man is coming at the officer with a knife, but because of the crowd, the officer cannot get a clear shot. The officer

    (A) should not fire until certain that the lives of innocent persons will not be endangered.
    (B) should fire a warning shot in the air to stop the man.
    (C) should fire a warning shot into the floor to stop the man.
    (D) should retreat outside so as to get a clear shot when the man comes out.

99. Officers are issued firearms to

    (A) protect themselves from injury.
    (B) defend themselves against attack.
    (C) protect innocent persons from injury and attack.
    (D) defend themselves or a third person from the imminent use of deadly physical force.

100. "Deadly physical force" most clearly means that which

    (A) kills.
    (B) defends.
    (C) is used as a last resort.
    (D) is used when all other means are insufficient.

ANSWER KEY FOR CITY OF WINDSOR POLICE OFFICER EXAMINATION

1.	C	26.	C
2.	C	27.	A
3.	B	28.	B
4.	B	29.	C
5.	A	30.	B
6.	B	31.	B
7.	D	32.	C
8.	D	33.	D
9.	D	34.	B
10.	B	35.	D
11.	C	36.	C
12.	C	37.	C
13.	C	38.	A
14.	C	39.	C
15.	A	40.	C
16.	C	41.	B
17.	B	42.	D
18.	C	43.	D
19.	A	44.	D
20.	D	45.	D
21.	C	46.	A
22.	A	47.	D
23.	C	48.	C
24.	A	49.	D
25.	A	50.	C

51. C	76. D
52. C	77. C
53. C	78. B
54. D	79. A
55. A	80. A
56. A	81. A
57. C	82. D
58. D	83. A
59. A	84. D
60. A	85. B
61. C	86. B
62. B	87. C
63. A	88. B
64. C	89. C
65. B	90. A
66. D	91. B
67. D	92. C
68. A	93. C
69. C	94. C
70. B	95. A
71. C	96. C
72. B	97. D
73. A	98. A
74. D	99. D
75. C	100. D

ANSWERS AND ANALYSIS FOR CITY OF WINDSOR POLICE OFFICER EXAMINATION

Section 1

1. (C) Firing a warning shot (B) is inherently dangerous, far out of proportion to the seriousness of the incident, and a prohibited use of firearms by most departments. The officer observed the indecent exposure, so witnesses to the incident (D) are not critical. Police officers do not *allow* people who have committed criminal acts to *escape,* as offered in selection (A). The correct answer is (C), pursue and apprehend the man.

2. (C) The question asks for the *least* acceptable form of identification to write a summons, so you need to prioritize the answer choices. Answers (A), a state majority card, and (D), a photo identification from a local employer, are superior forms of identification in comparison to the others since the driver's picture is on them. Social security cards (C) are easily obtained and not normally sufficient forms of identification for police purposes. However, given the choice between a social security card and an out-of-state library card (C), the least acceptable form of identification is the library card.

3. (B) A four-year-old child standing alone and crying is cause for immediate police concern. Answers (C) and (D) are unacceptable because they indicate that the officer will leave without making direct contact with the child. Answer (A), using the radio to determine if any children have been reported missing, appears to be a correct answer until you consider that, regardless of the reply, there is still a four-year-old child alone and crying. The correct answer is (B), approach the child and ask where his parents are.

4. (B) Answer (D) is the easiest to eliminate. Police supervisors don't test officers by applying pry marks to windows. The question informs you that there had been a *rash of burglaries* in the area. Workers don't normally mar a window by leaving pry marks (C). Since it is *late at night,* the window has pry marks, there has been a rash of burglaries, and the window is slightly open, it would be more logical to think that the warehouse has been burglarized (B) than that the owner is inside (A).

5. (A) The question asks what the *first* thing you should do is. When a criminal hurts a victim in front of a police officer, there is always a tendency to pursue the assailant (B) and (D). The correct answer is to render first aid to the victim (A), even at the expense of allowing the criminal to escape.

6. (B) You are looking for the *least* descriptive factor among the answer choices to pick a person out of a crowd. All of the selections contain the suspect's height, weight, and hair color. All also contain the fact that the suspect is wearing a sweatshirt, jeans, and sneakers. The fact that the suspect is wanted for murder is *not* a factor in picking him out of a crowd. The main difference between choice (B) and the other answers is that (B) includes the suspect's name, which would matter least in picking him out of a crowd.

7. (D) Circle the words *easiest to spot* and *heavy traffic* in the question. Answers (A) and (C) are easily eliminated. A crack in one of the headlights and labeling on a tire are difficult to spot, even if the car *isn't* moving. Answer (D) is better than (A) because the dice can be seen whether the officer is behind or in front of the vehicle, while the emblem in the rear window can be seen only from the rear.

8. (D) Answer (A) can be eliminated. Unless it is a life-or-death situation, police officers are never justified in firing a gun to alert other officers to their location. If you answered (B), you're saying it's OK for police officers to kill to prevent a bloody nose. Killing a person is never justified to stop a person from killing an animal (C), as reprehensible as it may be. The only correct answer is (D), to prevent a suspect from striking a man in the head with a baseball bat because there is a likelihood that serious physical injury or death would result from the blow.

9. (D) In order to create an impression in the minds of criminals that there is no chance to commit a crime and that they would quickly be apprehended if they do, they must be *aware* of a police presence but not exactly certain when or where the police will be. Answer (B) can obviously be eliminated. Patrol *does* have a relationship to preventing crime. Answer (C) can be eliminated because of the words *primarily* and *residential areas*. The words *high-crime areas* in answers (A) and (D) provide a key that one of them is the correct answer. The choice between the two is the use of marked or unmarked police vehicles. The correct answer is (D). Marked police vehicles will deter crime more effectively than unmarked vehicles.

10. (B) If the fuel tank holds 18.4 gallons when full and one-fourth has been used, divide 18.4 gallons by four, which equals 4.6 gallons. Subtracting 4.6 from 18.4 gallons gives you the correct answer of 13.8 gallons remaining in the gas tank.

11. (C) Answers (A), (B), and (D) are all either forms of punishment or forms of retaliation. The correct answer is (C). Even if the person is in handcuffs, officers have the right to use a minimum amount of force to protect themselves from being assaulted.

12. (C) The question does not provide enough information to take any of the actions in (A), (B), or (D) until the officer finds out the answer to (C), determining why the driver is slumped over the wheel. Has the driver suffered a heart attack? Is the driver ill? Intoxicated? The victim of a crime?

13. (C) Answers (B) and (D) are incorrect because in each the officer leaves without checking the condition of an unconscious person lying in an alley. If in fact this *is* a medical emergency, then seconds count. The officer can't entrust another person with the care of a citizen (A). The most correct answer is (C), determine the condition of the unconscious man.

14. (C) The reading section is speaking about crimes being committed in an officer's presence when off duty or in emergency situations such as disasters, accidents, and medical emergencies. The most correct answer is (C). Officers have a responsibility to intervene if a crime occurs in their presence, even when off duty.

15. (A) To *preserve* is to maintain or keep from harm. The correct answer is (A), maintaining it in the same physical condition as it was left by the criminal. Answers (B), (C), and (D) can be accomplished only after (A).

16. (C) To answer the question correctly, the same theory is used as in answering question 5. The officer's primary obligation is to the heart-attack victim. In answers (A) and (B), the officer leaves the victim and pursues the vehicle. Answer (D) has a motorist acting as an agent for the police. Asking a civilian to give chase is not only foolhardy, but the potential for civil liability on the part of the officer and the department is great. The correct answer is (C)—continue giving first aid to the victim and use your portable radio to advise the police dispatcher of what happened and what the suspect vehicle looked like.

17. (B) If one pace equals three feet, then fourteen and one-half paces equals forty-three feet, six inches.

18. (C) According to the reading section, a person can be charged with manslaughter in the second degree with a motor vehicle only if (1) death occurs and (2) the death is a consequence of the driver being under the effect of an intoxicating liquor, drug, or both. This eliminates answers (A) and (B) because neither involves a death. Answer (D) involves three deaths, but there is no indication the driver was intoxicated. The correct answer is (C). The person was under the influence of a drug (cocaine) and struck a pedestrian, causing his death.

19. (A) To berate (B) is to scold severely. Police officers do not scold children. Answers (C) and (D) are plausible, but the common sense thing to do is open the wallet and see if anything is in it (A).

20. (D) The officers were dispatched to 1438 D Nelton Court (D). If you chose the wrong answer, you're not underlining or circling key words in the reading sections.

21. (C) The complainant was Janice Rodriguez.

22. (A) The officers were admitted to 1438 C Nelton Court by Silvia Ortiz.

23. (C) Don't read into the answer choices looking for a complicated answer. (D) is obviously wrong. Alarms don't cause windows to shatter. If the rock was thrown from over six feet (A), where did the blood come from? Answer (B) is plausible, but even if this is what occurred, it could *cause* the person who broke the window to be cut (C). Answer (C) makes the most sense.

24. (A) You have discovered that a person who you thought committed a crime is innocent. Answers (B), (C), and (D) prolong an innocent person's custodial arrest. The correct answer is (A), release him and inform him of the new evidence proving his innocence.

25. (A) Circle the words *elderly person, just returned from a trip, found her home burglarized, immediately notified the police,* and *first thing you should do is.* Before determining if anything is missing (D), locating the point of entry used by the burglar (C), or preserving the crime scene (B), make sure the burglar isn't still in the home (A).

26. (C) If you got this question wrong, you either forgot to add the value of the briefcase ($150) or you added the value of only one roll of 35-mm camera film ($3.99) when four were stolen, equalling $15.96.

27. (A) The reading section specifically states: *Upon arrest, all prisoners shall be handcuffed with their hands behind the back.* The correct answer is (A). Officer Barnes should have placed the prisoner in handcuffs when the arrest was made.

28. (B) Circle the word *false.* All of the answer choices are true according to the reading passage except (B). The reading section specifically says that prisoners should be kept in front and always be considered armed, even after a careful search.

29. (C) The reading section specifically states: *When circumstances permit, always obtain assistance when arresting an armed or dangerous criminal.* The question informs you that the driver is wanted for *murder* and should be considered *armed and dangerous.* The correct answer is (C). If possible, wait for assistance prior to placing the suspect under arrest.

30. (B) Circle the words *does not* in the question. You're looking for an answer that isn't *a noncriminal, social-service function.* Answers (C) and (D) obviously fall into this category and can be eliminated. This leaves a choice between (A) and (B). If you chose (A), you didn't circle the word *noncriminal.* Is parking over the limit at a meter *criminal*? The correct answer is (B), processing a prisoner after an arrest.

31. (B) Circle the words *minimizing the opportunity for criminal behavior.* It makes sense this would be done in proportion to (B), the amount of crime occurring within a specific area.

32. (C) The problem cited in the first line of the question is one of *speeding*. Circle the words *tactic* and *to prevent*. This should point you to (C), act as a deterrent.

33. (E) All of the answer selections relate to serving and protecting the public. The correct answer is (E), none of the above, because the question includes the word *not*.

34. (B) The youth committed a criminal act which could have resulted in another person's death. Granting the youth special treatment (because he plays baseball with your son), (A) and (D), is improper. A warning is not sufficient in this instance (C). The correct answer is (B), arrest the youth.

35. (D) Since all of the items in the answers could be used by the prisoner to harm himself or others, the correct answer is (D), all of the above.

36. (C) The diagram of the accident scene indicates that thirty-three feet of skid marks were left in the roadway by the Caprice.

37. (C) Answer (A) is incorrect. John Simmons's D.O.B. is 7/14/49, *not* 6/21/52. Answer (B) is incorrect. John Simmons was driving south on Union Place, but the vehicle operated by Ralph Johnson left thirty-three feet of skid marks, *not* the vehicle operated by Simmons. Answer (D) is incorrect. Johnson's D.O.B. is 6/21/52 and he does live at 110 Main Street, but he states that his vehicle was going approximately twenty miles per hour, *not* twenty-five miles per hour. The correct answer is (C). The registration number of the vehicle going west on Allyn Street is BL 694.

38. (A) Based on the totality of information available, the cause of the accident was (A), the driver of the Caprice going through the stop sign at the intersection of Allyn Street and Union Place. While the witness reports that the Caprice was moving *at a fast speed,* there is no reason to believe that both vehicles were doing so, as suggested in choice (B).

39. (C) Answer (A) is incorrect. Johnson was driving a 1991 Caprice west on Allyn Street, *not* a 1992 Vega south on Union Place. Answer (B) is incorrect. The driver of the vehicle with damage to the left front received a laceration to the forehead, *not* the driver of the vehicle with damage to the right front. Answer (D) is incorrect. The weather was clear and the roadway was dry. The correct answer is (C). Anderson was standing at the southeast corner of Union Place and Allyn Street.

40. (C) Answer (A) is incorrect. Simmons lives at 1411 Hanover Street, *not* 141 Hanover Street. Also, he was driving a 1993 Vega, *not* a 1991 Caprice. Answer (B) is incorrect. Anderson was not driving a vehicle. Answer (D) is incorrect. The vehicle with registration AU 134 had moderate damage to the left front, *not* minor damage. The correct answer is (C). Simmons was driving south on a one-way street.

41. (B) Robert Anderson provided the primary evidence indicating fault as an eyewitness to the accident.

42. (D) Circle the words *physical evidence* in the question. A witness (B) is not *physical* evidence. Look closely at the diagram of the accident scene. The skid marks start before the intersection and end slightly past the stop sign, indicating that the driver went through the stop sign without stopping. The correct answer is (D), the skid marks. Even if the stop sign were not present, the driver of the Caprice had an obligation to yield the right of way to the driver of the Vega.

43. (D) The accident diagram has a symbol indicating direction in the top left-hand corner. The parked vehicle is facing south on Union Place.

44. (D) The diagram indicates that the width of Union Place is fifty-three feet.

45. (D) The driver of the 1991 Caprice was most at fault in this accident.

46. (A) Physical evidence and eyewitness statements are always superior to statements made by the persons involved in an accident.

47. (D) The reading section specifically states that a *single photo should never be used.*

48. (C) Circle the words *incorrect procedure.* Answers (A), (B), and (D) are all *correct* procedures according to the reading section. The correct answer is (C) because of the word *dissimilar* in the answer. Photographs *should be of persons with similar physical appearances.*

49. (D) All of the statements are correct.

50. (C) According to the reading section, the primary purpose of showing photographs to witnesses and victims of crimes is to determine who committed the crime.

51. (C) Common sense is the key to selecting the correct answer to this question. Let's review the information the question provides. We know the operator of the vehicle is driving over the posted speed limit, but has the vehicle's emergency flasher on. The purpose of the emergency flasher is to warn other motorists. We know the operator is driving his wife to the hospital, that she is in labor, and that the officer observes her to be in "obvious distress." With the information provided, it should be obvious that the correct course of action is to get the woman medical care as quickly as safety will allow. Calling for an ambulance (D), or taking the time to issue a summons (A), needlessly delays getting the woman to the hospital. Answer (B) is incorrect because it does not fulfill the need to get to the hospital *safely.* The correct answer is (C), give the driver of the vehicle a police escort to the hospital.

52. (C) Circle the words *shotgun shell casing* and also *loaded .38 caliber, six-shot revolver with one empty cylinder*. Based on this information, we know that (A) is incorrect. The shotgun shell casing could not have come from the revolver. Nor could a .38 caliber revolver eject a shotgun shell casing onto the ground (B). The assumption should not be made that because a shotgun shell casing and a revolver with one empty cylinder are found in the parking lot that either a shotgun or the revolver were *fired* there (D)—although that might be the case. The correct answer is (C). The shotgun shell casing did not come from the revolver.

53. (C) Information provided in the question indicates that the person was strangled three hours *before* receiving the wound to the head, so the most logical answer is (C). The victim was strangled, struck on the head, and then thrown into the water.

54. (D) The officer seized fourteen ounces of cocaine.

55. (A) All of the answers except (A) are insensitive methods of handling the situation. The victim is *not* the suspect. The correct answer is the obvious one. Have a female police officer interview the victim.

56. (A) This question must be answered based on the totality of circumstances offered in the question. There is no indication that the car was involved in an accident (B) or that the car is abandoned (C). If all four windows are rolled down, the front plate is gone, the car has been backed up against a building so the rear plate can't be seen, the glove compartment is open, and papers are scattered throughout the car, it's most logical to assume the car is stolen.

57. (C) Police officers don't ask people if they live in the city (A) or whether they are taxpayers (B) prior to providing them police services. In answer (D), the word *serve* doesn't fit with *criminal behavior*. The correct answer is (C), serve and protect any person the officer encounters.

58. (D) The police vehicle traveled thirteen blocks, then another six blocks past the alley, plus another six blocks to return to the alley. This equals twenty-five city blocks. If each block equals one-tenth of a mile, the police vehicle traveled 2.5 miles (D).

59. (A) Police community relations are the direct result of each individual officer's interaction with members of the community.

60. (A) The term closest to *regulation* is *rule* (A).

61. (C) A man has been shot and points out a woman, saying she did it. The woman put something in her purse and ran. A reasonably prudent person would have cause to believe it is a gun. Answers (A), (B), and (D) all involve waiting because the officers are male and the suspect went into a women's restroom. The officers should pursue the woman and take her into custody (C), not only because she just shot someone, but because she may harm herself or another person in the restroom.

62. (B) Circle the words *first thing the officers should do*. There is reason to believe the suspect has a gun in her purse. Before (A), (C), or (D), the officers should ensure their safety by taking the purse from the suspect.

63. (A) The defense attorney has an obligation to try to make the jury doubt the guilt of his or her client.

64. (C) Police officers don't lie. Answers (A) and (B) would be lying to the reporter. Your supervisor just told you not to give the name of the child to the press, so (D), referring the reporter to your supervisor, would be incorrect. The correct answer is (C), tell the reporter you will not give out the name of the child until proper notification of next of kin has been made.

65. (B) Circle the words *elderly man* and *the fire is rapidly spreading* in the question. This is obviously an emergency situation calling for immediate action. The correct answer is (B), remove the elderly man to a position of safety.

66. (D) Regardless of what you have seen in the movies or on television, the police do not make deals, (A) and (B), with people they arrest. There is no reason to turn the case over to the narcotics squad (C). The correct answer is (D), proceed with the arrest process, making no deals or promises.

67. (D) The question states that *crime can never be totally eliminated*. The answer then must be (D), none of the above.

68. (A) Even though crimes happen to people and property, legally the crime is against the state, not the victim. Answer (C) suggests a common myth. The police officer is the initial person who decides whether charges will be preferred, not the victim. Answer (B), when, and (D), where, both come after the correct answer, ask the victim the name of her assailant (A).

69. (C) The first obligation of a police officer after administering first aid is to determine if a crime has been committed.

70. (B) It doesn't make sense to interview the customers gathered—(A), (C), or (D)—if they weren't there when the robbery occurred. The correct answer is (B), determine if the person you're interviewing was there when the robbery happened.

Section 2

71. (C) Rita Moreno was convicted of murder.

72. (B) Jose Melendes is missing the index finger on his left hand.

73. (A) Raymond Armeti has a tattoo of an eagle on his left shoulder.

74. (D) Frank Scarleti has a large mole on his left forearm.

75. (C) Barbara Johnson's alias is Richard Brown.

76. (D) The person convicted of bank robbery is John Cunningham. Answer choices (A), (B), and (C) are all true statements, so the correct answer is (D), all of the above.

77. (C) Jose Melendes was convicted of possession of narcotics.

78. (B) Barbara Johnson was born 9/18/55, *not* 6/18/45.

79. (A) Raymond Armeti was convicted of insurance fraud.

80. (A) Frank Scarleti was convicted of assault in the first degree with a firearm.

Section 3

81. (A) Circle the words *not an advantage*. You're looking for an advantage of foot patrol over vehicular patrol. Of the answer choices offered, only (A), increased opportunity to perform community relations work, is an advantage.

82. (D) Circle the words *primary benefit*. Of the answer choices offered, the primary benefit of foot patrol is (D), it relieves vehicle patrol units from responding to minor calls.

83. (A) Circle the word *not* in the question. Answers (B), (C), and (D) *are* contributing factors in deciding in *favor of* establishing a foot beat, so (A) is the correct answer.

84. (D) The reading section states that officers should not establish a pattern which can be observed by a criminal.

85. (B) Circle the word *except* in the question. Answers (A), (C), and (D) *are* all factors in determining the boundaries of foot patrol. Answer (B), the political make up of the area to be patrolled, is not a factor.

86. (B) Two officers walking together on foot is more costly than any of the other answer choices.

87. (C) Answer (A) is incorrect because an officer on foot would not be able to pursue a speeding vehicle. Answer (B) is incorrect because an officer on foot can't carry first-aid and oxygen equipment. Answer (D) is incorrect because it's a personal injury accident, and first-aid equipment will be needed. (Report forms will also be needed and officers on foot don't carry reports.) The correct answer is (C), report of a vehicle blocking a downtown driveway.

88. (B) Circle the word *disadvantage* in the question. Answer choices (A), (C), and (D) are *advantages*. The correct answer is (B), vehicular patrol, unlike foot patrol, does not allow for frequent citizen contact.

89. (C) The key to the answer is *where* the most people would likely be. The correct answer is (C), a large shopping mall.

90. (A) The reading section states that patrol should be conducted at random.

91. (B) If you answered (A), you're stating a police officer can kill someone for shoplifting a candy bar. The dog in answer (C) is on a leash and is not a threat to anyone. In answer (D), the man has a *plastic* bat. Answer (B) is correct because the dog is *biting* and *dragging* an *infant* by the *neck*. A reasonably prudent person would expect this to cause serious physical injury or death to the infant, so deadly force may be used.

92. (C) The key to answering this question is the word *imminent*. It's not enough for there to be danger—(A), (B), and (D). To kill, there must be *imminent* danger to life (C).

93. (C) The reading section specifically states that the only time an officer can fire at a moving vehicle is when the officer or a third person is in imminent danger of death or serious physical injury.

94. (C) The same rationale is used to answer this question as question 93. Answer (C) is correct because there is no imminent danger of deadly force being used against the officer by the vehicle's occupant.

95. (A) Whenever you see the words "deadly physical force" or "deadly force" on a police examination, substitute the word "kill." Answer (B) is incorrect because the word "deadly" is not present. A police officer would not be justified in killing a person because the person pushed him (used "physical force"). The same reasoning holds true for answer (C). Force, when used in this context, means the same thing as "physical force." Again, the word "deadly" is not used. The reading passage limits the use of a firearm to kill an animal to those presenting an "immediate, serious threat." Answer (D) is incorrect because there is no indication that the threat was either imminent or serious.

96. (C) Circle the words *young child, pointing,* and *loaded BB gun.* While it's true that a BB shot into the officer's eye *could* cause serious physical injury, the chances of this happening must be balanced against the officer's shooting the child. The correct answer is (C). The officer would not be justified in using his firearm.

97. (D) All of the answer choices are true statements. The correct answer is (D), all of the above.

98. (A) The reading section clearly prohibits the firing of warning shots, answers (B) and (C). The correct answer is (A). The officer should not fire until certain that the lives of innocent persons will not be endangered.

99. (D) The reading passage clearly states that the reason police officers have firearms is to protect themselves or a third person from the imminent use of deadly physical force.

100. (D) Deadly physical force most clearly means that which kills.

City of Newcastle

Department of Personnel

Police Officer Examination
Test #1453

Name: _____

SSN: _____ / _____ / _____

Date: _____

General Examination Directions

This examination consists of three separate parts. Use the answer sheet and pencils provided. *Print your full name and social security number on both the answer sheet and each separate part of the examination. Failure to do so will result in your examination being voided and your elimination from the testing process.*

Time: 3 hours
100 Questions

**DO NOT OPEN THE FIRST TEST BOOKLET UNTIL
TOLD TO DO SO BY THE TEST PROCTOR**

SECTION 1 OF 3

Booklet 1 of 4: Questions

Directions

This part of the examination consists of seventy questions designed to test your ability to apply judgment, reasoning, and analytical thinking to practical police situations. You have *one hour and forty-five minutes* to complete this part of the examination. Choose the *most* correct answer. Your time has begun. You may now begin.

1. You have been assigned to foot patrol in a busy section of downtown. A woman complains to you about a man standing in front of a department store making lewd, offensive remarks to women as they walk by. As you approach, the man begins to run. You should

    (A) pursue and apprehend the man.
    (B) draw your weapon and order the man to stop.
    (C) fire a warning shot to stop the man.
    (D) yell a warning to the man and resume patrol.

2. While walking your beat, you're approached by a man who says he slipped on the icy sidewalk in front of the city hall. The first thing you should do is

    (A) inspect the sidewalk to determine if it's icy.
    (B) notify police headquarters.
    (C) determine if the man is injured.
    (D) determine the man's identity.

3. As a police officer, you stop the operator of a 1993 Ford for a minor traffic violation. A check of the vehicle's registration via police radio indicates that the license plate is not stolen but belongs on a 1988 Chevrolet. Your most logical course of action is to

    (A) issue the driver of the vehicle a summons for driving with the wrong license plate on the vehicle.
    (B) tow the vehicle and issue the driver a summons.
    (C) advise the driver of the vehicle about the license plate and ask for an explanation.
    (D) call for a backup officer and place the driver under arrest for misuse of the license plate.

4. While on patrol, you observe that a red light at a busy intersection is inoperable, causing a dangerous condition. Your most appropriate course of action is to

   (A) notify headquarters and direct traffic until portable stop signs arrive.
   (B) notify headquarters to have someone fix the light and then continue on patrol.
   (C) position your police vehicle so motorists will slow down.
   (D) position your police vehicle to act as a deterrent.

5. While on patrol, you're approached by a citizen who advises you his car was broken into while parked in another city. Police regulations prohibit the investigation of incidents out of the city in which you're a police officer. You should

   (A) explain to the citizen why you can't take his complaint and direct him to the appropriate agency.
   (B) take the complaint and forward the paperwork to the city where the crime occurred.
   (C) advise the citizen that you're prohibited by department regulations from getting involved.
   (D) drive the citizen to the place the incident occurred and facilitate his filing a police report.

6. Prior to going on patrol, you're instructed by your sergeant to give extra attention to the parking lots in your area. Reports have been received that stolen vehicles are being brought to parking lots behind housing projects and are being stripped of their parts. While on patrol you observe a newer-model Cadillac up on jacks in a parking lot behind a housing project. Two young men are removing its tires. Your most appropriate course of action is to

   (A) approach with your weapon drawn and order both men down on the ground.
   (B) notify headquarters, approach with caution, and order both men down on the ground.
   (C) notify headquarters, request a backup, and plan an approach with the second officer from two separate directions.
   (D) advise your sergeant of the situation and wait for the sergeant's arrival.

7. You respond to a call from the manager of a bus station. Upon arrival, you're informed by the manager that she received an anonymous call that a bomb is in locker 42. The manager used a key to look inside and saw a briefcase in the locker. You should

   (A) have the manager remove the briefcase from the locker and take it to a secure area.
   (B) ask the manager if she wants to evacuate the building.
   (C) notify headquarters, request a bomb expert, and evacuate the building.
   (D) x-ray the briefcase to see what's inside.

8. If a police vehicle is traveling fifty-two miles per hour, how many miles would it travel in fifteen minutes if its speed remained constant?

   (A) 8 miles
   (B) 10 miles
   (C) 13 miles
   (D) 18 miles

9. At 10:00 P.M., you go to 114 Main Street, apartment A-2, responding to a complaint from Ronald Vaughn of loud music coming from apartment A-3. Upon arrival you can hear that the music is very loud. Mr. Vaughn complains that he can't sleep and has asked Mr. Anderson in apartment A-3 to turn the music down, but he has refused. Your most appropriate course of action would be to

   (A) take a written complaint from Vaughn and secure an arrest warrant for Anderson.
   (B) ask Anderson to turn the music down to a reasonable level.
   (C) advise Anderson to turn off the music or you'll arrest him.
   (D) use a tape recorder to record the decibel level of the music for evidence in court.

10. You're a police officer working the front desk of police headquarters. Donald Higgins walks in and says that he wants to report a hit-and-run accident. Higgins states that four days ago his car was struck while parked in a local parking lot, causing moderate damage to the left front end. He has no idea who struck his car. Which of the following should you determine first?

    (A) Is the car insured for damage?
    (B) Why did Higgins wait four days to report the accident?
    (C) Exactly where did the accident take place?
    (D) Where is the vehicle located now?

11. While on foot patrol, you hear the sound of glass breaking and observe two youths running from next to a parked vehicle with its driver's window broken out. It would be most logical to think that

    (A) the youths broke the vehicle's window.
    (B) the youths heard the sound of the vehicle's window breaking and were afraid.
    (C) the window imploded due to the elements.
    (D) there is no relationship between the youths and the vehicle's broken window.

12. You're on patrol and drive by a home which the owners have reported to the police will be vacant while they are on vacation. You observe a ladder, which wasn't there the day before, propped up against the house and leading to a second-floor bedroom window. Your most appropriate course of action is to

    (A) make a note in your log of the date and time the ladder was observed for future reference.
    (B) investigate and determine if the home has been burglarized.
    (C) notify headquarters and ask them to call the owner.
    (D) remove the ladder from the house so it can't be used to gain entry.

13. A mail carrier stops you while you're walking your beat and hands you a purse he found in the mailbox. The purse contains photographs, cosmetics, and a business card with this information: Eileen Ceresky, Vice President, Sales, 232-7119. No money is in the purse. Your most appropriate course of action is to

(A) interrogate the mail carrier to determine if he stole money from the purse.
(B) advise the mail carrier to turn the purse over to postal authorities.
(C) telephone Eileen Ceresky and determine if the purse is hers.
(D) put the purse in the trunk of a police vehicle to secure it until its owner notifies the department.

14. An off-duty police officer on a city bus observes a passenger take out a knife, rob another passenger, and get off the bus. The officer makes no attempt to intervene or take action relative to the robbery. The officer's conduct is

(A) appropriate. A police officer is just a private citizen when off duty.
(B) appropriate. The officer could have been injured if he had intervened.
(C) appropriate. The officer has jurisdiction only when he is working.
(D) inappropriate. The officer should notify police headquarters of the suspect's description and direction of travel.

15. While on patrol, you drive your police vehicle behind several stores to check the doors to the backs of the buildings. You find a large screwdriver on the ground next to the entrance of a closed restaurant. There are jimmy marks on the door. Your most appropriate course of action is to

(A) make a notation in your log and continue on patrol.
(B) determine if the restaurant has been burglarized.
(C) notify headquarters via radio to call the owner.
(D) return to your vehicle and establish a surveillance.

16. Police regulation 15-1 states, "Uniformed police officers are prohibited from smoking in department vehicles and/or in view of the public." It most clearly follows that

(A) all members of the force must be nonsmokers.
(B) a uniformed officer directing traffic should not smoke.
(C) uniformed officers may smoke in department vehicles on meal breaks.
(D) detectives may not smoke in police headquarters.

17. While on patrol, you observe a man stopping pedestrians and asking for money. You should

(A) ignore the situation. Panhandling has become common.
(B) arrest the man for panhandling.
(C) advise the man that his actions are illegal and that a repeat offense may lead to his arrest.
(D) submit a report to headquarters relative to the matter.

18. Police officers should keep their radio transmissions as brief as possible to avoid

    (A) having criminals record their conversations.
    (B) taking up valuable radio time.
    (C) confusion.
    (D) monitoring by citizens with police scanners.

19. You're taking the description of a robbery suspect from a victim. Which of the following would be the most difficult part of the suspect's description for him to alter?

    (A) a tatoo on his right forearm
    (B) a beard and mustache
    (C) the color of his hair
    (D) the missing nails on two of his fingers

20. Officer Peters is interviewing the victim of an assault. Of the following, which is least important?

    (A) the name of the person who witnessed the assault
    (B) a complete description of the person who committed the assault
    (C) the name of the person who committed the assault
    (D) the name of the person who was assaulted

21. One definition of probable cause is "less than proof, but more than mere suspicion that a person committed a crime." In order to make an arrest, a police officer must have probable cause that a person committed a crime. This most clearly means that

    (A) police officers need proof of a crime before a person can be arrested.
    (B) an arrest may be made only if an officer observes a crime being committed.
    (C) a police officer must have probable cause a person committed a crime in order to arrest.
    (D) evidence that a crime has been committed is sufficient to arrest a person.

22. Officer Richard Burns responds to a call regarding a burglary that took place at a gift shop. The store owner, Mr. Boyce, reports that a backpack valued at $49.95 was stolen and probably used to carry the following stolen property out of the store:

4 signed and numbered paperweights, each valued at $325.00	
2 crystal vases, each valued at	45.00
2 opal rings, each valued at	62.00
cash	125.62

    Officer Burns is completing a report of the burglary. What is the total value of the items stolen?

    (A) $1,390.00
    (B) $1,515.62
    (C) $1,639.62
    (D) $1,689.57

23. While walking your beat, you observe a man and a woman arguing loudly outside a restaurant. You walk over to investigate, and the man, the manager of the restaurant, says that the woman didn't pay for her meal. Your first action should be to

   (A) arrest the woman and take her to headquarters.
   (B) ask the woman to pay for her meal.
   (C) advise the manager that it's not a police matter.
   (D) determine the facts of what occurred.

24. A police officer responds to a call of a sick person in an apartment. Upon arriving, the officer is rushed into the bathroom by the victim's wife, where the officer finds an unconscious man on the floor with a syringe sticking out of his arm. A small glassine bag, containing the residue of what the officer suspects is heroin, is lying next to the man. The first thing the officer should do is

   (A) arrest the man and his wife.
   (B) arrest the man.
   (C) call an ambulance for the man.
   (D) remove the syringe from the man's arm.

25. While walking your beat, you observe a vehicle double park. The driver of the vehicle asks you to watch his car while he runs into the bank to cash an "important" check. You should

   (A) agree to monitor the vehicle, since it's the fastest way to remedy the situation.
   (B) instruct the driver to move the vehicle and find an appropriate parking space.
   (C) issue the driver a ticket for improper parking.
   (D) place the driver under arrest for impeding traffic.

26. While on patrol, you stop a motorist for going through a stop sign. Running the driver's name through "stops and warrants," you learn she has two outstanding arrest warrants on file for passing bad checks. She states that if she misses work she will lose her job, but if you let her go she will turn herself in after work. You should

   (A) allow her to proceed after obtaining the name and address of her employer.
   (B) place the woman under arrest, but tell her you will not execute the arrest warrants until she turns herself in.
   (C) place the woman under arrest and serve the warrants.
   (D) notify headquarters that the woman will turn herself in, but obtain a specific time.

Answer question 27 based on the following state statute.

State Statute 50a-121—Criminal Lockout: A landlord, owner, or agent of such landlord or owner shall not deprive a tenant of access to his or her dwelling without a court order allowing the landlord, owner, or agent to do so. Violation of this statute shall be treated as a criminal misdemeanor, punishable by less than one year in prison.

27. Based on state statute 50a-121, it would be most logical for a police officer to effect an arrest in which of the following circumstances?

    (A) A building superintendent will not allow a person claiming to be the relative of a tenant into an apartment.
    (B) A landlord, without a court order, puts a padlock on a tenant's door, refusing him access for failure to pay his rent.
    (C) An agent of a landlord, who does have a court order to deny access, refuses to allow an evicted tenant entry into her former apartment.
    (D) A landlord refuses to repair a leaking faucet in an apartment.

28. You're a police officer sent to investigate the report of a crowd gathered at a city intersection. Upon arrival, the first thing you should do is determine if

    (A) a crime has been committed.
    (B) any evidence should be preserved.
    (C) there are any witnesses to the crime.
    (D) the crowd is illegally gathered.

29. How many words in the following sentence are spelled incorrectly? "The body was found with abrasions to the head and several auxillary marks and contusions to the lower extremities."

    (A) one
    (B) two
    (C) three
    (D) four

30. While responding to a radio call relative to an abandoned car, you're flagged down by a citizen who says that a youth just stole his briefcase and ran down an alley. You should

    (A) notify headquarters to send another officer to the scene to take the citizen's complaint.
    (B) advise the citizen that you're on another call but will come back after you're finished to take the complaint.
    (C) advise headquarters of the crime and attempt to apprehend the youth.
    (D) take the man with you to investigate the abandoned car and take his complaint on the way.

31. Officer Jerry Downing makes his rounds using the same pattern at the same time every day. Merchants often remark that they can set their watches to Officer Downing walking by their windows. This practice is

    (A) appropriate. It's good community relations for the officer to be thought of as punctual.
    (B) inappropriate. Officers who fill in on Officer Downing's days off will be unfamiliar with his schedule.
    (C) appropriate. Citizens will know where and when to contact Officer Downing.
    (D) inappropriate. Officer Downing should vary his routine so criminals can't anticipate his actions.

32. Police officers wear uniforms so they

    (A) can easily be identified.
    (B) can integrate into a semimilitary system.
    (C) can be properly supervised.
    (D) will instantly recognize one another.

33. While walking your beat, you're approached by a youth who advises you that his friends are playing in an abandoned building and he thinks it's dangerous. You should

    (A) tell the youth it's not good to inform on his friends.
    (B) call the station to determine if the abandoned building is dangerous.
    (C) investigate whether the youths are in the abandoned building.
    (D) bring the youth to headquarters to take a written statement.

34. You have been assigned by your sergeant to relieve an ill school-crossing guard at an elementary school. You're to assist children crossing the street. Your tour of duty ends at 3:00 P.M., and it's now 3:05 P.M. It would be most appropriate to

    (A) report back to headquarters. Your tour of duty is over.
    (B) ask one of the children to go into the school and advise a teacher that you will be leaving.
    (C) stay at your post and use your radio to request a relief.
    (D) ask a teacher to cross the children, as your tour of duty is over.

35. While walking your beat, you issue several cars parking tickets for parking in a "tow zone." As you're doing so, a man approaches, informing you that the car you just ticketed belongs to a state senator and that he is the senator's driver. He asks you to take back the ticket. Your most appropriate course of action is to

    (A) obtain the senator's name, take the ticket back, and submit a written report.
    (B) inform the senator's driver that you will not void the ticket.
    (C) advise the man not to worry because you won't turn in your copy of the ticket .
    (D) tell the driver that if he complains further you will tow the vehicle.

36. A twenty-year-old woman has been reported missing by her husband. Which of the following would be most helpful in positively identifying the woman?

    (A) the missing woman's full name and date of birth
    (B) the fact the woman has a large mole on her face
    (C) a complete description of the clothing last worn by the woman
    (D) the woman's maiden name

Answer question 37 based on the following.

    Police officers are precluded from using more force than reasonably necessary to overcome and subdue a resisting person in facilitating a lawful arrest.

37. In which of the following situations did the officers act correctly, according to the above statement?

    (A) Officers Jones and Gonzales chase a shoplifting suspect along the street and down an alley. The suspect tries to climb a chain-link fence but falls, breaking his ankle. Both officers kick the suspect and handcuff him.
    (B) Officer Johnson chases a youth who "bails out" of a stolen car. The officer catches the youth and slaps him several times in order to "retrain" him.
    (C) Officer Nelson interrupts a drug transaction. One of the men pulls a gun, and the officer hits the man on the wrist with his nightstick, knocking the gun to the ground. The man suffers a broken wrist.
    (D) Officer Sanchez tells a suspect, wanted on a warrant for passing bad checks, not to move. The suspect takes a step forward, and the officer hits the suspect in the stomach with her nightstick.

38. You are assigned to tow vehicles illegally parked within a specific area of downtown where many complaints have been received. You have given a vehicle a ticket, and the tow truck has arrived to tow the vehicle. The owner of the vehicle runs up to you, and he offers to move the car. You should

    (A) tow the vehicle. Its owner should have thought of the consequences prior to parking it illegally.
    (B) advise the owner that it's too late now. The wrecker has arrived.
    (C) allow the owner to move the vehicle and warn him about parking illegally in the future.
    (D) have the wrecker operator start to tow the vehicle but then release it to the owner so as to teach him a lesson.

39. While on vehicle patrol late at night, you notice that one of the headlights on the police vehicle is inoperative. Your shift ends in one hour. You should

    (A) notify headquarters and immediately have the headlight fixed.
    (B) continue on patrol. The next officer can have the headlight repaired.
    (C) contact your supervisor and ask what his or her recommendation is.
    (D) finish the rest of your tour of duty on foot and turn the vehicle in when you get off work.

40. You respond to the scene in which an oil truck has flipped over, spilling a large amount of oil onto the roadway. The driver of the truck is not injured. The first thing you should do is

(A) notify the fire department.
(B) secure the scene and detour traffic away from the spill.
(C) put up flares next to the spill to alert motorists.
(D) call a wrecker for the truck.

Answer question 41 based on the following.

Only in exigent circumstances or emergency situations shall officers (male or female) search persons of the opposite sex who have been placed under arrest.

41. In which of the following situations would it be incorrect for an officer to search a person under arrest?

(A) A male officer searches a female arrested for shoplifting.
(B) A female officer searches a male arrested for possession of narcotics and suspected of carrying a concealed weapon.
(C) A male officer searches a male youth after arresting him for sale of crack cocaine.
(D) A female officer searches a female prostitute after arresting her for soliciting.

42. While transporting a prisoner arrested for larceny to the detention facility, the prisoner advises you he has severe chest pains. The prisoner is doubled over in the back seat groaning. Your most appropriate course of action would be to

(A) transport the prisoner to the nearest hospital for medical treatment.
(B) ignore the prisoner. He is probably faking.
(C) continue on to the detention facility and check his condition upon arrival.
(D) notify headquarters and ask for instructions on where they want you to take the prisoner.

43. You are instructed by your sergeant to participate in a narcotics raid with a squad of detectives. While conducting the raid, you observe a detective put his finger in a plastic bag and taste a substance believed to be cocaine. This method of testing is

(A) appropriate. The detective is giving the substance a field test.
(B) inappropriate. It will now be difficult to accurately measure exactly how much cocaine was in the bag.
(C) appropriate. This is an inexpensive method of testing for drugs.
(D) inappropriate. Police officers should never put suspected drugs in their mouths.

44. While you are on foot patrol, a merchant complains to you about two sidewalk vendors in front of her store operating without city permits. The first thing you should do is

    (A) tell the merchant that vendors have as much right to sell their products as she does.
    (B) ask the vendors if they have permits.
    (C) arrest both vendors for selling merchandise without a permit.
    (D) call city hall to determine if the vendors are authorized.

45. The axiom "officers should keep their private lives unsullied" most clearly means that

    (A) officers should conduct their private lives in a decent and honorable fashion.
    (B) officers off duty should ensure that they are appropriately attired prior to leaving their homes.
    (C) officers should be careful in their private lives not to disagree with established authority.
    (D) off-duty officers must be clean and neat at all times.

46. All of the following are examples of police corruption except a police officer who

    (A) provides an informant with money in order to make a controlled purchase of narcotics in an undercover operation.
    (B) rewards addicts by giving them narcotics.
    (C) sells criminals narcotics in exchange for stolen goods.
    (D) accepts free meals at a restaurant on his or her beat.

47. Part of a police officer's responsibility is to investigate suspicious conduct. Of the following, the least likely person for an officer to stop due to suspicious conduct is

    (A) a person driving by the same location several times and who appears to be referring to a street map.
    (B) a fourteen-year-old female loitering in front of a bar.
    (C) a man emerging from an alley who looks all around and then darts back down the alley.
    (D) an older man sitting in a school parking lot for a long period of time with his car's engine running.

48. A large part of a police officer's duties involve providing noncriminal services. All of the following are examples of services performed by police officers and which are noncriminal in nature with the exception of

    (A) searching for a missing person.
    (B) investigating a complaint of harassing phone calls.
    (C) directing traffic.
    (D) reporting safety and fire hazards.

49. "To detect" most clearly means

    (A) to discover.
    (B) to investigate.
    (C) to find.
    (D) to locate.

50. While on patrol in the early morning hours, you observe that a car has struck a fire hydrant. The vehicle is vacant, but the headlights and radio are on and the engine is still hot. Based on these facts, it would be most logical to think that

    (A) the driver of the car left the vehicle in order to evade responsibility for the accident.
    (B) the accident was the result of drunk driving.
    (C) the accident occurred a short time ago.
    (D) the driver of the vehicle is injured.

51. You're a newly-appointed police officer. You respond to a disturbance, along with other officers, in which several firearms have been confiscated. Your sergeant hands you a loaded shotgun, instructing you to eject the shells from the weapon. You're not sure how to do it. You should

    (A) attempt to eject the shells. If your attempt fails, put the weapon aside.
    (B) tell your sergeant you don't know how to eject the shells.
    (C) hand the weapon to another officer and ask him to do it.
    (D) put the weapon in the trunk of a police vehicle and read up on how to eject the shells later.

52. You're on patrol and observe an ambulance being operated with its flashing lights and siren on. The ambulance stops for a red light and then proceeds through it. The driver and passenger are seen to be laughing and both drinking from bottles. A short distance later the ambulance turns off its flashing lights and siren. Your most appropriate course of action is to

    (A) continue on patrol. An ambulance has a right to use its flashing lights and siren.
    (B) follow the ambulance to see if the pattern is repeated.
    (C) stop the ambulance and investigate the driver's and passenger's behavior.
    (D) submit a report to the company that owns the ambulance.

53. Officer Peter Hopkins is preparing a report about a sexual assault. On which of the following should Officer Hopkins focus his report?

    (A) the factual circumstances relative to the crime
    (B) the officer's opinion concerning why the crime occurred
    (C) the perception of a relative that the victim fabricated the assault
    (D) the length of time spent by the officer in collecting physical evidence

54. You're directing traffic at a busy downtown intersection. You put your hand up for a motorist to stop. The motorist, an elderly man, stops and then continues, almost causing an accident. The driver tells you he thought that you motioned him forward. Your most appropriate course of action would be to

(A) guide the driver safely on his way.
(B) issue the driver a summons for failure to obey your signal.
(C) severely admonish the driver but allow him to leave.
(D) have the driver pull to the curb and observe your signals as training for the future.

55. You're instructed by your supervisor to guard the door of an apartment in which a homicide has taken place. You're told not to let anyone in and to make no statement to the press about what has occurred. Several reporters arrive at the scene and ask you what has happened. Your most appropriate response would be to tell the press

(A) that you have been told by your supervisor not to speak with the press.
(B) that you are not authorized to comment on the investigation.
(C) that several bodies have been found, but you're not certain what's going on.
(D) to leave the scene or you'll place them under arrest.

56. While on foot patrol, you observe an empty vehicle with its engine running parked outside of a bank. Your most appropriate course of action is to

(A) notify headquarters and immediately investigate.
(B) issue the vehicle a parking ticket and tow it.
(C) wait for the vehicle's operator to appear.
(D) make a note in your log and continue on patrol.

Answer question 57 based on the following.

Larceny in the fifth degree—53-121: A person commits larceny in the fifth degree when the value of the property or service exceeds $250.

Larceny in the sixth degree—53-121a: A person commits larceny in the sixth degree when the value of the property or service is $250 or less.

57. Officer Barbara Jefferson responds to a department store where she finds that two store detectives have apprehended a woman who left the store with the following merchandise without paying:

2 blouses, one valued at $29.35 and the other valued at $32.00
1 headband valued at $3.65
1 14-karat gold bracelet valued at $185.00

The suspect should be charged with

(A) shoplifting.
(B) larceny.
(C) larceny in the fifth degree.
(D) larceny in the sixth degree.

58. While off duty, an officer is seated in a restaurant where he observes an argument between a man and a woman. The man is seen to violently slap the woman on the face several times, grab her by the hair, and drag her from the restaurant. The woman is crying and trying to push herself away from the man, but she is unable to do so. The officer watches while he pushes her into a car and leaves the scene. The officer takes no action, later telling his supervisor that he is a private citizen when off duty, and he thought it was just an argument between husband and wife. The officer's conduct was

(A) appropriate. The woman did not ask for the police to be summoned.
(B) inappropriate. The officer should have called the police station.
(C) appropriate. It is the restaurant manager's job to notify the police.
(D) inappropriate. A crime was being committed in the officer's presence, and he should have intervened.

59. You're a police officer in uniform on foot patrol. You observe a man hurriedly exit a jewelry store and, upon seeing you, turn and rapidly go in the other direction, repeatedly looking back over his shoulder at you. Of the following, the most appropriate course of action would be to

(A) proceed immediately into the store and determine if a crime occurred.
(B) make a note in your log of the man's description.
(C) follow the man from a distance and see where he goes.
(D) notify headquarters that a robbery is in progress at the jewelry store.

60. While on patrol, you notice that the interior of a package store is dark, hours before it normally closes. The front door is closed but not locked. You see through the glass door that the counter is littered with broken bottles and that there appears to be blood on the floor. The first thing you should do is

(A) break down the front door and enter.
(B) check the rear door and see if it's locked.
(C) notify headquarters via radio and take up a position outside.
(D) enter and determine if a crime has been committed.

61. In which of the following circumstances would it be least desirable for a police officer to unholster his or her weapon and have it at the ready?

(A) when approaching a suspect who is believed to be armed with a firearm
(B) when approaching a suspect in order to serve an arrest warrant
(C) when entering a department store where it has been reported that shots have been fired
(D) on a narcotics raid where the occupants of an apartment are alleged to have automatic weapons

62. Crime would cease within our society if there were no

(A) offenders
(B) recidivists
(C) adjudication proceedings
(D) prisons

63. Which of the following criminals is most likely to be armed with a handgun?

   (A) a shoplifter
   (B) a con artist
   (C) a flimflam artist
   (D) a narcotics trafficker

64. Officers Pawlina and Jepesen go to 114 White Street to serve an arrest warrant for Samuel Jones for carrying a deadly weapon in a motor vehicle. The most critical thing the officers should be certain of is that

   (A) they arrest the right person.
   (B) they go to the correct address.
   (C) they ensure their own safety.
   (D) the correct vehicle is at the location.

65. A sergeant was heard to remark in a training class, "Remember, your radio is faster than your police cruiser. If you have a serious crime and are chasing someone, call it in." It follows that

   (A) officers should use their radios whenever it appears that a crime has been committed.
   (B) through use of the radio, other officers can get in position ahead of the suspect.
   (C) not using the radio is a direct violation of the sergeant's orders.
   (D) the radio should be used only in emergency situations.

66. You're obtaining the description of a stolen vehicle. Which of the following information is most important?

   (A) the vehicle's license plate number
   (B) the vehicle's color
   (C) the vehicle's engine identification number
   (D) the make and year of the vehicle

67. Which of the following descriptive factors concerning a man wanted for murder would be most valuable for an officer on motorized patrol?

   (A) The suspect is twenty-eight years old.
   (B) The suspect has a tattoo on his left shoulder.
   (C) The suspect is Asian and six feet, three inches tall.
   (D) The suspect is an illegal alien.

68. You are on foot patrol and hear the sound of vehicles colliding. Within seconds, you're at the scene and see that two vehicles have struck each other in an intersection. As you approach, the man who was driving one vehicle gets out and runs away. The other driver is unconscious. Your most appropriate course of action is to

(A) pursue the man who is running and capture him before he gets away.
(B) fire a warning shot to stop the man.
(C) notify headquarters of the fleeing man's description and render first aid to the injured driver.
(D) have a citizen check the injured driver, notify headquarters to send an ambulance, and pursue and capture the driver who ran.

69. You're on foot patrol in a housing project. You enter an apartment complex from the back door and observe a man sitting on the steps injecting himself with a needle. You detain him, conduct a field test, and determine the syringe contains heroin. You should

(A) call an ambulance for the man. He is addicted to a drug.
(B) ask the man if he obtained the needle through the shared-needle program.
(C) request that the narcotics squad respond to the scene.
(D) place the man under arrest.

70. Upon arriving at the scene of a reported street shooting, you observe a man lying in the street, bleeding from a gunshot wound to the head. A second man is standing over him with a gun in his hand. The first thing you should do is

(A) determine if a crime has been committed.
(B) draw your weapon and order the man to disarm himself.
(C) check on the victim.
(D) tell the man with the gun that you will shoot him if he blinks an eye.

SECTION 2 OF 3

Booklet 2 of 4: Readings and Questions

Directions

This part of the examination consists of two reading sections. At the end of each section are questions relative to the subject matter you have read. There are eight questions following reading section 1 and twelve questions following reading section 2. You may retain the reading sections while you answer the questions. Your time has begun. You now have *sixty minutes* to answer questions 71 through 90.

READING SECTION 1: THE CIVIC CENTER INCIDENT

Definitions:

- Robbery

   A person commits robbery when, in the course of committing a larceny, he uses or threatens the immediate use of physical force upon another person.

- Larceny

   A person commits larceny when, with intent to deprive another of property or to appropriate the same to himself, he wrongfully takes, obtains, or withholds such property from an owner.

- Arrest

   Arrest is the taking into custody of a person by a police officer to bring said person before a court to answer for a crime he is alleged to have committed.

   Officer Joseph Kubiak is assigned to a foot beat located in the downtown area. A major part of his responsibility is patrolling in and around a large civic center. More than one hundred stores, restaurants, and specialty shops are in the civic center. It also has a huge sports arena which draws large crowds from throughout the state.

   At 7:00 P.M., Officer Kubiak was in the civic center walking past Cameron's Pharmacy when he heard the sound of a commotion coming from inside. Looking through the front window, the officer saw Robert Jones, whom he knew to be the store manager, chasing a man down the store's center aisle and yelling something at him. As

235

the man ran out of the store, Jones yelled to Officer Kubiak, "Stop him! He just stole some money!"

Kubiak quickly asked Jones what had happened, and Jones informed the officer that he was in the process of giving a customer her change from a purchase when the suspect suddenly reached over and snatched a twenty-dollar bill out of his hand.

Kubiak used his portable radio to advise the police dispatcher that he was in pursuit of a suspect in the main corridor of the civic center. He then moved rapidly along the corridor and caught a glimpse of the suspect darting down a stairway leading to the building's basement. Kubiak knew the stairway led to a chained door and that there was no way the suspect could get out of the building without coming back up the stairway.

Kubiak was joined by Officer Patricia Jenkins, who had heard Kubiak's message over the radio. He informed her of what had transpired at Cameron's Pharmacy. Both officers had begun descending the stairway leading to the basement when they observed the suspect slowly coming up the stairs toward them.

The suspect stopped and shrugged. "You got me. There's no way out."

Kubiak placed the suspect under arrest and searched and handcuffed him. Jenkins then advised the suspect of his constitutional rights. While searching the suspect, who identified himself as Paul Somers, D.O.B. 11/20/70, of 313 South Street, Kubiak found a single twenty-dollar bill in Somer's left, front jacket pocket. The suspect had no other currency in his possession.

Kubiak notified the police dispatcher via portable radio that the suspect was in custody at 7:10 P.M. Kubiak accompanied Jenkins and the suspect outside, where he was placed in Jenkin's police cruiser to be transported to the booking room. Returning to the pharmacy, Kubiak interviewed Jones, the store manager, and two witnesses to the incident, Mrs. Beatrice Fleming, D.O.B. 9/19/19, of 114 West Street, and Mrs. Ramona Johnson, D.O.B. 4/16/45, of 141 Park Street. Fleming told Kubiak that she had purchased some shampoo and had given Jones a fifty-dollar bill to pay for the item. As Jones was handing her the change from the fifty dollars, the suspect suddenly reached over and snatched some money out of Jones's hand and began to run. Johnson verified Fleming's account of what had occurred and added she thought the suspect got away with "a lot of money." Jones, who is thirty-two years old and lives at 131 Sigourney Street, advised Kubiak that the suspect snatched only one of two twenties he had in his hand from the $47.29 in change he was giving to the customer. The suspect stole only twenty dollars.

Kubiak wrote an arrest report relative to the incident and turned in the twenty dollars he took from the suspect to the property room at the end of his shift as evidence to be used in court.

Answer questions 71 through 78 based on the reading passage.

71. The suspect was

   (A) advised of his constitutional rights by Kubiak.
   (B) not advised of his constitutional rights.
   (C) advised of his constitutional rights by Jenkins.
   (D) advised of his constitutional rights by Fleming.

72. All of the following statements are true except:

    (A) The suspect's name is Paul Somers, and he lives at 313 South Street.
    (B) The manager of Cameron's Pharmacy is thirty-two years old.
    (C) Kubiak found currency in the suspect's front, right jacket pocket.
    (D) Ramona Johnson was born April 16, 1945.

73. Beatrice Fleming

    (A) lives at 114 West Street and had a twenty-dollar bill snatched from her hand.
    (B) was born 4/16/45 and lives at 141 Park Street.
    (C) told Kubiak that she thought the suspect got away with "a lot of money."
    (D) was not the victim of a crime.

74. The price of the purchase made by Fleming was

    (A) $2.12
    (B) $2.21
    (C) $2.71
    (D) $3.24

75. Based on the reading section, the suspect should be charged with

    (A) threatening
    (B) shoplifting
    (C) larceny
    (D) robbery

76. The suspect was

    (A) searched by Kubiak and handcuffed by Jenkins.
    (B) advised of his constitutional rights by Jenkins and arrested by Kubiak.
    (C) advised of his constitutional rights and searched by Kubiak.
    (D) searched, then arrested, then handcuffed.

77. According to the reading passage, all of the following are true except:

    (A) Threatening the immediate use of physical force while committing a larceny is a robbery.
    (B) Kubiak saw the store manager chasing the suspect inside Cameron's Pharmacy.
    (C) The suspect snatched money from the hand of Beatrice Fleming.
    (D) The money found on the suspect was turned in to the property room.

78. Which of the following people lives at 141 Park Street?

    (A) Ramona Johnson
    (B) Paul Somers
    (C) Beatrice Fleming
    (D) Robert Jones

READING SECTION 2: QUAKER HEIGHTS HOUSING PROJECT

Officers Salvatore Mercante, unit 119, and Donald Evans, unit 120, are beat officers assigned to the Quaker Heights Housing Project. At 8:10 P.M., the officers heard the following radio broadcast from the police dispatcher.

"Units 119 and 120, respond to 148 Bellevue Street, apartment D4, on a report from Mrs. Jennifer Salerno in apartment B4 of a person shot. An ambulance has been notified. Unknown if the suspect is still at the scene. You're looking for one Raymond Gonzales, age forty-two, a Hispanic male, five feet, eight inches, one hundred and seventy pounds, brown hair, wearing jeans, black sweatshirt, and sneakers, armed with a handgun. Other units are on the way."

Upon arriving at the scene, Mercante and Evans observed four people in the hallway and heard screams coming from inside apartment D4. Entering, they observed a Hispanic female, later identified as Isabella Cortez, holding a Hispanic youth, later identified as Domingo Sanches, fifteen, of 148 Bellevue Street, apartment D4, in her arms. Sanches had been shot in the abdomen, but was still alive. While Evans gave Sanches first aid, Mercante asked Cortez what happened. She stated that her husband, Raymond Gonzales, accidently shot their son as both struggled over a handgun Sanches had brought home. An ambulance arrived at 8:17 P.M., and Sanches was transported to Mount Vernon Hospital. Cortez told Mercante that Gonzales ran from the apartment and was probably at his mother's home, located at 123 Sigourney Street, apartment A11.

Evans interviewed a witness to the shooting, Jennifer Salerno, who stated Sanches and Gonzales argued over the proceeds from Sanches's sale of crack cocaine, and when Sanches wouldn't pay his father his cut, Gonzales shot him in the stomach. Thomas Brown, of 146 Bellevue Street, apartment B2, told Mercante that Salerno's version of what happened was true. While Mercante was speaking with Brown, Officer Paul Cummings entered the apartment and gave Officer Evans a .38 revolver he said a person who identified himself as James Younger, age twenty-seven, of 146 Bellevue Street, apartment B3, had handed him, saying he found it in the bushes next to the apartment building. Closer questioning of Younger by Evans revealed that he had observed Gonzales throw the weapon there as he ran out of the building.

Mercante had notified headquarters via telephone of the address of the suspect's mother's home and, at 8:43 P.M., was advised by Officer James Garrett that Raymond Gonzales, also known as Pedro Hernandes, was in custody. At 8:47 P.M., unit 119 was advised that Domingo Sanches had been pronounced dead at 8:37 P.M. Raymond Gonzales was subsequently charged with murder. The scene was secured by unit 120 while unit 119 accompanied the witnesses to headquarters.

Answer questions 79 through 90 based on the above reading section.

79. Which of the following statements is true?

    (A) Jennifer Salerno witnessed the shooting and lives at 146 Bellevue Street, apartment D4.
    (B) James Younger lives at 146 Bellevue Street, apartment B3.
    (C) Domingo Sanches was the victim and lives at 123 Sigourney Street.
    (D) Unit 120 was advised by Garrett that the victim was pronounced dead.

80. The revolver was given to

    (A) Evans by Cummings.
    (B) Mercante by Evans.
    (C) Cummings by Mercante.
    (D) Mercante by Cummings.

81. Raymond Gonzales's alias is

    (A) Raymond Sanches.
    (B) Raymond Cortes.
    (C) Pedro Hernandes.
    (D) James Younger.

82. Domingo Sanches was given first aid by

    (A) Cummings.
    (B) Mercante.
    (C) Evans.
    (D) unit 119.

83. The ambulance arrived how long after unit 120 was told to respond to the scene?

    (A) fourteen minutes
    (B) eighteen minutes
    (C) twenty-two minutes
    (D) none of the above

84. The shooting was originally reported to police headquarters by

    (A) Isabella Cortez.
    (B) Jennifer Salerno.
    (C) James Younger.
    (D) James Garrett.

85. The officer to whom James Younger originally gave the revolver is

    (A) Salvatore Mercante.
    (B) Donald Evans.
    (C) James Garrett.
    (D) Paul Cummings.

86. Upon arriving at the scene, the officers first observed

   (A) four people in the hallway.
   (B) a Hispanic female holding a Hispanic male.
   (C) Jennifer Salerno.
   (D) screams coming from an apartment.

87. With the exception of the victim, how many people witnessed the shooting?

   (A) two
   (B) three
   (C) four
   (D) five

88. Which of the following people claimed that the shooting was accidental?

   (A) Jennifer Salerno
   (B) Isabella Cortez
   (C) James Younger
   (D) Pedro Hernandez

89. Of the following, the prime suspect in the shooting was

   (A) Raymone Gonzalez
   (B) Thomas Brown
   (C) Domingo Sanches
   (D) Pedro Hernandes

90. Isabella Cortez told which officer that the suspect ran from the apartment?

   (A) unit 119
   (B) unit 120
   (C) James Garrett
   (D) Paul Cummings

SECTION 3 OF 3

Booklet 3 of 4: Information

Directions

This portion of the examination is designed to test your ability to retain observable information and facts and to draw inferences and make conclusions. The following page consists of a series of pictures and data about the persons in the pictures, which you will be allowed to study for *five minutes*. After five minutes, the page containing the pictures and facts will be taken from you, and you will not be able to refer to them while answering the questions. Answer questions 91 through 100 based on the pictures and data you have studied. You will have *ten minutes* to answer the questions.

Name: Frank Charmante   Alias: Frank the Shark
D.O.B.: 9/5/48   Hair: black   Eyes: brown
Height: 6'2"   Weight: 185 lbs.
Scars or Marks: bullet wound scar, left shoulder
Convicted of: conspiracy to commit murder

Name: Alice Franklin   Alias: Mary Johnson
D.O.B.: 4/18/74   Hair: brown   Eyes: brown
Height: 5'5"   Weight: 135 lbs.
Scars or Marks: none
Convicted of: possession of narcotics

Name: Joseph Lorenzo   Alias: Mighty Joe Young
D.O.B.: 11/6/54   Hair: black   Eyes: brown
Height: 5'11"   Weight: 190 lbs.
Scars or Marks: 3" scar on palm of right hand
Convicted of: patronizing a prostitute

Name: Paul Douglas   Alias: Paul Donovan
D.O.B.: 2/27/68   Hair: brown   Eyes: brown
Height: 5'8"   Weight: 165 lbs.
Scars or Marks: none
Convicted of: robbery, first degree

Name: Diane Thompson   Alias: Paula Archer
D.O.B.: 8/24/67   Hair: black   Eyes: brown
Height: 5'2"   Weight: 125 lbs.
Scars or Marks: tattoo of rose on left shoulder
Convicted of: kidnapping

SECTION 3 OF 3

Booklet 4 of 4: Questions

91. Which of the following statements is true?

    (A) All the persons in the pictures have brown eyes.
    (B) Paul Douglas's alias is Mighty Joe Young.
    (C) Frank Charmante has a three-inch scar on the palm of his right hand.
    (D) Diane Thompson was convicted of possession of narcotics.

92. The person convicted of kidnapping is

    (A) Frank Charmante.
    (B) Alice Franklin.
    (C) Diane Thompson.
    (D) Paul Douglas.

93. Paul Douglas is also known as

    (A) Frank the Shark.
    (B) Joseph Lorenzo.
    (C) Paul Donovan.
    (D) Frank Charmante.

94. Which person has a tattoo of a rose on the left shoulder?

    (A) Alice Franklin
    (B) Paul Douglas
    (C) Diane Thompson
    (D) Frank Charmante

95. The person convicted of conspiracy to commit murder is

    (A) Frank Charmante.
    (B) Alice Franklin.
    (C) Joseph Lorenzo.
    (D) Paul Douglas.

96. Which person has no scars or marks and was born on February 27, 1968?

   (A) Alice Franklin
   (B) Joseph Lorenzo
   (C) Paul Douglas
   (D) Diane Thompson

97. The person convicted of patronizing a prostitute is

   (A) Frank Charmante.
   (B) Joseph Lorenzo.
   (C) Paul Douglas.
   (D) Paul Donovan.

98. Which of the following statements is true?

   (A) Alice Franklin's alias is Paula Archer.
   (B) Joseph Lorenzo's alias is Paul Donovan.
   (C) Diane Thompson's alias is Mary Johnson.
   (D) Pauls Douglas's alias is Paul Donovan.

99. The person convicted of bank robbery in the first degree is

   (A) Paul Douglas.
   (B) Frank Charmante.
   (C) Joseph Lorenzo.
   (D) Mary Johnson.

100. The person who has a bullet-wound scar on the left shoulder is

   (A) Frank the Shark.
   (B) Mighty Joe Young.
   (C) Paul Donovan.
   (D) Joseph Lorenzo.

ANSWER KEY FOR
CITY OF NEWCASTLE
POLICE OFFICER EXAMINATION

1.	A	26.	C
2.	C	27.	B
3.	C	28.	A
4.	A	29.	A
5.	A	30.	C
6.	C	31.	D
7.	C	32.	A
8.	C	33.	C
9.	B	34.	C
10.	B	35.	B
11.	A	36.	B
12.	B	37.	C
13.	C	38.	C
14.	D	39.	A
15.	B	40.	B
16.	B	41.	A
17.	C	42.	A
18.	B	43.	D
19.	A	44.	B
20.	B	45.	A
21.	C	46.	A
22.	D	47.	A
23.	D	48.	B
24.	C	49.	A
25.	B	50.	C

51.	B	76.	B
52.	C	77.	C
53.	A	78.	A
54.	A	79.	B
55.	B	80.	A
56.	A	81.	C
57.	D	82.	C
58.	D	83.	D
59.	A	84.	B
60.	D	85.	D
61.	B	86.	A
62.	A	87.	B
63.	D	88.	B
64.	A	89.	D
65.	B	90.	A
66.	C	91.	A
67.	C	92.	C
68.	C	93.	C
69.	D	94.	C
70.	B	95.	A
71.	C	96.	C
72.	C	97.	B
73.	D	98.	D
74.	C	99.	A
75.	C	100.	A

ANSWERS AND ANALYSIS FOR CITY OF NEWCASTLE POLICE OFFICER EXAMINATION

Section 1

1. (A) Answers (B), draw your weapon and order the man to stop, and (C), fire a warning shot to stop the man, are prohibited in most police departments. Drawing a weapon means you're prepared to kill someone. If you answered (B) or (C) then what you're really saying is that you would kill a person for making an offensive remark. Answer (D) implies that if the man doesn't stop, you don't feel that the woman's complaint is serious enough to pursue him. That's incorrect. The correct answer is (A), pursue and apprehend the man.

2. (C) Circle the words *the first thing you should do is* in the question. Before (A), (B), or (D), it would be common courtesy and correct procedure to determine if the man is injured (C).

3. (C) An officer checking a license plate over the radio and finding that current records indicate that the plate doesn't belong on a vehicle doesn't necessarily mean the operator has committed a violation. The driver may have just purchased the vehicle and a new registration was issued. Issuing a summons (A), towing the vehicle (B), or arresting the driver (D), may result, but first you should ask the driver why the license plate doesn't match the vehicle (C).

4. (A) An inoperable traffic signal is a very dangerous condition. To notify headquarters to fix the light (B) isn't enough. After you leave, a fatality could occur. Parking your cruiser, (C) and (D), will not prevent an accident. The correct answer is (A), notify headquarters and direct traffic until portable stop signs arrive.

5. (A) Circle the words *Police regulations prohibit the investigation of incidents out of the city in which you're a police officer.* This eliminates answer (B), and the obvious intent of the regulation also eliminates answer (D). Answer (C) is technically correct, but leaves the citizen not knowing what to do. The *best* answer is (A), explain why you can't take the complaint and direct the citizen to the agency that *can* investigate his complaint.

6. (C) You don't really have enough information to be certain a crime is being committed. It may be the man's car, a relative's, or a friend's. To point your gun at them (A) and order them down on the ground (B) is use of force and improper. Even if they *were* stealing the parts or had stolen the vehicle, would it be appropriate to "kill" both of them? Calling your supervisor to the scene (D) is inappropriate. Nothing has happened yet. The correct answer is (C)—wait for another officer, plan your approach from two different directions in case the young men *do* run, and assess the situation based on their reaction to the approach of a police officer.

7. (C) Don't touch anything which might be a bomb unless you've been specially trained in handling explosives. Answers (A) and (D) both involve moving the briefcase and are incorrect. Answer (B) is partially correct, but answer (C) is far superior. Notify headquarters, request a bomb expert, and evacuate the building.

8. (C) Divide four into fifty-two and the correct answer is thirteen miles.

9. (B) Answer (D) is obviously wrong. Recording sound on a tape recorder in which the volume can be turned up or down is useless. It's not against the law to listen to music. Answer (A) is incorrect. Arrests are made only when all other methods of handling the situation don't work. Answer (C) is incorrect. Police officers don't *threaten* people with arrest; they explain alternatives. The commonsense answer is (B), ask Mr. Anderson to turn down the music.

10. (B) Circle the words in the question *Which of the following should you determine first?* It's unusual for someone to wait four days to report an accident, and the *first* thing the officer should ask is *why* Mr. Higgins waited. The answer to that question could change the meaning of the answers given to (A), (C), and (D).

11. (A) Answer (C) is obviously wrong. When was the last time you saw a vehicle's window implode due to the elements (weather)? People don't usually run after hearing glass breaking (D)—more likely they'd stop what they are doing and look where the sound emanated. The answer could be (B), but the question would have to offer something more, such as another person near the car. It would be more logical to think that the youths broke the vehicle's window (A) than that they were afraid of the sound of glass breaking.

12. (B) Since the owners of the house have reported to the police that their home will be vacant, and a police officer didn't see the ladder there the day before, it's inherent in the way the question is worded that the police have a responsibility to act. Note that the ladder is leading to a point of possible access into the home. Merely making a note in a log and driving off (A) or moving the ladder (D) would be very embarrassing if burglars were inside or had been there and left after stealing the owners' property. Calling the owners on vacation to advise them a ladder is up against the house (C) accomplishes nothing. The correct answer is (B), investigate and determine if the home has been burglarized.

13. (C) Why would the mail carrier bother to give the purse to a police officer if he stole money from it (A)? Since you have the name and phone number of a person to call, it doesn't make sense to put the purse in the trunk of a car and wait for the owner to notify the police department (D). Many people don't report lost or stolen items to the police. Answer (B) needlessly delegates a task to another agency, which may or may not be the proper authority. The commonsense answer to the question is (C), telephone the person whose business card is in the purse and ask if it's hers.

14. (D) A very serious criminal act was committed in the presence of a police officer. Police officers have an obligation to take action when a crime is committed in front of them, even when off duty. This eliminates (A), (B), and (C). The minimum the officer should do is notify police headquarters that a robbery has taken place and provide a description and direction of travel of the criminal.

15. (B) Finding jimmy marks on a door and a screwdriver means either someone tried to get in or *did* enter. To just make a notation and continue on (A) is incorrect. Establishing a surveillance by yourself (D) will do little good if the burglar exits from a window or door you can't see. Calling the owner (C) would come after the correct answer, determine if the restaurant has been burglarized (B).

16. (B) The question and police regulation makes it clear that officers are not to smoke in public view while in uniform. There are few occasions when a police officer is considered *not* to be in public view. Of the answer selections, the most flagrant violation of this policy would be (B), an officer smoking while directing traffic.

17. (C) Again, think of arrest as a last resort, when all other methods of handling the situation don't work or when an arrest is obviously called for, such as in a robbery with violence. Police officers don't ignore crimes (A) or merely submit reports when a crime occurs in front of them (D). To arrest (B) is viable, but the most correct answer is (C), advise the man that his actions are illegal and that a repeat offense *may* lead to an arrest.

18. (B) Answer (C) is obviously wrong, and people have a right to monitor police broadcasts (D). Answer (A) would be correct except for the word *recording*. The use of that word doesn't make sense. The best answer is (B). The radio should be kept clear for emergency use, not casual conversation.

19. (A) A beard and mustache (B) are easily shaven, and hair color (C) can simply be changed. Missing nails (D) can be replaced with fake nails. The correct answer is (A). A tattoo would be the most difficult to alter.

20. (B) Circle the word *least* in the question. Prioritize the answer choices. Without the victim, there is no crime. Answer (D), the name of the person who was assaulted, is the most important of the answer choices. The next most important fact is (C), the name of the person who committed the assault. The name of a witness to the assault (A) is next most important. The *least* important fact of the answer choices offered is (B), a complete description of the person who committed the assault.

21. (C) Officers do not need *proof* of a crime to make an arrest (A). If this were the case, we wouldn't need courts. If (B) were correct, there wouldn't be many arrests. Most crimes are not committed in front of police officers. Answer (D) is incorrect because the officer must have evidence that a *particular* person committed a crime to make an arrest, not just the fact that a crime was committed. The correct answer is (C), a police officer must have probable cause that a person committed a crime in order to arrest. This is almost word for word from the question.

22. (D) If you got the answer to this question wrong, you forgot to add in the value of the backpack ($49.95) or failed to notice that there were *four* paperweights, *two* vases, and *two* rings. Pay attention to what you're reading. The answer to the question is simple math, and you can't afford to get questions like this one wrong. The correct answer is (D), $1,689.57.

23. (D) The manager saying that the woman didn't pay for her meal isn't enough information for you to arrest her (A). Maybe she did pay, and the manager is mistaken. It could be that there was a disagreement over what was ordered or about the quality of the food. The question asks for the *first* thing (action) you should do. The correct answer is (D), determine the facts of what occurred. Find out what happened before you make a decision to *do* anything.

24. (C) Circle the words *unconscious man on the floor* and *first thing the officer should do is* in the question. Unless there is another life in immediate danger and the officer's action would keep the situation from becoming worse, the correct answer to these types of questions is almost always to render aid or summon help to care for a sick person. Even if the person did commit a crime, arrest can come later if necessary. Before doing anything else, the first thing you should do is call an ambulance for the man.

25. (B) If you agree to *monitor* the vehicle (A), then you have assumed responsibility on behalf of yourself and the police department for the vehicle and everything in it. Police officers don't watch vehicles for people while they run errands. The commonsense answer is (B), instruct the driver to move the vehicle and find an appropriate parking place.

26. (C) An arrest warrant is an order from a judge to take a person into custody. Once an officer knows there is a valid arrest warrant for the woman, the officer should place the woman under arrest (C).

27. (B) Answer (A) is incorrect. The landlord is *not* depriving a tenant access into the apartment, but a person *claiming* to be a *relative* of a tenant. Answer (C) is incorrect. The agent of the landlord does have a court order as outlined by the state statute allowing him to refuse access to the apartment. Answer (D) has nothing to do with depriving a tenant access to a dwelling. The correct answer is (B). A landlord, who does not have a court order allowing him to do so, denies a tenant access by placing a padlock on the tenant's door. Failure to pay rent is a civil matter. The lockout, as defined by the state statute, is a crime.

28. (A) Circle the words *the first thing you should do is* in the question. The first thing you should do is (A), determine if a crime has been committed. Answers (B), (C), and (D) would not logically follow until after (A) has been determined.

29. (A) The only word not spelled correctly is *auxillary*. It should be spelled *auxiliary*.

30. (C) Responding to a radio call about an abandoned car is minor in comparison to a person who was *just* the victim of a theft. The key words in the question are *a youth just stole his briefcase and ran down an alley*. The crime occurred moments before your arrival, and you have an opportunity to apprehend the person who did it. Answers (A), (B), and (D) will almost certainly allow the criminal to escape. The correct answer is (C), advise headquarters of the crime and attempt to apprehend the youth.

31. (D) The primary objective of foot patrol is to prevent crime from occurring. The correct answer is (D), the officer should vary his patrol patterns (routine) so criminals can't anticipate his actions.

32. (A) Police officers wear uniforms so they can easily be identified by the public.

33. (C) We want to encourage people to approach police officers, not (A), tell the youth it's not good to inform on his friends or (D), bring the youth to headquarters to take a written statement. Answer (B) is obviously wrong. All abandoned buildings are dangerous. The correct answer is (C), investigate whether the youths are in the abandoned building.

34. (C) Obviously, you can't leave elementary school children to cross the street by themselves (A). Nor can you delegate your responsibility to anyone else, (B) and (D). The correct answer is (C), stay at your post and use your radio to request a relief.

35. (B) Police officers can't allow anyone to use political pressure to stop them from doing their jobs. That's why the lady holding the scales of justice wears a blindfold. Police officers must perform their jobs impartially, applying the same standard to all persons. The correct answer is (B), inform the senator's driver you will not void the ticket.

36. (B) Circle the words *positively identifying the woman* in the question. Although (A), (C), and (D) are important, *positive* identification almost always requires a *physical* attribute, such as fingerprints, dental records, or in this case, the fact that the woman has a mole on her face (B).

37. (C) In answers (A) and (B) the officer's actions are an abuse of force and are criminal. Answer (D) is an improper use of force by the officer. The correct answer is (C) because the suspect pulled a gun and the officer's actions were reasonable. His life was in imminent danger.

38. (C) The objectives are to get the vehicle moved from a position in which it's illegally parked and to deter the driver from illegal parking in the future. If a parking ticket has been issued, it doesn't make sense *not* to allow the owner of the vehicle to move the car. To tow the vehicle, (A) and (B), after the owner has offered to move it, is improper. Answer (D) is not only improper, but an abuse of police power. The correct answer is (C), allow the owner to move the vehicle and warn him about parking illegally in the future.

39. (A) Police officers cannot knowingly allow mechanical defects to exist on *their* vehicles which they would ticket a private citizen for. The correct answer is (A), notify headquarters and immediately have the headlight fixed.

40. (B) Circle the words *the driver of the truck is not injured* and *the first thing you should do is* in the question. Answer (D), call for a wrecker is incorrect. It's the last thing a police officer would do among the choices offered. Flares (C) next to an oil spill could ignite the oil, causing a fire and the truck to explode. You would want to call the fire department (A) but not before securing the scene and detouring traffic away from the spill (B). In these types of questions, the correct answer is almost always to render first aid to the injured or keep the accident scene from getting worse.

41. (A) Circle the word *incorrect* in the question. Answer (B) is *correct* procedure because the female officer arrested a person *suspected of carrying a concealed weapon*, which creates an exigent circumstance. The female officer's life would be in danger if she *didn't* search the man. Answer (C) is *correct* procedure because it's a *male* officer and a *male* youth. Answer (D) is *correct* procedure because it's a *female* officer and a *female* person arrested. The answer to the question is (A). It would be *incorrect* procedure, according to the reading section, for a *male* officer to search a *female* shoplifter. There is no emergency situation or exigent circumstance.

42. (A) Circle the words *severe chest pains* and *the prisoner is doubled over in the back seat and groaning* in the question. Prisoners have as much right to medical attention as anyone else. These are the symptoms of a possible heart attack. The correct answer is (A), transport the prisoner to the nearest hospital for medical treatment.

43. (D) Police officers test drugs by putting some on their finger and tasting it only in the movies. Street cocaine is usually only eight to fourteen percent pure. That means it's at least eighty-six percent something else, such as strychnine. Most police officers wear plastic gloves on narcotics raids and don't even feel comfortable touching the bags these substances are in! The correct answer is (D). This method of testing is inappropriate. Police officers should never put suspected drugs in their mouths.

44. (B) Just because the merchant says the vendors don't have permits doesn't make it so. Once again, the simple, commonsense answer is correct. Ask the vendors if they have permits. It logically follows that you would ask them to produce it, and if they couldn't, then (D) and (C) might follow.

45. (A) The word *sullied* means soiled or tarnished. In the context of the axiom, the most correct answer is (A), officers should conduct their private lives in a decent and honorable fashion.

46. (A) Answers (B) and (C) are both criminal acts. Answer (D) is a violation of all police departments' codes of conduct. The correct answer is (A), a police officer who provides an informant with money in order to make a controlled purchase of narcotics in an undercover operation.

47. (A) Circle the word *least* in the question. Prioritize the answer selections. Answers (B) and (C) are obviously very suspicious behavior. This leaves a choice between answers (A) and (D). Answer (A) is the correct choice because it provides a *reason* for the person to be driving by the same location several times. The driver is referring to a street map. This is much less suspicious than (D), an older man sitting in a car in a school parking lot for a long period of time with the engine running.

48. (B) Searching for missing persons (A), directing traffic (C), and reporting safety and fire hazards (D), are all noncriminal functions performed by the police. The correct answer is (B), investigating a complaint of harassing phone calls. The use of the word *investigating* should have been a strong clue to you that (B) is the correct answer.

49. (A) *To detect* means to discover.

50. (C) Circle the words *early morning hours* and *vacant, but the headlights and radio are on and the engine is still hot* in the question. There is no reason to believe (A), (B), or (D) at this point in the investigation. The driver may have left to call the police. The correct answer is (C), the accident occurred a short time ago.

51. (B) A loaded gun doesn't forgive mistakes. The correct answer when you don't know how to do something is to tell your sergeant you don't know how to do it (B).

52. (C) In order for an ambulance to use its flashing lights and siren, it must be on an emergency call. If on an emergency call, the ambulance can legally go through a red light after stopping and making sure it's safe to do so. Although the call may have been canceled, causing the driver to turn the flashing lights and siren off, the laughing, drinking, and totality of circumstances surrounding everything the officer saw is cause for the officer to investigate (C).

53. (A) Police officers focus their investigations and the reports they generate about them on the factual circumstances relative to a crime. Although (C) and (D) are factors and (B) is important, (although the use of the word *opinion* negates it somewhat), answer (A) is most correct.

54. (A) Circle the words *elderly man* in the question. The correct answer to this question (A) would be appropriate for a driver of any age, but it's especially so for someone elderly.

55. (B) Circle the words *You're told not to let anyone in and to make no statement to the press* in the question. Answer (C) is then obviously wrong. The reporters have not committed a crime, so (D) is incorrect. Answer (B), you're not authorized to comment on the investigation, is a much better choice than (A), you have been told by your supervisor not to speak to the press.

56. (A) An empty car with its engine running outside of a bank has all the elements of a getaway car in a bank robbery. Answers (B) and (D) are incorrect because they don't address the problem posed in the question, and there is no reason to believe the car is parked illegally. The correct answer, notify headquarters and immediately investigate (A), is a superior course of action to merely waiting for the vehicle's owner to appear (C).

57. (D) If you add up the value of the stolen property, it comes to exactly $250. The correct answer is (D), larceny in the sixth degree. If you got the question wrong, you didn't circle the words *$250 or less* in the reading section preceding the question.

58. (D) An obvious crime has been committed in the presence of a police officer. An off-duty police officer has an obligation to intervene if a crime is committed in his or her presence.

59. (A) The information provided in the question would arouse the suspicion of anyone observing the man's behavior that he had done something wrong. However, you don't *know* the jewelry store has been robbed (D). Even so, people in the store *may* be hurt or have been the victims of a crime. This eliminates answers (B) and (C). The appropriate course of action would be to proceed immediately into the store and determine if a crime occurred (A).

60. (D) If you answered (A), break down the front door and enter, you're not reading the question carefully. The question states that the front door is closed but *not* locked. There is no reason to check the rear door (B). There appears to be blood on the floor and someone might be hurt inside, so why would you take up a position outside as offered in answer (C)? The correct answer is (D), enter and determine if a crime has been committed.

61. (B) Circle the words *least desirable* and *unholster his or her weapon* in the question. In answers (A), (C), and (D) it *would* be appropriate for a police officer to have the gun out and at the ready. It would *not* be appropriate for a police officer to have the gun drawn when approaching a suspect to serve an arrest warrant (B), unless the officer believed his or her life or the life of another person was in imminent danger.

62. (A) If people didn't violate the law there would be no crime. The correct answer is (A), offenders.

63. (D) A narcotics trafficker (a person using and/or selling drugs) is much more likely to be armed with a handgun than is a shoplifter, con artist, or flimflam artist.

64. (A) When serving an arrest warrant, it's important to make sure that the person you're arresting is the same person listed on the warrant as committing the crime.

65. (B) Just because a crime has been committed (A) doesn't mean it's necessary for an officer to use the police radio. The sergeant's remarks in a training class were not an order (C), nor are police radios used *only* for emergency situations (D). The correct answer is (B), through use of the radio, other officers can get in position ahead of the suspect.

66. (C) The color of a vehicle (B) is easily altered, and license plates (A) can simply be changed. The make and year of the vehicle (D) are important, but the correct answer is (C), the vehicle's engine identification number, because it's very difficult for a person to alter.

67. (C) Circle the words *officer on motorized patrol*. Of the answer choices, an Asian who is six feet, three inches tall would be easiest to spot.

68. (C) Once again, you're given a choice between rendering first aid or pursuing a suspect. The correct answer is (C), notify headquarters of the man's description and render first aid to the injured driver. Rendering first aid is always the first concern, even at the expense of allowing a suspect to get away.

69. (D) The person is committing a crime in your presence. You should place the man under arrest.

70. (B) Information provided in the question would lead you to believe a crime has been committed, so eliminate (A). Before you can check on the victim (C), the correct response is to draw your weapon and order the man to disarm himself (B).

Section 2

71. (C) The suspect was advised of his constitutional rights by Jenkins.

72. (C) Circle the word *except* in the question. Answers (A), (B), and (D) are all true. Answer (C) is *not* true. Kubiak found currency in the suspect's *left*, front jacket pocket, not in his *right*, front jacket pocket.

73. (D) Beatrice Fleming does live at 114 West Street but did *not* have a twenty-dollar bill snatched from her hand (A). (It was snatched from Jones's hand.) She was born 9/19/19, *not* 4/16/45 (B) and does *not* live at 141 Park Street. Johnson, *not* Fleming, told Kubiak that she thought the suspect got away with "a lot of money" (C). The correct answer is (D). Fleming was not the victim of a crime. The victim of the crime was Jones.

74. (C) Fleming gave the store manager, Jones, a fifty-dollar bill to purchase some shampoo. Jones stated that he was giving Fleming $47.29 in change. The price of the purchase was $2.71.

75. (C) There was no force or threat of force by the suspect. The correct answer is (C). The suspect should be charged with larceny.

76. (B) Answer (A) is incorrect. The suspect was searched by Kubiak but *not* handcuffed by Jenkins. He was handcuffed by Kubiak. Answer (C) is incorrect. The suspect was *not* advised of his constitutional rights by Kubiak. He was advised of his rights by Jenkins. Answer (D) is incorrect. The suspect was arrested, then searched, then handcuffed. The correct answer is (B). The suspect was advised of his constitutional rights by Jenkins and arrested by Kubiak.

77. (C) The suspect did not snatch money from the hand of Beatrice Fleming. He snatched the money from the hand of Robert Jones.

78. (A) Ramona Johnson lives at 141 Park Street.

79. (B) Answer (A) is incorrect. Jennifer Salerno witnessed the shooting, but she lives at 148 Bellevue Street, apartment B4, *not* 146 Bellevue Street, apartment D4. Answer (C) is incorrect. Domingo Sanches lives at 148 Bellevue Street, apartment D4. Answer (D) is incorrect. Unit 119, *not* unit 120, was advised the victim was pronounced dead, and the reading section doesn't say that it was Garrett who made the notification. The correct answer is (B). James Younger lives at 146 Bellevue Street, apartment B3.

80. (A) Cummings gave the revolver to Evans.

81. (C) Raymond Gonzales's alias is Pedro Hernandes.

82. (C) Domingo Sanches was given first aid by Evans.

83. (D) Unit 120, Evans, was dispatched to the scene at 8:10 P.M. The ambulance arrived at the scene at 8:17 P.M. The correct answer is (D), none of the above. Seven minutes is not one of the answer choices.

84. (B) The shooting was originally reported to police headquarters by Jennifer Salerno.

85. (D) James Younger gave the revolver to Paul Cummings.

86. (A) They observed four people in the hallway.

87. (B) Isabella Cortez, Jennifer Salerno, and Thomas Brown witnessed the shooting.

88. (B) Isabella Cortez claimed that the shooting was accidental.

89. (D) The only correct answer is the alias used by Raymond Gonzales, Pedro Hernandes.

90. (A) Isabella Cortez told Mercante, unit 119, that the suspect ran from the apartment.

Section 3

91. (A) All of the suspects have brown eyes.

92. (C) Diane Thompson was convicted of kidnapping.

93. (C) Paul Douglas is also known as Paul Donovan.

94. (C) Diane Thompson has a tattoo of a rose on her left shoulder.

95. (A) Frank Charmante was convicted of conspiracy to commit murder.

96. (C) Paul Douglas has no scars or marks and was born February 27, 1968.

97. (B) Joseph Lorenzo was convicted of patronizing a prostitute.

98. (D) Paul Douglas's alias is Paul Donovan.

99. (A) Paul Douglas was convicted of robbery in the first degree.

100. (A) The person who has a bullet-wound scar on the left shoulder is Frank the Shark.

WRITING SKILLS AND VOCABULARY TEST QUESTIONS

There is a recent trend in police testing to include questions on the written examination requiring candidates to identify correct and incorrect spelling, grammar, word usage, and punctuation within a sentence. The proper preparation of police reports in support of criminal investigations often determines whether a crime will be solved or an arrested person successfully prosecuted. The ability of a police candidate to demonstrate simple rules of grammar, sentence construction, and spelling is directly related to good job performance.

This section is designed to provide examples of the type of test questions used to evaluate candidates' written and vocabulary skills and provide you with some tips to prepare yourself to achieve the highest possible score. Some departments intersperse writing skills and vocabulary questions within the police judgment section, while others group these questions in a separate booklet or section.

WRITING SKILLS EXAMINATION

Directions

This examination consists of one hundred questions designed to test your ability to identify words spelled correctly and incorrectly; use proper grammar, punctuation, and vocabulary; and recognize the correct use of a word or group of words. The test has three parts. Follow the directions immediately preceding each part.

Time: 95 minutes
100 Questions

Part I

Directions

Questions 1 through 50 contain five answer selections. Indicate whether there is an error in one of the underlined sections by choosing (A), (B), (C), or (D). If the question does not contain an error in spelling, grammar, punctuation, or word usage, mark (E), no error, for that question.

Mark all answers on the answer sheet. You have *forty minutes* to complete this part of the examination.

1. Police officers should never acept gifts or favors for doing their duty. no error
   (A)   (B)   (C)   (D)   (E)

2. It's especialy important for police officers to apply the law equally to all persons.
   (A)   (B)   (C)   (D)

   no error
   (E)

3. The officer submitted an afidavit in support of the arrest warrant. no error
   (A)   (B)   (C)   (D)   (E)

4. The officer inspected the patrol vehicle and found the first aid kit flares
   (A)   (B)   (C)

   and oxygen tank missing. no error
   (D)   (E)

5. Police manuals systematize policy and procedure in an orderly fashion. no error
   (A)   (B)   (C)   (D)   (E)

6. It's sometimes necesary for a police officer to use force when making an arrest.
   (A)   (B)   (C)   (D)

   no error
   (E)

7. To interupt people when they are speaking is not polite. no error
   (A)   (B)   (C)   (D)   (E)

8. Police officers should not fire their weapons unless their lives are in
   (A)   (B)   (C)

   iminent danger. no error
   (D)   (E)

9. A committe of citizens was formed to review the incident. no error
   (A)   (B)   (C)   (D)   (E)

10. The offense occured directly in front of the officer. no error
    (A)   (B)   (C)   (D)   (E)

11. The officer took down the names and addresses of all the witnesses.   no error
    (A)   (B)   (C)   (D)   (E)

12. Police officers are represenatives of the communities they serve.   no error
    (A)   (B)   (C)   (D)   (E)

13. The sherif served an eviction notice on the tenants of the building.   no error
    (A)   (B)   (C)   (D)   (E)

14. The police department consisted of regular and auxillary police officers.
        (A)   (B)   (C)   (D)
    no error
    (E)

15. The thief admitted to producing false identification.   no error
    (A)   (B)   (C)   (D)   (E)

16. The witness failed to coroborate the suspect's alibi.   no error
    (A)   (B)   (C)   (D)   (E)

17. The old drunk was inocuous but mentally incompetent.   no error
    (A)   (B)   (C)   (D)   (E)

18. Absenteism and a failure to be punctual are often corrected through
        (A)   (B)   (C)
    positive discipline.   no error
        (D)   (E)

19. The suspect used a pseudonym as an integral part of his plan to disapear.
            (A)   (B)   (C)   (D)
    no error
    (E)

20. The police commissioner used a private chanel to radio headquarters.   no error
                (A)   (B)   (C)   (D)   (E)

21. The victim was struck on the forehead but not seriously hurt.   no error
    (A)   (B)   (C)   (D)   (E)

22. One of the patience in the emergency room was a suspect in the shooting.
            (A)   (B)   (C)   (D)
    no error
    (E)

23. Accross the street from city hall is a commuter parking lot.   no error
    (A)   (B)   (C)   (D)   (E)

24. Three of the childrens bicycles were stolen.   no error
    (A)   (B)   (C)   (D)   (E)

25. The accident occurred four foot south of the telephone pole.   no error
    (A)   (B)   (C)   (D)   (E)

26. The officer did a through investigation of the crime scene.   no error
        (A)   (B)   (C)   (D)   (E)

27. The man attempted to embessle money from his company.   no error
         (A)   (B)   (C)   (D)   (E)

28. The man matched the description of the suspect but he had
        (A)   (B)   (C)

    an alibi for the time of the crime.   no error
              (D)   (E)

29. The officer found the knifes in the car.   no error
       (A)   (B)   (C)   (D)   (E)

30. The fraudulent obtaining of money is a larceny.   no error
        (A)   (B)   (C)   (D)   (E)

31. The person who perpetuated the crime was arrested by the officer.   no error
        (A)   (B)   (C)   (D)   (E)

32. The woman was on trail for shooting her husband.   no error
        (A)   (B)   (C)   (D)   (E)

33. If your arrested, you may need a lawyer.   no error
       (A)   (B)   (C)   (D)   (E)

34. When you're excepted into the police academy, you'll learn how to fire a gun.
              (A)   (B)   (C)   (D)
    no error
     (E)

35. The officer felt it was a privilege to be chosen to guard the president.   no error
        (A)   (B)   (C)   (D)   (E)

36. The officer obtained a warrant to sieze the car used in the crime.   no error
       (A)   (B)   (C)   (D)   (E)

37. Due to the absents of evidence, the case was dismissed.   no error
         (A)   (B)   (C)   (D)   (E)

38. The officer wieghed the cocaine to determine how much had been found.
             (A)   (B)   (C)   (D)
    no error
     (E)

39. Its four blocks from the police department to city hall.   no error
      (A)   (B)   (C)   (D)   (E)

40. The officer wasn't their when the order was given.   no error
       (A)   (B)   (C)   (D)   (E)

41. The officer had a great deal of familiarity with firearms. no error
    (A)   (B)   (C)   (D)   (E)

42. Illict narcotics are a violation of the statute. no error
    (A)   (B)   (C)   (D)   (E)

43. The addict had a perscription for the pills. no error
    (A)   (B)   (C)   (D)   (E)

44. The container in the car was red green and blue. no error
    (A)   (B)   (C)   (D)   (E)

45. There badge of office is a symbol of trust. no error
    (A)   (B)   (C)   (D)   (E)

46. The shotgun was accidentaly discharged. no error
    (A)   (B)   (C)   (D)   (E)

47. The sergeant asked for a statis report. no error
    (A)   (B)   (C)   (D)   (E)

48. The license plate was partialy obscured. no error
    (A)   (B)   (C)   (D)   (E)

49. The truck struck a dear crossing the road. no error
    (A)   (B)   (C)   (D)   (E)

50. The officer was instructed to protect the crime scene. no error
    (A)   (B)   (C)   (D)   (E)

Part II

Directions

Questions 51 through 90 contain a word or words left out. Fill in the blanks by choosing an answer which contains the correct spelling or word usage. You have *forty minutes* to complete this part of the examination.

51. The man was arrested for unlawful _____.

   (A) assembily
   (B) asembily
   (C) asembaly
   (D) assembly

52. The officer _____ responded to the scene.

   (A) promtaly
   (B) promtally
   (C) promptly
   (D) promtilly

53. The thief _____ to stealing the watch.

   (A) admitted
   (B) admited
   (C) amitted
   (D) admittead

54. The officer _____ checked the building.

   (A) carefally
   (B) carfully
   (C) carefully
   (D) carefuly

55. It was _____ gun.

   (A) somebody elses
   (B) somebody else's
   (C) somebody elsis
   (D) somebody elses'

56. The _____ stole the lawnmower.

   (A) nieghbor
   (B) neighbor
   (C) naybear
   (D) neigher

57. The suspect was charged with _____ of narcotics.

    (A) possesion
    (B) possessien
    (C) poseession
    (D) possession

58. The officer _____ the suspect.

    (A) pursuad
    (B) pursued
    (C) persued
    (D) persuede

59. The _____ of the bullet exceeded one thousand feet per second.

    (A) velocity
    (B) velicity
    (C) vilicity
    (D) volocite

60. The fuel _____ was broken.

    (A) gaige
    (B) gague
    (C) gaged
    (D) gauge

61. Both people in the mug shots looked _____.

    (A) similer
    (B) semilar
    (C) similar
    (D) simelar

62. The school _____ called the police.

    (A) principle
    (B) principal
    (C) principil
    (D) principale

63. The written order _____ the verbal instruction.

    (A) supersede
    (B) supercided
    (C) superceded
    (D) superseded

64. The officer was asked to _____ parking in the area.

    (A) facilitate
    (B) fecilitate
    (C) feciltate
    (D) facilitete

65. The building's _____ were excellent.

    (A) acousticks
    (B) acoustics
    (C) accoustics
    (D) acuesticts

66. The officer received a _____ to appear in court.

    (A) supeona
    (B) supoena
    (C) subpena
    (D) subpoena

67. The officer gained _____ to the building.

    (A) acess
    (B) access
    (C) acces
    (D) aksess

68. The officer was directed to _____ the neighborhood.

    (A) canvas
    (B) kanvas
    (C) canvass
    (D) canvess

69. The officer directed traffic at the _____.

    (A) pageant
    (B) pagent
    (C) pagant
    (D) pagaent

70. The officer was assigned to patrol a _____ area.

    (A) comercial
    (B) commercial
    (C) comershall
    (D) commershell

71. The police officer was found _____ for his actions.

   (A) libel
   (B) liable
   (C) libil
   (D) lieble

72. The car was struck by _____.

   (A) lightning
   (B) lightening
   (C) lightaning
   (D) lighting

73. The _____ department reviewed the test scores.

   (A) personal
   (B) personnal
   (C) persennel
   (D) personnel

74. The officer is a _____ of the city.

   (A) residence
   (B) resident
   (C) resedent
   (D) risident

75. The _____ arrested the woman for failure to appear in court.

   (A) marchall
   (B) martial
   (C) marshal
   (D) marshel

76. The class _____ was on fingerprint identification.

   (A) lesson
   (B) lessen
   (C) leson
   (D) lesen

77. The _____ clearly defined the crime of robbery.

   (A) statue
   (B) statuete
   (C) statute
   (D) staute

78. The officer suffered a _____ wound.

    (A) miner
    (B) minor
    (C) mienor
    (D) minar

79. The vehicle was _____ when it was struck.

    (A) stationery
    (B) stationnery
    (C) stationary
    (D) statonary

80. The officer _____ worked as a security guard.

    (A) formally
    (B) formerly
    (C) formaly
    (D) fomerly

81. The officer _____ off the porch.

    (A) falled
    (B) fall
    (C) fell
    (D) fallen

82. The officer was _____ relative to the manner in which he handled the incident.

    (A) counsil
    (B) counseled
    (C) counciled
    (D) consoled

83. The prisoner had a thick belt around his _____.

    (A) waist
    (B) waiste
    (C) waste
    (D) wiast

84. One of the responsibilities of the police is to keep the _____.

    (A) peice
    (B) peace
    (C) piece
    (D) peaced

85. The officer was requested to _____ his vacation period.

    (A) chose
    (B) chosen
    (C) choose
    (D) chooses

86. The officer was _____ certain he had seen the suspect before.

    (A) quite
    (B) quiet
    (C) queit
    (D) kwite

87. The officer was concerned the ambulance would not _____ in time.

    (A) arrived
    (B) did arrive
    (C) arrive
    (D) had arrived

88. It was the _____ time the criminal had been arrested.

    (A) forth
    (B) fouth
    (C) four
    (D) fourth

89. The _____ of the blow could not be determined.

    (A) angel
    (B) angle
    (C) angil
    (D) angile

90. The officer didn't _____ his radio.

    (A) loose
    (B) lost
    (C) lose
    (D) losed

Part III

Directions

Questions 91 through 100 consist of vocabulary words. Choose the closest correct meaning to the following words. You have *fifteen minutes* to complete this part of the examination.

91. Ascend

    (A) to lower
    (B) to rise
    (C) to agree
    (D) to permit

92. Formally

    (A) in time past
    (B) before
    (C) in a conventional manner
    (D) once

93. Eminent

    (A) impending
    (B) notable
    (C) protruding
    (D) threatening

94. Conscious

    (A) aware
    (B) moral
    (C) right action
    (D) genuine

95. Bewilder

    (A) scare
    (B) confuse
    (C) frighten
    (D) complicate

96. Command

    (A) instruct
    (B) tell
    (C) charge
    (D) direct

97. Moral

    (A) ethical
    (B) prevailing mood
    (C) right
    (D) spirit

98. Prosecute

    (A) request in writing
    (B) oblige by law
    (C) sue
    (D) require

99. Principle

    (A) highest
    (B) basic rule
    (C) main
    (D) first

100. Consensus

    (A) survey
    (B) group
    (C) poll
    (D) agreement

ANSWER KEY FOR
WRITING SKILLS EXAMINATION

1.	B	26.	B
2.	A	27.	B
3.	B	28.	C
4.	C	29.	C
5.	E	30.	E
6.	A	31.	B
7.	A	32.	B
8.	D	33.	A
9.	A	34.	A
10.	B	35.	E
11.	E	36.	C
12.	B	37.	B
13.	A	38.	A
14.	C	39.	A
15.	E	40.	B
16.	C	41.	E
17.	B	42.	A
18.	A	43.	C
19.	D	44.	C
20.	C	45.	A
21.	E	46.	C
22.	A	47.	D
23.	A	48.	C
24.	B	49.	C
25.	B	50.	E

51.	D	76.	A
52.	C	77.	C
53.	A	78.	B
54.	C	79.	C
55.	B	80.	B
56.	B	81.	C
57.	D	82.	B
58.	B	83.	A
59.	A	84.	B
60.	D	85.	C
61.	C	86.	A
62.	B	87.	C
63.	D	88.	D
64.	A	89.	B
65.	B	90.	C
66.	D	91.	B
67.	B	92.	C
68.	C	93.	B
69.	A	94.	A
70.	B	95.	B
71.	B	96.	D
72.	A	97.	A
73.	D	98.	C
74.	B	99.	B
75.	C	100.	D

ANSWERS AND ANALYSIS FOR WRITING SKILLS EXAMINATION

Part I

1. (B) Spelling error. *Acept* should be *accept*.

2. (A) Spelling error. *Especialy* should be *especially*.

3. (B) Spelling error. *Afidavit* should be *affidavit*.

4. (C) Punctuation error. There should be a comma after the word *kit*.

5. (E) No error.

6. (A) Spelling error. *Necesary* should be *necessary*.

7. (A) Spelling error. *Interupt* should be *interrupt*.

8. (D) Spelling error. *Iminent* should be *imminent*.

9. (A) Spelling error. *Committe* should be *committee*.

10. (B) Spelling error. *Occured* should be *occurred*.

11. (E) No error.

12. (B) Spelling error. *Represenatives* should be *representatives*.

13. (A) Spelling error. *Sherrif* should be *sheriff*.

14. (C) Spelling error. *Auxillary* should be *auxiliary*.

15. (E) No error.

16. (C) Spelling error. *Coroborate* should be *corroborate*.

17. (B) Spelling error. *Inocuous* should be *innocuous*.

18. (A) Spelling error. *Absenteism* should be *Absenteeism*.

19. (D) Spelling error. *Disapear* should be *disappear*.

20. (C) Spelling error. *Chanel* should be *channel*.

21. (E) No error.

22. (A) Word usage error. *Patience* should be *patients*.

23. (A) Spelling error. *Accross* should be *Across*.

24. (B) Word usage error. *Childrens* should be *children's*.

25. (B) Word usage error. *Foot* should be *feet*.

26. (B) Word usage error. *Through* should be *thorough*.

27. (B) Spelling error. *Embessle* should be *embezzle*.

28. (C) Punctuation error. A comma should follow the word *suspect*.

29. (C) Spelling error. *Knifes* should be *knives*.

30. (E) No error.

31. (B) Word usage error. *Perpetuated* should be *perpetrated*.

32. (B) Word usage error. *Trail* should be *trial*.

33. (A) Word usage error. *Your* should be *you're*.

34. (A) Word usage error. *Excepted* should be *accepted*.

35. (E) No error.

36. (C) Spelling error. *Sieze* should be *seize*.

37. (B) Spelling error. *Absents* should be *absence*.

38. (A) Spelling error. *Wieghed* should be *weighed*.

39. (A) Punctuation error. *Its* should be *It's*.

40. (B) Word usage error. *Their* should be *there*.

41. (E) No error.

42. (A) Spelling error. *Illict* should be *Illicit*.

43. (C) Spelling error. *Perscription* should be *Prescription*.

44. (C) Punctuation error. A comma should follow the word *red*.

45. (A) Word usage error. *There* should be *Their*.

46. (C) Spelling error. *Accidentaly* should be *accidentally*.

47. (D) Spelling error. *Statis* should be *status*.

48. (C) Spelling error. *Partialy* should be *partially*.

49. (C) Word usage error. *Dear* should be *deer*.

50. (E) No error.

Part II

51. (D) assembly

52. (C) promptly

53. (A) admitted

54. (C) carefully

55. (B) somebody else's

56. (B) neighbor

57. (D) possession

58. (B) pursued

59. (A) velocity

60. (D) gauge

61. (C) similar

62. (B) principal

63. (D) superseded

64. (A) facilitate

65. (B) acoustics

66. (D) subpoena

67. (B) access

68. (C) canvass

69. (A) pageant

70. (B) commercial

71. (B) liable

72. (A) lightning

73. (D) personnel

74. (B) resident

75. (C) marshal

76. (A) lesson

77. (C) statute

78. (B) minor

79. (C) stationary

80. (B) formerly

81. (C) fell

82. (B) counseled

83. (A) waist

84. (B) peace

85. (C) choose

86. (A) quite

87. (C) arrive

88. (D) fourth

89. (B) angle

90. (C) lose

Part III

91. (B) to rise

92. (C) in a formal manner

93. (B) notable

94. (A) aware

95. (B) confuse

96. (D) direct

97. (A) ethical

98. (C) sue

99. (B) basic rule

100. (D) agreement

Tips to Improve Your Writing Exam Skills

You can do several things to increase your test-taking ability in the written skills area. For example, remember the verse you learned in elementary school? It went like this:

> I before E
>> except after C
>>> or when sounded like *A*
>>>> as in neighbor and weigh.

Remembering this verse will assist you with words like receive, chief, freight, field, etc. Try these other clues to improve your other writing test skills.

1. In word usage and spelling questions, concentrate on each of the words in the question and answer choices. Circle or highlight words which are unfamiliar to you or which don't look right. Analyze the different parts of the word. Sound the word out. Write the word on a separate piece of paper and see if it fits properly with the sentence.

2. To improve your vocabulary, choose a book, newspaper, or magazine and jot down the first fifteen words you're not completely familiar with. Examine how the word was used in the sentence. Now write a definition for the word on a sheet of paper. Overcome your fear of the dictionary and look up each word you wrote down. Compare the meanings to the definitions that *you* wrote.

3. Enlarge your vocabulary by doing crossword puzzles. Become "word conscious." Don't skip over words you don't know the meaning of. Look them up. Following are words often used in writing skills tests.

absence	conceive	imitation	proceed
abundance	conquered	imminent	receive
accept	conquering	interrupt	relieve
access	control	judgment	repel
accidentally	controlling	knelling	resistance
achieve	corroborate	leisure	rise
acknowledgment	corruptible	liable	seize
across	counseled	likewise	sensible
address	counterfeit	limitation	separate
admissible	deceive	marveled	siege
affidavit	devise	marveling	significance
all right	disappear	marvelous	similar
analyze	disappoint	necessary	sincerely
anoint	disguise	neither	skillful
arrive	dissipate	noticing	stationary
assassin	either	occur	status
auxiliary	embezzle	occurred	statute
balloon	enforceable	occurrence	subpoena
believe	especially	paralyze	succeed
benefit	ethical	partially	supervise
business	exceed	perpetrated	surmise
calendar	failing	personnel	their
changing	field	possession	trafficker
channel	foreign	possible	traveled
chief	forfeit	precede	traveling
choose	fourth	prefer	violation
chose	freight	preferring	yield
commercial	grammar	prescription	weigh
committee	grieve	privilege	weird
comparative	illicit	probable	wield

NOTIFICATION OF WRITTEN EXAMINATION RESULTS

After taking your written examination, there will be a four to six week wait until you're notified of your test results. *Don't make the mistake of just continuing on with your life waiting to see what happens!* While you're waiting for *your* test results, other candidates will be studying for the oral examinations and getting in shape to take the physical agility and medical examinations. Even after you receive notification from the department of personnel that you passed the written test, it may be an additional two weeks or more before the next step in the process, either the medical exam or the physical agility test. It will be at least a month between tests and you can't afford to waste this valuable time. Motivate yourself to continue studying!

So four to six weeks after taking your written examination you will receive a letter from the personnel department advising you of the results. How much information is contained in the letter varies from city to city. Most cities advise candidates of the numerical score they achieved on the test. Some merely notify candidates whether they passed or failed. Those who do pass are given a date, time, and location for the next step in the examination process, usually the medical examination. Other departments give the numerical score *and* a rank ordering of how the candidate did in comparison with others who took the test. An example of a score notification letter from a personnel department to a candidate follows.

Regardless of your score or rank, *don't misinterpret the results and drop out of the process*. Let's say you receive a letter from a personnel department that your score on the written examination is seventy-seven percent and your rank order is number sixty-three. You also know they are only going to hire twenty police officers. Many people look at numbers like these and figure sixty-two people are ahead of them on the list; why bother continuing? *DON'T DROP OUT.* Many people are police officers today because they continued on with the testing process while others who were ahead of them in the initial stages withdrew! The testing process is specifically designed to screen people out along the way. The written examination is just the *first* stage. Candidates who may be ahead of you on the list *now*, will fail their medical, physical agility, polygraph, and psychological examinations. Others will be eliminated during the background investigation. The oral examination often counts for fifty percent of the final score and changes the rank order of the list dramatically. Also, as previously discussed, veterans preference and residents points and the "rule of three" will change the final ranking of candidates on the list.

If you're number sixty-three on the list after the written examination, and they're going to hire twenty police officers, it means forty-three candidates are between you and your goal of becoming a police officer. How many candidates will have taken other jobs between the time they applied, took the written examination, and received the results? How many will drop out because they're number forty? How many will score lower than you on the *other* examinations? How many will be appointed after completing the testing process and then decide not to enter the police academy? When I was commander of a police academy, two candidates who had made it through the entire testing process didn't show up on the first day of classes. The next two people on the certified list were notified and are police officers today! So, if you take no other advice from this book, listen to this coach right now and *please don't drop out of the process!*

THE CITY OF DORCHESTER
Department of Personnel
125 Main Street
Dorchester, —

July 18, 19—

Mr. Sean Matthews
125 Shaker Pine Lane
Dorchester, —

Dear Candidate:

    The results of your recent examination for the position of police officer are as follows:

POSITION TITLE:	Police Officer	
YOUR SCORE:	92.00%	
YOUR RANKING:	4	

    This is not a notice of appointment. Your name will be placed on a list of persons eligible to take the MEDICAL EXAMINATION. You are scheduled to take the MEDICAL EXAMINATION for the position of POLICE OFFICER on July 29, 19— at 10:00 A.M. Report to the City of Dorchester Health Clinic, Room 413, located at 175 West Main Street. Failure to report for your Medical Examination on the date and at the time specified will result in your disqualification as a candidate for the position of POLICE OFFICER.

Sincerely yours,

Michael M. Davis

Michael M. Davis
Personnel Department

At the narrow passage, there is no brother and no friend.
—Arabian Proverb

PERSONAL DEVELOPMENT AND ACTION PLAN

What have I done today to prepare myself for a career in policing?

1. _____

2. _____

3. _____

4. _____

5. _____

6. _____

7. _____

8. _____

9. _____

10. _____

6

CROSSROADS
ALONG THE PATH

THE MEDICAL EXAMINATION

You have received your letter from the department of personnel, have scored very high on the written examination, and now have a date, time, and location to take the medical examination. The medical examination is as much a "test" as any of the other stages of the examination process. Failure to pass the medical examination will result in your disqualification as a candidate, so make sure you carefully follow any instructions contained in the letter from the personnel department.

Most police departments provide candidates with the medical standards and physical agility test requirements prior to scheduling the medical examination. If you've followed the advice in this book, you knew what the medical requirements were before applying for the job. There are many medical conditions which can be treated and corrected prior to taking your medical examination. Even if you're *not* experiencing any health problems, I highly recommend that you contact your personal physician and have a physical prior to taking the medical examination. For example, you may be surprised to discover that your blood pressure is elevated. There are diet, exercise, and lifestyle changes your doctor can recommend which may lower your blood pressure into the normal range.

Like the written test, the medical exam doesn't grade you on appearance, so wear comfortable clothing. You can expect to be put through the following tests:

- extensive medical history
- height and weight and/or body fat composition measurement
- vision examination, including color vision
- cardiovascular examination, including a blood pressure measurement and an electrocardiograph
- blood test
- hearing test and ear examination
- respiratory examination, including a chest x-ray
- hernia examination
- urinalysis, including a drug test

WHAT TO EXPECT AT YOUR MEDICAL EXAMINATION

In most small and in some medium-sized cities, the medical examination is conducted at the office of a local physician under contract with the city. In larger cities, candidates for police positions usually have their physicals at city-operated health clinics or medical centers. At city-operated clinics, the process will take several hours, and you'll spend most of your time filling out forms and being shuffled from place to place to stand in line for routine tests. In other words, it's the "hurry up and wait" routine. Bring the following with you to the medical examination:

- a good book to read while you're waiting
- notes on your family's medical history
- several pens (black ink)
- your glasses or contact lenses for the vision test
- your motor vehicle operator's license

Expect other candidates and people who have routine doctor appointments to be in the office or medical center at the same time you're scheduled to take your medical examination. Upon arrival, you'll report to a secretary or nurse who may ask you for identification. Eventually you will be given an extensive medical history questionnaire to complete. This form will be reviewed by one or more physicians and also by the background investigation team. Your health record is already on file with your high school or college, family doctor, military branch, and prior employer, so *don't lie on the medical history questionnaire*. Fudging on the medical history is exactly the sort of thing the background investigation team is trained to spot. A deliberately false entry on *any* document in the testing process will disqualify you. On the other hand, don't volunteer information on the questionnaire unless it's specifically requested. Clear, concise, factual statements are the best.

As mentioned previously, the medical requirements for police officers vary from city to city. However, let's go through a medical examination recently used by a major city in hiring its police officers to make absolutely certain you're thoroughly prepared.

After filling out the medical history questionnaire, you'll eventually be shown to a waiting room to begin your physical. Many parts of the examination will be conducted by a nurse or aide, not by a physician. There's nothing wrong with asking questions at the medical examination, and I encourage you to do so. Some of the tests, such as the blood, urine, and x-ray exams, take time, and an on-the-spot determination can't be made. However, *do ask* what your blood pressure reading is and ask about your eye and color vision tests. Did you pass? Also ask about your height/weight and/or body fat composition results. Asking pertinent questions will relieve your anxiety about whether you're passing. The nurse or doctor won't be able to give you all your test results, but some results are readily available, and you certainly have a right to ask about them.

In our sample city, the physical examination consisted of the following tests.

Height and Weight Measurement

Many, but not all, police departments no longer have minimum height requirements for police officers. Minimum height standards have been decreased to permit smaller-statured women, Asians, and Hispanics to qualify for positions in policing since there is no evidence that height is an effective prediction of successful job performance.

Regarding weight, most departments use a formula based on weight in proportion to height and frame size. Others use body fat composition determined by skinfold measurement. There isn't anything you can do to change your height, but if being overweight is a problem, schedule an appointment with your doctor and get on a weight reduction program which combines diet and exercise. Given the time frame between submitting your initial application and being scheduled for your medical exam, you may be able to shed enough body fat to qualify. Also, most departments allow ten to fifteen percent excess body weight over the ideal weight shown on the charts. This allowance, coupled with a weight-reduction plan, may put you within the parameters for qualification. If you are prone to being overweight, you had better do some studying on nutrition and exercise because you need to be in prime condition for your entire career, not just on weigh-in day. Policing is a stressful way of life, and you won't be able to protect others unless you can physically protect yourself. Long periods of inactivity are often followed by the split-second need for maximum physical exertion. Driving up to the scene of a robbery in progress and then chasing a suspect down a dark alley and over a series of chainlink fences requires excellent physical and cardiorespiratory fitness. Being overweight could mean losing a suspect or compromising your personal safety and exacerbating bodily and psychological wear and tear over a tough career. So get in shape and stay that way. It will pay huge dividends for you over your career.

For candidates applying to departments using a standard height/weight chart (as opposed to body fat composition), charts for both men and women follow.

HEIGHT AND WEIGHT TABLES ACCORDING TO FRAME
(Weight in pounds, indoor clothing)

MEN

| Height (in shoes) | | Small Frame | Medium Frame | Large Frame |
Feet	Inches			
5	2	128–134	131–141	136–150
5	3	130–136	133–143	140–153
5	4	132–138	135–145	142–156
5	5	134–140	137–148	144–160
5	6	136–142	139–151	146–164
5	7	138–145	142–154	149–168
5	8	140–148	145–156	152–172
5	9	142–151	148–158	155–176
5	10	144–154	151–160	158–180
5	11	146–157	154–163	161–184
6	0	149–160	157–170	164–188
6	1	152–164	160–174	168–192
6	2	155–168	164–178	172–197
6	3	158–172	167–182	176–202
6	4	162–176	171–187	181–207

WOMEN

| Height (in shoes) | | Small Frame | Medium Frame | Large Frame |
Feet	Inches			
4	10	102–111	109–121	118–131
4	11	103–113	111–123	120–134
5	0	104–115	113–126	122–137
5	1	106–118	115–128	125–140
5	2	108–121	118–130	128–143
5	3	111–124	121–132	131–147
5	4	114–127	124–135	134–151
5	5	117–130	127–141	137–155
5	6	120–133	130–144	140–157
5	7	123–136	133–147	143–159
5	8	126–139	136–150	146–163
5	9	129–142	139–153	149–170
5	10	132–145	142–156	152–173
5	11	135–148	145–159	155–176
6	0	138–151	148–162	158–179

(Indoor clothing weighs 5 pounds for men and 3 pounds for women; shoes with 1-inch heels.)

Body Fat Composition Measurement

Some police departments use body fat composition (as opposed to height/weight charts) in their medical examinations. Body fat composition is expressed as a percentage of the total composition of a person, and it allows comparison with others in a statistical grouping. Estimating how much of a person's body is made up of fat gives a preliminary idea of how fit they are. Generally, people who have a low body fat percentage tend to be in better shape than people who have more fat. A doctor or nurse will use special calipers to measure skinfold thicknesses at six locations, usually on the triceps, subscapular (below the shoulder blade), side, thigh, abdomen, and chest. Approximately half of our fat is located just beneath the skin, and by grasping a fold of skin and fat and measuring it with calipers, the sum of the six skinfolds can be used to classify and rank individuals. Following is a chart depicting body fat norms using the skinfold test.

BODY FAT NORMS BASED ON SUM OF SIX SKINFOLDS

Percentage Body Fat	Rating
Less than 15	Excellent
15.1 to 23	Good
23.1 to 28	Average
28.1 or more	Below average

The Vision Test

Good vision is an important requisite for police work. Police officers continuously use eyesight in performing their duties, and mistakes due to poor vision could result in terrible consequences. Police officers carry and use firearms, and the safety of the public and the officer might depend on an officer's eyesight. Court testimony about an action taken by an officer often begins with the premise of what an officer "saw." So, although there are variations in requirements across the country, most police departments require candidates to have 20/40 or better vision in one eye and 20/20 in the other. Other departments require vision correctable with glasses or contact lenses to 20/20 in both eyes. If you wear glasses or contacts, it's not a problem in most jurisdictions as long as your vision can be corrected to the minimum standard. It's a good idea to schedule a visit to an optometrist prior to taking the eye test as part of your medical examination to become a police officer. If you need glasses, get them ahead of time.

Most vision tests consist of viewing a "Snellen chart" hung on the wall in the doctor's office. Each row of letters in the chart is smaller than the ones above. You'll be asked to stand twenty feet away from the chart (usually there is a strip of tape on the floor indicating the correct distance), cover one eye, and read the letters. If you can read the letters of a size considered normal for a person twenty feet away this is expressed as 20/20 vision. If at twenty feet you can only read the letters which the normal eye can see at forty feet, you have 20/40 vision. The procedure is repeated for your other eye.

Color Vision Test

Many people don't realize they can't see colors or shades of colors normally. Others know that some colors present difficulty for them, but they have learned to use the proper name of a color in association with specific objects. For example, if shown a painting of a basket of fruit, they will say that the fruit shaped like an apple is red. It may actually be green in the painting.

Some police departments have strict color-vision requirements. They argue that a person who confuses reds and greens, for example, would be able to distinguish a traffic signal only by the position of the lights and brightness of the bulbs. Or, a person could confuse a suspect's clothing description, etc. (It's estimated that four out of every one hundred men and one out of every two hundred women are color blind.)

The type of test you will be given is called an "Ishihara test." It consists of cards covered with small dots of color that vary in hue and intensity. Letters or numbers are "hidden" in the dot pattern through the variation in hue or color intensity of neighboring dots, and you will be asked to identify the characters. If you have normal color vision, the letters or numbers will jump right out at you. When you visit your optometrist, have your color vision checked along with your eyesight.

Heart and Blood Pressure Tests

Heart disease is one of the leading causes of death and disability for police officers. In addition, the claiming of police disability pensions because of hypertension (chronic high blood pressure) has become a major economic issue in many states and cities. The cardiovascular condition of candidates for police positions is looked at very closely during the medical examination. If an examining physician concludes that heart disease or hypertension would prevent a candidate from being able to withstand the physical and/or emotional stresses required to be a police officer, then the person can and should be eliminated from the process.

The doctor will review your medical history questionnaire to see if cardiovascular disease runs in your family or if you have experienced past problems with your heart or vascular system. He or she will use a stethoscope to listen to the beat of your heart as the blood passes through its valves to determine if you have a heart murmur.

Your blood pressure (the pressure blood exerts against the walls of the arteries) will also be checked. Blood pressure is recorded in a fraction. Normal blood pressure is considered to be 120/80. The number 120 is the systolic reading (when the heart contracts) and the number 80 is the diastolic reading (when the heart rests between beats). A systolic reading greater than 150 and/or a diastolic reading greater than 90 is considered high. Diagnosed hypertension usually disqualifies a candidate for the position of police officer. For many people, elevated blood pressure can be reduced through diet, exercise, and lifestyle changes. Others may need medication.

Have your blood pressure checked by your physician before your medical examination for police officer. Although the rules vary across the country, the doctor performing the medical exam for the town or city to which you've applied may be reluctant to disqualify a candidate who has a letter from his or her personal physician indicating a hypertensive condition is temporary or highly treatable.

Your examination may also include an electrocardiograph, which records the electrical charges occurring as the heart beats. The examination consists of having several plastic disks (they look like suction cups) placed on your upper body. The disks are attached to wires which lead to a machine that prints out a graph. Don't worry, the examination is painless. It provides the doctor an indication of whether your heart is functioning properly.

Blood Test

Your blood will be drawn (usually just a pin prick to the finger) to conduct a series of serology tests which are used to diagnose a wide variety of diseases, such as anemia and damage to the kidneys or liver. A blood test would also indicate if you were HIV-positive. Similar to the other medical tests, the finding of a condition which would seriously affect your ability to perform the duties of a police officer may eliminate you from further consideration. By testing and examining your blood, the healthy functioning of most organs and tissues can be determined.

Hearing Test

Normal hearing is required to be a police officer. The doctor will begin your hearing test by speaking with you to see if you can hear and understand normal ranges of speech during conversation. Ordinary conversation ranges from 200 to 3000 vibrations per second in pitch at 50 to 60 decibels. Your hearing will be considered good if you can hear all sounds between approximately 60 and 8000 vibrations at 20 decibels. The doctor may use a tuning fork, which is held against the outer ear, to measure your response to tones, or an audiometer, in which case you'll wear earphones to detect sounds at various volumes.

Respiratory Test

The doctor will check your respiratory system by using a stethoscope to listen to the expansion and contraction of your lungs. A chest x-ray will also be taken to ensure that you are free of such diseases as tuberculosis, pleurisy, pneumonia, and bronchitis. Police officers must be in good cardiorespiratory condition due to the physical demands of the job. For example, chasing suspects and running up and down flights of stairs while wearing up to fifteen pounds of uniform accessories (firearm, holster, flashlight, bullet-proof vest, radio, handcuff, and so forth) require good respiratory conditioning. An asthmatic condition, or one of the lung diseases previously mentioned, might eliminate you from the process if the doctor concludes it will affect your ability to perform the duties of a police officer.

Hernia Examination

A hernia is a protrusion of part of an organ through the tissues that usually contain it. Usually hernias occur in abdominal organs, and the most common are inguinal and femoral hernias. An inguinal hernia is the protrusion of a loop of intestine into the groin and is most common in men. Femoral hernias are most common for women and they are a loop of intestine protruding into the femoral canal, which carries the nerves and blood vessels from the abdomen into the upper thigh and groin area. Hernias may be congenital or may result from straining—lifting heavy weights, jumping off a high wall, or coughing, for example—or from obesity or pregnancy.

Having a hernia will disqualify you from becoming a police officer. The potential strenuousness of the job could exacerbate the condition, which may then require surgery and limited activity which would affect job performance.

At the medical examination, a doctor will interview you and physically examine you to determine if you have a hernia. Most likely, a repaired hernia would not eliminate a candidate as long as the doctor did not think it would affect the person's ability to perform the job of a police officer.

Urinalysis and Drug Test

You will be required to give a urine sample at your physical examination to test primarily for diabetes and illicit drug use. Diabetes is a disease characterized by an abnormal amount of sugar in the blood or urine. It is an incurable disease and in some cases results in a loss of strength. Milder forms can be controlled by diet. Since the characteristics of the disease vary, a mild case may not eliminate you from becoming a police officer. As with high blood pressure, if you are a diabetic it's a good idea to discuss this with your personal physician prior to the medical examination. You'll have to convince the doctor performing your medical exam that it will not affect your ability to perform the job of a police officer.

Obviously, if you fail the drug test it will disqualify you for becoming a police officer. Examples of the types of drugs tested for are marijuana; opiates, such as heroin, morphine, and methadone; cocaine; amphetamines; barbiturates; and phencyclidines.

Final Thoughts

You won't be told by the doctor that you've failed the medical examination unless it's obvious—for example, your vision is inadequate. In that case, you would not continue taking the other tests. Many of the tests (blood, urine, etc.) require laboratory analysis and take time. The results are sent to the personnel department.

If you fail the medical examination, the director of the personnel department will send you a letter indicating you didn't pass. Some cities go into detail about the reason why, while others do not because they don't want to provide a candidate with information for a possible lawsuit. Large cities are notorious for not notifying cadidates about the medical examination until a list is formulated for the next step in the testing process. In that case, the notification consists of inviting candidates to the next test and no mention is made of the medical examination. Other departments formally notify candidates they passed by sending a letter from the director of personnel.

During the medical examination, ask the nurse or doctor if you passed after each of the tests. Often they will tell you that they can't say "officially," but that everything "looks good." If you don't hear from the personnel department within ten days after taking the medical exam, call and ask if you passed.

PERSONAL DEVELOPMENT AND ACTION PLAN

What have I done today to prepare myself for a career in policing?

1. _____

2. _____

3. _____

4. _____

5. _____

6. _____

7. _____

8. _____

9. _____

10. _____

7
JOUSTS
ALONG THE PATH

THE PHYSICAL AGILITY TEST

After receiving notification that you have passed the medical examination, you will be given a date, time, and location to take the physical agility test. The test is given at a local high school or college gymnasium, or at the police academy, if the department is large enough to have one.

Test administrators like to schedule the physical agility test as early in the testing and interviewing process as possible because, like the written examination, large numbers of applicants can be tested at the same time. It's also an economical test and it screens out a surprisingly large number of unqualified candidates. Some departments even have candidates sign waiver forms, relieving the department of medical responsibility, and give the agility test prior to the medical examination. Usually, the physical agility examination is graded pass/fail and failure means disqualification as a candidate for police officer.

The composition of the test has several variations, but all of them have similar criteria. Most physical agility tests examine a candidate's muscular endurance, flexibility (especially in the lower back and hamstrings), muscular explosiveness, grip strength, speed, balance, coordination, and cardiovascular conditioning. They do this by using a series of physical exercises combined with job-related obstacles and situations. The test may consist of the following:

- sit-and-reach flexibility test
- one-mile run
- agility run
- obstacle course
- push-ups
- dynamometer hand-grip test
- vertical jump
- fifty-yard dash
- pull-ups

You could be instructed to crawl under and climb over obstacles, walk on a balance beam, zigzag through a maze of cones, drag or carry a one-hundred-pound dummy for a distance, or dash up or down flights of stairs. While doing all of this, you may be instructed to do sit-ups, push-ups, pull-ups, dashes, or any combination of these exercises.

PREPARATION FOR THE PHYSICAL AGILITY TEST

Many candidates don't properly prepare themselves for the various parts of the testing process. I'm going to make sure this doesn't happen to you by describing each of the exercises, explaining what you will have to do to excel, and by detailing an exercise plan to prepare you for each of the individual tests. Female readers should pay particular attention to the suggestions in this chapter for building the type of upper-body and grip strength required to pass the physical agility test.

What to Wear to the Test

You will receive written instructions from the personnel department about what you can wear for this test. Within those restrictions, the type of clothing you'll want depends on the test component, its location, and whether some components will be outdoors, such as the one-mile run. Remember, this is a *test,* not a fashion show. The objective isn't to look good, it's to excel at each and every one of the tests. Following are recommended items of clothing to wear or bring with you, along with some helpful hints on a few of the key items.

- gym bag to carry and store your workout clothing
- 2 pairs of sneakers or running shoes
- 1 extra pair of laces
- 2 pairs of quality socks
- 2 pairs of gym shorts
- 2 pairs of sweatpants
- 2 T-shirts
- 1 sweatshirt
- 1 bottle of water
- motor vehicle operator's license

Footwear—You will be running a lot at the physical agility test, so have a quality pair of sneakers or running shoes that fit properly with the type of socks you will be wearing. Since you may be doing some stair climbing, the fit of the running shoe or sneaker is especially important. You don't want your foot slipping and sliding when running stairs. Don't make the mistake of wearing brand new footwear that isn't properly broken in. Bring an extra pair of sneakers and socks with you. If it rains, and the running portion of the exam is outdoors, you will be able to change into a fresh pair of sneaks. Also, bring an extra pair of shoelaces in case one breaks halfway through the day.

Sweatpants and Gym Shorts—You will have to decide whether to wear sweatpants or gym shorts when going through the various exercises. I recommend that you wear what you practice in. If it rains, and the running events are held outdoors, sweats can get very heavy, and seconds might make the difference between passing and failing. If the exercise is a "step test," you may want the freedom of movement of gym shorts. The test may include exercises where you'll be in contact with the gymnasium floor or other hard surfaces, such as when doing sit-ups, a wall climb, or a dummy drag, and you may want to wear sweatpants for those exercises. It's a good idea to have both sweatpants and gym shorts to give yourself the option of what to wear depending on the particular agility test you're taking.

T-shirts—Bring a couple of lightweight T-shirts. Full range of motion is important when going through the exercises, so make sure the T-shirts you bring aren't too tight and that they allow maximum freedom of movement. You're going to be sweating throughout the day, so make certain you have clothes to change into between exercises if necessary.

Sweatshirt—Because of the large number of candidates who might be tested at the same time, there may be significant delays between the different stages of your examination. Approach the physical agility test like an Olympic athlete; between exercises put on a sweatshirt to keep your muscles warm.

Fluids—The physical agility test often takes an entire day. Don't drink something between exercises that might inhibit peak performance. I recommend you bring a plastic bottle filled with water or an electrolyte replacer for replenishing fluids between exercises.

Contact With Police Officers and Test Administrators

The physical agility test often consists of five or six separate exercises with several applicants going through them at the same time. This, plus the one-mile run, if it's included, requires quite a few people to administer the test, ensure safety, and record each applicant's results. Police officers often assist in this stage of the examination process. Other than at the oral examination, at the chief's final interview, and through the background investigation team, this test is usually the only part of the process in which you'll encounter police officers. Having police officers present at the test adds another level of "testing" that you should be aware of. Those officers could affect you in the later stages of the testing process and at the police academy.

How to excel at the police academy is covered later in this book, but for purposes of the physical agility test, it's important that you understand how to interact with police officers. One or more of the people conducting your physical agility test could be sitting on your oral examination board several weeks down the road or be one of your future instructors at the police academy. Those police departments having their own academy (as opposed to smaller departments which send recruits to a state-operated, generic police academy), often use its instructors to assist in conducting the physical agility test.

Policing is a semimilitary profession, and police applicants are as far down on the hierarchy as you can get. Expect to be treated like a recruit at a military boot camp. You may be directed to stand in line or formation. Don't chew gum. Don't talk in line and don't talk when any of the test proctors are speaking. The test proctors will probably be in civilian attire. You may not be able to tell which proctors are city personnel department employees and which are police officers. Proper etiquette is important. Address everyone as either "sir" or "ma'am." Expect to be addressed by your last name. Police officers expect applicants to immediately respond when told to do something. Be attentive to what's going on. If you're not absolutely certain of the instructions for any part of the physical agility test, raise your hand and ask for clarification. Be on your best behavior during and between the tests; you can bet that you are being observed if the proctors are police officers.

Let's go through several variations of the physical agility test to familiarize you with the process.

Physical Agility Test 1

Station 1: Sit-and-reach Test

This test is designed to evaluate your flexibility in the lower back and hamstrings. The sit-and-reach test is used because it eliminates candidates who are susceptible to lower back and muscle injuries. Flexibility is thought to be a predictor of successful physical performance of daily tasks in the workplace.

The sit-and-reach test is done without shoes. Two common test methods are used. The first has the candidate sit on the floor with legs extended and feet flat against a box. The box has a metric ruler attached to the top with the twenty-three-centimeter mark located above the feet and the zero mark nearer the candidate's knees. The candidate is instructed to slowly reach with the fingertips as far forward as possible for a measurement.

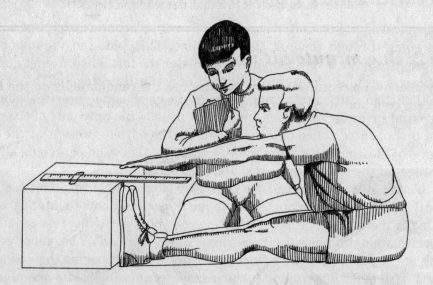

The second method doesn't use a box. A line or piece of tape is placed on the floor and the candidate is instructed to sit and extend his or her legs until the heels touch the line. A ruler is placed at the line with the measurement beginning at fifteen inches (again, zero is toward the candidate). The candidate is asked to slowly reach forward as far as possible. The candidate's score is determined by how far the fingertips reach past the starting point of either the box or the line. Following are two sit-and-reach charts, one in centimeters and one in inches.

SIT-AND-REACH FLEXIBILITY TEST 1

Rating	Measurement (cm)
Good	35 and greater
Acceptable	20–30
Failing	less than 20

(Without shoes, heels at 23 cm; test results in centimeters.)

SIT-AND-REACH FLEXIBILITY TEST 2

Rating	Measurement (inches)
Good	22 and greater
Acceptable	14–21
Failing	less than 14

(Without shoes, heels at 15 inches; test results in inches.)

Station 2: One-minute Sit-up Test

The type of sit-up required in this exercise has the candidate lie on the back and keep the knees bent and at approximately shoulder width apart.

A test proctor holds the candidate's ankles as the sit-ups are performed. At a signal, the candidate does as many bent-knee sit-ups as possible in *one minute*. Some tests require candidates to perform the sit-up by touching both knees with the elbows, while others require alternately touching the opposite knee with an elbow. Following is a chart listing standard requirements.

ONE-MINUTE SIT-UP TEST

Good	33
Acceptable	25–32
Failing	less than 25

Station 3: Dynamometer Hand-grip Test

Some departments equate hand-grip strength with successful qualification with the police firearm. Many police academy firearm training programs are forty hours or more in length; candidates spend lengthy periods on the practice range, and some studies do show a positive correlation between grip strength and scores achieved by candidates in shooting at targets on the practice range.

Hand-grip strength is measured at some physical agility tests and not at others. If it is tested, you will be asked to hold a grip-strength testing device called a "dynamometer" in whichever hand you choose. Usually, you are asked to hold the device with your arm extended downward by your side and to squeeze as hard a possible.

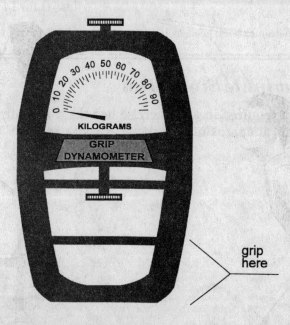

A dial will register your score in kilograms. You are allowed three tries and the highest score is recorded. Following is a chart with standard requirements.

DYNAMOMETER GRIP-STRENGTH TEST

Rating	Force (kilograms)
Good	52–65
Acceptable	44–51
Failing	less than 44

Station 4: One-mile Run

This test is designed to evaluate the efficiency of a candidate's cardiorespiratory system. The course is normally on one mile of flat terrain. The maximum time allowed is nine minutes.

Station 5: Vertical Jump

This exercise is designed to evaluate a candidate's muscular explosiveness and leg strength. The test consists of measuring how high a candidate can jump from a standing position. A wall in the gymnasium is marked off in inches. Candidates are instructed to jump and touch the highest point on the wall they can reach with the fingertips of either hand.

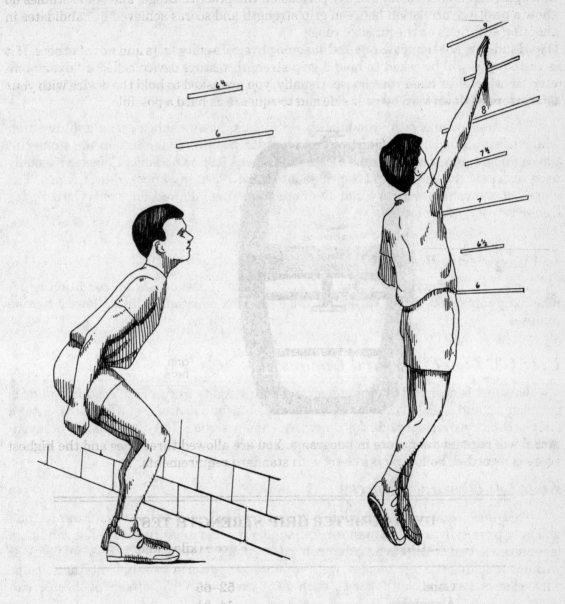

Sometimes candidates are asked to place colored chalk on their hands so the mark they make will be easily discernible. Three jumps are normally allowed. The best of the three jumps, minus the candidate's standing reach, is recorded as the score. Following is a chart listing standard requirements for the vertical jump.

VERTICAL JUMP TEST

Rating	Highest Jump (inches)
Good	19–24
Acceptable	15–18
Failing	less than 15

Physical Agility Test 2

Event 1: Agility Run

This test evaluates the candidate's ability to quickly change speed and direction while maintaining balance. Starting from a prone position (lying flat on the stomach), the candidate jumps up and runs a zigzag course as fast as possible. Cones are usually used to create the course, and the candidate must reset any knocked-over cones. The length of the course can vary, but the maximum time allowed for a fifty-yard zigzag course is twenty-four seconds.

Event 2: One-mile Run

This test is designed to evaluate a candidate's cardiovascular conditioning. A mile-long course on a flat surface is created. The maximum time allowed is nine minutes.

Event 3: Two Fifty-yard Dashes

This test is designed to evaluate a candidate's ability to run fast. A starting line is established, and a candidate runs as fast as possible for a distance of fifty yards. After a sixty-second recovery period, the candidate runs a second fifty-yard dash. The maximum time allowed is 8.5 seconds per fifty-yard dash.

Event 4: Obstacle Course

This test evaluates a candidate's strength, flexibility, balance, endurance, and ability to physically adapt to unknown and suddenly occurring situations. The candidate is required to run twenty-five yards, open a door, enter, crawl under a three-foot barrier without touching the top or sides, walk twenty feet, perform twenty bent-knee sit-ups with elbows touching both knees, dash fifty yards, perform fifteen push-ups, run twenty-five yards while jumping over obstacles without touching them, walk on a balance beam for twelve feet without falling off, climb a four-foot-high wall, and run twenty-five yards to a finish line. The maximum time allowed to finish the course is two and a half minutes. Candidates who do not successfully pass the obstacle course are allowed one more attempt.

Physical Agility Test 3

Some physical agility tests assign each event a range of numerical scores. These are totaled to determine if the candidate passes or fails the test as a whole. The advantage of this method is that it allows a candidate who fails one event to still pass the entire test by excelling in other events.

Test 1: One-minute Sit-up Test

With the back on the floor and knees bent, the candidate performs as many sit-ups as possible within one minute. The sit-up must be performed by touching both knees with the elbows. A test monitor will hold the candidate's ankles. Following is a table listing achievement levels and points.

ONE-MINUTE SIT-UP TEST

Rating	Sit-ups	Score
Excellent	38 or more	5 points
Good	33–37	4 points
Acceptable	25–32	3 points
Failing	less than 25	0 points

Test 2: Three-minute Step Test

This test evaluates a candidate's cardiovascular condition. It's conducted by using a twelve-inch-high bench for the candidate to step up onto and off. A stepping rate of twenty-four steps per minute is required for three minutes.

After stepping, the candidate is instructed to immediately sit down and the heart rate is taken for one minute. The lower the number of heartbeats, the higher the candidate's score. Following is a table listing the pulse requirements and assigned points.

THREE-MINUTE STEP TEST

Rating	Pulse (1 minute)	Score
Excellent	75–84	5
Good	85–94	4
Acceptable	95–129	3
Failing	130 or higher	0

Test 3: Dummy Drag

This test is designed to evaluate a candidate's muscular strength. A starting line is established where a human dummy weighing approximately one hundred pounds is placed. At a signal from the test proctor, the candidate must grab the dummy under the shoulders and drag it, while moving backward, around several cones a distance of thirty feet. Following is a table listing achievement levels and assigned points.

DUMMY DRAG

Rating	Time (seconds)	Score
Excellent	less than 90	5
Good	90–110	4
Acceptable	111–145	3
Failing	more than 145	0

Test 4: One-mile Run

This test is designed to evaluate the efficiency of a candidate's cardiorespiratory system. The course is on a flat surface for a distance of one mile. The following table shows achievement levels and assigned points.

ONE-MILE RUN

Rating	Time (minutes)	Score
Excellent	less than 9	5
Good	9.01–10.00	4
Acceptable	10.01–11.00	3
Failing	more than 11	0

In this third physical agility test, a candidate would have to score a minimum of twelve points in order to pass.

TRAINING FOR THE PHYSICAL AGILITY TEST

Although the physical agility test evaluates a broad range of physical fitness characteristics, the exercises and situations used are narrow in scope. It's not enough to for you to just be *aware* of the types of activities and exercises used to evaluate candidates. You need to immediately begin a physical conditioning program which is *exercise specific* in order to excel in this type of testing. Don't make the mistake of thinking that because you're in great shape you'll automatically pass the test. For example, you might be a long-distance runner who routinely competes in marathons. How's your grip strength? Or you could be a body builder capable of bench pressing three hundred pounds. How's your flexibility? You may have a highly tuned cardiorespiratory system from going to aerobics classes four days a week. How's your speed in the fifty-yard dash?

Because most physical agility tests require passing *all* of the phases of the examination, your ability to excel in one type of exercise could still result in your failing the test if you're weak in another type of exercise. You can break the world record in the one-mile run, but if you can't do the required number of sit-ups or climb a four-foot wall within the time the test allows, you will still fail the examination! *What will really matter on test day is how you do on each specific exercise and how you handle situations and overcome obstacles.*

This book offers an exercise preparation plan specific to the type of tests, obstacles, and situations used by most police departments in evaluating the physical fitness of candidates. You may receive notification from the personnel department of a slightly different series of exercises. If so, use the following format as a framework to design your own exercise program.

PHYSICAL AGILITY TEST PREPARATION GUIDE

Exercise plans work only if they are consistently followed. If you've already taken your written examination, you have only four to eight weeks to get ready for the physical agility test. Significant gains can be made in thirty days, but you had better motivate yourself to make every day count! My suggested exercise plan consists of the following four major components.

COMPONENTS OF AN EXERCISE PLAN

Warm-up Exercises *(in conjunction with flexibility exercises)*	Performance is improved if the muscles are progressively warmed up prior to maximum activity.
Flexibility Exercises	For full range of motion and mobility without injury.
Event-specific Routines	Practicing the exercise, situation, or obstacle to overcome will improve both skill level and fitness.
Cool Down	Allowing the muscles and respiration to slowly return to normal after exercising promotes maximum recuperation and flexibility retention.

Warm-up and Flexibility Exercises

The term "warm-up" means preparing the body for physical activity by increasing the body's temperature. A minimum of fifteen to twenty minutes should be spent moving from light to progressively more active warm-up and stretching exercises. A light sweat is usually a good indicator the body is sufficiently ready to begin more strenuous conditioning. Since we all have individual differences in the flexibility of different areas of the body (for example, loose in the hamstrings, but tight in the shoulders), you should experiment with different warm-up activities specifically suited to your stage of physical and cardiorespiratory conditioning. However, a good rule of thumb is to work from the head down to the feet, increasing the range of motion and the vigor of the routine as your body heats up. Again, your warm-up routine should last from fifteen to twenty minutes. Offered below is a list of standard warm-up exercises. Based on your needs and preferences, select four or five of the following to begin your exercise routine.

Warm-up Exercises

- neck rolls
- shoulder shrugs
- hips around
- side bends
- toe touches
- jumping jacks
- lunges
- rope skipping
- push-ups
- sit-ups
- leg raises
- stationary bicycling
- bench stepping
- power walking
- treadmill walking
- stair climbing
- chin-up bar hanging
- knee lifts

If you have only a limited amount of time to prepare for the physical agility test, I recommend a five-day-per-week split-exercise routine, working on different parts of the physical agility test each workout. An example would be to work out on Monday, Tuesday, Thursday, Friday, and Saturday and take Wednesday and Sunday as rest days.

PHYSICAL AGILITY EXERCISE ROUTINE
FIVE-DAY SPLIT

Monday	**Tuesday**	**Thursday**
Warm-up routine	Warm-up routine	Warm-up routine
One-mile run (9 minutes)	Sit-ups (33 in 60 seconds)	Three-minute step test
Walk one mile	50-yard dash	(pulse 75–84)
Sit-ups (33 in 60 seconds)	Push-ups	Sit-ups (33 in 60 seconds)
Push-ups	Upper-body weight routine	Lower-body weight routine
Cool down (stretching	Cool down (stretching	Pull-ups
exercises)	exercises)	Cool down (stretching
		exercises)

Friday	**Saturday**
Warm-up routine	Warm-up routine
Vertical jump (15–18 inches)	One-mile run (9 minutes)
Sit-ups (33 in 60 seconds)	Walk one mile
Push-ups	Sit-ups (33 in 60 seconds)
Obstacle course (2 minutes,	Agility run (24 seconds)
30 seconds)	Cool down (stretching
Cool down (stretching	exercises)
exercises)	

Two exceptions to the schedule should be *flexibility* and *grip strength* training, which should be done *daily* right up to the day of the agility test. Improvement in these areas is gradual and even a small gain has important significance on test day. Suggestions for improving in these two areas follow.

Flexibility Exercises

The exercise used most often to evaluate a candidate's flexibility is the sit-and-reach test. Performing this exercise involves primarily the lower back and hamstrings. Flexibility exercises don't actually stretch the muscles, but the connective tissue surrounding the muscle fibers and the tendons. The best way to increase flexibility is to perform slow, deliberate, stretching movements and to hold stretched positions for sixty seconds. To increase the range of motion of the connective tissue and muscle fibers, it's necessary to push slightly beyond the normal range. Concentrate on improving your flexibility in the hamstrings and lower back by performing the following exercises daily after a sufficient warm-up period.

Exercise 1

Sit on the floor with your legs as far apart as possible. Begin slowly bending forward at the waist. When you reach your limit, maintain that position for sixty seconds. Return to the starting position, then stretch toward your left foot. Hold that position for sixty seconds. Then stretch toward your right foot and hold for sixty seconds. Repeat this exercise several times every day.

Exercise 2

Place your palms against a wall and, while keeping your feet flat, move your feet backward until you feel tension in the back of your legs. Hold the position for sixty seconds. Repeat this exercise several times every day.

Exercise 3

Lie flat on your back and, while keeping your legs straight and together, raise your heels off the floor until you feel tension and/or increased stretching in the areas of your lower back and hamstrings. Hold this position for thirty seconds. Repeat this exercise several times every day.

Exercise 4: Sit-and-Reach

Nothing improves performance like actually doing the exercise you'll be tested on. Perform the sit-and-reach test daily and keep a log of your achievements so you can see the improvement you're making.

Grip-strength Exercises

Your local sporting goods store has several commercial products which will improve your grip strength. However, squeezing a golf ball or a piece of clay will produce the same result. Pick a device that you can carry with you from now until test day and continuously squeeze it as hard as you can throughout the day. You can do this exercise while riding in your car, sitting at your desk, or taking a walk. You can purchase a dynamometer to record your progress, although the expense isn't necessary.

Event-specific and Weight Routines

One-mile Run

A good place to do your running is at a high school or college; they usually have a quarter-mile track. Four times around and you've done your mile. If it's been awhile since you've done any running, I suggest starting by briskly walking the first quarter mile, running the second, walking the third, and running the last quarter mile. At the next workout, try to lengthen the running part of the routine and shorten the walking distance. Your goal is to run the entire mile in less than nine minutes.

Fifty-yard Dash and Agility Run

Mark off fifty yards somewhere. Create a clearly observable finish line by using a cone or chalking a line. Have someone time your run. In the obstacle course, there is usually at least one fifty-yard and one twenty-five-yard dash. In training for the fifty-yard and twenty-five-yard dashes, take a break after each run, but repeat them as many times as possible. You'll know when you've passed your peak in training for this exercise when your times begin to increase rather than decrease. When this occurs, it's time to move to another exercise.

In the agility run, a zigzag course is used. Fifty yards is one hundred fifty feet, so every ten feet or so place one of fourteen cones, empty paint cans, etc. in zigzag fashion. The cones and empty paint cans should be eight to ten feet off center. When running the course, if you knock over a cone, you must stop and right it. The maximum time allowed is twenty-four seconds.

Push-ups

Since the obstacle course is a timed event, the more rapidly you perform correct push-ups, the faster your time will be for completing the entire course. Some departments will allow female candidates to do knee push-ups (where the knees are the

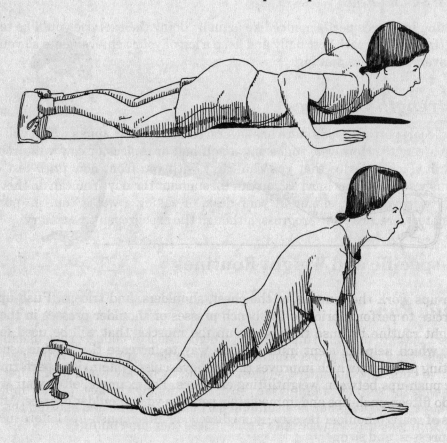

lower-body stationary point, rather than the toes in traditional push-ups) and others don't. I recommend that female candidates do both traditional and knee push-ups as part of their routine so they will be prepared for whichever is required.

To perform a knee push-up, begin on your hands and knees, as illustrated, with hands parallel to each other and a little more than shoulder width apart. Lower your body, keeping your trunk and legs in a level plane, until your chest barely touches the floor, then push yourself straight up to the starting position.

To perform a traditional push-up, make the same motion except begin from a prone position with the lower body supported on the toes. Remember to keep the trunk and legs in a level plane throughout the repetitions. I recommend a goal of fifteen repetitions.

Push-ups work the muscles of the chest, shoulders, and triceps. Push-ups are a good exercise to perform prior to the bench presses or shoulder presses in the upper-body weight routine because they warm up the muscles that will be used for those exercises, which helps prevent injuries. One way to increase the aerobic aspect of a weightlifting program (which improves the cardiovascular system) is to perform one set of fifteen push-ups between weightlifting exercises. For example, after your warm-up routine, do fifteen push-ups and immediately perform your shoulder presses. After your three sets of seated shoulder presses, immediately do fifteen push-ups before moving on to bench presses, and so on.

Upper-body Weight Routine

To prepare for the physical agility test, our goal is to increase the range of motion and strength of the entire body. It's *not* to see how much weight you can lift. These exercises are done most effectively at a gym. If possible, join a gym or fitness center. Many centers have special rates for three-month periods and, if not, the cost of a workout is usually about five dollars per day. If you can't afford to work out in a gym, two dumbbells of sufficient weight to make you work, but not strain, may be used.

In Tuesday's routine we begin with warm-ups, sit-ups, and a fifty-yard dash. After completing those exercises, the following upper-body weight routine is recommended.

Seated Shoulder Presses (3 sets of 10–12 repetitions)

From a seated position, raise the dumbbells or bar from just below the shoulders by extending the arms to straight overhead. Return to the starting position. Repeat ten to twelve times to make up one set.

Bench Presses (3 sets of 10–12 repetitions)

Lie on your back on a bench and hold the dumbbells close to and just below the shoulder level. Extend your arms straight up. Return to the starting position. Repeat ten to twelve times to make up one set. If using a bar, lie on your back, remove the bar from the rack to a position at the upper chest and push the bar straight up, extending the arms, then return to the starting position. Repeat ten to twelve times to make up one set.

Arm Curls (3 sets of 8–10 repetitions)

Stand with the feet placed shoulder width apart. With arms hanging straight down at your sides, hold a dumbbell in each hand. Bring the dumbbells forward and up, bending at the elbow, to a level just below the shoulders. You should be tensing the biceps muscle. If using a bar, begin with it resting across the top of your thighs and swing it upward to a position just below the shoulders, tensing the biceps muscles.

Lower-body Weight Routine

As part of your Thursday workout routine, perform the following lower-body exercises.

Squats (3 sets of 15–20 repetitions)

If possible, use a squat machine at a gym to perform this exercise. If you can't, stand erect with your feet shoulder width apart. Hold a dumbbell in each hand at your sides. Keeping the body erect, lower yourself until the thighs are parallel with the floor, then rise back up to the starting position. Repeat this exercise fifteen to twenty times to make up one set.

Leg Extensions (3 sets of 15–20 repetitions)

This exercise can be done only on a leg extension machine. From the seated position, extend the leg upward and outward, tensing the thigh muscles, with a weight sufficient to make you work but not strain. Return to the starting position and repeat this fifteen to twenty times to make up one set.

Hamstring Extensions (3 sets of 15–20 repetitions)

This exercise can be done only on a weight machine, also. Lie on your stomach and hook your ankles under the padded roll. Raise your heels toward your buttocks and return to the starting position. Use a weight sufficient to make you work but not strain. Repeat fifteen to twenty times to make up one set.

Pull-ups

Strength in the shoulders, arms, chest, and back are required to perform pull-ups (chin-ups). The exercise is performed by facing the bar, rising up to grasp the bar with the hands about shoulder width apart (overhand grip), pulling your body up so your chin clears the bar, then lowering yourself back down to the starting position (arms straight). Many police departments use the pull-up station on a weight machine to test candidates, while others use a traditional pull-up bar as illustrated.

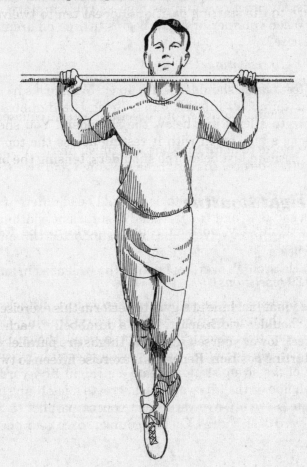

Pull-ups are difficult for many women to perform because they require a lot of upper body strength. Some departments allow female candidates to begin the exercise by stepping on a box in order to reach the bar, others don't.

Pull-ups are a difficult exercise, but the muscles required to perform them respond well to consistent training, and you'll be surprised to see how rapid your progress is. Set your goal for ten to twelve repetitions, which is the normal range required in most physical agility tests or obstacle courses. Strengthening the muscles required in this exercise will also be of great benefit to you if your test requires any type of wall climb or object pulling (such as a weighted dummy) over a distance.

Vertical Jump

Determine your standing reach by extending your arm overhead and marking the spot on a wall. Keep your feet flat on the ground and reach as high as you can. Then, from a standing position, jump as high as you can and touch the wall. The highest point your fingertips touch past the mark you made for your standing reach is your score for the vertical jump. An acceptable score is a jump reaching between fifteen and eighteen inches.

In training for the vertical jump, you may want to use ankle weights to increase resistance to the muscles used in this exercise. Like other exercises requiring the coordination of many different muscle groups, improving performance in the vertical jump requires consistent practice. Jump as high as you can, take a short break, then repeat the exercise. When your performance begins to drop off dramatically, it's time to move to another exercise.

Obstacle Course

You'll need the following to create your practice obstacle course:

- ten cones or other objects to mark the start and finish lines
- one sawhorse, or other device, that is three feet high and two to three feet wide to crawl under
- three obstacles to jump over—the obstacles should be of different heights, preferably one foot, one and a half feet, and two feet, and of sufficient width to create a barrier
- one board ten feet long and twelve inches wide supported three feet off the ground, creating a balance beam
- one four-foot obstacle to climb over, replicating the wall used in an obstacle course

Look at the following drawing of a mock physical agility test obstacle course. You'll need a large enough area for the nine stations depicted in the drawing. Create the course by first marking off twenty-five yards. Eight feet beyond the finish line, place your sawhorse to crawl under. Move another twenty feet and establish a sit-up station. About five feet to the right of the sit-up station create a straight fifty-yard dash. About eight feet beyond the finish line of the fifty-yard dash, create a push-up station. Moving over about five feet, create a twenty-five-yard dash course parallel to and in the reverse direction of the fifty-yard dash course. On this course, space your obstacles to jump over

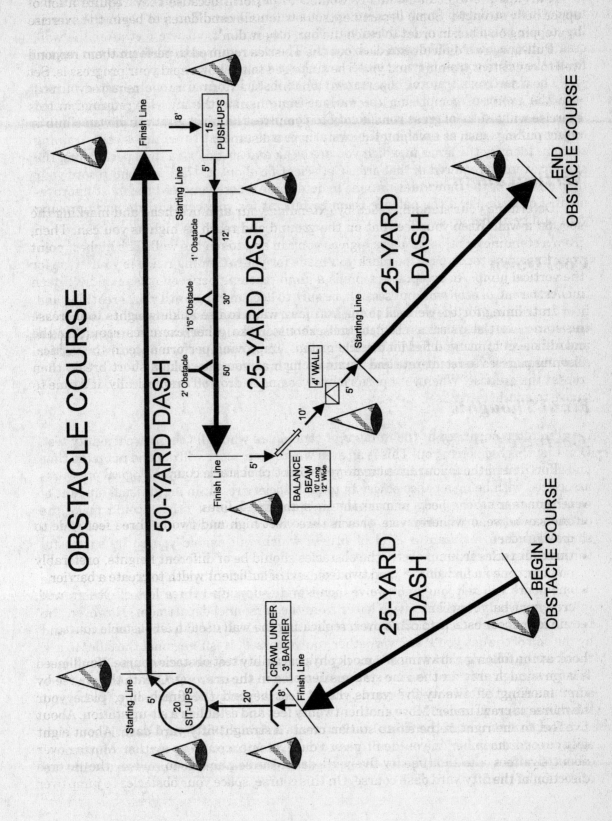

OBSTACLE COURSE

50-YARD DASH

25-YARD DASH

25-YARD DASH

25-YARD DASH

Finish Line

Starting Line

8'

PUSH-UPS
15

5'

1' Obstacle

12'

16" Obstacle

30'

2' Obstacle

50'

5'

BALANCE
BEAM
10' Long
12" Wide

10'

4' WALL

5'

Starting Line

END
OBSTACLE COURSE

BEGIN
OBSTACLE COURSE

Finish Line

CRAWL UNDER
3' BARRIER

8'

20'

SIT-UPS
20

5'

Starting Line

Finish Line

at twelve feet, thirty feet, and fifty feet. To the left and about five feet from the twenty-five-yard dash finish line, set up your balance beam. Ten feet beyond the finish line of the balance beam, establish your four-foot wall. About five feet after the wall, create another twenty-five-yard dash course. The maximum amount of time you have to finish the entire course is two minutes and thirty seconds.

The objective in training on your own mock obstacle course is to familiarize yourself with the exercises comprising the various stations, to identify your strengths and weaknesses, and to increase your ability to complete the course within the time limits required. Set a goal of finishing the obstacle course at least three times each training session. Identify the areas in which you are weak and spend extra time performing the specific exercise required in that area. Get scientific about it! Have a friend record your time on each of the individual stations to determine where you need the most improvement. For example, if the balance beam is difficult for you, concentrate on improving your ability in that area.

Cool Down

At the end of each workout session, be sure to keep moving until your breathing and heart rate have quieted. Go back to the list of warm-up exercises and perform several of the slower exercises, such as the neck rolls, shoulder shrugs, bends, and lunges. Stretch and walk about until you feel limber and rested. Again, cooling down properly is vital for allowing muscles to recuperate and for retaining maximum flexibility.

Final Thoughts

I'm often surprised at the number of candidates who fail the physical agility test. Don't let this happen to you! This is an area where your score will depend upon the time and effort you put into your training program. The physical and psychological pressures associated with being a police officer in today's society result in an unusual amount of wear and tear to the body and mind. An optimum level of fitness could make the difference between whether you, or someone you're protecting, lives or dies. Get in shape and then maintain a level of fitness which will enable you to be successful throughout your career.

When do you find out if you've passed or failed the physical agility test? Some departments will tell you right on the spot and follow up with a letter. Others will inform you that you will receive a letter from the personnel department. However, the requirements for each portion of the test are almost always told to the candidates, and by the end of the day you'll know whether you've passed. It isn't against the rules to ask those administering the various tests if you passed, and in most cases they'll tell you. The physical agility test isn't a *you* against *them* situation. Often, those who are administering the tests will be urging you to succeed and pulling for you to go beyond the minimum requirements.

The letter from the personnel department advising that you passed the physical agility test (remember, if you don't pass, you're eliminated from further contention) often contains a date and time for the next part of the examination process, usually the oral examination.

PERSONAL DEVELOPMENT AND ACTION PLAN

What have I done today to prepare myself for a career in policing?

1. _____

2. _____

3. _____

4. _____

5. _____

6. _____

7. _____

8. _____

9. _____

10. _____

8

VOICES
ALONG THE PATH

THE ORAL EXAMINATION

By this stage in the testing process, many candidates have been screened out because they weren't qualified, found other jobs, or didn't have the perseverance and self-discipline necessary to make it through all the steps of police officer testing. The field is narrowing, and more candidates will be rejected at the oral examination.

In most cities, the oral examination counts for fifty percent of the final average score. You *can* do things to prepare for the oral examination, and this chapter is devoted to explaining the process, advising you of what to expect, and teaching you how to excel on this particular type of test. How well you'll do depends greatly on how much *time* and *effort* you put into preparing for this examination.

The Difference Between Written and Oral Tests

Remember that the written examination was designed to test your ability to apply analytical thinking, demonstrate practical judgment, analyze facts, use deductive reasoning to prioritize; to read and understand; and to observe and retain information. But written examinations lack the capability of accurately evaluating your intrinsic qualities, such as leadership potential, organizational integrity (the ability to put departmental goals ahead of personal goals), ability to relate with others, and appearance. A candidate's ability to communicate verbally, perhaps the most important trait of a good police officer, also can't be evaluated through written instruments. Policing is a "doing" profession and "doing" behaviors must be evaluated. They are a combination of verbal responses and body language, gestural, and appearance factors which people administering an examination can observe. So, this is why oral examinations are given: to test for desirable qualities, knowledge, skills, and abilities which the written examination cannot test.

Oral examinations provide the tester the opportunity to

- meet a candidate face-to-face and ask open-ended, role-playing-type questions.
- ask questions which probe and evaluate the content and reasoning behind a candidate's answers.
- ascertain a candidate's beliefs, attitudes, maturity, intentions, and depth of convictions.
- determine a candidate's lack of knowledge or confusion in specific areas.
- observe whether a candidate does or does not possess a wide range of qualities—for example, stable behavior, ethics, and personal integrity.

You can exercise a great deal of control over your score in the oral examination. Knowing how these tests are constructed and the process used to conduct the oral examination will help you prepare for your test.

The Oral Board

Typical oral boards have three panel members. If there are many candidates, several boards may be convened with each handling a fraction of the pool of candidates. Each board will ask exactly the same questions and use the same criteria to grade their candidates. Some oral boards are composed of police sergeants and lieutenants, while others are composed of a mixture of police officers and sergeants. There is a trend to further diversify panels by having civilian police analysts, police psychologists, or other nonsworn personnel serve along with police representatives. Sometimes officers and/or city officials from other locales are asked to be panelists on entry-level oral board examinations in order to assure objectivity. The people chosen to serve on your panel may have a great deal of experience serving on oral boards or very little. None of them will be professional interviewers. Regardless of whether they're from out of town or are members of the police department you have applied to, they will have received material from the personnel department containing the following:

- the position description
- the procedure to be used to conduct the oral examination
- interviewing techniques
- rating instructions

The Position Description

The primary duties and responsibilities of police officers are the same across the country. However, different departments may emphasize some job tasks more than others. For example, a large city may emphasize some knowledge or skills that would be relatively unimportant to a small town. For this reason, the position description (also called the job description) for the job you are applying for is vital for you to have (several are illustrated on pages 75–78). Panelists and/or test administrators use the position description as a guide in formulating the questions they will ask you at the oral examination. They want to make sure the questions are both appropriate and related to the knowledge, skills, and abilities necessary to perform the job of a police officer in the city to which you have applied. Be sure to completely familiarize yourself with the position description; it provides valuable clues about the types of questions you will be asked.

Conducting the Oral Examination

In some cities, oral board panelists attend a class on the various aspects of conducting the oral examination. Other cities merely have the people who have been selected arrive several hours early for a briefing on the procedure to be used. The meeting is usually conducted by the test administrator. During that time, the panelists get to know one another (if they're from different cities or if civilians are on the panel) and review the questions they'll ask the candidates during the examination.

Some cities allow panelists to construct their own test questions. The questions are reviewed by the test administrator to make sure they are appropriate and job related. However, *most* cities create the test questions for the panelists because care must be taken to avoid inappropriate or illegal questions. Panelists may not question you about race, color, national origin, ancestry, marital status, political party membership or activities, or religious affiliation or church attendance.

Since the board has only a short time to spend with each candidate (from twenty to forty minutes, depending on how many candidates there are to interview), only a limited number of questions may be asked. Each panelist selects two or three questions which become the *mandatory* test questions. Each candidate *must* be asked these questions; however, the panelists are free to ask optional or follow-up questions, and they frequently choose to do so.

At the exam, one of the panelists or the test administrator is selected to greet each candidate and introduce him or her to the others. A tape recorder will be operated by either a panel member or the test administrator. Another panelist often acts as timekeeper to ensure that each examination is approximately the same length.

The Panelists' Viewpoint

Let's review what takes place at the oral examination from the viewpoint of the people who hold your future career in their hands—the panelists. People who are chosen to serve on examination panels are achievers. They take themselves and their responsibilities seriously. It's a safe bet that they are traditional in their values, beliefs, and thinking. Because they have been in policing for years, they are likely to ask you questions that would be old hat to them, but will seem difficult to you.

Serving on an oral board is mentally and physically draining. Every thirty minutes or so another candidate comes through the door and is asked exactly the same questions in the same sequence. You may be the first person they interview or the fifty-third. When large numbers of candidates are involved in the process, fatigue from the uniformity and tediousness of the procedure takes its toll. Regardless of their personal motivation and good qualities, the panelists are inevitably affected.

So when *you* walk into the room, what will make *you* better than the eighteen or fifty-two candidates who may have come before you? Convincing the panel that you have *value* and *worth* to the *organization* is the secret to achieving a high score at the oral examination. Let's learn how to do this by first taking a look at how the examination is graded.

Grading the Test

The purpose of this examination is to measure a candidate's intrinsic qualities. As you might imagine, assigning a number to grade intrinsic qualities is difficult. The rating device should not allow a range of scores so wide that the test becomes invalid or unreliable. Although grading forms vary from department to department, the types of mechanisms used are similar. Following are two samples of rating forms commonly used to evaluate candidates at entry-level oral examinations.

RATING FACTORS

1. Overall Impression
General appearance, enthusiasm, speech,
vocabulary, mannerisms, communication
skills, clarity of expression.

| 40 | 50 | 60 | 70 | 80 | 90 | 100 |

2. Alertness, Self Confidence
Readiness in grasping the meaning of
questions, self-confidence, surety of answers.

| 40 | 50 | 60 | 70 | 80 | 90 | 100 |

3. Interest, Attitude
Genuine interest in the position sought,
positive attitude about the functions of the job.

| 40 | 50 | 60 | 70 | 80 | 90 | 100 |

4. Judgment/Problem Solving, Presenting Ideas
Ability to exercise good judgment, make decisions,
be dependable and consistent, use logic, get to
the root of the problem, weigh alternatives,
analyze situations, come to conclusions.

| 40 | 50 | 60 | 70 | 80 | 90 | 100 |

5. Responsibility, Maturity
Possession of maturity necessary to handle the
responsibilities of the position sought, integrity
required of the job, awareness of the seriousness
of the position.

| 40 | 50 | 60 | 70 | 80 | 90 | 100 |

6. Working Relationships, Ability to Perform
Ability to meet stress, promote worker cooperation,
and handle the public relations requirements
of the position sought.

| 40 | 50 | 60 | 70 | 80 | 90 | 100 |

7. Job Knowledge
Understanding of the duties and requirements
of the position sought.

| 40 | 50 | 60 | 70 | 80 | 90 | 100 |

RATING FORM					
10	20	30	_____	Decision-making Ability
6	8	10	_____	Communication Skills
6	8	10	_____	Judgment
4	5	6	_____	Poise and Appearance
4	5	6	_____	Comprehension and Alertness
4	5	6	_____	Resourcefulness
4	5	6	_____	Attitude
4	5	6	_____	Maturity
4	5	6	_____	Interest and Initiative
4	5	6	_____	Knowledge About the Job Sought

During the oral examination, the panelists take notes on the candidate's performance. Immediately after the candidate leaves the room, each panelist privately reviews his or her notes and assigns a numerical rating for each of the categories. After the panelists' individual ratings are completed, they discuss any significant differences between their ratings. One or more of the panelists may have observed some performance, positive or negative, that was overlooked by another board member. The board members don't have to reach a consensus, however, and they are not encouraged to alter their ratings unless they are convinced their preliminary score was off.

After the board members have thoroughly reviewed the ratings of a candidate, they total and average the scores and assign a final score, which is the candidate's oral examination mark.

> *If a man empties his purse into his head no one can take it from him.*
>
> —Benjamin Franklin

First Impression—Lasting Impression

The impression you make with the oral board in the first few minutes is critical. This is an opportunity to "sell yourself." You never get a *second* chance to make a good *first* impression. The oral panel will begin forming an impression about you based on *what they see, what you say,* and *how you say it.* The moment you enter the room you're on center stage and the panelists will be influenced by everything about you, either positively or negatively. The image you project (how you come across) to the panelists is largely dependent on:

- how you walk into and out of the room
- your posture
- your appearance
- your speech and its tonal qualities
- your body movements and gestures

- the words you choose and how you say them
- your facial expressions
- the amount and intensity of eye contact with the panel

All these factors communicate information about you to the panel. Since you're not expected to know the technical aspects of policing, the panel members are judging your *potential value and worth* to the department. Communicating your value and worth to the organization must be done by *speaking in a clear, concise, and understandable manner* to the panelists. You must be able to communicate your best and strongest traits with confidence, energy, and enthusiasm. Most accomplished speakers spend hours practicing before they get up in front of an audience. The more you rehearse, the better you'll perform on test day. If your appearance, body language, and mannerisms are appropriate, the panel will be free to concentrate on what you are saying.

> *Your expression is the most important thing you can wear.*
>
> —Sir Ascher

Using the Advantage You Have Already Gained

By following the suggestions offered in previous chapters of this book, you have gained a distinct advantage over other candidates in the oral testing process. Let's quickly review what those advantages are and discuss how to maximize the research and activities you have been engaged in to prepare yourself for becoming a police officer.

1. You have gained knowledge about the department by researching its history, organizational structure, crime statistics, and method of policing and by reading newspaper articles to gain an understanding of significant issues facing the department.

2. You have taken advantage of the department's citizen rider program and have toured the city in a police cruiser on both the day and evening shift.

3. You have enrolled in or graduated from a criminal justice program at a college or university.

4. You have attended seminars in criminal justice.

5. You have served an internship with the department, working in its various units, divisions, and bureaus.

6. You are a member of the department's Police Athletic League, Police Explorers, or are currently a Police Cadet.

Having done all of this is meaningless if all that you've learned remains locked in your head and never comes out of your mouth at the oral examination. Don't lose the opportunity to tell the board what you know and what you have done to prepare yourself to become a police officer. You must now begin systematically reviewing all the material you have gathered; study the contents as intently as you would for a written examination.

PREPARING FOR YOUR ORAL TEST

Developing Questions

Now that you have a basic understanding of the oral board system, you can formulate a method to prepare for this test. Although numerous practice questions are discussed later in this chapter, it will be *most* beneficial to you if you begin by creating your own questions and answers as a study tool. For example, the panel is likely to begin the process by using a question designed to both ease your anxiety and provide an opportunity for you to talk affirmatively about yourself. Examples of these types of questions are:

Tell us a little bit about yourself.

Why do you want to become a police officer?

What have you done to prepare yourself for a career in policing?

After this lead-in question, the board might ask several general questions such as:

As a police officer, you may find yourself in a situation where you have to take a life to prevent others from being killed. How do you feel about that?

You may arrest a person for committing a crime only to have the court find the person innocent. How do you feel about that?

Then, the panel may put you in situations and ask how you would handle them. For instance, you might be asked:

You observe the driver of a vehicle strike a parked car, causing considerable damage. The vehicle's operator backs up and flees the scene. Upon stopping the vehicle, you find it's operated by a close friend. How would you handle this situation?

Take out some paper and create another four questions yourself. You now have a set of ten questions, which would be a likely number for a panel to ask. Take all the time you need and write out the answers as if your being hired depended only on how well you answer these questions.

Practicing Your Spoken Answers

Now comes the difficult part. Since the exam responses will be oral, to prepare effectively you *must* be able to communicate your answers to the panel members in a clear, concise, and understandable manner, without referring to your notes. If the information (for example, the fact that you graduated with honors from the criminal justice program at Boston University) remains locked in your head and never comes out of your mouth, or does so haltingly, you've lost the opportunity to convince the board of your value and worth to the organization! So, you have to continually practice *verbally* communicating. Even if the questions you're asked at the oral board aren't *exactly* the same as those in this text or those which you've created, they will be very similar, and you will have taken a substantial step forward in achieving a very high score by practicing this way.

The next step in your preparation process is to *create your own mock oral board*! Pretend you're actually at the oral board. Using a tape recorder, practice answering the questions you've developed or that are in this text. Play the tape back and put yourself in the place of a panelist judging your answer. Did you answer the questions completely? How would you rate your communication skills? Are your thoughts well organized? Do they flow easily and project confidence in your answers or are your main points disjointed and confused with "ums" and "ahs" and gaps between ideas? Do you say "you know" or "like" over and over again?

Take the exercise a step further by taping ten or twelve of the questions you have created. Space the questions with approximately five minutes of blank tape between them. Get a table and place three chairs behind it. Put a large stuffed animal in each of the three chairs (a lion, tiger, and bear would be good). They are now your panel. Set a fourth chair in front of the table facing your three stuffed animals and put your tape recorder on the table in front of it. Practice entering the room, smiling at your stuffed animal panelists as you firmly shake their hands (maintaining eye contact, of course), and seating yourself in front of the panel. Turn on the tape recorder and begin with the first question. Answer the questions exactly as you would at a real exam. Continue through all of the questions and repeat this exercise until you do it perfectly. If you can do this with three stuffed animals, you can do it with ease and confidence at your oral examination!

Another technique is to have your spouse, another family member, or a friend ask the questions so you can practice your responses. If possible, use a video camera to photograph your practice sessions so you can see yourself as others see you. Watch closely to see if you're engaging in "image distortion." Image distortion occurs when your words say one thing but your posture, gestures, and voice inflections say something else. You create an image different from the one you think you are creating. Ask yourself the following questions:

- What do I look like? Am I crossing my arms over my chest in a closed, protective position?
- What do I sound like?
- Am I sitting properly? Am I fidgeting in the seat or holding the arms of the chair tightly?
- Are my facial expressions and gestures appropriate for an oral test? Are my gestures artificial?
- Do I make eye contact with all three panel members when answering the questions?

You may be surprised and dismayed after reviewing the video to discover you have more weak points than you realized. Seeing yourself as others see you is a very positive practice tool. At first, you may feel awkward practicing with your mock oral board, but you'll quickly see a vast improvement in your performance as you adjust for your weaknesses. Be sure to make use of all the oral exam practice material beginning on page 341, following these same techniques. However you choose to practice, practice you must, or you won't score at the level you're capable of at your test.

> *Mistakes are their own instructors.*
>
> —Horace

Perfecting Your Physical Appearance

For all of the concentration in this chapter on the ability to communicate well verbally, another factor also weighs heavily in this type of subjective testing process: appearance. The panelists have about thirty minutes to make a decision that will affect whether you become a police officer. Leave nothing to chance. Remember, policing is a semimilitary profession. Board members will consciously or subconsciously judge you on many of the following appearance factors:

Business Attire—Dress conservatively for your oral examination. Men should wear a dark blue or gray suit. Women should wear a conservatively styled and colored business suit with skin-colored nylon stockings. Suits should be fresh from the cleaners and free of lint, both front and back. Men's trousers should be sharply creased and fit properly at the shoe line. Don't put anything in your pockets. Remove your wallet, keys, and loose change. You don't want to jingle when you enter and exit the examination room or have any unnecessary bulges that take away from a streamlined, military appearance. Women should not carry a purse. Men's belts, shoes, socks, and ties should match their suits. The tie must be wrinkle free and neatly knotted. Do not wear a tie clasp. A starched, white, long-sleeved shirt should be worn, regardless of the season. Both men's and women's shoes must be spotless and highly shined. Women should wear low shoes.

Cologne and perfume—Don't wear any for the oral examination.

Earrings—Under no circumstance should a male candidate wear an earring to an oral test. If you usually do wear an earring, allow enough time for even the hole to be unnoticeable before the oral exam. Women should make sure their earrings are small and appropriate for work; dangling earrings call attention to themselves, not to question responses.

Facial Hair—If you have a beard or mustache, shave it off.

Fingernails—Your fingernails should be clean and trimmed. Women should avoid long nails and colored polish; short, clean nails with no polish or a clear gloss would be best.

Gold Chains—Men, leave them home. Women should not wear more than one necklace as a suit accessory and it should be understated. Limit bracelets to your wristwatch.

Hair—Get a haircut just before the oral exam. Men should wear their hair short. The hair should not extend over the ears on the sides or past the shirt collar in back. Sideburns should extend no farther than the middle of the earlobe. Female candidates' hair is best in a short, neat style but at longest should be no more than shoulder length.

Make-up—Most female police officers wear little make-up or none at all, so it's best to keep make-up to a minimum. Just remember that you want to call attention to your answers.

Rings—If you have a college ring, by all means wear it. If you're married, wear your wedding band, but your wedding band only—for women, sparkling diamond rings, especially ones that stick up above the hand, are best left at home. Don't wear more than one ring on each hand. Pinky rings are not appropriate for men or women.

Tips

- Bring an extra suit in your car on test day. If you get a flat tire driving to the exam or have some other unfortunate mishap, you can change into a fresh suit.

- It's a good idea to pack a gym bag with a hairbrush, sticky lint roller, nail file, and a handkerchief or cloth diaper to touch up the shine on your shoes just before going in for the test. Find a bathroom and make certain you're squared away before your name or number is called.

- When you find out where your examination will be, drive there and see what the parking situation is. Will you have to walk several blocks? You'll have to allow time for that. What if it rains or snows and makes a mess of your clothes? Plan for that too; bring along an umbrella.

- Try not to let other candidates who may be present distract you. Get yourself ready mentally.

- You'll probably be required to check in with a test administrator who will ask you for your number or whatever piece of paper has been sent to you in the mail. Don't be surprised if you're told the board is running late and your time will be later than scheduled. This often happens. Self-confidence is important, especially at this stage in the process. Don't allow petty inconveniences to disrupt your concentration. Whatever means you use to get yourself psyched up, now is the time to do it!

Checklists

Post the following checklists at home and make sure you've taken care of each item before you leave for the test.

MALE CHECKLIST

- [ ] attendance card or code number
- [ ] beard (shave)
- [ ] belt (to match suit)
- [ ] college ring/wedding band
- [ ] comb
- [ ] diaper or handkerchief (for shoes)
- [ ] earrings (leave home)
- [ ] fingernails (clean and trimmed)
- [ ] gas (fill up car)
- [ ] gold chains (leave home)
- [ ] gym bag or carrying case
- [ ] hairbrush
- [ ] haircut
- [ ] know what time the test is
- [ ] know where to go
- [ ] know where to park
- [ ] leave early
- [ ] lint roller
- [ ] mustache (shave)
- [ ] money
- [ ] nail file
- [ ] shirt (white, long-sleeved, starched)
- [ ] sideburns (trim to middle of ear lobe)
- [ ] shoes (to match suit, clean and polished)
- [ ] socks (to match shoes and suit)
- [ ] suit (dark blue or gray)
- [ ] trousers (military creases)

FEMALE CHECKLIST

- ☐ attendance card or code number
- ☐ college ring/wedding band
- ☐ comb
- ☐ diaper or handkerchief (for shoes)
- ☐ earrings (if desired, appropriate for a business meeting)
- ☐ fingernails (clean, clear polish)
- ☐ gas (fill up car)
- ☐ gym bag or carrying case
- ☐ hair (style appropriate for a business meeting)
- ☐ hairbrush
- ☐ know what time the test is
- ☐ know where to go
- ☐ know where to park
- ☐ leave early
- ☐ lint roller
- ☐ make-up (appropriate for a business meeting)
- ☐ money
- ☐ nail file
- ☐ shoes (to match suit, clean and polished)
- ☐ suit (appropriate for a business meeting)

APPEARING BEFORE THE ORAL BOARD

Remember, after the candidate who goes in before you leaves the testing room, it's normally ten or fifteen minutes before you're called in. The panelists are human too and often come out to get coffee or use the bathroom. This isn't the time for one of them to see you slouched against the wall or pacing nervously up and down the corridor.

When it's your turn to take the test, one of the panelists or the test administrator will come out to get you. A panelist introduces himself or herself and leads you into the room. A test administrator may ask you to go in alone or may enter to introduce you to the board. Occasionally, the test administrator stays in the room to operate the tape recorder or observe the testing process. Expect to see people other than the panelists in the room. The board members rise as you enter the room in order to be introduced or introduce themselves to you.

It's show time from the second you enter the room until you leave. You're on stage. Make immediate eye contact with each of the panelists. Smile. Extend your hand and give a firm, friendly handshake. If you could do it with your stuffed animals, you can do it with the people around this table! Don't be surprised to see a tape recorder, folders, or rating forms on the table in front of the panel. Usually, one of the panelists asks you to sit down. Courtesy counts. Say, "Thank you, sir" or "ma'am." Pull your chair directly up to the table. Sit up straight. Clasp your hands together on the table in front of you (prominently displaying your college ring if you have one) and make eye contact with each of the panelists.

One of the board members, usually the one sitting in the middle, has been assigned to begin the examination with either an explanation of the procedure to be used or the question designed to be an icebreaker: "Would you tell the panel a little about yourself?" As the examination continues, you may see panelists smoking. They may ask you if you'd like to smoke. Don't! Chewing gum is also inappropriate. If paper clips, pencils, pads, or other items have been placed in front of you, don't nervously play with them. Appear relaxed, confident, and sure of yourself. Don't start to slouch or lean back in the chair. Panelists like to see plenty of teeth at interviews, so give them your best smile whenever it's appropriate.

> A bad beginning makes a bad ending.
>
> —Euripedes

Questions Frequently Asked at Oral Examinations

After you've been introduced to the panel and are seated, one of the panelists usually makes a general statement to the candidate such as:

> You're here to take your oral examination for the position of police officer. It's natural for you to be nervous and we want to relieve your anxiety as much as possible so you will feel comfortable answering our questions. We will be asking you a series of questions relating to the position for which you have applied. Answer the questions to the best of your ability.

The following questions are typical of those asked at oral examinations throughout the country. They are followed by responses. You may have to adjust your own response to suit the particular department to which you have applied. Since the same question can be asked in several ways, different versions of the same question are sometimes offered.

1. **Tell us a little bit about yourself.**

1. **What have you done to prepare yourself to become a police officer?**

1. **Why do you feel the City of Newcastle should hire you as a police officer?**

Possible response (city resident):

I'd be happy to, sir. I've lived here in Newcastle all my life. After graduating from high school, I applied for and was accepted into the criminal justice program at Newcastle Community Technical College. My cousin is a state police officer, and I've ridden with him several times on patrol in the cruiser. We talk about police work all the time, and I've wanted to be a police officer for many years.

While attending Newcastle College, I took advantage of its internship program with the police department and spent four months working in several police divisions, including narcotics, evidentiary services, and records. This past summer, I worked with the Police Athletic League supervising the basketball program. I was fortunate to be chosen to attend a PAL-sponsored seminar on dealing with youth gangs.

For income until I become a police officer, I've been working part-time as a waiter at a local restaurant. I've tried to do everything possible to prepare myself for a career as a police officer and look forward to serving on the Newcastle Police Department.

Possible response (non-city resident):

I'd be happy to, sir. While attending high school, I became an emergency response technician and volunteered my time to work for a local ambulance company. This type of work brought me into frequent contact with police officers, and the more time I spent with them, the more convinced I became that this is the type of work I want to pursue as a career.

So after graduation from high school, I entered Brookdale College and began working toward my bachelor's degree in criminal justice. Brookdale has a very small police department, and the chief of police informed me he doesn't anticipate hiring additional officers in the near future. I began researching area departments and, as part of that research, rode with several officers in the Newcastle Police Department. I was very impressed with the officers, the department, and the city which it serves, and I decided this is where I wanted to pursue a career in policing.

I'm currently working for a department store in Brookdale during the week, but I'm on call for ambulance duty on the weekends. I'm looking forward to serving as a police officer in the city of Newcastle and upon appointment intend to move here from Brookdale.

2. **You've applied for a position as a police officer in a city with residents from many different cultures and backgrounds. What strengths do you have which will allow you to deal effectively with people from diverse cultures and backgrounds?**

2. **Newcastle is in a metropolitan area and has a culturally diverse population. There is a high rate of unemployment, and a large percentage of our residents are living at or below the poverty level. Do you feel you will be successful in serving under these conditions?**

Possible response:

One of the reasons I want to become a police officer is to help people. From what I've read and the limited experience I've managed to obtain, police officers are in a unique position to make a difference in other people's lives. It seems to me that the key is to treat people as you would want to be treated, or the way you would expect a police officer to treat a member of your family. I think the opportunity to deal with people from all walks of life is both exciting and challenging. It's my belief that if police officers provide a high level of quality service and are courteous and respectful to whomever they meet, then this will be reciprocated. I'm eager and willing to apply these principles throughout the community and will do my best to treat everyone honestly and fairly!

3. What do you feel is the most important personal quality a police officer should have?

3. What characteristics do you think the ideal police officer should possess?

Possible response:

Ma'am, from what I've seen and read, police officers have been given a great deal of authority and responsibility. They apply the law to situations, arrest people, carry guns, and represent the city. So I think the personal ethics, honesty, and integrity of police officers are very important. I also think those chosen to be police officers should be mature, responsible people who have common sense. Since police officers spend a lot of their time dealing with people, I believe the ability to communicate and interrelate with people from all walks of life is very important.

Follow-up question:

If you had to choose one personal characteristic from among those you mentioned as being most important, what would it be?

Possible response:

If I had to choose one, it would be honesty! Because of the type of job police officers have, and the fact they're public servants, it's absolutely essential that police officers be completely honest and not be subject to corruption in any form.

Follow-up question:

Is accepting a free cup of coffee offered to a police officer by a merchant dishonest? Is it a form of corruption?

Possible response:

Yes, sir. In my opinion, a police officer should never accept anything for free.

4. Under what circumstances do you think it would be appropriate for a police officer to use force in making an arrest?

4. There may be circumstances in which you'll have to use force as a police officer. How do you feel about that?

Possible response:

I would use the minimal amount of force necessary as a last resort, when all other means of controlling the situation have proven to be inadequate. For example, if I saw one man assaulting another and he ignored my instructions to stop, I would physically stop him.

Follow-up question:

When you say you would "physically stop" the man from committing an assault, how much force would you use?

Possible response:

Sir, as a police officer, I would use whatever force was reasonable and prudent under the circumstances to stop the man from committing the assault.

5. **You're a police officer on patrol and are sent to back up another police officer on an active robbery. Upon arriving at the scene, you observe that the other officer has placed a man under arrest and has handcuffed him. The officer is beating the prisoner with his nightstick, even though the prisoner is not resisting arrest in any way. The prisoner is suffering severe injuries. How would you handle this situation?**

Possible response:

I would tell the officer to stop beating the prisoner, give the prisoner first aid, and call for an ambulance and a supervisor. I would then tell the supervisor what I had observed.

Follow-up question:

What if after you tell the officer to stop beating the prisoner, he doesn't stop? What would you do if the officer ignores you and continues to beat the prisoner with his nightstick?

Possible response:

Then I would use whatever force was prudent and necessary to protect the prisoner from being assaulted by the police officer!

6. **You arrest a man for creating a disturbance and place him in handcuffs. During the course of the investigation, you learn he is HIV-positive. As you're leading the man to your cruiser, he turns and spits in your face. What would you do?**

Possible response:

I would place the man in the cruiser and report the fact that he spit in my face on the report relative to the incident.

Follow-up question:

You wouldn't use any force against a prisoner who spit in your face?

Possible response:

Since the prisoner is in handcuffs, I'd position myself behind the man so it would be difficult for him to turn back toward me. I would verbally warn the prisoner not to spit, and if he continued to do so, I would place a hand on the back of his neck and guide him to the cruiser.

7. **You have been told by your supervisor to direct traffic at a busy intersection adjacent to a construction site. Your sergeant has instructed you not to leave the intersection without his approval. While directing traffic, you hear a loud explosion at the construction site and are informed by workers that several people have been seriously injured. What would you do?**

Possible response:

I would advise headquarters via portable radio of the situation, request that an ambulance and the fire department be sent to the scene, and render first aid to the injured construction workers. Later, I would explain to the sergeant why I had to leave the intersection.

Follow-up question:

You would leave the intersection without your supervisor's permission, even though he had told you not to?

Possible response:

Yes, sir. It's an emergency situation. I think the sergeant would be more upset if I didn't respond and continued directing traffic when lives were at stake a short distance away.

8. **While walking your beat late at night, you hear a woman's screams for help coming from a dark alley. As you walk down the alley, you see a man holding a lead pipe. He is standing over a woman who is lying on the ground. The woman appears to be unconscious and is bleeding profusely from a wound to her head. How would you handle this situation?**

Possible response:

I would use my radio to notify headquarters and request that a back-up and ambulance be sent to the scene. I would then instruct the man to drop the pipe, raise his hands in the air, and back away from the woman. I would render first aid to the woman and, if she regained consciousness, would ask her what had happened. If she didn't, I would ask the man what had occurred. Based on the responses I received and the man's actions, I would decide what further steps to take.

Follow-up question:

What would you do if the man refused to drop the pipe and began walking toward you, holding the pipe in a threatening manner and saying he was going to kill you?

Possible response:

I would order the man to stop and drop the pipe. If he didn't, I would make a decision whether I could stop the man physically or if I needed to draw my gun.

Follow-up question:

OK, let's say you do draw your gun and the suspect is still threatening to kill you. He's very close to you now and raises the pipe in the air as if to hit you on the head with it. What would you do then?

Possible response:

I would probably back up in order to buy time until help arrived. However, if I was convinced the female victim was in danger of dying, or the man with the pipe was going to kill me or prevent me from saving the woman's life, then I would have no choice but to use my gun to stop him.

Follow-up question:

So, you would kill the man?

Possible response:

My intention would be to stop him from killing me or preventing me from saving the woman's life. If there was no other way to deter the man from his actions, I would have to shoot him.

9. **You're off duty attending a party with some friends in the town where you're a police officer. One of your friends takes out some cocaine and begins snorting it in front of you. How would you handle this situation?**

Possible response:

I would have no alternative but to place him under arrest. He was committing a crime right in front of me. I know that once you become a police officer, your responsibilities don't end just because you're not working.

Follow-up question:

You would place a friend under arrest? Why not put the cocaine in the sink and wash it down the drain?

Possible response:

Yes, sir. I would place him under arrest. Throwing away the cocaine acknowledges that the person committed a crime, but it places the police officer in the position of helping to destroy evidence that a crime was committed. In my opinion that's unethical and wrong.

10. **You are on patrol and stop a motorist for speeding. The motorist offers you a hundred dollars to not give him a speeding ticket. How would you handle this situation?**

10. **You arrest a person for carrying a pistol without a permit. Only you and the man know about the arrest. He offers you a hundred dollars to let him go, saying he will never do it again. How would you respond?**

10. **While walking your beat, you interrupt a crap game in the hallway of a housing project. Everyone runs as you approach. You apprehend one of the players. There is one hundred dollars on the floor. The man says, "Take the money and let me go. No one will ever know." How would you handle this situation?**

Possible response:

I would arrest the man and not accept the money. I don't know the specific laws yet, but it's common sense that the person was trying to bribe me. If there is an additional charge I can place against the person for offering me money in exchange for my not doing my job, I would arrest him for that too. If so, I would confiscate the money and turn it in to the police department. If there is no bribery law, I would call my supervisor, explain the situation, and ask what I should do.

Follow-up question:

What if you knew that accepting a bribe *was* a violation of department guidelines and a criminal act? You're with another police officer and *she* takes the money and lets the person go, telling you not to mention it to anyone. As a matter of fact, she offers to split the money with you. What would you do?

Possible response:

I would intervene in the situation and arrest the person myself. I would then call a supervisor and advise the supervisor of what had happened.

Follow-up question:

You would turn in another police officer, knowing there is a likelihood she would be arrested?

Possible response:

Yes, sir. I would. If the police officer committed a criminal act, I would have no choice but to take action. The police have taken an oath to enforce the law and uphold the highest standards. I would take that oath very seriously and wouldn't allow anyone else to violate it.

11. **There may come a time in your career as a police officer when you have to take a life to protect your own life or the lives of others. How do you feel about that?**

Possible response:

I've given the matter a lot of thought. To take another human being's life would be terrible, and I don't know how I would react afterward. However, if someone were trying to kill me or another person, I would do whatever was necessary to stop him or her. If the only way to stop a person from killing me or someone else was to take his or her life, I would have to do it.

12. **As a police officer, you will be dealing with people in traumatic circumstances. You're going to be called derogatory names, be shouted at, and be told you're not doing your job. If you arrest a person, some will say you shouldn't have, and if you don't, others will say you should have. How do you think you will be able to handle these types of reactions from the public?**

Possible response:

Ma'am, I know that being a police officer is a tough job. When dealing with the public, not everyone is going to be satisfied all of the time. If I enforce the law equally and impartially, then I'll know I took the right action. From riding with and talking to police officers, I've observed they have to have a pretty thick skin and not let name-calling and people who yell at them affect their decisions. People get upset in emergency situations and say things they may not really mean. That's one of my definitions of being a professional—the ability to do your job under difficult circumstances.

13. **Your supervisor instructs you to use a method of handling a situation which you think is wrong. However, you know your supervisor has the authority to order you to do it that way, and it's not illegal, immoral, or unethical. How would you handle this situation?**

Possible response:

If the supervisor has the authority to direct me to use a specific method to do something, and it's not illegal, immoral, or unethical, then I would do it that way. I would choose an appropriate time to discuss it later with the supervisor and inform him or her why I think there is a better way to do it. However, I understand that policing is a semimilitary profession and that I will have to take orders.

Follow-up question:

When you say you would wait for an "appropriate time," what do you mean by that?

Possible response:

It depends on the circumstances. If it was an emergency situation or if the public was listening to what was being said, I don't think it would be appropriate to question what my supervisor was directing me to do. I don't have the training or experience in police work. I would wait until later. If we were alone, or in another appropriate setting, I would offer my suggestion.

14. **What are your goals in becoming a police officer? Where would you like to see yourself five or ten years from now?**

Possible response:

I want to become the best police officer on the force! I plan to study very hard and come out number one in the police academy. I want to learn everything I can about police work, and I plan to continue on at college and work toward my master's degree in criminal justice. Someday, I would like to become a detective. I've always been fascinated with the forensic aspects of criminal investigation, and if I learn enough and obtain the proper experience, I would like to work in the detective division.

15. **You're on patrol and sent to an active robbery taking place at a convenience store. There is a report that the owner of the store has been shot and an ambulance is on the way. Upon arriving at the scene, you observe a small crowd gathered in front of the store. The people yell to you that the robber just fled down an alley next to the store. What would you do?**

Possible response:

I would radio headquarters that citizens had reported that the robber fled down an alley adjacent to the store. My first responsibility is to determine the condition of the owner of the store and, if necessary, render first aid. If I could get a description of the robbery suspect while doing so, I would broadcast it over the radio so other police officers could look for the suspect.

Follow-up question:

Why not have one of the people in the crowd care for the store owner until the ambulance arrives, and you pursue the robbery suspect?

Possible response:

My primary responsibility is to save the store owner's life. I don't believe that responsibility can be delegated to another person.

16. **While on patrol, you observe a vehicle go through a stop sign and almost strike a pedestrian crossing the street. You stop the vehicle, and the driver informs you he is the mayor's son. He demands your name and badge number and says he will have you fired if you give him a ticket. How would you handle this situation?**

Possible response:

I would give him a ticket for going through the stop sign and write down my name and badge number for him. I would include his remarks in my written report relative to the incident.

Follow-up question:

What if the man then demands to see your supervisor?

Possible response:

I would give the man the name of my supervisor and advise him I would call him via radio. I would then radio my supervisor, advise him or her of the situation, and see if he or she wanted to respond to the scene or meet the man elsewhere.

17. **While walking a beat in the downtown area, you notice that a small crowd has gathered at an intersection. The crowd is laughing and pointing toward something in the street. Upon arrival, you observe a man dressed in a clown's outfit stopping cars and putting on a comedy routine. Traffic is backed up, and motorists are blowing their horns. That very morning the chief read a memo about the prohibition of this type of street entertainment. How would you handle this situation?**

Possible response:

If the person had a right to conduct this sort of entertainment, and the only problem was where he was doing it, then I would approach him and ask him to conduct the show at a more appropriate location—perhaps at a city park or on a side street closed to vehicular traffic. I would advise him that his performing in the street was creating a dangerous situation.

Follow-up question:

Suppose the clown began arguing with you, and the crowd began yelling for you to leave the man alone?

Possible response:

I would try to reason with the man, and if that didn't work, I would advise him that his continuing to perform in the street could lead to his arrest. The last thing I would want to do is arrest the man, but if he persisted, would not listen to reason, and his presence was causing a dangerous situation, I would place him under arrest as a last resort.

18. **You respond to the scene of a sexual assault. The victim is Hispanic, and even though she speaks English, she requests that a Hispanic female officer handle her complaint. How would you handle this situation?**

Possible response:

If a Hispanic female officer was available, I would request she be sent to the scene to handle the complaint. In a sensitive investigation such as a sexual assault, I believe every consideration should be given to the victim. If a Hispanic female officer was not available, I would explain this to the victim, and I would ask if any female officers were available so the victim would feel more comfortable answering questions about what occurred.

Follow-up question:

What if no female officers were available to respond to the scene? How would you handle that?

Possible response:

I would explain to the victim that no female officers were available to respond to the scene. I would ask the victim if there was someone she would like to be present when I asked her about the incident. If not, I would try to get a female nurse at the hospital to be present while I questioned the victim. I would also assure the victim that specific details about the assault could be handled later, when a female officer was available. My questions would be only who had assaulted her, when and where she had been assaulted, and what the assailant looked like, so we could try to locate him.

19. **Our formal questions are concluded. Is there anything you would like to state to the panel before you leave?**

Possible response:

Yes, sir, there is. I want the panel to know that I very much want to be a Newcastle police officer. I hope I've answered the questions that you've asked me to your satisfaction. I want the panel to know that if you recommend my being hired as a police officer, I won't disappoint you, myself, or my family. I will work very hard to become the type of police officer you will be proud to have recommended. Thank you very much for your time.

Leaving the Oral Board Examination Room

The examination isn't over until you've left the room. The panelists still have to score you, and the *last* impression you leave the panel with is important. After your final response, be certain to make eye contact with each panel member, give each a firm handshake, and thank them individually for their time. Square your shoulders and exit the room in a dignified fashion.

PERSONAL DEVELOPMENT AND ACTION PLAN

What have I done today to prepare myself for a career in policing?

1. _____

2. _____

3. _____

4. _____

5. _____

6. _____

7. _____

8. _____

9. _____

10. _____

9

SURVIVING THE GAUNTLET

Congratulations! You've passed the written examination, medical evaluation, physical agility test, and oral examination. Your written and oral test scores have been combined and your final average calculated. Your name is now on a rank-ordered list in the city's personnel department along with those of other candidates who have made it this far in the selection process.

Most cities mail candidates a letter indicating their final score and numerical standing in comparison to the other finalists. An eligible-to-be-hired list has been created. However, the selection process isn't over yet. More candidates will be weeded out during the psychological evaluation, background investigation, and polygraph test. Having made it this far in the *formal testing process,* you're now entering a critical stage in the *hiring process.* Many otherwise qualified candidates are eliminated in these last steps because they mistakenly think the testing is finished. *Every contact* with *anyone* connected with the selection process and *each document* or *form* you fill out is very much a *test. Don't let your guard down!* Let's make certain you understand what's involved so you can take steps to protect your hard-earned position on the list and even move up as other candidates are eliminated.

THE PSYCHOLOGICAL EXAMINATION

The objective of the psychological examination is to identify and reject individuals who may lack the emotional stability and maturity required to perform the duties of a police officer. Policing is a unique profession in American society. Officers are often confronted with life-and-death situations in which they must interpret the law, decide what is right or wrong, and take immediate action. These situations happen at lightning speed, and officers must react just as quickly. Police officers don't have time to discuss a situation with their supervisor or consult a procedural manual to decide the best way to handle the matter. Cops carry guns! They intervene in people's lives. The possibility that they will be required to use force to enforce the law always lurks in the background. A certain amount of psychological hardiness is required to withstand the pressures and emotional requirements of policing. Not everyone is suited to wear the badge and carry the gun.

Some cities routinely use the psychological examination as part of the selection process, while others don't. Many test administrators regard it as a poor method of screening potential police candidates because it's expensive and is capable of providing only an indication of future behavior. It will screen out those suffering from severe mental illness, but many administrators argue that the background investigation will provide the same results. Most departments rely on the background investigation and/or polygraph test to determine candidates' mental and emotional stability.

Nevertheless, to be prepared for a psychological examination, you need to know that there are various ways of conducting them, ranging from paper-and-pencil tests to an interview with a psychologist or psychiatrist. If large numbers of final candidates need to be tested, many cities use standardized personality-based tests. These tests are designed to indicate the potential for a candidate's personal feelings or preferences interfering with his or her ability to perform the duties required of a police officer. The test is usually administered in booklet form, or sometimes on computer, in which case you'll be asked to sit at a terminal and respond to questions as they appear on the monitor's screen. In most cases, this type of test is given at the personnel office or a high school or college. The test consists of approximately one hundred questions, but only two answer choices are given for each question. Unlike traditional multiple-choice tests, no answers are right or wrong. Rather, your answers to sets of similar questions will reveal your preferences and reflect how you feel about the world around you. For example, a question might read:

When confronted with an unpleasant situation are you more apt to

(A) avoid it
(B) confront it

As you can see, there isn't a *correct* answer; it all depends on what you as an individual prefer. Your best course of action is to answer the questions in a straight-forward and honest manner.

The reason these types of tests are considered "standardized" is that so many people have taken them, it allows a trained psychologist or psychiatrist to predict a person's tendency toward irrational thinking and/or behavior patterns. In the unlikely event the test *did* indicate this tendency on the part of a candidate, the candidate would be scheduled to visit a psychologist or psychiatrist for a more extensive evaluation.

Realistically, the chances of this happening to you are slim. You wouldn't have made it this far in the process if you weren't a stable, mature individual. For a candidate to be rejected solely on the basis of a psychological evaluation, the doctor would have to specifically show why the candidate was being rejected and how the test mechanism that was used relates to the candidate's ability to perform the job tasks of a police officer.

Another type of psychological examination is conducted by the psychologist or psychiatrist in his or her office. This type of evaluation is similar to the oral examination. You'll be asked open-ended and hypothetical questions: "What would you do if . . .?" Like being before the oral board, you may be asked questions which place you in the role of a police officer to determine what you would do and why in a particular situation. For example, one question might be, "How would you feel if you had to take a life while performing your duties as a police officer?" An extreme response, such as "It wouldn't bother me a bit. The guy probably needed killing," is the type of answer indicating emotional immaturity. That's an exaggerated example; nevertheless, you will want to stay away from *extreme responses and points of view* and use the skills you learned to excel on the oral examination in taking the psychological evaluation. Answer the questions completely but don't *volunteer* your strong, *personal* feelings on any subject.

THE BACKGROUND INVESTIGATION

The past behavior of a candidate is considered to be a good predictor of future behavior and job performance. The primary purpose of the background investigation is to identify candidates who are not suited for police work because of patterns, events, or characteristics reflected in their background. The investigation is conducted by police detectives who have been detached from their other duties to concentrate on completing background investigations on finalists for police positions. Because of the time and costs involved, the background investigation is the most expensive part of the screening process. Statistics indicate candidates have a much higher chance of being rejected as a result of a background investigation than a psychological evaluation.

The background investigation seeks to:

1. Verify information on the employment application (especially sections awarding candidates additional points) and medical history questionnaire.

2. Evaluate the candidate's honesty, integrity, and lawfulness.

3. Evaluate knowledge, skills, abilities, or personal traits not previously evaluated.

4. Determine if anything in the candidate's personal or family situation would interfere with successful job performance.

5. Evaluate a candidate's work experiences as reflected in such factors as punctuality, absenteeism, or indications of abnormal psychological characteristics.

As part of the background investigation process, candidates are required to complete a detailed personal history statement. The personal history statement asks much more in-depth questions than did the application for employment and is used by the background investigation team as a source document in its investigation.

Following is a standard checklist used in conducting a police background investigation to ensure all steps in the process are completed.

BACKGROUND INVESTIGATION CHECKLIST

Investigator's name: _____ Candidate's name: _____

Investigator's name: _____

Initial yes	Date completed		Comments
☐	_____	1. Has a release of information form been signed by the candidate?	_____
☐	_____	2. Have you received from the candidate or the personnel department:	_____
☐	_____	a. application for employment	_____
☐	_____	b. medical history questionnaire	_____
☐	_____	c. birth certificate	_____
☐	_____	d. driver's license information	_____
☐	_____	e. marriage certificate, divorce or separation papers	_____
☐	_____	f. diplomas or equivalency certificate	_____
☐	_____	g. DD-214 military record	_____
☐	_____	h. other? _____	_____
☐	_____	3. Have you reviewed the candidate's file and identified other records to be requested and areas and persons to be investigated/interviewed?	_____
☐	_____	4. Have you scheduled an interview with the candidate, reviewed and discussed application and documents?	_____
☐	_____	5. Fingerprinted candidate?	_____
☐	_____	6. Criminal record requested/received/ reviewed from local, state, and federal agencies?	_____
☐	_____	7. Motor vehicle record requested/ received/reviewed?	_____

BACKGROUND INVESTIGATION CHECKLIST (CONTINUED)

Initial yes	Date completed		Comments

☐ _____   8. Written requests for additional infor-
                  mation or records sent?   _____

☐ _____   a. educational transcripts   _____

☐ _____   b. employment   _____

☐ _____   c. personal references   _____

☐ _____   d. credit references   _____

☐ _____   e. other? _____

☐ _____   9. Interviews scheduled:
                  (name/relationship)   _____

                  a. employers (list)
                     1. _____
☐ _____   2. _____
                     3. _____

                  b. work peers (list)
                     1. _____
☐ _____   2. _____
                     3. _____

                  c. family (list)
                     1. _____
☐ _____   2. _____
                     3. _____

                  d. neighbors/friends (list)
                     1. _____
☐ _____   2. _____
                     3. _____

                  e. educators, coaches, etc. (list)
                     1. _____
☐ _____   2. _____
                     3. _____

                  f. community organizations (list)
                     1. _____
☐ _____   2. _____
                     3. _____

BACKGROUND INVESTIGATION CHECKLIST (CONTINUED)

Initial yes	Date completed		Comments

g. others (list)
1. _____
2. _____
3. _____

☐ _____

10. Polygraph scheduled?
    Date taken:_____   _____

☐ _____

11. Is the background investigation file complete?   _____

☐ _____

12. Have your reviewed all of your findings and justified your conclusions?   _____

☐ _____

13. Are there any particular areas which should be further probed?   _____

☐ _____

a. at another interview with candidate?   _____

☐ _____

b. at the chief's interview?   _____

☐ _____

14. Prepare the background investigation narrative and send to background investigation supervisor.
    Date: _____

☐ _____

In addition to completing the background investigation checklist, the investigator(s) will prepare a narrative report. The report will be based on all the information obtained about you to date: all the previous test results, the employment application, the medical history questionnaire, and the information gathered about your background by the investigative team. All of their findings, both positive and negative, will be framed in the report to answer questions like these about your abilities and qualities.

Does the candidate have

- the ability to adjust from one situation to another?
- the ability to perform detailed work using a structured method?
- the ability to communicate orally and interact effectively with a variety of people, even in conflict situations?
- the ability to work under minimum supervision?
- the ability to work as part of a team and obtain the help of others?
- a keen sense of judgment?
- a willingness to work within the criminal justice system?
- a sense of community responsibility?
- a true interest in public service and needs?
- a respect for authority?
- good health, strength, agility, coordination, and physical stamina?
- empathy and compassion, yet the ability to remain objective in sensitive social situations?
- no extreme attitudes (positive or negative) about types of people, groups, or situations to be encountered in sensitive or enforcement situations?
- no personal attributes, habits, and activities which would compromise the integrity of the candidate or the department?
- no abnormal psychological characteristics?

I didn't provide all of this information about the background investigation to you just for interesting reading. It's important you understand how thorough the investigation really is so you *won't be tempted to state or write anything false* during the process! Now that you know the type of investigation that will be conducted, the people who will likely be interviewed, and what documents will be reviewed by the background investigation team, take the following steps to make certain everything goes well:

1. Contact the people who will be interviewed by the background investigation team and tell them you've applied for a position as a police officer. It's especially important to contact past employers and inform your current employer.

2. Clean up your financial situation and credit report.

3. Be prepared to discuss motor vehicle violations and/or a minor misdemeanor arrest record. Don't try to rationalize with the detectives that it wasn't your fault. Admit your mistake, convince them it won't happen again because you're now a mature, responsible person, and move on.

4. Present yourself at every interview as if you were appearing before an oral panel. Review the chapter on how to excel at oral examinations. (The detectives conducting your background investigation have more to do with the final hiring process than test administrators or personnel analysts would care to admit.)

The reasons candidates for police officer are rejected as a result of the background investigation vary across the country. However, candidates are most commonly screened out because of a:

- conviction of a felony
- conviction of several misdemeanors
- conviction of sale or transfer of an illegal drug or a repeated pattern of illicit drug use
- conviction of crimes involving sex offenses, pornography, and/or moral turpitude
- dishonorable discharge from military service
- repeated pattern of dishonesty
- repeated pattern of serious motor vehicle violations

Because of the legal jargon associated with court records, many people are confused about whether they have a criminal record. The following definitions are often used for court and police records. (The definitions may be slightly different in your state, so check with an attorney for advice about answering written or oral questions about an arrest or conviction record.)

Accelerated rehabilitation—A kind of probation that can be granted for up to two years to first-time offenders. If the person completes the probationary period with no further problems, the charge is erased. At the point the record is erased, it would be truthful to say you do not have a conviction record.

Alcohol education program—Another first-time offender program, but for people arrested for drunken driving. After attending the program, the charge can be dismissed. At the point when the charge is dismissed, it would be truthful to say you do not have a conviction record.

Dismissal—The charge is dropped and the person's record is wiped clean. Often a charge is dismissed when a person completes the two programs listed above and remains out of trouble for a specified period. At the point the case is dismissed, it would be truthful to say you do not have a conviction record.

Disposition—The outcome of a charge against a person, whether it be a prison sentence, fine, dismissal, or something else.

Not prosecuted—Usually a charge is not prosecuted because of an error in the arrest or a lack of evidence. A state has thirteen months to reopen the case if more evidence is found or a mistake is discovered. Contact an attorney to have your record expunged.

Suspended sentence—Usually used as an incentive to ensure people follow the conditions of their probation. If they don't, they have to serve the original sentence.

Time served—The time someone spends imprisoned after an arrest, from one day to several months. A judge may decide that the time spent waiting in prison was sufficient punishment for the crime and give the person a sentence of "time served." The person would then be free.

Unconditional discharge—This is most often used after a person is found guilty of a minor offense but is unable to pay the fine. Instead of taking money from a person, the judge can decide to let the person go; however, the guilty finding is still placed on the person's record.

THE POLYGRAPH TEST

As with the psychological examination, many cities choose not to use the polygraph test (lie detector test) to screen police officer candidates. It's expensive and many question its reliability, pointing out that most results obtained through the use of a polygraph must still be corroborated through further investigation. Polygraph results are not admissible in court as evidence. Proponents of using the polygraph test argue that it's a very useful "investigative tool" which assists the background investigation team in resolving discrepancies about a candidate. It also provides areas for further investigation.

The best way to prepare for a polygraph test is to have a thorough understanding of how the test works so you won't have any undue anxiety about taking it. The polygraph is a machine that charts physiological changes in the body as a person is asked a series of questions. These physiological responses include heart rate, blood pressure, galvanic skin resistance, and rate and depth of respiration. The theory behind the polygraph is that the emotional stress caused by lying is reflected in significant autonomic changes in the body which can be graphed and which a trained examiner can interpret to determine if a person is being truthful.

Some large police departments have officers who are trained to perform polygraph examinations. If this is the case in the department to which you've applied, you'll be taking your test either at the police department or the police academy. However, most departments contract with a licensed polygraph examiner. In this case, you would be instructed to report to an office similar to that of a doctor or dentist, with a waiting room, receptionist, and so forth.

The polygraph examination takes about an hour, but a large portion of that time consists of a pretest interview. At the interview, you'll sign a form stating that you're appearing voluntarily and that you consent to be tested. The polygraph examiner will explain his or her qualifications and will tell you how the polygraph instrument works. Part of the process is to convince you that he or she is an expert in detecting falsehoods and that the instruments really work. The examiner will answer any questions you have about the procedure. The polygraphist might have you sit in the examination chair while explaining this and will begin connecting the various attachments, such as the blood pressure cuff, to you. The examination room may contain a one-way mirror into another room so others will be able to see and hear your responses to the questions. If so, one or more members of the background investigation team are likely to be present.

In addition to wrapping the blood pressure cuff around your arm (the cuff is identical to those used by physicians), two rubber tubes are placed around your trunk to record the rate and pattern of respiration. The third attachment is placed on one of your fingers or the palm of your hand to measure the changes in the electrical resistance of the skin.

The polygraph examiner will inform you prior to beginning the actual examination of every question to be asked. This is important because a question may be, "Have you ever been convicted of a crime?" If your answer is yes, you'll want to discuss the circumstances with the examiner prior to the actual test so his or her report will reflect the content of your answer and not just your affirmative response. The polygraph test normally has ten to twenty questions. Sometimes a control test is given prior to the actual examination. You would be instructed to answer no to all questions. For example, you might be given several cards numbered one through eight. The examiner might ask you if you have a certain card (one or more of which you do have) and if all the answers must be negative, then at least one of them is not truthful. The polygraph examiner will note your autonomic response to false answers for later comparison.

During the actual examination you will be asked such questions as:

- Have you ever been convicted of a crime?
- Is your first name Henry?
- Have you ever received a parking ticket?
- Did you drive here today?
- Have you ever stolen anything from your employer?
- Do you have a blue shirt on?

Since you will be asked to answer yes or no to each question, the pretest period with the examiner is very important. The questions you will be asked which determine whether you pass or fail the polygraph test must relate to the background and qualifications of a candidate for the position of a police officer.

You don't have to be perfect to pass a polygraph examination. Approach this test as you would any other in the selection process. Tell the truth! Explain your answers to the questions when appropriate. You have a right to know if you've passed or failed, so ask. By this point in the testing process, you will have been asked the same questions so many times that you probably would have already been rejected as a candidate if there were a major problem. Make certain your answers at this exam are consistent with what you have written, with the records you have submitted, and with what you have told various officials throughout the entire selection process.

THE CHIEF'S INTERVIEW

Believe it or not, there is still one more hurdle for you to leap before the screening process is finally over. After successfully completing the psychological interview, background investigation, and polygraph test, you'll be scheduled for a job interview with the chief of police!

We previously discussed the fact that many cities have what's known as the "rule of three." (A few personnel departments have the "rule of five.") As the final hiring authority, the chief of police is presented with a "certified-to-be-hired" list. This is a rank-ordered list containing the names of all police candidates who have successfully completed the testing and screening process and have been certified by the personnel department as meeting the requirements necessary to become a police officer. If your city uses the "rule of three" it means the chief can select any of the top three candidates on the certified list for each position to be filled. In other words, if the chief was going to hire two police officers, the list would consist of the names of the four highest-scoring candidates. However, the chief could choose any two of the four names on the list. The chief could decide not to hire the two candidates at the top of the list and instead select candidates three and four.

What does this mean to you? It means you have to prepare for this fifteen-minute interview as well as you did for the other tests involved in the selection process. Once again, the techniques you used to excel with the oral panel are the same you'll use in the chief's interview. Here's how the process works.

There are several ways you can be notified of where and when to appear for your interview with the chief or a designee. You might receive another letter from the personnel department or, by this stage in the process, receive a telephone call from a member of the background investigation team or a human resource coordinator working for the police department. The actual interview will be conducted either in the chief's office or a conference room at police headquarters. The chief is usually joined by one or more high-ranking members of the department. If the chief has delegated the process, which is often the case in large departments, an assistant chief or captain will conduct the interview.

On the day of your interview *arrive early*. All departments have a visitor parking area. Make certain you park where you're supposed to. The last thing you want to happen is to get a parking ticket or have your car towed while you're interviewing for a police officer position. You'll enter the front lobby of police headquarters. The officers at the desk will know you're coming and will direct you to the chief's office or a waiting area. The same rules apply that did while you waited to take your oral examination. Sit erect, don't speak unless you're spoken to, and respond to everyone with courtesy.

The same sort of questions asked by your oral panel will be asked again:

- Why do you want to be a police officer?

- What have you done to prepare yourself for a career in policing?

- How do you feel about the fact you may have to use force in conducting your duties as a police officer?

- What are your most positive strengths? What are your weaknesses?

By now you'll be able to breeze through these questions and highly impress the chief or the designee. You've arrived! A career filled with honor, pride, and integrity awaits you. I wish I could do it again!

PERSONAL DEVELOPMENT AND ACTION PLAN

What have I done today to prepare myself for a career in policing?

1. _____

2. _____

3. _____

4. _____

5. _____

6. _____

7. _____

8. _____

9. _____

10. _____

10

THE GATE
TO THE WAY

THE POLICE ACADEMY

When I was commander of the Hartford Police Training Academy in Connecticut, fifteen to twenty percent of the recruits didn't make it through the twenty-two weeks of training. Nationally, this statistic is slightly lower now, but still a large number of those who complete a very selective screening process and are supposedly "qualified" to become police officers never get sworn in. Why? Is it because most of the people who became police officers when I did had a military background, and they were better prepared for the unique atmosphere and training techniques used to produce police officers? Is it that our society is no longer capable of producing the type of men and women with the "right stuff" necessary to carry the badge and the gun? Is it because the standards and requirements to become a police officer are higher today?

No. The reason everyone doesn't make it through the academy is that, like the screening process, the entire twenty-two weeks is a *test*! Not everyone is *supposed* to graduate. Until now, you have been tested through pencil-and-paper exams and interviews. Civilians had a lot to say about the requirements to become a police officer. The police academy is different. It's run by cops! You're entering a world few get to see. It's tribal and semimilitary; there are rights of passage and codes of honor. The vestiges of Old World values remain—personal integrity, living up to your word, inner courage, and self-sacrifice. The academy is part military boot camp, part college, part junior Olympics, and part seminary. It's not the academics that eliminates recruits, or makes them resign, it's the *discipline* that's required.

Certification of Police Academies

Each state has its own laws about certifying and training police officers. Most states have enacted legislation creating state councils responsible for mandating academy requirements, such as curriculum, certification of instructors, number of training hours, and testing of recruits. Many states have their own police academy, which trains both state and municipal police officers, although usually separately. Any city or town within the state can send its candidates to the state-operated academy. Large cities often have their own training academy, which is certified by the state but operated by its own police officers. These academies exist because large cities have unique inner-city policing concerns requiring training not usually offered at state-operated academies. In order to give this additional training, local police academy training is often longer than state-operated municipal police academy training. Usually, twenty-two weeks (880 hours) of instruction followed by an addition eighty hours of field instruction are required for certification. The number of training hours required may be higher or lower in your state.

NOTIFICATION OF RECRUIT STATUS

Now you know that it's tough to get through the academy and that it's regulated by the state. You want to know what happens at the police academy and how to prepare for it, right? It begins by your receiving another letter, but this time it's from the chief of police or the commander of the police academy congratulating you on being chosen to become a member of the police department. A sample of a letter sent to new recruits follows.

September 15, 19—

Leslie Jones
122 Buckingham Street
Newcastle, —

Dear Leslie Jones:

Congratulations on being selected to become a member of the Newcastle Police Department. You are now a police recruit and a student at the Newcastle Police Academy. The objective of the Police Recruit Training Course is to provide future police officers with a working knowledge of human relations, basic police science, law enforcement principles and procedures, and specific police skills so that they can deal effectively with calls for police service, as well as those which are a result of crime and disorder. The twenty-two week training program will provide you with the basic skills needed to perform the duties of a Newcastle police officer.

The police academy will begin on September 25, 19—, at 0745 hours. The academy is located at 143 Newcastle Road, adjacent to police headquarters. Parking is available in the visitor parking lot. **Do not park in any other location.** Proceed to the police academy and into classroom 4 on the first floor. You are expected to be present in the "uniform of the day," which for police recruits consists of the following:

khaki shirt, long-sleeved
khaki pants
black tie
black shoes with black laces
black socks
black or brown belt

Recruits are required to report for duty with a three-ringed notebook, paper, and a pen which writes in **black ink.** You will also be required to present your motor vehicle operator's license upon reporting to the facility.

Sincerely,

Ralph A. Simmons

Captain Ralph A. Simmons
Commander
Newcastle Police Training Academy

The Recruit Uniform

Appearance is critical at the police academy. Police officers wear uniforms and are inspected daily by their superior officers. Your academy instructors will make an initial judgment about you based on how "sharp" you look. It's not uncommon for the first day to begin outside the classroom with a military roll call and uniform inspection. Make certain you take the following steps to create the best first impression possible:

1. Men, get a haircut, and the shorter the better. Women should consider wearing their hair so it will not fall over the ears, eyebrows, or extend over the collar.

2. You can purchase your khaki shirts and pants at a department store. I recommend that you purchase at least three shirts and pants and two ties. It takes time to get clothes back from the cleaners and you will want to make certain you have a clean uniform each day. The way your uniforms fit is important; have them tailored if needed. Tell the cleaners you want military creases ironed into the shirts and extra sharp creases in the pants.

3. Look in the yellow pages of the telephone book to find a store that sells police equipment. They'll have the type of military shoe that maintains a high gloss shine without your having to polish them every day. They will also have the type of belts and ties worn by police officers. If you can't find a police equipment store in your area, most major department stores carry the type of shoes, belts, and ties worn by police academy recruits.

Your First Day

There are different philosophies about how a police academy should be operated. Some academies are like college, where the primary purpose is to transfer academic knowledge from instructor to student. Others are more like a military boot camp, with heavy emphasis on strict discipline, physical fitness, self-defense training, and police tradition. Most police academies are a mixture of both. Often the early emphasis is on acquainting recruits with military-type structure and discipline through a variety of traditional boot camp mechanisms. As the academy progresses, the emphasis shifts to academic training and education. At some police academies, recruits are introduced to a semimilitary environment the moment they step into the building. You might encounter a situation like this:

On the first day, as recruits wearing their khaki uniforms enter the police academy lobby, they are met by a very large officer in full police uniform who yells at them to move rapidly through a door leading to a hallway. Upon entering the hallway, recruits are met by another police academy instructor who directs them to back up against the hallway wall, stand at attention, look straight ahead, and not speak unless spoken to by a police officer. As more recruits enter, the line forms down the hallway on both sides. The instructor begins berating all the recruits about how terrible their uniforms look, how the recruits will never make it through the police academy, and on and on. Heaven help the person who is *one second* past 0745 hours coming through the door. That gets twenty push-ups and a long, long lecture about self-discipline, punctuality, and dependability. Then, the instructors leave all the recruits alone in the hallway, still standing at attention, for ten minutes.

The recruits are left wondering what they have gotten themselves into. For many, this is the first time they will have been subjected to discipline of this type. They are experiencing some anxiety and apprehension! Some recruits can't handle this treatment and don't make it through the first week!

What's the reason for this type of hazing? It's to see if the recruits *have what it takes*. Most people entering a police academy will be sworn in as police officers and will carry a gun every day for twenty-five years. If a recruit can't take a little yelling in the training environment of a police academy, what will he or she do on the street when someone does more than just yell at them? Pull the gun out of the holster and kill someone? Part of this "rite of passage" is to determine if you have the self-discipline and psychological hardiness which will be necessary to withstand the pressures of policing on the street. Better to find out in the academy than some dark alley at two o'clock in the morning.

So how do you handle this type of pressure? It's simple. Keep your eyes and ears open and your mouth shut. Mentally prepare yourself. Do what you're told, when you're told to do it. Follow instructions. Watch, listen, and learn. It's all a mind game at the academy. Don't take it personally. Your instructor's main objective is to teach you the art of policing and to provide you with the skills needed not only to serve the public, but to *keep you alive* when you hit the streets. Self-discipline is a major part of it.

Eventually you'll enter a classroom which will be similar to those at a high school or college. The first day is mainly devoted to acquainting you with your obligations as a police recruit: police academy regulations; academy conduct; and academic, certification, and graduation requirements. You'll receive a police recruit manual specifically detailing all of this. At some point you will be welcomed by the chief of police and/or the police academy commander. Your academy instructors will also be introduced. You'll begin to get used to standing and coming to attention (shoes with heels together and toes out at a forty-five degree angle, hands along the sides, thumbs at the trouser seam, shoulders back, eyes forward) when a police officer enters the room. You'll answer "Yes, sir; yes, ma'am" and "no, sir; no ma'am." You'll march single file to lunch with an academy instructor and be told not to converse with anyone unless spoken to first. You'll be issued textbooks and eventually will be allowed to go home ("dismissed for the day"), at which point you'll be completely dazed. People will ask you how it went, and you'll say, "I'm not sure." Within three days, you'll be hooked. Within two weeks, graduating and becoming a police officer will be the most important thing in your life.

THE RECRUIT TRAINING MANUAL

The best way to understand how to excel at the police academy is to study a recruit training manual so you'll know what to expect and can take steps to prepare. In the typical training manual that follows, I've included tips (in italics) in those sections especially important for successful academy completion.

NEWCASTLE POLICE DEPARTMENT RECRUIT MANUAL

Contents

I. Introduction
II. Personal Qualifications and Standards
III. Recruit Obligations
IV. Curriculum
V. Police Academy Performance Standards
VI. Police Academy Rules and Regulations
VII. Termination of Training

I. Introduction

You are now a Newcastle Police Academy recruit. As such, you do *not* have police powers or authority until you have successfully completed the prescribed course and are certified by the Newcastle Police Department and other appropriate authorities. During the time that you are assigned to the Newcastle Police Academy, you are under the direct supervision of the police academy commander and the commander's staff.

You are commended for choosing law enforcement as your profession. You can be proud that you were selected from numerous applicants to begin an exciting and rewarding career with this department. Your success in meeting the rigorous standards of the police selection process is an indication that you possess many of the qualities required of police officers in a complex society. Academy training will enhance these characteristics and provide the necessary foundation upon which to build your future career.

The academy staff is committed to your development and ready to assist you in every possible way. You should view your relationship with your instructors as a mutually supportive partnership, the common purpose of which is your successful completion of a demanding and challenging training program. As with any professional endeavor, achievement depends on your dedication, maturity, and determination. You are expected to put forth your maximum effort.

A police officer's role is unique and requires a variety of skills and abilities to deal with a myriad of sensitive and volatile issues. You must be objective, fair, impartial, and of exemplary character. You will be required to make critical decisions concerning life and death, personal liberty, and major crimes, relying on your intelligence, judgment, self-discipline, and training.

II. Personal Qualifications and Standards

Recruit officers must demonstrate a level of professional conduct, both on and off duty, which is in keeping with the high standards of police service and the department. Recruits will be evaluated on personal qualifications and standards which include, but are not limited to:

1. Adherence to the rules and regulations of the Newcastle Police Academy and the Newcastle Police Department
2. Ability to get along with people and establish cooperative relationships
3. Appearance, personal hygiene, and demeanor
4. Maturity and poise
5. Alertness
6. Positive and professional communication skills
7. Dependability—the extent to which a recruit can be relied upon to complete assigned tasks and meet expectations
8. Punctuality
9. Honesty and integrity
10. Work habits—including organization of work, promptness, teamwork, and diligence
11. Proper off-duty conduct

Tip: Pay special attention to number 11, "proper off-duty conduct." The fastest way to get booted out of the police academy is to be arrested or otherwise become entangled with the criminal justice system while a police recruit.

Police officers are expected to perform their duties to the public in a prompt, fair, professional, impartial, and courteous manner. The personal qualifications learned or reinforced during training provides a framework for the standard of service expected.

III. Recruit Obligations

1. To adhere to the principles contained in the "Law Enforcement Code of Ethics," the rules and regulations of the department, and those of the academy. The public expects the integrity of its law enforcement officers to be exemplary. The dishonesty of a single officer may impair public confidence and cast suspicion upon the entire department. A recruit has the same obligation as a police officer to scrupulously avoid any conduct which might compromise personal integrity, the integrity of the department, or the integrity of fellow officers.

   Tip: The "Law Enforcement Code of Ethics" can be found in the supplement section.

2. To embrace the commitment to serve the public, to protect civil liberties, and to promote public peace and welfare. Each recruit must be dedicated to impartial enforcement of the law.

3. To develop a sense of self-confidence in personal abilities and to take responsibility for personal actions and behaviors, on and off the job.

4. To maintain control under pressure, avoiding loss of temper, impatience, rudeness, vulgarity, and sarcasm.

5. To promote a positive image to the public by maintaining proper uniform and grooming standards.

6. To develop the ability to deal effectively with all members of the community in a fashion reflecting respect and dignity. Recruits should deal with people in a sensitive and understanding manner. Courtesy is fundamental to sound public and community relations and to the department's objectives.

7. To develop an understanding of the role of the public in the prevention of crime and apprehension of criminals.

8. To understand the use-of-force policy and to apply only reasonable and necessary force to accomplish the police mission.

Tip: The concept of using reasonable and necessary force will be on many tests at the academy. The answer is always to use the minimum force necessary that is reasonable under the circumstances.

9. To develop the ability to make decisions, taking into account ethical, legal, and tactical considerations.

10. To develop an appreciation for the cultural diversity of the community and for the department's goal of delivering impartial police service for all.

IV. Curriculum (Syllabus provided separately)

Area 1: Introduction to Criminal Justice

The History and Evolution of the Police
Federal and State Agencies
The Judicial System
Corrections, Parole, and Probation

Area 2: Police and the Law

United States Constitution
Criminal Law/Source of Law
Introduction to Criminal Law
State Penal Code and Unclassified Crimes
Human Rights and Opportunities
Law of Evidence
Laws of Arrest
Search and Seizure
Search Warrant Preparation

Area 3: Practical Police Skills

Firearms Training
Emergency Medical Services
Defensive Tactics

Mechanics of Arrest
Defensive Driving
Application Sessions (Stations Days)
Police Report Writing

Area 4: Police—Human Relations

Human Behavior
Police Ethics and Professionalism
Police and the Public
Police and Troubled Youth
Community Agencies

Area 5: Criminal Investigation

Principles of Investigation
Crime Scene Procedure
Interviews and Interrogation
Criminal Statements
Fingerprinting
Photography
Case Investigative Techniques
Crimes Involving Alcohol, Tobacco, and Firearms
Explosives and Incendiary Devices
Narcotics and Dangerous Drugs
Counterfeiting/Forgery
Gambling/Organized Crime
Case Preparation
Developing Informants
Motor Vehicle Theft

Area 6: Patrol Procedure and Traffic Services

Accident Investigation
Courtroom Demeanor and Testifying
Crime Prevention
Crisis Intervention
Crowd Control/Civil Disorders
Domestic Complaints
Motor Vehicle Law/Summonses/Infractions/Warnings
Patrol Techniques/Functions and Procedures
Police Communications
Police Report Writing
Precautionary Measures/Approach to Danger
Recognition and Handling of Abnormal Behavior
Roadblocks
Stopping Suspects
Traffic Control

Area 7: Departmental and Field Training Experience

V. Police Academy Performance Standards

The recruit training program is composed of twenty-two weeks of instruction followed by eighty hours of field training with a field training officer. The academic and practical field training segments of the Newcastle Police Academy Recruit Program are designed to go beyond the minimum requirements prescribed by the state for certification as a police officer. Additional training is provided in order to better prepare officers to deal effectively with all members of the community in a manner which will maintain their support and cooperation.

In order to successfully graduate, all recruits must

1. Maintain at least a seventy percent grade average in each of the below-listed test areas, which include material taught within the curriculum.

   Introduction to Criminal Justice
   Laws of Arrest
   Search and Seizure
   Laws of Evidence
   Penal Code
   Motor Vehicle Law
   Accident Investigation
   Human Relations
   Patrol Techniques
   Police Orders and Procedures
   Emergency Medical Services

2. Successfully complete the Police Report Writing course.

   A major element of police work is the proper preparation of reports that detail field situations encountered by individual officers, including investigations of crimes and arrests of suspects. The accuracy and attention to detail with which these reports are prepared often determine whether a crime will be solved or a perpetrator successfully prosecuted. It is essential that police report-writing skills be developed which enable recruits to record the details of their actions as police officers.

Requirements

Following instructions, recruits will be required to prepare reports which will be graded on the recruit's thoroughness in examining all relevant information; the taking of accurate, complete notes; the analysis and organization of the findings; and the ability to communicate all relevant information in a written report. Adherence to the rules of English grammar, construction, and spelling is required of recruit officers. Additionally, a report of a preliminary investigation of a crime must accurately reflect the elements and circumstances of the crime, as well as the seizure, handling, and disposition of evidence, and notifications made. Arrest reports must follow the proper narrative format and accurately reflect admonitions by officers, waivers, and statements obtained from arrestees and witnesses. Failure to adequately demonstrate these skills will result in dismissal. Recruits will be required to obtain scores of seventy percent or higher on three report-writing examinations. These exercises will be graded by subject matter experts to ensure consistency in scoring.

Tip: Report writing is a critical skill for successful completion of the academy. Always bring a dictionary to the classroom. If writing is an area that has been a problem for you, hire a tutor or attend a night course to upgrade your skills.

3. Successfully pass the Emergency Medical Services Practicum.

   Tip: This is an advanced first aid and cardiopulmonary resuscitation course.

4. Successfully complete the Firearms and Revolver Qualification course.

   In the skills application phase, recruits must attain a minimum passing score of 220 out of a possible 300 points. Remediation shall be mandatory for those recruits who fail to qualify with the department-issued firearm before the end of normal firearms training. Recruits must also achieve a score of one hundred percent on a written test of the "Newcastle Police Department Firearms Guidelines." It is inappropriate for a recruit to know only seventy percent or even eighty percent of these critical guidelines; therefore a perfect score is required.

   Tip: It's absolutely critical that you pass the firearms qualification course. If you have no previous experience with firearms, enroll in a training program certified by the National Rifle Association. Use the same firearm as that issued by the department. Explain to the instructor that you are entering the police academy and need assistance in qualifying in the police firearms training course. Almost anyone can learn to fire a gun with precision, but it does take lots of practice.

5. Sucessfully complete Defensive Tactics, Defensive Driving, and Physical Fitness Training.

   Tip: Continue the physical conditioning program you began in preparing for the physical agility test.

6. Successfully complete exercises in shotgun and tear gas familiarization.

VI. Police Academy Rules and Regulations

1. All police recruits are subject to the provisions of the "Newcastle Police Department Code of Conduct."

2. All police recruits are subject to all Newcastle Police Department policies and procedures.

3. The Newcastle Police Academy is operational Monday through Friday (excluding holidays) from 0730 to 1600 hours. Recruits who wish to consult with academy

staff during other-than-normal operating hours shall make prior arrangements with the proper staff member.

4. Absence: Attendance at all classes is *mandatory*. Each recruit is responsible for all requirements related to assignments, test dates and times, and participation in situational exercises and field training programs. Absence from class does not excuse or relieve recruits of their responsibility. It is a recruit's responsibility to make up any missed classes or tests. If, in the opinion of the police academy commander, based on a recommendation from the Academic Review Board, any recruit has missed more work than he or she is capable of making up prior to the class graduation date, or whose use of leave is deemed excessive or frivolous, he or she may be terminated from employment.

5. Illness/Injury: Absences will be allowed for illness or injury that incapacitates the recruit. The police academy may require proof of illness or injury from a qualified physician.

6. Recruits are required to be punctual for all roll calls and classes. Absences or lateness will be recorded and *will be considered a factor for dismissal from the academy*. Recruits arriving late for 0745 roll call will report to the academy supervisor prior to entering the classroom.

7. The police recruit's uniform for academic instruction will be kept in excellent condition. A daily inspection of the police recruits will be made at roll call for uniforms, shoes, and grooming. Prescribed gym clothing shall be worn for physical training and self-defense classes. *Men's hair shall be neatly trimmed, with sideburns no longer than the middle of the ear lobe. No facial hair is allowed. Female recruits with long hair shall wear their hair up. No earrings will be worn. Shoes shall be shined to a high gloss.*

8. During the recruit tour of duty, recruits shall

   - report to the classroom at 0745 for roll call and inspection.
   - take their assigned seats. Seating arrangements shall not be altered without permission of the instructor.
   - refrain from eating, drinking, or smoking in the classroom.
   - be respectful to all loaned property, be courteous to all personnel, maintain decorum and military bearing, and address all personnel by designated rank and last name or the words "Sir" or "Ma'am." This includes all outside speakers.
   - participate in all instruction and ask meaningful questions.
   - take complete class notes and maintain them in a three-ringed, loose-leaf notebook. All notes shall be transferred to typewritten sheets. Notebooks will be examined and evaluated at frequent intervals.

9. A recruit's signature on announced or unannounced quizzes, tests, examinations, or other evaluation instruments attests to unaided work. Cheating in any form shall result in immediate dismissal.

10. To enter an office, recruits shall knock firmly prior to entry. They shall approach whomever they have business with, addressing them by title and name. Recruits shall then state their name, stand at ease, and state their business.

11. Recruits may not participate in other employment.

12. Recruits shall not grant interviews or make public statements regarding academy or department policies, procedures, or training activities without prior approval of the academy commander.

13. Profanity, derogatory language, and loud or boisterous conduct is unprofessional and not acceptable.

VII. Termination of Training

Training may be terminated on either a voluntary or involuntary basis.

Voluntary: Recruits who wish to withdraw from the Newcastle Police Academy shall submit their resignation in writing to the chief of police through the commander of the Newcastle Police Academy.

Involuntary: Recruits may be terminated for any of the following reasons:

1. Violation of the "Newcastle Police Department Code of Conduct."
2. Being late for class or assignments on more than three occasions.
3. Violation of the "Newcastle Police Department Firearm Safety Guidelines."
4. Conduct detrimental to the learning environment of the police academy, to the discipline of the recruit class, or to the efficiency or operations of the academy or the police department.
5. Failure to maintain an overall academic average of seventy percent in each of the specified course areas.
6. Lack of proficiency in self-defense or failure of the self-defense techniques course after remediation.
7. Inability to achieve or maintain a qualifying score with the service revolver.
8. Failure to achieve proficiency sufficient to meet department and state standards in driving a police vehicle under various driving conditions.
9. Misconduct that would bring embarrassment or discredit to the department.
10. Dishonesty and cheating in any test situation.

(This sample recruit manual was adapted from the *Hartford Police Training Academy Recruit Manual* by the author.)

Additional Tips for Excelling at the Police Academy

Arrive early every day

The typical police academy starts each day at 0745 hours with roll call. Roll call is a military formation in which recruits stand side by side in close ranks at the "attention" position. However, prior to roll call, academy instructors will be present in and around the classroom. Your arriving early each day *will* be noticed and regarded as a positive sign of your commitment to becoming a police officer. It's also an excellent opportunity for you to ask questions relative to areas in which you may need additional assistance. *Wait for the instructors to approach you.* If you arrive early every single day, they eventually will.

Maintain control under pressure

Part of the role of the police academy instructor is to test your ability to maintain control of your emotions under pressure. What does it take for you to lose your temper? Emergency situations require inner discipline. How will you react to an angry crowd venting its frustration at you simply because you wear the uniform of a public servant?

Understand ahead of time that you will be pushed to your physical and emotional limits. Academy instructors will most often put individual recruits under pressure during physical fitness and self-defense activities. These situations will *always* arise when a recruit is *perceived* to be giving less than one hundred percent. The willingness to *try*, even when exhausted, is prized at the academy. *Always* be the first to volunteer for everything. Even if you try and initially fail, you will have won points for self-confidence, leadership, and determination. The pressure will be taken off of *you* and placed on someone else.

Keep up with the academics

There is nothing more important than getting off to a good academic start at the police academy. Scoring well on the first couple of tests is critical to sustaining a high average. Although textbooks are issued, major emphasis is placed on handouts and manuals. Lecture is the preferred instructional method. Take copious notes. Much of the material you'll be tested on won't come from your textbooks. Use the same study method that was explained in the chapter on preparing for written examinations. You'll need to discipline yourself to consistently study after class and on weekends. Other recruits will want to form study groups. *Don't.* These groups almost always end up as social events and very little studying gets done. Your objective is to come out number one in the academy. The higher you graduate, the more *seniority* you'll have. This will affect your career for years to come. Seniority dictates what shift you work, when you can go on vacation or take a day off, and to some extent your job assignment. If there are forty recruits in class and you graduate first, you have seniority in job classification over thirty-nine other officers, even though you will be sworn in on the same day. If the department is ever subjected to layoffs, it's "last hired, first fired." Thirty-nine other officers would be laid off before you. Commit yourself totally to the police academy. Make it the most important thing in your life for the entire twenty-two weeks.

PERSONAL DEVELOPMENT AND ACTION PLAN

What have I done today to prepare myself for a career in policing?

1. _____

2. _____

3. _____

4. _____

5. _____

6. _____

7. _____

8. _____

9. _____

10. _____

11
TOUCHSTONES

GLOSSARY

Ability—An ability is an intrinsic trait further developed through training, education, or experience that allows performance of a function which is either mental or physical.

Annual Report—An annual report is prepared by a city to describe its accomplishments for a period of one year. The report contains information about each department, including the number of employees.

Arrest—Arrest involves taking a person into custody to answer for a crime he or she is alleged to have committed.

Authorized Strength—The number of people in a police department authorized to do a particular job is called authorized strength.

Background Investigation—The background investigation is part of the screening process for police candidates. The primary purpose of the investigation is to eliminate candidates who are not suited for police work because of patterns, events, or characteristics reflected in their personal histories. The investigation is conducted by the police department and involves checking candidates' work experiences, arrest records, diplomas, and so forth.

Bid Shift—A bid shift is a system in which officers are allowed to choose a specific work shift (time of day) based on their seniority.

Body Fat Composition—Body fat composition is the percentage of fat a person carries, and it is compared to others through statistical groupings. The body fat composition test, part of the medical examination, has replaced height to weight comparisons in many departments.

Budget—A police budget details the amount of money needed to deliver police services in a community.

Call for Service—A call for service results in police response to a problem. A call for service may be initiated by the public or by a police officer who has detected a problem.

Certified Hiring List—A certified hiring list is a rank-ordered list of candidates who have passed all testing and other requirements and are eligible to be hired.

Citizen Rider Program—The citizen rider program is a community relations program in which citizens are allowed to accompany a police officer in a patrol car while responding to calls.

Community Relations—Good community relations promote feelings of trust, pride, and rapport between a police department and the community it serves.

Cop—A cop is a police officer. During the 1800s, police officers were called constables and many people believe the word *cop* came from the initials for "constable on patrol." Others think it is a shortened form of the word "copper," a reference to the copper badges worn by many police officers.

Crime—A crime is anything that society says is a crime and has the authority to punish.

Crime Analysis—Crime analysis involves compiling and scrutinizing information in order to plan, organize, direct, and coordinate police services, for example, crime statistics, crime patterns, and calls for police services.

Crime Prevention—Crime prevention is reducing the opportunity for criminals to commit crimes.

Crime Repression/Suppression—Crime repression (suppression) involves creating an atmosphere in which criminal offenders believe that the opportunity to commit a crime doesn't exist or that the crime will result in immediate arrest.

Crime Scene Preservation—In proper crime-scene preservation, the location at which a crime has occurred is kept in exactly the same condition as it was left by the criminal.

Deadly Physical Force—Force used by a person which can reasonably be expected to cause death or serious physical injury is deadly physical force. In most cases, police officers can use deadly physical force only to protect themselves or a third person from the imminent use of deadly physical force.

Deadly Weapon—A weapon designed specifically to kill, such as a gun, is a deadly weapon.

Discovery—Discovery is the process of learning something through reading, observing, and thinking.

Felony—A felony is a crime punishable by more than one year in prison.

Force, Use of—In making an arrest, only the minimum amount of force necessary to overcome a person's resistance may be used.

Image Distortion—Image distortion occurs when a person's words say one thing and his or her posture, gestures, and voice inflections say something else, creating an image different from the one intended.

Job Description—See **Position Description.**

Job Task Analysis—Job task analysis is a systematic process of defining the tasks and/or behaviors needed to perform a job successfully over a period of time.

Knowledge—Knowledge is a systematic body of information which a person possesses as a result of formal education, life experience, and training.

Larceny—Larceny is committed when a person intentionally and wrongfully takes, obtains, or withholds property from an owner.

Line Function—The term *line function* describes those officers in a police department engaged in activities directly related to immediate response to citizens' calls for police service. For example, officers assigned to the patrol division are line officers, while those engaged in the training or records division, which supports the work of the patrol division, are staff officers.

Lines of Authority—In a semimilitary profession, lines of authority clearly delineate the responsibility for completion of job tasks throughout the department and describe those individuals who have the authority to delegate work to lower levels.

Medical Examination—The medical examination is part of the screening process for police candidates and is given to determine if candidates have the physical requirements needed to perform the job of a police officer.

Medical History Questionnaire—Part of the medical examination, the medical history questionnaire is a form candidates fill out detailing their past and present medical conditions.

Metropolitan Police Act of 1829—The Metropolitan Police Act of 1829 established the first organized, modern police department in Westminster, England. It was headed by Sir Robert Peel.

Minimum Requirements—Minimum requirements are the basic qualifications necessary to fulfill the requirements of a job; some examples in policing might be having 20/20 vision, being at least eighteen years of age, having a high school diploma, and living in the city where the job is.

Misdemeanor—A misdemeanor is a crime punishable by less than one year in prison.

Modus Operandi—*Modus operandi* is a Latin term meaning *method of operation*—the method in which a criminal operates and the habits and procedures used repeatedly by a criminal to commit crimes.

Municipal Police Officers—Municipal police officers are officers employed by cities. They are responsible for crime prevention, crime detection, and arresting people who commit criminal acts.

Patrol—Patrol refers to having police officers moving about in defined areas to provide security and assistance and to observe and inspect.

Foot patrol refers to officers who walk an area, called a *beat,* responding to calls for service. Foot patrol allows greater contact with the public, but is limited in the area that can be covered and the speed of response.

Vehicular patrol refers to officers moving about an area in a police car, responding to calls for service. Vehicles allow officers to carry additional equipment and to respond to calls for service quickly over a wide area.

Random patrol is patrol, whether on foot or in a car, that establishes no regular pattern so that criminals cannot know where police officers are at any given moment.

Patrol Division—The patrol division is the backbone of a police department and is directly responsible for the delivery of police services to the community.

Personal Trait—A personal trait (or characteristic) is a predisposition on the part of a person to behave in a certain way.

Police Athletic League—The Police Athletic League is an outreach program to provide mentors for young adults within a sports framework. Leagues are sponsored by police departments.

Police Cadet Program—The Police Cadet Program provides apprenticeship positions with police departments to individuals aged eighteen to twenty-one. Cadets work in the various divisions of police departments to prepare for becoming police officers.

Police Explorer Program—The Police Explorer Program is a Boy Scout troop sponsored by a police department. Scouts work with police officers and perform minor duties such as directing traffic and marching in parades.

Police Internship—Police internships are usually coordinated between a police department and a college, allowing students to work part-time to gain an understanding of police department functional components and operations.

Police Mission—The mission of the police is to protect life and property against criminal acts, preserve the peace, and ensure the safe movement of traffic. The abbreviated version of this is to "serve and protect the public."

Police Omnipresence—The term *police omnipresence* refers to the perception on the part of criminals that the police are everywhere and that if they commit a criminal act, they will immediately be apprehended.

Polygraph Examination—The polygraph examination is part of the screening process and background investigation for police candidates. The polygraph is a machine which charts physiological changes in the body as a person is asked a series of questions.

Position Description—A position description is a document about a job describing its function, the tasks associated with its successful completion, and the minimum requirements a candidate needs to possess to apply for the position.

Probable Cause—Probable cause is reasonable grounds for belief that an offense (crime) has been committed. A police officer must have facts, observations, or trustworthy information establishing probable cause before making an arrest.

Probationary Period—A probationary period is a working test period, usually one year in length from the date of swearing in, in which an officer may be discharged for performance-related issues without access to a unionized grievance process.

Psychological Examination—The psychological examination is part of the testing process for police candidates. Its objective is to eliminate individuals who may lack the emotional stability and maturity required to perform the duties of a police officer. The test is either a standardized, personality-based, multiple-choice test or an interview with a psychologist.

Recidivist—A person who repeatedly commits criminal acts is a recidivist.

Residency Preference Points—Points are awarded to the final passing grade of candidates who are residents of a department's city. Normally, city residents are eligible for an additional ten percent of their final average score.

Residency Requirement—A prerequisite of police work is either residency within the city or residency within a specified distance and/or driving time to the department headquarters.

Robbery—A person commits robbery when, in the course of committing a larceny, the person either uses or threatens the immediate use of physical force upon another person.

Rule of Three—The "rule of three" is a personnel department device used in many cities in which a department head (chief of police) may select *any* one of the top three candidates on a hiring list to fill each open position.

Seniority—The amount of time that an officer has been working for a police department, usually calculated from the date he or she was sworn in, is called seniority.

Skill—A skill is a proficiency that is acquired through training, experience, and practice.

Staff Function—The term *staff function* describes all work in a police department that doesn't deal directly with the public in the field, such as the records division, training, and fiscal management.

State Police Officer—State police officers are employed by state governments and are responsible for criminal and traffic-control-related activities occurring on state highways. State police officers have jurisdiction throughout a state and can make arrests in any city or town.

SWAT—SWAT stands for special weapons assault team. The team is a highly trained group of police officers called upon to handle dangerous situations, such as those involving hostages and barricaded persons.

Tests—Any examination, interview, or form that eliminates candidates from the police officer selection process is a test.

Drug test—A drug test is required as part of the screening process in most departments—candidates are required to submit to a urinalysis. The drugs most commonly tested for are marijuana; cocaine; opiates, such as heroin and morphine; amphetamines; barbiturates; methadone; and phencyclidines.

Generic test questions—Generic test questions are those which do not reflect a specific department's method of operations but instead deal with universally accepted principles and concepts.

Oral test—This testing process evaluates a candidate on knowledge, skills, abilities, and personal characteristics which have been determined necessary for the performance of a job. The test is an interview before three or more panel members who evaluate a candidate's intrinsic and behavioral qualities, communication skills, appearance, and organizational integrity.

Physical agility test—This test, another part of the screening process for the position of police officer, evaluates a candidate's muscular endurance, flexibility, muscular explosiveness, grip strength, speed, balance, coordination, and cardiovascular conditioning by using a series of exercises combined with job-related obstacle courses.

Police entry-level test—The entry-level test for police is a systematic process in which the individual being tested is presented with a set of constructed questions that will allow the tester to make a prediction of whether that individual has what the test is designed to measure.

Test reliability—For a test to be *reliable,* it must consistently and dependably measure those characteristics needed to perform a job properly over a period of time.

Test validity—For a test to be *valid,* the questions must specifically relate to performing the job for which the test is given.

Written test—Entry-level *written* examinations consist of multiple-choice questions designed to measure a candidate's analytical thinking, reasoning, judgment, observation, memory, common sense, grammar, writing, and problem-solving abilities.

Tour of duty—A tour of duty is a police officer's work day—the number of hours an officer works in one day.

Veterans Preference Points—Veterans preference points are added to the final average test score of an honorably discharged war veteran. Five points are usually awarded.

Violation—A violation is a crime punishable by a fine only.

Vision Requirements—Most police departments require vision correctable to 20/20; others allow 20/40. A vision test is part of the medical examination. Some departments require normal color vision and will test for that also.

Visualization—Visualization is a technique used to keep the mind focused on a specific goal.

Way—*The Way* is a martial arts philosophy that pursues wisdom through a series of life-long challenges, each of which is set at a slightly higher plateau.

LAW ENFORCEMENT CODE OF ETHICS

As a law enforcement officer, my fundamental duty is to serve people: to safeguard lives and property; to protect the innocent against deception, the weak against oppression or intimidation, and the peaceful against violence or disorder; and to respect the constitutional rights of all people to liberty, equality, and justice.

I will keep my private life unsullied and as an example to all; maintain courageous calm in the face of danger, scorn, or ridicule; develop self-restraint; and be constantly mindful of the welfare of others. Honest in thought and deed in both my personal and official life, I will be exemplary in obeying the laws of the land and the regulations of my department. Whatever I see or hear of a confidential nature or that is confided to me in my official capacity will be kept ever secret unless revelation is necessary in the performance of my duty.

I will never act officiously or permit personal feelings, prejudices, animosities, or friendships to influence my decisions. With no compromise for crime and with relentless prosecution of criminals, I will enforce the law courteously and appropriately without fear or favor, malice or ill will, never employing unnecessary force or violence, and never accepting gratuities.

I recognize the badge of my office as a symbol of public faith, and I accept it as a public trust to be held so long as I am true to the ethics of the police service. I will constantly strive to achieve these objectives and ideals, dedicating myself to my chosen profession—law enforcement!

CANONS OF POLICE ETHICS

Article I: Primary Responsibility of Job

The primary responsibility of the police service, and of individual officers, is the protection of the people of the United States through the upholding of their laws; chief among these is the Constitution of the United States and its amendments. Law enforcement officers always respect the whole of the community and its legally expressed will and are never the arm of any political party or clique.

Article II: Limitations of Authority

The first duty of law enforcement officers, as upholders of the law, is to know its bounds upon them in enforcing it. Because they represent the legal will of the community, be it local, state, or federal, they must be aware of the limitations and proscriptions which the people, through law, have placed upon them. They must recognize the genius of the American system of government which gives no single person, nor group, nor institution, absolute power, and they must ensure that they, as prime defenders of the system, do not pervert its character.

Article III: Duty to be Familiar with the Law and with Responsibilities of Self and Other Public Officials

Law enforcement officers shall assiduously apply themselves to the study of the principles of the laws that they are sworn to uphold. They will make certain of their responsibilities in the particulars of their enforcement, seeking aid from their superiors in matters of technicality or principles when they are not clear; they will make special effort to understand their relationships to other public officials, including other law enforcement agencies, particularly on matters of jurisdiction, both geographically and substantively.

Article IV: Utilization of Proper Means to Gain Proper Ends

Law enforcement officers shall be mindful of their responsibility to pay strict heed to the selection of the means in discharging the duties of their office. Violations of law or disregard for public safety and property on the part of officers are intrinsically wrong; they are self-defeating in that they instill in the public mind a like disposition. The employment of illegal means, no matter how worthy the end, is certain to encourage disrespect for the law and its officers. If the law is to be honored, it must be honored by those who enforce it.

Article V: Cooperation with Public Officials in the Discharge of Their Authorized Duties

Law enforcement officers shall cooperate fully with other public officials in the discharge of authorized duties, regardless of political party affiliation or personal prejudice. They shall be meticulous, however, in assuring themselves of the propriety, under the law, of such actions and shall guard against the use of their office or persons, whether knowingly or unknowingly, in any improper or illegal action. In any situation open to question, they shall seek authority from their superior officers, giving them a full report of the proposed service or action.

Article VI: Private Conduct

Law enforcement officers shall be mindful of their special identification by the public as an upholder of the law. Laxity of conduct or manner in private life, expressing either disrespect for the law or seeking to grant special privilege, cannot but reflect upon police officers and the police service. The community and the service require that law enforcement officers lead the life of decent and honorable people. Following the career of a police officer gives no one special perquisites. It does give the satisfaction and pride of following and furthering an unbroken tradition of safeguarding the American republic. Officers who reflect upon this tradition will not disgrace it. Rather, they will so conduct their private lives that the public will regard them as an example of stability, fidelity, and morality.

Article VII: Conduct Toward the Public

Law enforcement officers, mindful of their responsibility to the whole community, shall deal with individuals of the community in a manner calculated to instill respect for its laws and its police service. Law enforcement officers shall conduct their official lives in a manner such as will inspire confidence and trust. Thus, they will be neither overbearing nor subservient, as citizens have neither an obligation to stand in awe of them nor a right to command them. Officers will give service where they can, and require compliance with the law. They will do neither from personal preference or prejudice but only as duly appointed officers of the law discharging their sworn obligations.

Article VIII: Conduct in Arresting and Dealing with Law Violators

Law enforcement officers shall use their powers of arrest strictly in accordance with the law and with due regard to the rights of the citizen concerned. The position gives officers no right to prosecute violators nor to mete out punishment for offenses. Officers shall, at all times, have a clear appreciation of their responsibilities and limitations regarding detention of the violator; they shall conduct themselves in such a manner as will minimize the possibility of having to use force. To this end they shall cultivate a dedication to the service of the people and the equitable upholding of their laws whether in the handling of law violators or in dealing with the law-abiding.

Article IX: Gifts and Favors

Law enforcement officers, representing government, bear the heavy responsibility of maintaining, in their conduct, the honor and integrity of all government institutions. They shall, therefore, guard against placing themselves in a position in which any person can reasonably assume that special consideration is being given. Thus, they should be firm in refusing gifts, favors, or gratuities, large or small, which can, in the public mind, be interpreted as capable of influencing their judgment in the discharge of duties.

Article X: Presentation of Evidence

Law enforcement officers shall be concerned equally in the prosecution of the wrongdoer and the defense of the innocent. They shall ascertain what constitutes evidence and shall present such evidence impartially and without malice. In so doing, they will ignore social, political, and other distinctions among the persons involved, strengthening the tradition of the reliability and the integrity of an officer's word. Law enforcement officers shall take special pains to increase their perception and skill of observation, mindful that in many circumstances theirs is the sole impartial testimony to the facts of a crime.

Article XI: Attitude Toward Profession

Law enforcement officers shall regard the discharge of their duties as a public trust and recognize their responsibility as a public servant. By diligent study and sincere attention to self-improvement, they shall strive to make the best possible application of science to the solution of crime and, in the field of human relationships, strive for effective leadership and the public influence in matters affecting public safety. They shall appreciate the importance and responsibility of their office and hold police work to be an honorable profession rendering valuable service to the community and the country.

DUTIES AND RESPONSIBILITIES OF POLICE OFFICERS

This list is not comprehensive, but is intended to give you a general sampling of the tasks performed by police officers in their daily work.

Police officers

- patrol residential areas and business districts on foot and in patrol vehicles.
- continuously monitor conditions within patrol areas conducive to criminal activity.
- inspect business locations for open doors, illegal activity, crimes in progress, and hazardous conditions.
- monitor schools, parks, and playgrounds for illegal activities.
- respond to fires and direct and control traffic.
- inspect streets for defective lights, signs, signals, etc.
- are constantly alert to suspicious behavior, take action to prevent and deter crimes from occurring, and perform field investigations of all suspicious persons and conditions.
- use radio communication equipment to report activities, receive assignments, and communicate with other officers.
- prepare written reports and complete departmental forms about arrests, traffic violations, incidents observed, and actions taken.
- enforce traffic laws and ordinances, stop vehicles committing traffic violations, issue citations or warnings, and direct traffic at emergency scenes.
- respond to assigned calls for service, activating vehicular emergency equipment (light, sirens, horn, etc.) when appropriate.
- conduct investigations; determine whether crimes have been committed; and take any actions necessary, such as making an arrest, issuing a warning, or referring someone to another agency.
- perform emergency medical services, such as rendering first aid and performing cardiopulmonary resuscitation.
- respond to scenes involving murder, suicide, assault, burglary, robbery, rape, illegal drugs, kidnapping, larceny, noise complaints, family disputes, prowlers, intoxicated persons, missing persons, trespassing, breach of peace, disorderly conduct, auto theft, etc. and determine the who, what, when, where, why, and how relative to an investigation.
- protect the scenes of crimes; secure descriptions of persons responsible and property involved in criminal activity; and identify, collect, preserve, and maintain custody of physical evidence and found property, such as fingerprints, weapons, tool impressions, and bullets.

- investigate traffic accidents, including fatalities and hit-and-run accidents; gather physical evidence; chart and measure skid marks, points of vehicular contact, etc.; diagram accident scenes; determine cause; and determine if enforcement actions (summons, warning, etc.) are appropriate.

- determine when and how to effect an arrest, search prisoners, prepare charges and arrest reports, transport prisoners to the police station, and fingerprint and photograph prisoners.

- use batons, handcuffs, billies, blackjacks, firearms, etc.

- obtain arrest and search warrants and take written statements from victims, complainants, and offenders.

- investigate cases involving juvenile offenders, crimes against children, child neglect, morals offenses, abuse, etc.

- handle crowd control and labor disputes.

- testify in court and guard prisoners.

STEPS IN THE JUSTICE PROCESS AND INVESTIGATION

Steps in the Criminal Justice Process

1. Commission of a crime
2. Report of crime to the police
3. Investigation of the crime by the police
4. Application for an arrest warrant
5. Arrest of criminal by the police
6. Arraignment of criminal in court
7. Bail, trial date set
8. Criminal trial
9. Verdict by judge or jury
10. Sentence or disposition

Steps in Preliminary Investigations

P. Proceed to the scene promptly and safely
R. Render assistance to the injured
E. Effect the arrest of the criminal
L. Locate and identify witnesses
I. Interview the complainant and the witnesses
M. Maintain the crime scene and protect the evidence
I. Interrogate the suspect
N. Note all conditions, events, and remarks
A. Arrange for the collection of evidence
R. Report the incident fully and accurately
Y. Yield responsibility to the follow-up investigator

STATISTICS

NUMBER OF OFFICERS AND CIVILIAN EMPLOYEES IN THE TWENTY LARGEST POLICE DEPARTMENTS IN THE UNITED STATES

City, State	Officers	Civilian Employees
1. New York City, New York	26,856	9,371
2. Chicago, Illinois	12,132	3,126
3. Los Angeles, California	8,198	2,666
4. Philadelphia, Pennsylvania	6,424	894
5. Washington, D.C.	4,502	646
6. Houston, Texas	4,077	1,655
7. Detroit, Michigan	3,954	618
8. Baltimore, Maryland	2,893	562
9. Dallas, Texas	2,857	809
10. Boston, Massachusetts	1,989	627
11. Phoenix, Arizona	1,982	672
12. Milwaukee, Wisconsin	1,895	455
13. Honolulu, Hawaii	1,887	425
14. Cleveland, Ohio	1,682	362
15. San Antonio, Texas	1,571	316
16. Atlanta, Georgia	1,533	568
17. St. Louis, Missouri	1,516	624
18. Memphis, Tennessee	1,390	415
19. Denver, Colorado	1,361	262
20. Jacksonville, Florida	1,253	892

Department of Justice, Federal Bureau of Investigation, *Uniform Crime Report for the United States,* 1992.

NUMBER OF POLICE OFFICERS AND CIVILIAN EMPLOYEES IN THE UNITED STATES IN 1991

United States population	238,000,000
Number of police officers	535,629
Number of civilian police employees	199,883

Department of Justice, Federal Bureau of Investigation, *Uniform Crime Report for the United States,* 1992.